Oh My GOD

Genetics **O**f **D**ivinity

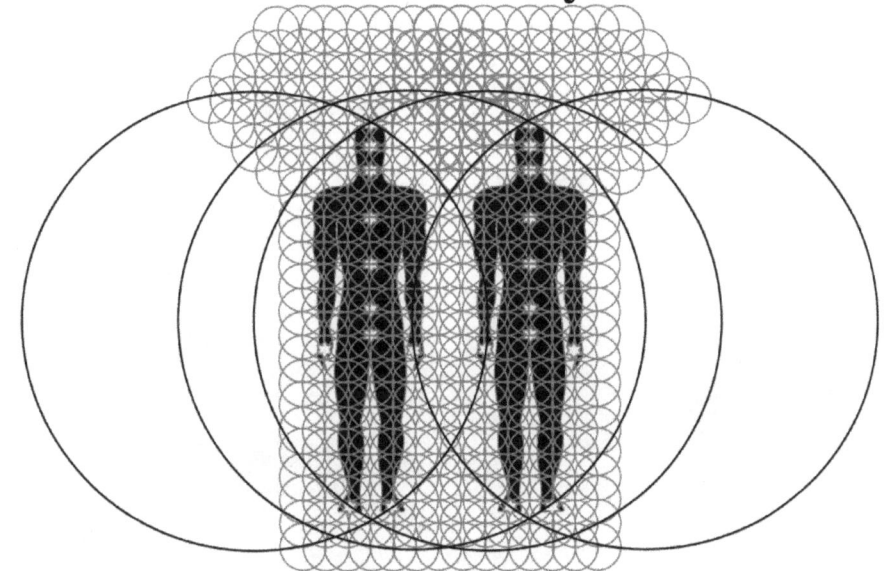

Joy Ghosh

The Code Of Eternal Consciousness

Copyright © 2012 ICREATE TECHNOLOGIES, LLC

Genetics Of Divinity™ is a trademark owned by ICREATE Technologies, LLC.

Companion Website at www.OhMyGeneticsOfDivinity.com

Root Website at www.GeneticsOfDivinity.com

Multiversity of Genetics Of Divinity at www.icreatecorp.com

Connect at -

- Facebook: http://facebook.com/geneticsofdivinity
- Twitter: http://twitter.com/divinegenes
- Youtube: http://youtube.com/user/geneticsofdivinity

Note to the Owner : As the owner of this book, you also have been granted access to Level 1 Training content at the Multiversity of the *Genetics Of Divinity* as an included bonus with your purchase. This is a significant resource of valuable information in the online Multiversity at www.GeneticsOfDivinity.com to enhance the reactivation process of the code of Eternal Consciousness that is already embedded in your DNA. We encourage you to take advantage of this resource to maximize your learning experience. Simply "Like" us at http://facebook.com/geneticsofdivinity on Facebook or "Follow" us at http://twitter.com/divinegenes on Twitter, whichever you use the most and email a scanned copy of the original receipt of purchase of this book to coordinator@GeneticsOfDivinity.com. Please remember to provide your Facebook or Twitter ID that you used to Like or Follow us, to identify yourself in your email. We call this *SocialMediaBucks* ☺ that you can use to pay for your access to the online training portal at the Multiversity. Upon receipt of your information, we will respond within 72 hours with your login details to access the Multiversity training portal.

All rights reserved.

DEDICATION

This work is dedicated to every man, woman and child in this most magnificent brilliant blue marble of the cosmos that we call Earth, who have boldly asked the elusive questions about Creation and Existence, Purpose of Life, Secrets of the path to the Shangri-La of Abundant Life in an insatiable search for the Truth. *At the core of Creation and Existence lies the foundation of symbiotic collaborative relationships established through the free will of mutual consent between the relating partners for the purpose of collective coexistence.* I applaud and celebrate your quest which has brought you to this book today and in the process, you are about to embark on a journey built on the same foundation of a symbiotic collaborative relationship between you and I through our free will of mutual consent. Once you read this book you will discover the Truth about yourself in particular and Existence in general. The Truth is already known to you and has been that way since eternity. However this Truth lays dormant, buried deep within the catacombs of your immortal subconscious memory. The book will guide you on an adventure to reveal the Truth and you will begin to resonate once again with the symphony of Creation of Existence. Therein lays the secret to the fulfillment of your immortal Life Purpose in this mortal Life Experience.

"YOU" ARE IMMORTAL

I CELEBRATE YOUR TRANSCENDENCE

Table Of Contents

The Conclusion 11
Chapter 1 – From The Abyss To Dizzy Heights 13
Chapter 2 - The Launchpad 22
Chapter 3 - Knock! Knock! Who's there? 44
Chapter 4 - Consciousness – Your Identity 56
    Defining Consciousness 59
    The Different Levels Of Consciousness 61
        COMATOSE 62
        POWERLESS 64
        FRUSTRATED 66
        ANALYTICAL 68
        CARING 70
        EMPOWERED 71
        AWAKENED 75
        CREATIVE 78
        SOURCE OF THOUGHT 81
    Kinesiology 87
    Evolution of Human Consciousness 88
    Why Bother Upgrading Your Consciousness? 90
Chapter 5 - Laws Of Creation And Existence 92
    Core Attributes of Creation 93
        The CREATOR and the Creature 93
        Contrast 96

Free Will 98
Parallelism 102
The Cycle of Creation 110
Chapter 6 - Multi-dimensional Co-existence 115
The ZERO Dimension or 0-D 119
The First Dimension or 1-D 121
The Second Dimension or 2-D 123
The Third Dimension or 3-D 125
A Twist in the Third Dimension 128
The Fourth Dimension or 4-D 133
Parallelism of Creation 137
Quantum Mechanics Proves Parallelism 139
Beyond the Fourth Dimension 144
The Superstring Theory 145
The "M" (Membrane) Theory 148
Parallel Universes 151
Defining Your Personal Parallel Universe 156
Mechanics Of Defining A Parallel Universe 170
The 12 Strand Human DNA 172
Activating Your Parallel Universe Through Your DNA 178
Chapter 7 - Multi-dimensional Model of Creation and Existence 183
Mastering The Basics 188
Modeling The Multi-Dimensional Existence 193
Object Oriented Design At the Core 193
Twelve Dimensions of Existence 209
The Binding Dimensions – ZERO and ELEVEN 211

- The Bounded Dimensions – 10-D to 1-D 223
  - The Tenth Dimension 223
  - The Ninth Dimension 227
  - The Eighth Dimension 229
  - The Seventh Dimension 233
  - The Sixth Dimension 250
  - The Fifth Dimension 254
  - Your Immortal Self – The 5-D ACTIVEBODY 257
  - Your Mortal Self – The 3-D ADAPTIVEBODY 260
  - Revisiting Your 12 Strand Human DNA 265
  - Could We Have Misunderstood Religion 269
  - A Detour To The Law of Attraction 276
  - Back from the LOA Detour into the 5-D 288
  - The Fourth Dimension 290
  - The Third Dimension 299
  - Revisiting The ZERO Dimension 305
  - The First Dimension 307
  - The Second Dimension 307
- Chapter 8 - Perfect Masterpiece of Creation 310
  - Introduction To The Memory and The Mind 311
  - The Quad-Compartmental Mind 313
  - Understanding Memory Systems 316
  - Central Nervous System – Modus Operandi 324
    - Pattern Recognition 327
  - Knowledgebase, Belief Systems and Neural Pathways 330
  - The EGS - Emotional Guidance System 333

Effect of Lower EGS Emotions on the Adaptivebody 338
Neuro-plasticity and Neuro-elasticity 342
EGS as Your Personal EWACS 343
Multi-Dimensional Energy Vortices - Chakras 344
    Sacred Geometry and the Vessica Piscis 346
    The Crown Chakra 348
    The Third Eye Chakra 349
    The Foot (Split) Chakra 354
    The Hand (Split) Chakra 356
    The Other Five Chakras 358
Adaptive Energy Field of the Adaptivebody 362
Desirability Index Of The Adaptivebody 364
Brainwaves – Passport To Physical Reality 367
    The BETA Brainwave Frequency Band 373
    The ALPHA Brainwave Frequency Band 374
    The THETA Brainwave Frequency Band 374
    The DELTA Brainwave Frequency Band 375
    The 2nd BETA Brainwave Frequency Band 376
    The GAMMA Brainwave Frequency Band 376
    Transformation of Brainwave Energy 378
Applying Wave Mechanics to Existence 383
PUPS - Parallel Universal Positioning System 386
    The Mechanics of Your PUPS 392
    Interconnectedness between PUPS and EGS 394
Chapter 9 - Source Energy and the G.O.D 400
My Activebody and I – A Live Download 402

The Source Force 403
Independence From The Time Factor 404
Biophotons and the Lightbody 406
History of Existence – Source to Force 411
    Defining Space 413
    Wave Mechanics for Stabilization of Existence 414
    Birth of Contrast and Duality 416
Technology To Create The Dimensions 418
    Collaborative Relationships and Free Will 425
    Sinusoidal Waveforms - Signature of Existence 426
Wave Mechanics Of The EGS 430
Traveling Faster Than Light Speed 436
The G.O.D 'Particle' – Sourceon 441
Was There Really a "Big Bang"? 445
Chapter 10 – The Beginning 448
    Finding Your True Identity 450
    Defining Your Very Own Parallel Universe 452
    Four Types of Civilizations + The Fifth 458
    Next Steps 460
    ABOUT THE AUTHOR 466

ACKNOWLEDGMENTS

I thank the many modern day physicists, cosmologists, teachers, ordinary men and women with extraordinary skills and connections to their non-physical selves that I have had the opportunity to interact with, all my like-minded friends and family for their incessant research for the Truth about Creation and Existence and for their effusive and unrestrained willingness to share their knowledge with me and for their patience to listen to my rather esoteric ramblings from time to time. I thank all the enlightened and awakened individuals who graced this planet long before any organized religion was born, for their wisdom, insight, discoveries, analysis and knowledge about Creation and Existence. I thank the *ETERNAL CONSCIOUSNESS* for revealing to me through those countless hours of self-realization and self-revelation, the sublime information that I call the *Genetics Of Divinity,* that seem to simply flow into me since that winter December evening, that I call the defining moment of this lifetime, flooding my consciousness with such esoteric cognitions that have led me to the liberating path of Eternal Truth. I am humbled and filled with gratitude with the knowledge that was revealed to me that has transformed my life experience from unbounded plight to unbounded delight. Now as directed to be my life purpose, I convey the same knowledge to you to rekindle memories of this Eternal Truth that currently lays dormant in your subconscious mind, so that you too can enjoy a life experience filled with unbounded delight.

You and I are about to establish a symbiotic collaborative relationship with each other through our free will of mutual consent for the purpose of collective coexistence. This is the only reason why you have been presented with the material contained in this book. Welcome to the portal for your **Genetics Of Divinity**.

The Conclusion

The **<u>PERCEIVED</u> REALITY in your life is a Fantasy.**

Is <u>NOW</u> the Time to Step Into YOUR <u>TRUE</u> REALITY?

I Am Immortal... Not believing in this is Immoral.

YOU Are Immortal... Not believing in this is Immoral.

I Have **Not** Been Designed For Immorality.

You Have **Not** Been Designed For Immorality.

I AM IMMORTAL.

YOU ARE IMMORTAL.

WE ARE ALL DESIGNED TO ENJOY UNBOUNDED DELIGHT IN OUR PHYSICAL LIFE EXPERIENCE.

I RESPECT, HONOR and CELEBRATE YOU.

I had ten objectives for you while I was framing the information contained in this book:
1. Describe the Code of the *Genetics Of Divinity* that defines the complete design of Existence and upgrade your consciousness.
2. Illustrate how you can use the *Genetics Of Divinity* to find your definitive Life Purpose and be able to upgrade your level of consciousness.
3. Illustrate how by simply applying the Code of the *Genetics Of Divinity* you can make the right decisions in life every time all the time.
4. Explain how the definite direction of your Life Purpose is always based on service that you are to deliver *for others* to receive and consequently how others have a Life Purpose to serve *for you* to

receive through the establishment of *symbiotic collaborative relationships* through mutual consent.
5. Provide convincing evidence that you and everything else have been created with the sole design principle of all Existence for enjoying a life experience filled with unbounded delight.
6. Describe how the current challenges in your life are there only to show you by *Contrast* what a different life experience could be without those challenges. Once you become aware of this Contrast, applying the Code of the *Genetics Of Divinity* can enable you to live a life experience in that Contrast.
7. Clarify for you that you *always* have a choice to choose your life experience at every moment. Nobody has a right, according to the Laws of Creation and neither do you need to relinquish the right to others to dictate the quality of *your* life experience – only *you* have that right over *your* own life experience. Anything else is a violation of the Code of the Genetics Of Divinity.
8. Explain the true mechanics behind the Law of Attraction. The manner in which you have been taught to apply the Law of Attraction so far in all likelihood is flawed and non-repeatable – hence the LoA has proved less effective compared to your expectations. Once you apply the correct protocols as I describe here, the Law of Attraction will work for you consistently and expediently all the time.
9. Demonstrate to you that the Code of the *Genetics Of Divinity* is fair, providing for and empowering you in the same manner that it provides for and empowers others. There is no need for a life experience of lack and scarcity – there is always more where whatever you desire came from, as long as that desire is logical and ethically feasible.
10. Your physical body is mortal but your non-physical self is IMMORTAL and truth be told *you never pass away* – you are designed to *only pass on* to a different life experience with a different Life Purpose. It's time to get over the debate of IMMORTALITY and get on with a life according to the code of the *Genetics Of Divinity*.

Chapter 1 – From The Abyss To Dizzy Heights

"What is that white light?" I wondered as I lay limp on the bed, drained of almost all of my physical energy. I could neither feel my body nor the bed – just an unknown lightness and darkness everywhere, except that soothing white light which seemed to hover over my head, smoothly transitioning into the darkness around it. I can't even remember if my eyes were open or closed, but that the light was there nonetheless. Then I sensed a touch on my forehead as I felt my mother fondly run her fingers through my hair. The light was gone and I was home again – it was the third time in this lifetime that she gave me the gift of life.

What I am about to tell you now is personal and it has been quite an effort to convince myself that I should reveal my personal story in public. Please note as you read what's forthcoming, that my goal to disclose such personal information is not to impress you with my sob story or my plight, but to impress *upon* you the fact that the birthing pains inflicted on me by those days of unbounded plight were the beginning of the reactivation process of the dormant memories of the code of *Genetics of Divinity* from my subconscious mind into my conscious mind. Once that occurred, as I consciously started to conduct my life according to the code - my unbounded plight had changed to unbounded delight. It is my belief that you are lined up for the same transformation – by design of the "Code" of the *Genetics of Divinity*.

I was born in a family and grew up in a society where the concept of IMMORTALITY was confined to mythology and grandmother's bedtime stories. Those were the tales of Gods who supposedly reincarnated over and over again on Earth whenever humanity spiraled downwards into pain and suffering and got shrouded in the dark cloak of sin. According to those myths, those Gods came to Earth in mortal forms, to single-handedly defeat the evil and restore peace and prosperity in the life experience of the mortals. While those riveting stories served the entertainment value and the non-medicinal sleeping potion in the early years of childhood, they certainly lost their potency rapidly as I grew older and the filter of rationality took up guard on the entrance to my consciousness.

Questions, unanswered questions, had begun to cloud my young mind in my moments of pensive solitude, "What's the big deal about IMMORTALITY, when clearly I am a mere mortal?", "Why did these omnipotent Gods choose to be born as a mortal – sometimes in physical human form and sometimes otherwise, when they could very well have stayed back in their heavenly abodes and simply taken care of stuff through remote control?"

Reincarnation – what an esoteric concept. I could hardly pronounce that word in my youngster years, far less keep the letters in the right order. "Why bother coming back to this world where there was so much pain and suffering?", "What did I as a mortal lack in my body that those immortal Gods possessed? What made them so special? If they could do all that cool stuff as described in those compelling tales about extraordinary accomplishments as a mortal, why could I not do the same?" " Why is there so much pain and suffering in this world?" "Why can I not be, do or have anything and everything that I so dearly desire in my life?" "Why would someone else steal my dreams?" "Is it even possible to have lasting happiness in this life experience?" "Why can I not see the future?" "Why have I been born – what is my life purpose?" "Who would really care if I was never born?"

"Why does life seem to be so uncertain?" "Why won't my dreams come true?" "Am I really free to choose my life experience?" "Is this how life is supposed to be?"

Discouragingly frustrating is probably the most appropriate phrase that could explain the way I had felt when none of my questions could be answered with the slightest degree of credibility and conviction. "That's the way it is, my dear", did not go too far to quench the thirst of my budding consciousness. I sought out religious texts with the expectation that I could find answers to my questions in them. But alas, stories of miracles performed by the respective religious leaders continued, while the followers remained seemingly sterile, quasi-potent in comparison and apparently devoid of such fantastic abilities. It was not too long thereafter that I had stopped chasing the fantasy of immortality and like the average individual else succumbed to the whims of the invisible Gods and surrendered as an impotent hostage to the unilateral dictates of fate and destiny to control my life experience.

After completing my degree in electrical and electronics engineering, I had flirted aimlessly from one job to another before setting my sights on a career in software engineering, which had brought me many successes, recognition and wealth. I fell in love with a woman and tied the knot with the *hope* that I had finally turned over a new leaf in love and *Miss* Fortune finally decided to smile me (or did she really?). It was four years into my marriage that the cracks started to appear in the mirror for reasons that made no logical sense to me. I realized much later, *belief* and not hope creates reality.

Being brought up in a family and in a society where the sanctity of the marital bond is considered 'sacred', I spent a greater part of the next sixteeen years of my marriage asking the "Why me?" question, voluntarily assuming all the blame for the marital challenges, as our marriage degraded from what I had envisioned to be a symbiotic collaborative relationship when I had fallen in love, into one of stoic compromise and passive acceptance of the dictates of destiny and fate that I used to rely on at that time in my past. I feigned delight and love in the family in public while the decay inside was evident. I had lost my identity and had begun to question even my own name – I could not recognize myself since I had been living a life to appease others at the cost of my own definition of collective coexistence. I was sacrificing my own identity "Who am I and what have I become?" I had asked and received no answer. No, prayers to the religious God did not do much good. Religion still could not find the words to answer my questions credibly as the enigma of the unknown guided my life into the dark chasms of remorse and the helpless anticipation of the perfect storm.

It was in the darkest hour of my life in early December of 2010, when I literally lay helpless with a broken mind and seriously diseased body, that my red rose finally withered and collapsed. It was at that darkest moment that I made a decision to be born again and live the life that I always wanted. I clenched the hands of my desperately concerned parents by my bedside in a feeble grip and managed to whisper (or did I really have the strength to do even that?), "I want to be born again as your son and live my life one more time." I asked myself, "Have I lived? Have I loved? Have I served?" Still no answers came. Darkness enveloped me - I saw nothing but a soothing white light hovering over my head in the darkness and barely felt my mother's fingers run through my hair - it could well have been my hallucinations. Then I felt nothing.

What ensued afterwards I have no conscious recollection of. I regained my strength over the next few days as if I was swimming up to the surface of a sea of molasses – I had survived. How I survived, why I survived or what brought me back to life I could not tell at that time, although I do know now and I will reveal to you in this book. However, I just knew that there had to be a valid purpose, a very compelling reason why I survived through that darkest hour in my life. I remembered Muhammad Ali's rope-a-dope technique that he had used so effectively in his illustrious career – it was my time to rope-a-dope.

Empowered by the consciousness of the last decade of research on Applied and Theoretical Physics, Chemistry, Human Anatomy, Astronomy, Hypnotherapy, Religion, Prereligion Spirituality, Sacred Geometry, Multi-Dimensional Energetics and most importantly another Source that I will disclose to you in a later chapter of this book, my life purpose was revealed to me as I recovered from the depths of unbounded plight and set out on my journey towards the heights of unbounded delight. It was no longer a meager hope but a bold belief and conviction that I was given a second shot at life and this time I had to make every second count.

I filed for divorce after sixteen years of marriage of which the last twelve were the years of evolution in the revolution of my life experience to realize who I really was and why I was born (again). The consciousness of *Genetics of Divinity* made me realize that it was not my ex-spouse who was to blame and neither was I for those tumultuous years of grief that we both endured under the false pretense and social display of a blissful marriage. I came to know through the *Genetics of Divinity* that *we* were never compatible in the first place and that symbiotic collaborative relationship through the free will of mutual consent for the purpose of collective coexistence could not have occurred anyway. While I cannot speak for her, I know today I was responsible for the choices I had made during our dating days and hold myself accountable for everything good, bad or indifferent that transpired – my lack of knowledge of the *Genetics Of Divinity* could no longer be the pet excuse of going through a life experience far away from that objective of bliss and unbounded delight. I just knew that *my mess was to become the womb of my message.*

Had I known the *Genetics Of Divinity* all those years ago, had I known that all of Creation and Existence was based on the core principle of symbiotic collaborative relationships, had I known about the immortality of the non-physical part of this mortal physical body, had I known all that I reveal in this book and all the other content that I share through other media and through my websites, my life experience and that of all others who I had touched would have been vastly different. Through my *pain* I learned what *pleasure* is, through *lack of love* I learned what *free and effusive love* is, it was the *discord* that clarified for me what *accord* is. The

Laws of Creation had illustrated to me the attribute of Contrast as you will shortly learn about.

Within weeks of my decision to live my life again and eventual recovery later in December 2010 I started to consciously abide by and apply the code of the *Genetics Of Divinity*. It was around the middle of 2011 that I just knew without a shred of doubt, as surely as the sunrise on the East that there was a lady *out there* waiting for me who would bring peace, love and harmony in my life experience. I did not have a name, I did not know what her appearance was like, I had no idea where she lived or what she did for a living and more importantly what could be the compelling reason for her to wait to meet someone like me to establish a relationship together. Nonetheless, I felt the energy of her presence all the time. The symbiotic collaborative relationship with this imaginary love of my life was getting stronger and stronger by the day as my convictions grew bolder and unshakable. I remember telling my brother about this formless, nameless, imaginary lady *out there* with whom I was building a symbiotic collaborative relationship and I could almost sense his deliberate struggle to subdue an outburst of laughter - his dear big brother had finally *lost it*.

As the *Genetics Of Divinity* would have it, unerringly so when applied correctly, within a few months since then, we found each other in the most unusual and unexpected manner that one can imagine, in a different continent across the planet. Even without physically seeing each other or even speaking to each other, our relationship started through online chats – no commitments, just pure light hearted banter and friendship across the blue Pacific. Within days, my conviction of perceived reality became my knowledge of true reality of a symbiotic collaborative relationship established through the free will of mutual consent for the purpose of collective coexistence and a life experience filled with unbounded delight. What ensued thereafter can be regarded a modern fairy tale as the bond grew bolder and stronger, still living on opposite ends of the world. We met in person only a few times for brief periods as we both had to cater to professional and personal lives where we lived. After my marital status changed a year later, I proposed to her for the first time and I would leave it to your conviction, not imagination, to figure out the outcome. Coincidence? Logic and rational reasoning of the *Genetics of Divinity* indicates that such so-called coincidences are actually conscious alignment of collaborating partners mutually consenting to a symbiotic relationship at the non-physical plane occurring at speeds faster than the speed of light (as you will learn later on in this book)

I have applied the same code, the same principle of symbiotic collaborative relationships in my professional life, for finances, for my health, for my passion for martial arts and knowledge - every time without fail the *Genetics of Divinity* has delivered for me. Now my life purpose that was disclosed to me is to share this knowledge with the rest of humanity. I am not going to pass on from this physical mortal body with the magic inside me. I therefore share it with you and encourage you to share the knowledge that you will acquire, with others in your life in the spirit of symbiotic collaborative relationships established through mutual consent with the purpose of enjoying a collective co-existence.

That was my story that I wanted to share with you as a reader, to demonstrate just a few applications of the code of the *Genetics Of Divinity*. Do you relate to any of these life experiences? How different would your life experience be if you could know your life purpose and was able to see your personal future? What would your life be like if you could make the right decisions in life every time, all the time that you sought the guidance from the *Genetics Of Divinity*? I found my ideal soul mate through the *Genetics Of Divinity* and so can you (if you haven't already). If you are a couple, this technology can bring you closer together. What else can the knowledge of the *Genetics Of Divinity* do for you? I could provide a long list of applications and even then it would be unfair since I am certain I will leave something out.

The *Genetics Of Divinity* is based on the core design principle of all Creation and Existence – that of *symbiotic collaborative relationships*. Let me break that phrase down for you in reverse order. *Relationships* is the art and science of *relating*. What do you relate to? It may be a physical material object or a non-physical, intangible emotion or thought. *Collaborative* relationships imply partnership between the relating entities, which may be physical or non-physical. There is no *first among equals* in such a relationship – the partnership is among equals who voluntarily contribute and collaborate together for common goals. *Symbiotic* collaborative relationship refers to a mutually beneficial and complimentary partnership where the success and stability of the relationship is dependent on the parallel, reciprocal and complimentary contribution of the relating entities.

Just to clarify, I did not disclose details about my personal life to gain sympathy or impress you with the turbulent times that I had gone through year after year of my life. The reason to describe my life story is to impress upon you that regardless of where you are in your life experience, you are living in an artificial, perceived reality because your consciousness is not guided by the eternal Code of *Genetics of Divinity* – yet. However, the moment you decide to understand, internalize and reactivate the code from your subconscious mind into your conscious mind, your life experience will begin to transform and results such as mine and beyond become true reality and typical.

As you will learn in this book, relationships in Existence are not restricted between people. You have a relationship with your pet, the plants in your garden, the house you live in or want to live in, the car you drive or want to drive, the money that you have or want to have access to, the knowledge that you have or want to acquire, the help to the less endowed that you are providing or want to provide, the peace and prosperity that you desire to see in this planet, the quality of food that you want to consume, the clothes that you want to wear are all relationships. In fact every moment of your life experience involves a relationship with some physical or non-physical entity – the question would be, *is that a symbiotic collaborative relationship or otherwise?* If you feel challenged with a relationship with any of these entities, that can be resolved simply by understanding and applying the code of the *Genetics Of Divinity* – quite candidly the only effective way as granted by the Laws of Creation.

I encourage you to do this exercise with me before we dive in. Take a white sheet of paper and use blue ink to write the following in your best handwriting, This is the core principle of the Genetics of Divinity and provides the foundation for all Creation and Existence, which also includes the quality of your present and future life experience. Ready?

Handwrite this down, *"I pledge and commit myself from this moment onwards to seek and establish symbiotic collaborative relationships with anything and anyone that I believe will lead to unbounded delight in my life experience and theirs, through the free will of mutual consent of both parties for the purpose of collective co-existence."*

Now sign it and place the current date and time below it. This is going to be your guiding principle as you reactivate the dormant memories of the code of Eternal Consciousness and consciously leverage it to create a life experience filled with unbounded delight.

Chapter 2 - The Launchpad

I retrieved my bags from the conveyor belt and headed towards the exit doors of the airport. As pre-arranged, my friend was waiting for me among about a few hundred other happy looking people eagerly waiting for their loved ones. She waved at me as we spotted each other and I approached her swiftly. After customary greetings were done she said, "I apologize Joy. As you can see, it is overcast today and the forecast says heavy rain." I looked outside through the glass panels, almost as a reflex action and she was right. The drops had indeed begun to hit the ground.

I turned to look at her, smiled and said, "You know while I was in the air and above those clouds, I could see just the blue sky and the bright sun and those clouds looked so very gorgeous and ethereal beneath the airplane. It was so beautiful up there – quite honestly, I am still up there enjoying the experience." My friend, quite well aware of where this conversation was going, nodded, amused almost in anticipation of what's coming next. "Rise above those clouds, my friend," I continued, "They are transient anyway. The blue sky and the bright sun are permanent. Why focus on the dullness of the transient when the ecstasy of the permanent can bring you unbounded delight forever?" She laughed cognitively as we walked out in the rain towards her car.

It is my conviction that each one of us is completely responsible and accountable for anything and everything that we get attracted to in our life experience – good, bad or indifferent. Our individual state of happiness and fulfillment or otherwise is the sum total of all our uplifting and untoward thoughts, feelings and emotions from within our self and contrary to common belief, never the result of influence of the world external to us.

May I request you to turn your eyes (without turning your head) and look towards your top right corner and ponder for a moment, what the key reason for all the pain and suffering in this world could be? Why do we fight those wars? Why do we desire to acquire things material objects by force or deceit? "I want it, I must have it, I can't get it, so I must grab it" – why do we think that way? Why do we steal from others what we have no right? Why are we hungry for muscle power? Why are we willing to do whatever it takes to proliferate the greed and succumb to the lust for the lure of money? Why do we want more what others have and appreciate less what we already have? Why do we indulge in this hideous addiction of one-upmanship, to prove that we are better than the others? Why do we spend most of our waking hours chasing whatever mirage we are chasing without conviction or logical strategy? Why do we blame others for our plight and offer excuses for the purpose of false absolution of personal responsibility? Imagine a world where all the above was there but with the *contrasting* conditions? Would that not be a world you would be excited to live in? You actually can and as a matter of fact that Parallel Universe actually exists and you can navigate to that life experience through faculties that are already embedded within your body – more on this in Chapter 7.

All the pain and suffering perceived in this world and the one answer to all of these questions can be attributed to one dis-ease of human consciousness as it stands today - *unconsciousness*. We have deviated as a civilization from the core design principle of Creation and Existence that was instituted even before this physical Third Dimension even came into existence. The code of Eternal Consciousness defines all Existence to be built upon *symbiotic collaborative relationships through the free will of mutual consent between the relating partners for the purpose of collective coexistence.* In all likelihood, this is the first time you have even heard about this core principle of Creation. As an individual we are all integral parts of a whole – the entirety of Existence. This implies each one of us has this physical life experience for a specific purpose that is assigned to us by our non-physical self, prior to birth and that purpose is always based on service for others (animate or inanimate) who would share a contemporary life experience. If this seems too intense for you at this early stage, that is not uncommon. As you read this book, you will understand the true implications of this core design principle and when you apply the knowledge, the *magic* will start.

Paradigms, enforced laws, rules and regulations of totalitarian governments, social and cultural taboos over the centuries have overlaid debris over the code of Eternal Consciousness that today lays dormant and yet embedded in our subconscious mind. Consequently as the most endowed species of Creation in this planet, humanity is unable to enjoy a life experience filled with unbounded delight, for which we have been created in this physical form to begin with. Humanity is defying Creation, it is NOW time to desist.

Humanity today is not self-sufficient – correction, we *live under a delusion* that we are not self-sufficient to live a life where all that we need is within our reach anytime and anywhere. I am not a betting man but I will bet a dollar to a donut (an American figure of speech) that the reason why you are interested in this book is that you are feeling insufficient and deprived right now on at least one of the thirteen major areas of your life – more on these major thirteen areas of your life coming up in Chapter 3.

Imagine a world where every man, woman and child became self-sufficient by reactivating the embedded yet dormant knowledge of Eternal Consciousness of the *Genetics of Divinity*, by learning the techniques and leveraging those tools to become self-sufficient. What if all the lack and deprivation that we feel went away and everyone in this planet was fulfilled with whatever they desired as long as it is logical and ethically feasible in the spirit of establishing (1)*symbiotic*, (2) *collaborative relationships through the* (3) *free will of* (4) *mutual consent between the (5) relating partners, for the purpose of* (6)*collective coexistence*? In such a world, however hypothetical and esoteric it may sound to you at this point in your journey of reactivating the code in your subconscious mind, do you think there can be any pain and suffering left for humanity to stay plagued with? This book provides you with the guidance of how to actually create such a world collectively with those who have or are in the process of reactivating the code of the *Genetics Of Divinity* in their consciousness.

Think logically before answering that question. If you have what you want in your life and you kept getting what you wanted in your life, would you even bother to engage in acts of harm, aggression and trepidation on others? No, you won't because there would be no motivation left in you to engage in such acts of confrontation and discord. So my intent for you through this book is to guide you to that cognition that you have all the attributes by virtue of your birth as a human to be self-sufficient – you have been designed to enjoy a life experience filled with unbounded delight, why relinquish that birthright? Once you have that cognition of self-reliance and self-sufficiency, you can be, do or have anything and everything you want in this physical world as long as it is logical and ethically feasible, to fulfill your most heartfelt desires.

Existence has created you as a human, empowered with the will to receive and the will to bestow and enjoy unbounded delight in your life experience. If your life experience so far has been anything short of that, your perceived reality is actually a fantasy, a virtual and perceived reality. The knowledge in this book will elevate your consciousness to identify and experience your true reality.

What made you choose to read this book? Did you come across this book just by accident? Just browsing and you *'happened'* to stumble upon this book? Or is it that somebody for reasons best known to them thought it would be a great idea to refer this book to you? Hmmm... maybe you *happened* to come across an ad in a publication or the Internet or *happened* to tune on to a media channel where this book was being discussed. Of all the millions of books out there, of all the tens of thousands of thoughts that race through your mind every day, between the jam packed schedule that you have to contend with every day, this book just *happened* to find its way to grab your attention. Wow! You would not just dismiss this achievement, yes, this achievement of yours as sheer coincidence or happenstance, a quirk of fate, a wrinkle of destiny or OMG-ness - luck, would you?

Still reading? I find you interesting. Really, I do find you interesting. I think I can read your mind, right now, although in all likelihood we have never met in person and in even greater likelihood, I am probably nowhere in your line of sight right now. Would you care to know what I am reading in your mind? Ready to put science and the concept of multi-dimensional energy to test, are you? Ok, I'll tell you, but it's ok to be intrigued, just don't be disturbed or worried about privacy - promise?

Good! Let me ask you a question – how long has it been? I mean how long have you been searching? I am not referring to a search for this book necessarily. How long have you been searching for answers that have defied you until a few moments before you came across this book and have started to read it? What is the scarcity in your life right now for which you are searching (probably desperately) a solution? Where do you feel insufficient in life right now that is bothering you and adversely affecting your health and happiness? What do you lack in life right now that you could not do without? Who deprived you of what? Nah, none of those catabolic feelings and thoughts would have brought you to this book – quite candidly, you would have been driven away from this book with such destructive thoughts and emotions. In fact if all you were thinking about were those questions of lack and scarcity and the insufficiency, there is no way you would have come across this book.

Somewhere, sometime in your state of despair even if it was for a fleeting moment, you had a focused thought, you had a distant vision, albeit blurred, or maybe you even said a prayer about such a time in your future lifetime where that lack and scarcity was replaced with an experience of abundance and fulfillment. When you had that constructive thought, remember that moment – you felt good. You felt so good, that in all likelihood, you did not want to come off that zone, that vision of your happy and fulfilled self. There is also a fair chance, that you had thoughts and beliefs about some knowledge somewhere *out there* that will lead you to the answers to your questions that you have been asking about the world in general and your life in particular to help improve the quality of your life, find peace, security, love, stability or just freedom to be, do or have anything that your free will desires.

It might have been having a *daydream* but clearly was no *pipedream*. Whatever you were focusing on, with full or zero awareness, has brought you to people, events or circumstances that led you to this book. There was no accidental coincidence, no happenstance, no quirk of fate –

truth be told it was all your thinking and doing. It was no accident. Unbeknownst to your conscious awareness, you leveraged the core principle of Creation, establishing a symbiotic collaborative relationship with that knowledge. The end result - you were attracted towards this book and according to the core theme of the *Genetics of Divinity*, you are now in the process of establishing that relationship through mutual consent for the purpose of collective co-existence.

You have wants, needs, desires, goals, dreams in life and that is perfectly natural, you have been created in this physical form that way to aspire for more. But obviously you don't have all of them in your life experience – there is a feeling of lack and scarcity in you, isn't there? There is this bad taste in your mouth, probably even a sense of helplessness. Your best efforts to regain solid ground takes you at times or maybe most of the time to even more slippery terrain, would you agree? Albert Einstein said it best, *'You cannot solve a problem from the same level of the problem.'* In other words you have to rise above the problem and get a bird's eye view of the situation in your life. This book will take you to such an elevated platform and introduce you to a plethora of tools to not only get that bird's eye view of your life but also find solutions to whatever challenges that you have in your life now.

Your past is history and all the value that you could derive from that period in your life should be left restricted simply to comical relief if not for academic interest. Promise your best friend – oh, I mean that person who stares directly at you in the eye whenever you stand in front of a mirror, that you will never regress to whatever experiences of plight you have might gone through to arrive at this particular time and space as you read this book.

Why? First of all by the design of Creation, the past cannot be changed although every present moment is a defining moment for a future that is different than the past. *History repeats itself only when the circumstances that led to that historical event are recreated.* How many times so far have you repeated your history that continues to keep you stuck in life? Secondly, your past experiences have not been able to provide answers to your most pressing questions that you have been asking for such a long time. The purpose of the past was to demonstrate to you the operating principles of one of the core attributes of Creation – *Contrast* and hence led you to this body of knowledge.

The exchange of the baton in the relay race of your life experience has occurred, the role of the past that you perceive to be negative is complete – it has lost its breath, it is tired and worn out – it serves no more purpose than academic interest. You have a lap to run now since the baton has been passed to the present moment in the present space where you find yourself now.

Whether you win the race, whether you find the answers you have been seeking, is now entirely up to you. I can tell you that it will be challenging for you to acquire this knowledge as it will most likely be contrary to your current life script, philosophies and belief systems. The *neuroplasticity* of your current consciousness may tempt you to reject the knowledge that I share with you in this book. How long the race would last, depends on your tenacity and determination to hit the finish line. Remember that a race has only one first place, one winner, one champion.

The common person would be yawning by now, yielding to the first temptation to put this book down and go back into the shadows of grief, frustration and scarcity. For some reason they would believe there is no need to change anything, make no special effort to upgrade their current state of affairs – destiny, fate or even some external super power that apparently resides in the sky, would take care of everything. An old Chinese saying goes like this - *Insanity is the desire to keep doing the same thing over and over again and expect a different result.* An uninitiated person is a true champion of such insanity. The race that I mention smells like work and the uninitiated abhors work, even if there are promises of rewards of unimaginable proportions upon completion. The uninitiated has given up their rights bestowed upon them by virtue of their birth as a human and have voluntarily placed their trust on self-motivated external forces and entities.

But then that is NOT you. You are a champion, you are a go getter, you are open to acquire new knowledge, you are keen to evolve into that fulfilled, happy, giving, individual and realign with your life purpose. Although you are momentarily detached from your true reality and living in a world of your perceived reality, you know in the core of your being that there is more to life than what meets the physical eye. That is why you believe, that is why you seek, that is why you pick yourself up one more time, that is why you read this book. You might have gotten knocked *down* by circumstances in life but clearly nothing could or can knock you *out*. I salute your courage and your hunger to learn and evolve - *you always win because you can never lose.*

Allow me to share a quick and short answer to some of your questions that have remained unanswered until this very moment. Think of this answer as more of a reassurance that all is well and working exactly and perfectly as designed by the Eternal Consciousness of the *Genetics Of Divinity* regardless of your current situation in life.

---------------------------*****---------------------------

You are part of a grand design of Creation and Existence that stems from the Source Energy of INEFFABLE BLISS - the Source of infinite Creation, the Source of infinite WISDOM, the Source of infinite ABUNDANCE, the Source of infinite PEACE, the Source of infinite LOVE, a Source of infinite CARING, NURTURING and GIVING, the definition of the INFINITE and the ALL. In that grand design of Creation (refer to the Cycle Of Creation in Chapter 5), you are a Creature who is created through the transformation of Source Energy with the purpose to serve those entities of Existence with whom you are equipped to interact and seek to establish *symbiotic collaborative relationships through the free will of mutual consent for the purpose of collective coexistence.*

As a Creature you have been designed with an inherent desire or *will to receive and in the process enjoy unbounded delight in your life experience.* Your uniqueness and a core attribute that separates you from the other species in this planet, is that you are also a CREATOR with the inherent desire or *will to bestow and in the process too, enjoy unbounded delight* – a desire that has been implanted in you by virtue of your birth as a human.

Your desires as a human to receive and to bestow are also forms of energy that your brain generates as brainwaves. Whether what you desire to receive or desire to bestow will be reciprocated the subject of such a desire is dependent on whether the same reciprocal desire or energy is echoed back to you by your subject of the desire, under resonant conditions or under attenuated conditions. Remember the core principle of Creation – everything in Existence is mandatorily required to establish symbiotic collaborative relationships through the free will of mutual consent between the relating parties for the purpose of collective coexistence. Hence your desires transmitted as brainwaves are required to follow this core design principle of Creation in order to be fulfilled and in the process lead you to unbounded delight. I will describe brainwaves in great detail in Chapter 8 and what you learn there will blow your mind.

While you have primarily lived the life of a Creature so far, you have an inherent desire to connect to the infinite *Abundance* and ineffable *Bliss* of the CREATOR all for the purpose of enjoying infinite and unbounded delight in your life experience. How do you know what is unbounded delight? This is another magnificent aspect of creation – you have within you a very unique guidance system called the Emotional Guidance System© that I describe in Chapter 8 being as unique to you as your own DNA signature. This guidance system requires a *target* to be set – much like the destination of the GPS Navigational system in your car or in modern aircraft. This target acts like a homing beacon that your guidance system can be made to lock on and guide you through to that objective. The EGS was first presented in public by Esther and Jerry Hicks in their classic *'Ask and It Is Given'* © Using the EGS, you can define your perception of unbounded delight. Have you defined it yet? Now's the time.

--------------------------#####--------------------------

You may be asking, "Who is Joy Ghosh? What background does he have to write such a book and reveal this information? Why should I believe in him – is this information authentic? What is the guarantee that this is not another one of those self-styled gurus who has read a few books on spirituality and thinks he has the answers for my pressing questions about my life?"

By asking those qualifying questions about the credibility of information in this book, you have leveraged your inherent quality of a *Type A* Creature – the quality of discernment. You will learn all about Type A Creatures in Chapter 7. Good! I like it. I will answer your questions briefly for now and some of those answers may not be very clear at the moment. However as you go through the material contained in this book, the cognitions will set in as dormant memory systems within your subconscious mind get re-activated.

To your first question, my response is provided at the back of this book and you will know more and more about me as you read this material. The following statement may sound weird or a fantasy to you, which would be natural at this early stage of your expanding consciousness. However you will be able to appreciate this more and more as you go deeper and deeper into the knowledge contained here. *Consider me as the medium, the carrier of the knowledge that you are about to receive about Creation and Existence that has been revealed to me by my higher self in the Fifth Dimension of Existence in consultation with your very own higher dimensional self in the same Fifth Dimension of Existence.* I encourage you to be patient and yet hungry for the information that you are about to receive about the multi-dimensional architecture of Existence in Chapter 7, when this statement above will make much more sense.

To your second question, I reply, "My background will be revealed to you throughout this book as I would never contemplate making an effort to engage in the most magnificent and ambitious project of my life before personally experiencing all the cognitions, convictions and manifestations that I present to you in this book. Everything that had happened to me in my life in the past had led me to that moment in my life experience when my life purpose for this lifetime was revealed to me by my higher dimensional self. I will demonstrate to you the techniques on how to communicate with your very own higher dimensional self and identify your own life purpose. I have embarked on this project of a lifetime in conformance with that life purpose that was revealed to me, as you will shortly realize while reading this book."

To your third question, I reply, "You don't have to believe me – just allow the knowledge that you are about to receive the opportunity to reach your subconscious mind by remaining open to new beliefs and paradigms that you might not yet have been exposed to. I encourage you to make a commitment to yourself that you will go through this book word for word and feel the energy that will resonate with your subconscious memory systems about the code of the *Genetics Of Divinity*. You will realize that you need not believe me as that would not be necessary at all. You will realize that the consciousness of Creation will grow and expand inside YOU as you align yourself to the natural vibrations of your own existence. It is not a matter of 'if', but 'when' you get to that point when the consciousness within you becomes stronger with every reading of this book until you reach that coveted tipping point from disbelief to indestructible, unshakable belief, cognition and self-realization. You would then have received the answers to all those tough and pressing questions that you have been asking about your life."

To your fourth question, my response is - "The only guarantee is YOU and YOUR consciousness that is set to evolve and transform as you allow the frequency of this content to resonate with your dormant memories. I am not a self-styled *guru* by any means - I don't have any extra special powers or additional knowledge than you do. The only difference between you and I at least at this stage of your exposure to the code of the *Genetics of Divinity* is that my consciousness about Creation and Existence has been reactivated from the dormant memories *more* than yours has been. In fact I am still a student and will continue to remain an eager and insatiably hungry student of this magnificent reality show called LIFE (an acronym for *Living Infinitely For Eternity*). I still crave for and will continue to crave for more and more wisdom and knowledge that still lays dormant in my subconscious mind. Consider this book and me as the author, as your conduit between the world of *perceived reality* (or fantasy) where you live now and the world of your self-chosen *true reality* where you passionately desire to live. For those of you who have been exposed to the groundbreaking work of Dr. David Hawkins, *this book has graded to a score of 998* on 1000 on the Hawkins' Scale of

Consciousness – that should give you some reassurance about the authenticity and accuracy of the material provided here."

I know something about you – again although it is very likely that we have not physically met with each other – yet. At some point in your life, based on where you are in your life today, what your challenges have been, you have been asking some very profound questions about the way of the world in general and about your life in particular. As a Creature, these questions come to your mind when you are in solitude, or relationally alone, and ponder about how your life experience has been thus far, where it is now, where you are headed and if you are headed in the right direction of your life purpose. The nature of these questions indicates confusion in your mind and you are unable to find answers, which probably frustrates you. But then you are relentless in your pursuit and you just know in the core of your being that there are answers to those questions awaiting you to seek them out. ... and here we are.

Here's just a sampling of some of these pressing questions that you might have been asking and thoughts that you might have been thinking. "Why are all these negative things happening to me? I have been trying so hard and yet, practically nothing seems to work. I guess I was not born lucky. Nothing can defy destiny – oh well, this is my destiny! There are other people who I know with less qualities and faculties and yet they are doing so much better than I am. Why me of all people? Am I destined for failure? I am a good person and people love and respect me. So why does nothing work out for me? Why do I have to go through such pain and suffering in my life? When will it all end? Can I ever become really free and enjoy my life in a manner that I define as unbounded delight? I cannot bear so much stress in my life – nothing works out for me. Some guys have all the luck and look at me – the most unluckiest person in the world

– that's me. God does not like me. God does not listen to my prayers. What have I done to deserve this?"

I could go on, but I guess you get the point, don't you? Do you know what separates you from the uninitiated commoner? While they continue to keep asking these questions and blame everyone else taking no responsibility and accountability for their personal state of affairs, live a life of excuses and procrastination, you on the other hand have the humility to accept that you don't know it all, you don't have all the answers and yet have that hunger to seek out answers to your most pressing questions. You are convinced that there must be a reason for your current unfavorable state of affairs and there definitely is a solution for every challenge that you face in your life today. You are right – you are spot on. Your quest for knowledge and brought you to this point in your life when you have this material in your possession and here's the brief answer.

---------------------------*****--------------------------

Delight in fulfillment of your desires and enjoyment as a Creature and a CREATOR that you are, is subjective and is your own personal perception of reality. Pain and suffering, or the plight, are nothing but one of these perceptions that you have interpreted as an individual or that you have agreed to accept as a perception from another individual or society. What *you* consider as pain and suffering, may be total delight and enjoyment for the next person, each with individual free will and maturity level of consciousness.

The only reason for your perception of this life experience of plight, the only reason this perception is available to you is to demonstrate a *contrast* to another perception where there is the absence of pain and suffering. If the Creature in you, designed with the will to receive, is perceiving something as pain and suffering, then by contrast, you can also perceive what will eliminate that pain and suffering and bring you, the Creature, unbounded delight and enjoyment in your life experience.

---------------------------#####-------------------------

Although covered in greater details in Chapter 5, I wanted to allude to the concepts of *contrast, free will* and *perceived reality* to you right away, so that the excitement of self-realization continues to grow within you. You were designed for unbounded delight, which is your natural state of being. You have been engineered to be, do or have anything you want to receive and in your life experience and enjoy unbounded delight in the journey as long as what you seek is logical and ethically feasible.

Are you ready to embark on the most exciting voyage of your life? There will be storms, there will be temptations to procrastinate, there will be seemingly overpowering urges, yes, urges (in plural) to let go and jump ship, there will be people, events and circumstances that will be presented to you to defray you and knock you off course in your quest to align with your life purpose, there will be times when you won't physically see the light in the darkness around you, there will be times when FEAR (an acronym for *False Emotions Appearing Real*) will make attempts to gain a grip on you, there will be periods when your optimism and visions of fulfillment will be challenged.

The question is, can you weather those storms? Can you be that palm tree on an open beach that simply sways to the onslaught of strong winds and crushing waves? The palm tree that remains resolute long enough exactly where it is rooted, allowing the storm to inevitably lose its fury and wrath, to welcome the blue skies and the calm winds once again. The question is - can you be that palm tree as you embark on this journey to elevate your consciousness, find your life purpose and enjoy a life experience filled with unbounded delight?

---------------------------*****--------------------------

You must understand that what cannot be attained, cannot be named. Along the same lines, what can be named, can be attained without exception. The one and only reason you can want something in your life experience is because it exists in a different Parallel Universe where your physical body does not live just yet – more on Parallel Universes in Chapter 6. What you think about most of the time, *thinks* about you by default but is it most of the time as well? What you want with unshakable belief, *wants* you, but is that with the same unshakable belief as yours? What you need with absolute passion, *needs* you but is that need powered by the same level of passion as yours?

If you have played with the Law of Attraction and have been part of the billion dollar market as a consumer around this Law, I can tell you that the techniques that you have followed so far are quite ineffective, illogical and is more fiction than fact. The *Genetics of Divinity* will illustrate the true mechanics of the Law of Attraction and you will learn that this so-called "Law" is only a by-product of the core theme of this code of Eternal Consciousness.

---------------------------#####--------------------------

After reading this book and resonating with the contents, you will want to read this again and again and then again. Every time you do so, you will change, your world inside and outside you will change, you will morph into the thoroughbred of the human species. You will ascend into a maturity of Eternal Consciousness that came into Existence even before this physical Third Dimension was formed.

Your voyage will take you through the exciting realms of Theoretical and Applied Physics, Chemistry, Human Anatomy, specifically the brain and brainwaves, Genetics, Engineering, Hypnotherapy, Astronomy, Cosmology, Sacred

Geometry, Multi-Dimensional Consciousness and Multi-Dimensional Energetics. This is information that dates back to an era even before the physical Existence in the Third Dimension that you perceive through your five senses was created, and still continues to apply to every moment of your life experience.

Due to the fact you are being exposed to most of this information for the first time, especially in the areas of *Multi-Dimensional Consciousness and Energetics*, you may find the data rather esoteric and some of it may also seem impossible and incomprehensible. it did to me when the information was first revealed to me by my Fifth Dimensional self that I call my *Activebody* (described in Chapter 7). Stay patient and open to the information and use your rational discernment after you have all the facts, as your dormant memory systems get re-activated and resurface up to your conscious mind. You have the inherent ability to know that nothing is impossible as long as there is sound logic to back it up. So stay with me and you will be rewarded for your persistence and openness to receive this information.

You want things to change for the better in your life experience, right? Good! For that change in life experience to happen, you will need to change things in the manner in which you currently allow your consciousness to guide you through life. This is one of my core objectives for you in this book as you read and understand the information. I guarantee that if you stay attentive and reactivate those dormant memories, you will never be the same again as the Creature within you begins the process of alignment with the CREATOR within you and collectively you seek out and follow your life purpose. There is a lot of new information packed in this book that has never been revealed before, so I would encourage you to pace yourself through it.

Whenever I meet one of my mentors he asks, "I am excited. How about you?" So now I ask you that same question, "I am excited about you – are you?" I know you are excited and you should be since you are about to begin your alignment between the Creature or the *receiver* and the CREATOR or the *bestower* within you, collectively design your future life experience and fill it with unbounded delight. Once you have achieved alignment between the Creature and the CREATOR within you, your next step would be to start communicating with your non-physical and immortal *Activebody* in the Fifth Dimension of Existence.

Once that happens and you start receiving continuous guidance while making decisions in life, you will find that your life experience has changed dramatically and everything will seemingly go your way almost *magically*. This will happen literally at your command as long as your intent is to establish those symbiotic collaborative relationships through the free will of mutual consent for the purpose of collective coexistence. When you achieve such alignment, you will soar into a new and higher level of consciousness, from where you will be able to actually visualize your life in a future time and space – in a different Parallel Universe that you will define for yourself. All senses of self-pity, lack, scarcity and insufficiency will disappear and you will as a Creature and a CREATOR engulf your physical life experience with emotions of unbounded delight and enjoyment – exactly as the grand design of Creation intended it to be.

Since you are receiving this information as a Creature in this physical Third dimension of Existence, it is important for you to understand the basic governing laws of this physical world first before you can understand the laws of the non-physical world. It is in this understanding of duality of the physical and non-physical laws and the duality of contrast in life that you will arrive at the realization of the *singularity* of Creation and Existence.

To get started, I would like to guide you to a basic relaxation exercise - close your eyes, relax your jaws, allow your tongue to float and imagine that you are looking a blank, white screen or a natural waterfall. Inhale deeply for 3 to 4 seconds allowing your stomach to expand, hold that breath for 1 or 2 seconds and exhale slowly for 5 to 6 seconds allowing your stomach to contract. Repeat this rhythm for about five or six cycles. Just like a computer requires a reboot from time to time to refresh its memory (RAM unit and disk cache), your brain would have just rebooted through the above exercise and now, you are ready to receive. Ask yourself this question before we begin, "Am I worth it?" It is only you who can answer this question with full conviction.

Now find yourself a mirror, preferably one that is fixed to a wall where you will not be disturbed – we are going to engage in a little ritual. Look at your best friend, that is YOU by the way, straight in the eye and say this short prayer, if you will, with all sincerity and integrity,

---------------------------*****---------------------------

"I pledge and commit myself to receive this knowledge and have the humility to direct and control my energy for the alignment with my life purpose for the greater good of my life experience and for every life that I touch. I am humbled, thankful and grateful for every event and circumstance that has happened in my life so far as they have brought me to this point in my evolution by illustrating the contrast of Creation. I am ready to receive."

---------------------------#####---------------------------

Did you feel a chill or sense of calmness and a sense of bliss drift down from your head through your face and flush down onto your body as you finished that prayer? Good! This is indication through your conscious and deliberate prayer above, you have sent reactivation impulses to your dormant memories in your subconscious mind. If you did not feel this calmness engulf your body, repeat the above with true sincerity and integrity with full intent and conviction and you will feel the difference.

Why do you have to learn all this background information in this book? Why should I not give you the magic formula of success, wealth, health and relationships right now in a box wrapped in a bow and be over and done with? I understand your desperation and in all likelihood you have been feeling like this for a while now. Well, how much has that desperation, that eagerness for the non-existent magic shortcut, that so-called straight line between two points served you till date?

Allow me to make this fact abundantly clear – your perceived reality is just a fantasy because your true reality is yet to unfold in your life experience - otherwise you would not have come across this book. How do I know that? Simple, it is because you have not yet experienced unbounded delight – if you did, you would already have known this material. This book, along with the coaching available to you through the online Multiversity of the *Genetics Of Divinity*, will guide you in the direction to your chosen true reality as long as you remain teachable and open to concepts however esoteric they may appear to your conscious mind at the present moment.

I want you to have the maximum benefit of owning this book by not only acquiring the knowledge, but also by applying the techniques described herein. *Knowledge is Power but ONLY if you Use it*. Please make sure you complete the exercises presented in the remainder of this book to the best of your honest ability. Anytime you get stuck, or need some clarification or want to communicate with me, visit my website at www.GeneticsOfDivinity.com and secure access to Level 1 coaching content on every aspect of this book that I have made available to you at the Multiversity of the *Genetics Of Divinity*.

Consider this book as the turning point of your life and as one of my mentors say so bestowingly, '*May you never be the same.*' You are now ready to receive.

Chapter 3 - Knock! Knock! Who's there?

There was a time in my life, not too far away in the past when I was drifting like a rudderless ship in the stormy seas and boy was I getting tossed around! I was searching for the same answers that you are also probably searching for in your life. Little did I know about anything that you are about to read in this book. I was shrouded in mysticism, blaming everyone and everything external to me but myself. There is no shame when I admit openly that there were times in the past when I had looked up to the heavens with open arms, accused a *partial God* and asked in disgusted frustration, *"Why me of all people?"*

Those days of unbounded plight provide comical relief today and I have since then, answered my own questions (and more advanced questions keep coming up). Or is it that the code of Eternal Consciousness that I call the *Genetics Of Divinity*, led me to the answers and cognition of the truth *"It is me of all people because it **IS** I who is responsible for everything in my life experience."* Today I have not only apologized to the Eternal Consciousness for this folly of mine and made my peace, I am also getting better and better to understand the Laws of Creation and Existence – it is an ongoing learning process due to the infiniteness of this consciousness, as more and more sections of the code reactivates out of my subconscious mind and the consciousness bubbles up to my conscious mind to define my life experience of true reality.

Are you ready for an exercise? I'd like you to find a mirror and a quiet place where you will not be disturbed. If you are at home, in your parked car (no driving while reading please) or in a private place, make sure you are alone and nobody can see or even better, hear you. You will be talking to your best buddy - yes that person in the mirror in front of you is who I am referring to. People, especially those with an "immobilized or non-existent rudder" often find it weird and rather disturbing to find someone having an animated conversation with the image in a mirror. I definitely don't want any hushed and discrete phone calls to the local psychiatrist or to the lunatic asylum reporting that someone they know (you) has finally lost it. ☺. If you want to get in touch with your higher self that exists in the Fifth Dimension waiting to communicate with you, the mirror offers an excellent basic conduit to facilitate the communication – rest assured there are more advanced techniques as you will learn in future interactions with me.

---------------------------*****---------------------------

Exercise # 01

I am going to ask you a question and you will answer that question not to me, but to your best buddy in the mirror without losing eye contact, ok? There is no right or wrong answer and there is no time limit for your answer. It is important that you speak the truth and keep maintaining eye contact as you speak. There can be no secrets, no deceptions, between best buddies, right? So uphold the honor of friendship while you speak. Here's the question, "If all you had was one minute, how would you introduce yourself based on (1) *How you have lived,* (2) *How you have loved* and (3) *How you have served* so far in your life?" Think about the answers. When ready, look into the mirror and speak with all integrity and honesty.

----------------------#####--------------------------

This seemingly simple exercise could be the one of the more challenging assignments on self-reflection that you can perform for yourself. *Only after such a self-reflection at the present moment can you attempt self-projection to your future life experience filled with unbounded delight.*

When I first did this exercise during that period of extreme stress, frustration and borderline depression in my life that I described in Chapter 1, I could not speak for a few minutes – just kept staring at the 'me' in the mirror contemplating on the question as my mind raced haphazardly from memory to memory of my past. Then I remember tears welling up in my eyes as I looked at my best friend and barely managed to whisper, "I need help. Please help me." That's all I could say, I looked down, closed my eyes and had started to weep uncontrollably.

Now this may seem weird to you but I say exactly as it happened. It could well have been my imagination, but I did sense a light touch on my right shoulder, a gentle yet firm touch and then I heard *him* speak in a calm yet confident voice *"You don't know much about yourself do you, Joy? Learn to know more yourself and what lies embedded within you and that is all the help you'll ever need. I believe in you and I know you will deliver – all you need is already within you by design. Discover yourself and you will discover unbounded delight."* That was it.

While I was still trying to figure out what happened, confused in my severely compromised state of mind, I looked up, cleared my eyes and I obviously could see nobody around. I looked at the mirror again confused even more, speechless – almost hypnotized by the magnanimity of the moment. The blissful beginnings of realization of the *Eternal Consciousness* had descended on me, as the first resonant impulse was delivered to the dormant memories in my subconscious mind. I have never felt alone anymore, anywhere ever since that experience.

Even today when I recollect the experience and tell this story, emotions of the first conscious contact with my higher self, flood my mind – not of despair or desperation but emotions of sheer joy and reassurance. Even today and every morning when I wake up, I tee up a conversation with my non-physical and immortal Fifth Dimensional self or who I refer to as my *Activebody* that I describe in Chapter 7. Today our conversations are so different, so positive, so uplifting, so light hearted, so benevolent and so *'bestowing'*. My decision to write this book is also the end result of such a conversation that I had with *him*. He is not only always there *with* me, he is always there *for* me and he has all the right answers 100% of the time – no surprise there because in the dimension where he resides there is no factor of time as you will learn in Chapter 7.

You too can get answers from your own Fifth Dimensional self when you ask for it – nothing random, and I do not have any more special powers than you do. You have been designed from the Active Energy of your non-physical higher self, or *Activebody*, as I will describe in Chapter 7. It may take a little while, but once you achieve alignment with your *Activebody*, the accurate answers to your pressing questions will come to you without exception.

That was my story. How did you do with the exercise? I encourage you to take advantage of sending me your results through www.GeneticsOfDivinity.com or ideally through your secure area within the online Multiversity in Module 3. I can help and guide you more that way. Regardless of what your answer was, would you say that you know yourself really well? Think again – the answer is not as easy as it seems.

I will not take up space on this book explaining to you the structure and physiological functions of the human brain – feel free to research on your own. However I would like to draw your attention that your brain is composed of tiny cells called neurons which are interconnected to each other to constitute the nervous system. How many of these neurons does the adult human brain have? There is no accurate count, but hundreds of billions of them – more than the number of stars in the Milky Way. From basic mathematics using the principles of permutations and combinations, million-billion possible interconnections can potentially exist between these neurons. Each of these interconnections called neural pathways (described in Chapter 8), collectively define your entire life experience.

It has been speculated that if one embarked on a project to count the number of interconnections between these neurons in your brain, at a rate of counting one connection per second, it will take 32 million years to complete. Only then, would you have just completed an inventory count of the interconnections. I have not even discussed anything about the effort to understand what each of these interconnections mean to you in your life experience. Moreover, you can consciously change these neural pathways by reactivating new consciousness and acquiring new knowledge. So the effort of taking an inventory of these pathways would be futile, since by the time you counted one connection, it would probably have changed into yet another.

You really don't know yourself yet and the capabilities that you possess – you are not sufficiently self-aware. You may be aware of your current state of affairs but awareness and knowledge are vastly different. You may be aware, for example, of how to drive your car, but you may not have the knowledge of the actual technology that powers the vehicle. So you may be aware of your current state of affairs but that does not necessarily mean you know how and why you are where you are at the present moment in your life experience. Since you are reading this book, it is clear that there is some uneasiness and discomfort in your life experience and you have a desire to expand and enhance that experience.

When you think about yourself, what do you think of? What kind of a self-image do you project? Wow, these are loaded questions! Let's break it up. In the next exercise, your task is to make an assessment of your current state of life experience. The results will be the biggest eye-opener in your life, I promise you that.

One of the core founding principles of Creation and Existence mandates the establishment of symbiotic collaborative relationships for the purpose of a collective coexistence, which implies that nothing – physical or non-physical can exist in isolation. Following this principle, your entire life experience can be compartmentalized in the thirteen distinct relationship categories as shown in Figure 1.

Essentially your task in Figure 1, is to focus on each category which represents a particular collaborative relationship of your life where you invest some time and energy on. Spend a few minutes thinking about the people (alive or not), objects, emotions or experiences in that relationship under consideration. If you are wondering... yes, you do have a relationship with inanimate objects such as finances and other material objects that money can buy, just like you have a relationship with the society or community that you live in, your career and academics. What emotions flooded your mind when you first shifted focus on that relationship? Would you regard that relationship to be symbiotic and collaborative? Was the relationship created through the free will of mutual consent between you and your partner in the relationship? Would you say that relationship is one of collective coexistence that brings you both unbounded delight in your life experience? Write them down. Now visualize a virtual interaction with the *subject* in that relationship - you MUST see yourself in that picture when you visualize.

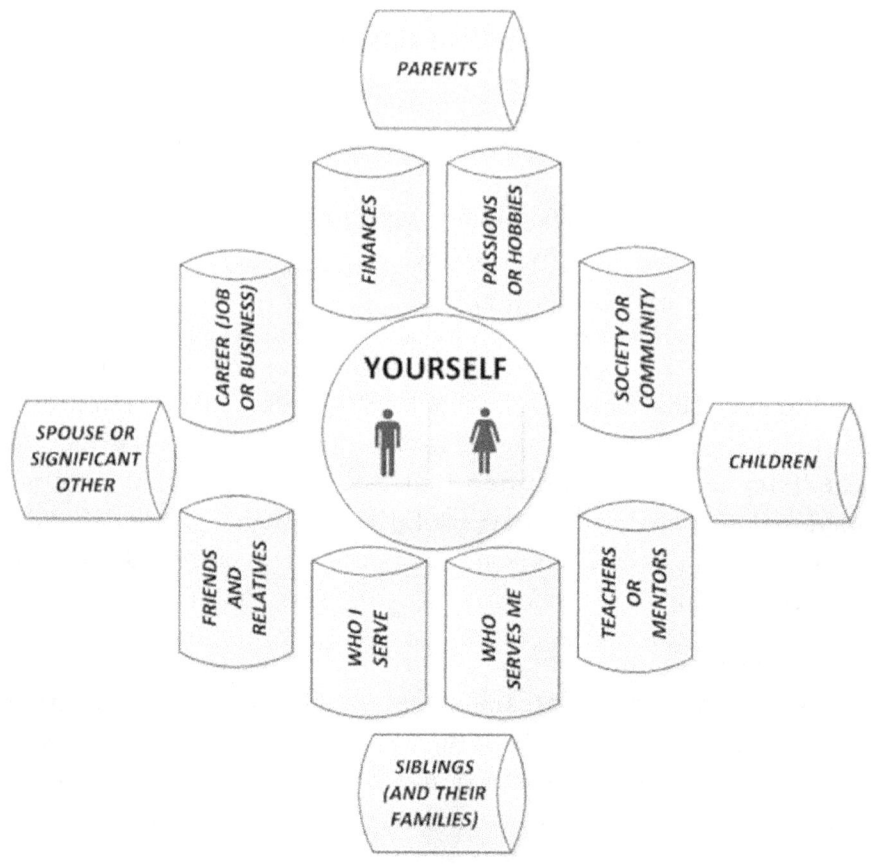

Figure 1

Look towards your top-right while you perform this task for better access to your *conscious* memory bank. Pick one memorable interaction from the past that you had with the partner in that relationship to help you with the process of visualization. You may ask, "Well, do I pick a good or a not so good interaction?" My answer is *"Yes"*. You get to pick just any one interaction from the past – your choice. Ready?

What kind of image have you portrayed or are now portraying to the other partner in that relationship in that interaction? I describe the concept of *Desirability Index* in Chapter 8 – this indicates how desirable you project yourself to the other party in the relationship. You have to understand that just because you desire something in life it does not necessarily imply that it desires you as well. In the spirit of this code of Eternal Consciousness, a relationship worth your time and energy is one that is symbiotic and collaborative in nature for your collective coexistence.

Coming back to the Exercise, if you are focusing on the "Children" category, what would be your first emotion? When you did the visualization of the interaction, what kind of image were you projecting to your child(ren)? The image that you project to the outer world is the same image that gets projected back to you. Recent studies have revealed the existence of mirror neurons that I refer to as *mirror memory patterns.* This will be clear to you when I discuss the architecture of memory systems in your body.

Are you projecting the image of a caring, nurturing, understanding, role model, supportive, loving and protective parent to your child(ren)? Or is it that you were projecting an image that is distant, disconnected, agitated, angry, punitive, non-committal or indifferent? Describe that image using keywords or key phrases such as the examples I have mentioned above. Once done with this relationship, go to the next category and repeat the process for each of the relationship categories indicated in Figure 1

A common question that you may ask is *'Where do I start'*? You can start anywhere and complete them in any order, except the *centerpiece* – that would be the last. My personal choice is to start with the four categories that you see positioned horizontally, since they are either the closest to your bloodline and/or you are more likely to invest a greater part of your time and energy with. Imagine all of the relationship categories as cylinders laid out on their curved surfaces as in Figure 1 with the central cylinder placed on its flat surface. Imagine you are looking down from the top so that you just see the flat surface of the central cylinder and the curved surfaces of the other cylinders.

---------------------------*****---------------------------

Exercise #02

There are no right or wrong answers in this exercise. You are simply taking stock of or doing a survey of your current state. Moreover this is a private task, so stay truthful to yourself.

For each relationship category in Figure 1 except the central one write down your first emotion when you started to focus on the partner(s) in that relationship. Then visualize a past interaction that you had with the partner(s) in that relationship and write down the image that you were projecting to the other party in that interaction.

Repeat this for all relationships but the central one in your chosen sequence. Then continue below

---------------------------#####---------------------------

I am assuming you have completed Exercise #02 by now, and have all relationships addressed except the central one. Now let's focus on the central relationship that represents YOU. This is the most important and significant relationship of all – *YOUR relationship with YOURSELF*. Is that relationship with yourself symbiotic and collaborative in nature? Do you take care of your body, your thoughts, your actions, your emotions, what you eat, what you drink, what do you voluntarily consent to put inside your body – is that sporadic or in regular intervals, who do you interact with, who do you love, what do you love – think about your life and how you *carry* yourself on a day to day basis. Let's tilt the three dimensional layout now and instead of a top down view where you saw everything flat in Figure 1 (technically called a 'plan' type of view in architectural engineering), we look at the above arrangement of the relationships in your life from the side as in Figure 2 (technically called and 'elevation' type of view in architectural engineering).

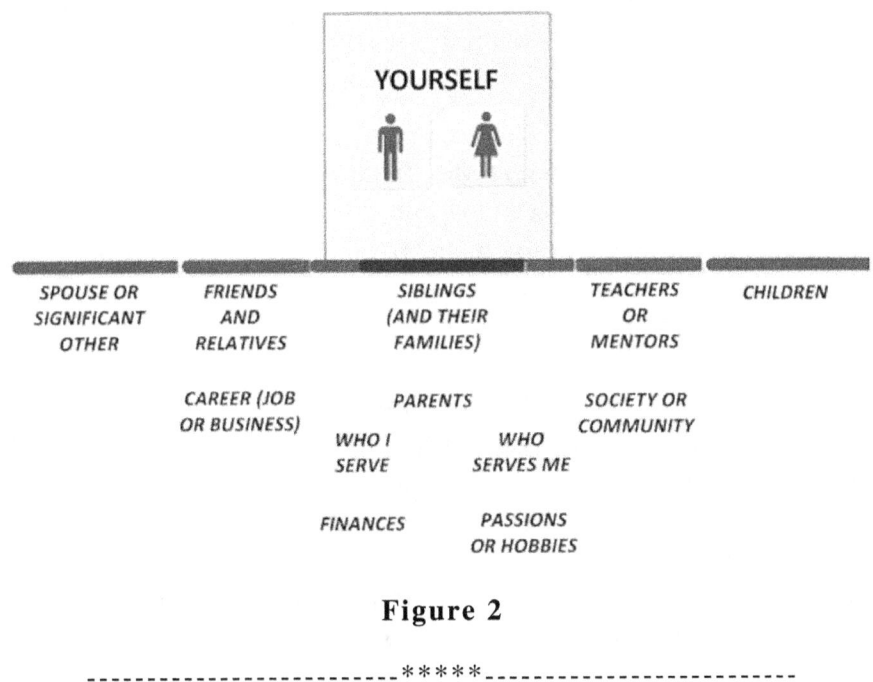

Figure 2

---*****---

Exercise #03

In Figure 2 where *you* stand out as the centerpiece, consider the image that you portray to yourself. How do you perceive yourself TODAY when you see yourself in the mirror? If you had to rate your quality of life experience in one sentence what would that be? Would that self-image be the sum total of the images that you outlined in the twelve relationships in Exercise 01 or would that be something different?

We are only assessing your current state of self-image.

Write down on the first emotion when you think about your best friend – *YOU*. How do you feel about yourself? Are you getting ahead in life or do you feel you are falling behind? Be honest in this exercise and understand yourself. Write any good and the not so good keywords or key-phrases about yourself. When you see yourself in the mirror, what do you feel? What emotions flood your mind?

--------------------------#####--------------------------

In all likelihood this is the first time you invested your time to take stock of your current state and your relationship with the other aspects of your life. Take a few minutes to scan what you have written in all relationships. Close your eyes, take a few long and deep breaths (about 4-5 breaths per minute following the breathing cycle of a 4-5 second inhalation, 2-3 seconds of hold and 6-7 seconds of exhalation) and allow your mind to wander as you visit all the relationships one at a time ending with the central relationship with yourself. This is probably the most detailed exercise on self-reflection that you have ever done before and you will realize by the time you are done reading this book, how important this effort has been.

You are on a journey here to elevate your consciousness and enjoy a life experience filled with unbounded delight. Like any other journey, it is mandatory to know your present coordinates before you can plan and navigate to your intended destination. We will revisit this exercise at the end of this book after you have undergone a consciousness upgrade. At that time I will be asking you to perform the exercise and evaluate the results again. I will ask you, if you had to establish a symbiotic collaborative relationship through the free will of mutual consent for the purpose of collective coexistence, which are the top three relationships that you would focus on first? Invariably those relationships would be the top three that you would desire to enjoy in a

Parallel Universe where you would want to spend your life experience in the future.

As an owner of this book you are eligible for access to the training portal in the Multiversity of the *Genetics Of Divinity* and I encourage you to enroll and take advantage of downloadable charts, worksheets and guides from that resource that were referenced in this Chapter. For further details I encourage you to visit the companion website at www.GeneticsOfDivinity.com.

Chapter 4 - Consciousness – Your Identity

You are well on the road to self-realization and self-revelation that there is much more to you than what currently meets the criteria of your currently perceived reality. This chapter is the defining moment of your life. As you progress through this chapter, you may find the contents incomprehensible and unintelligible and you may even feel the temptation to stop reading any further. If this happens, don't fight the emotions that you feel – it is natural and will be your defining moment as you will begin the process to remember who you are, where you came from and why you are here. The subsequent chapters will solidify such cognitions for you – this is the start.

Examine Figure 3 very closely. Consider each ring stacked up against the one next to it to form the shape of a bowl. If you stare at this image for a while, you may experience a hypnotic effect and almost actually see that stacked up three dimensional bowl-like shape. As you can see in Figure 3, the bottom edge of the ring represents the *consciousness* level, while the top edge represents the primary emotions and feelings that stand out in an individual who is at that level of consciousness. I call Figure 3 the *Consciousness Chart of Creation.*

Figure 3 also illustrates the bridge between the consciousness of the physical world that we can interpret around us on the basis of our five senses and the non-physical worlds, yes, *worlds* in plural that are beyond the reach and comprehension of those five senses. Why, you ask, should we even bother about understanding the non-physical worlds if our five senses cannot comprehend them? Read on and ask that question again by the time you have completed this book – the answer will be evident.

--------------------------*****--------------------------

It is only through the understanding of the non-physical Energy can a Creature endowed with the *will to receive*, begin to understand the true essence of Creation, recognize the CREATOR within and discover the *will to bestow*. Once a Creature arrives at this cognition of the non-physical Energy, *it* can begin the process of enjoying a physical life experience filled with elements that the Creature defines as unbounded delight.

--------------------------#####--------------------------

I guarantee you this – you have never seen anything like Figure 3 before. The concepts that you learn just from this one illustration may defy your current beliefs and thought patterns - some initial reluctance and possible rejection is natural. But then, you don't know what you don't know, do you? Stay receptive to this information and soon all that reluctance will go away as you get cleansed and cleared, thereby opening yourself up for inevitable transformation. From this point onwards in this book, you will experience a shift in your consciousness if you are willing to play on. It is your choice to have an open mind and take time to understand the basic different elements of Creation and unleash your true identity of a CREATOR.

Before we being to dive into the magnanimity of Figure 3, it is important to understand the meaning of *consciousness*. Let us take a simple example from the physical world to illustrate the concept. Since you are consuming this material, either by reading or listening, I would assume that you are wide awake and attentive to the material. What would happen if the temperature of your

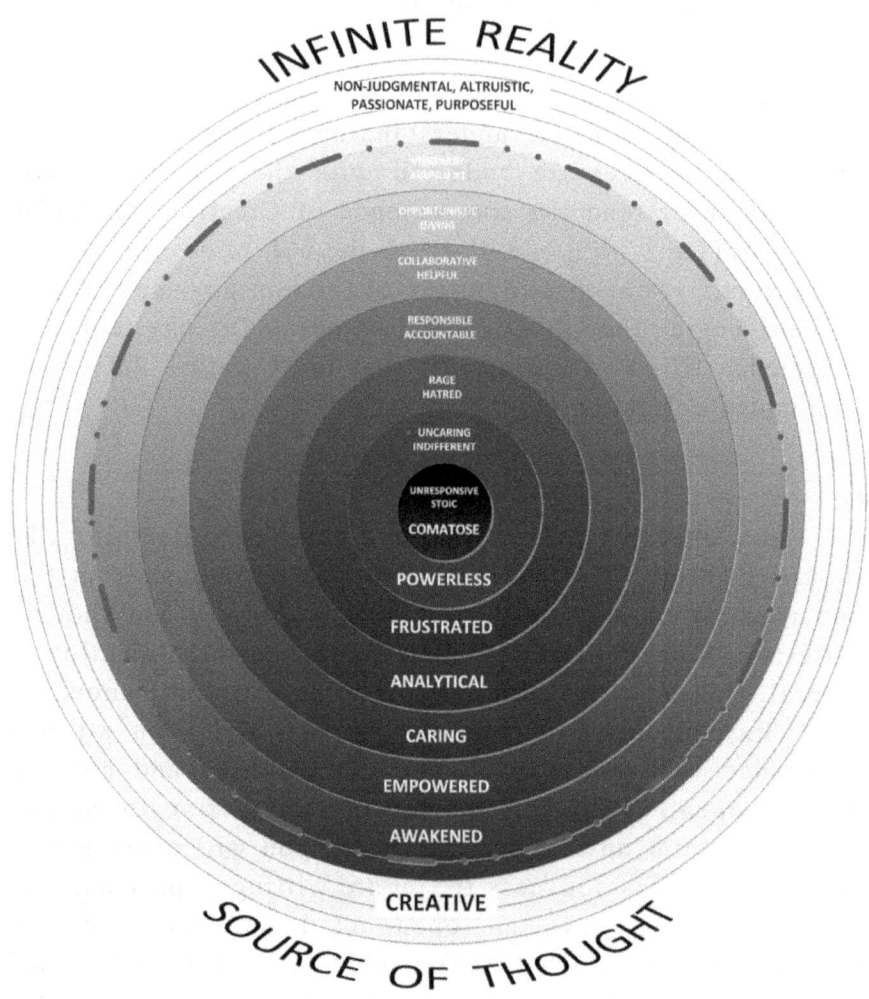

Figure 3

surroundings was suddenly dropped to a level that would make you really uncomfortable? In all likelihood, you will be looking for or reaching out to something to preserve your comfortable body heat, right? However consider a person in a state of coma, surviving on life support systems being exposed to such a change in environmental conditions - do you think the reaction would be similar to yours? Hardly! So where is the difference between you and that other person in a state of coma?

Your knowledge and understanding of what a comfortable temperature in the above example means to you and what you need to do to regain that feeling of comfort is almost an automatic response and action. The other person in that state of coma is unable to respond to that impulse or use any knowledge on the subject. This knowledgebase in your memory systems that facilitates your response or your reactions to your interactions with people, events and circumstances is called *consciousness*. It is this consciousness that determines literally any relationship currently active in your life experience or you will seek to establish in the future.

Defining Consciousness

---------------------------*****--------------------------

Consciousness is the knowledgebase and hence ability of an individual – physical or non-physical, to identify the self, determine its role and purpose in Existence to build symbiotic collaborative relationships with other entities in Existence through the free will of mutual consent between the relating partners for the purpose of collective coexistence and consequently be able to consciously and voluntarily influence and control the life experience.

In Chapter 7 you will learn about the Twelve Dimensions of Existence and the same definition of consciousness is applicable across this multi-dimensional architecture, whether the dimension is physical or non-physical. While the concept of *life experience* in the Third dimension where you and I are having this contemporary physical experience is finite and mortal, the life experience in the non-physical dimensions are immortal and hence infinite in nature since these dimensions are independent of the factor of time as I will explain shortly.

-------------------------#####-------------------------

Now that you understand the basics of consciousness, how does that relate to this chapter and the book? The consciousness I am referring to here in this book refers to your level of conscious understanding, acceptance, perception and automatic response to the grand design of Creation and your specific role and purpose in the grid of Existence as defined by the code of Eternal Consciousness that I call the *Genetics Of Divinity*.

Who are you? Why are you here? Where do you come from? Where will you be going after your physical body *passes on* (not passes away)? What would you be doing after you pass on? What is the purpose of your life? Why is there pain and suffering in your life and in the world? Why of all people have you (in your perception) been *'chosen'* to experience the hardships and challenges that you may be going through right now in your life? What have you done to deserve that experience in life? Why have things happened to you the way they happened to you? If you knew how, could you have made them happen differently? If you knew how, could you convince yourself that you can predict the future of your life experience based on the choices that you have made in the past that led you to your present moment? If you knew how, could you make a choice right now and carve out a different life experience in the future? If you knew how, can you be, do or have anything and everything that you want in life as long as it is logical and ethically feasible and conforms to the postulates of the *Genetics Of Divinity*? Are you in control of your life experience or is there some writing on the wall called *destiny* or *luck* that dictates everything? Is there someone *'out there'* (traditionally regarded to live somewhere in the open sky) who wants to punish you for your *'sins'*? Is that someone out there, responsible for your current quality of your life experience or is that someone you yourself? Can you answer one or more of these questions correctly without even thinking about it just like you know your name? Therein lies your level of consciousness that I am referring to in this book.

As you will read in this book, there are different levels of this consciousness of Creation, some of which are comprehensible and applicable in this physical dimension of Existence while some can only be attained in the non-physical dimensions of Existence.

The Different Levels Of Consciousness

I will start with the lowest level of consciousness that we as the Creature and a CREATOR of Creation can have a life experience with and work our way up – at least to the level where you can comprehend within the limits of your conscious intelligence. Once you get there, I will take you further. There is absolutely no need to fret if you cannot understand past a certain level – give it time and repetition and you will get past those blocks.

Before you dive in to understand and attempt to relate yourself to one of these different levels of consciousness, it is important to know that wherever your current level of consciousness is at, it is the result of your past belief systems and paradigms that have been implanted in your conscious mind ever since you were born in physical form. In your early years of life a lot of these belief systems and paradigms have been implanted by the environment where you grew up. As your consciousness and rationality developed, you consciously allowed additional belief systems and paradigms to develop these memory systems. Collectively today this consciousness is controlling the quality of your life experience – you decide if that experience is one of unbounded plight or of unbounded delight. You were designed by the Laws of Creation and Existence for unbounded delight in your life experience. If your current life experience is short of your personal definition of this unbounded delight, you will now learn the root cause and it is my belief and desire that you will take action to upgrade your consciousness.

If you do have a desire to upgrade your level of consciousness, I want you to know that you can, from the very moment you make that decision to do so. Your current level of consciousness is a memory system in your body that influences conscious thought and action as you will learn in Chapter 8. You have all the infrastructure you need to neutralize those inhibiting memories and reactivate new memories of higher levels of consciousness about the code of the *Genetics Of Divinity*. The code is already embedded in your subconscious mind by virtue of you being a human, but it lays dormant and hence ineffective to enable you to enjoy a life experience filled with unbounded delight.

COMATOSE – An individual having a life experience at this lowest level of consciousness can actually be likened to a person in a state of coma, being kept alive through life support systems only. Clinically this person is alive but the

five senses trigger no conscious and intelligent reaction, not even the basic animal reactions of flight, fight or freeze. The eyes that look but not see, the ears that hear but don't listen, the tongue that does not sense any taste, the nostrils that smell no fragrance, the skin that feels no touch, the mind that is empty as a dark black canvas, are all attributes of a person in this level of consciousness.

This person perceives everything with suspicion and lives with the expectation that everything and anything that happens in life has the underpinnings of greater grief and suffering. Such a person does not pay attention to advice and counsel regardless how sound and beneficial they may be. Lack of knowledge is often compounded by the lack of desire to acquire knowledge, which leads to an insurmountable and persistent fear of the unknown. Such a person has an attitude of false arrogance to not invest any energy on the improvement of the personal life experience, due to the falsely deep-rooted *'I-know-it-all-and-it's-my-fate'* belief. Such a person is not teachable, does not entertain nor accept change, would rather suffer and complain than consider options to enhance the personal life experience.

Bitterness, jealousy, hatred, revenge, anger, passive aggressiveness or even confrontational behavior, focus on all that is perceived as negative or flawed are all attributes that define the attitude of such a person. There is no inclination to learn about, far less understand the Laws of Creation but a strong reliance on mysticism and heresy. Such a person may also exhibit character traits where some belief exists in the concept of *God* as projected by religious doctrines, which could have been developed through observation of others at a similar level of consciousness. However there is little that can be considered *"Godlike"* in this person. Such a person may indulge in an elaborate external display of being a devout follower of a religious *God*, but exhibits no character, attitude or action that conforms to such a belief.

Such an individual survives in a self-destruct mode, taking heed to no warning and staying inattentive and callous towards self-improvement and self-realization. In the scale of consciousness such an individual can be considered to be living a life of unbounded plight with no direction and no set purpose.

POWERLESS – An individual at this level of consciousness has been living the life that may be likened to a rudderless ship in stormy seas. Life continues to incessantly remain filled with emotions of despair, unfounded fears, insurmountable and repeatable grief and a sense of seemingly everlasting lack of control. Such an individual feels unworthy, has surrendered to the disempowering doctrines of fate, fortune, luck and destiny, would resign and turn the other cheek for more when life slaps on one, submits to everything told or asked to do, suffers from guilt and blames everyone and everything else around, takes little responsibility or accountability in life.

This individual's sense of insecurity has a vice-like grip on the entire being and in all likelihood, suffers from chronic depression. There is so much of catabolic energy in this person's consciousness that it adversely affects the physical health (high blood pressure, diabetes, weight gain, insomnia, shortness of breath to name a few symptoms). Self-pity is this person's shadow and mirror. The unworthiness and total powerlessness in this person raises questions about the role and purpose in the life experience. Every moment is a struggle and a deliberate effort to survive that does not feel natural. Life is considered a burden rather than a journey. Such a person seldom has good friends or lovers and may often be a subject of abuse and ridicule from others.

Deep down this person's core there are moments when fleeting thoughts of a better life may appear, but the catabolic ball of energy is so great, that those moments are usually short-lived. Such a person may have reached a point of giving up, stopped caring for self or for others, has lost the urge to seek and set direction in life to a point that even positive events and circumstances are met with stoic indifference, non-appreciation and ingratitude. The intensity of the catabolic energy is so large that the individual is engulfed with the pre-disposition to ignore favorable experiences, consciously focus on the unfavorable and unconsciously attract more of what is unwanted.

The powerlessness of such an individual imparts a victim's mentality in outlook towards life, treating everything and everyone with suspicion and literally expecting and anticipating a negative experience at every interaction. Such an individual may exhibit frequent outbursts of hatred and rage in both inward and outward personalities. Conviction of unworthiness and near-total unconscious disconnection from the code of Eternal Consciousness may even cause such an individual to submit to emotions of jealousy and contempt. Such a person does not project a sustained willingness if any, to learn, change and improve even if there may be an awareness that in that knowledge and change lies the *secret* to recover from the fathomless chasm where the individual is currently having a life experience of unbounded plight.

Such a person would often submit to the concept of a religious *God* as the panacea to all problems in life and indulge in prayer and rituals prescribed by organized religion, however taking insignificant action to assume self-responsibility and accountability for the quality of life experience. The dependence on external factors for personal peace and happiness is almost total, however illogical and unfounded it may be. Such a person would always complain about lack and scarcity in life without any desire or willingness to learn or change the quality of life experience.

FRUSTRATED – In this level of consciousness a person understands that there is more to life that meets the eye of the average person with the Powerless consciousness. Such an individual *'suspects'* that there is a better and bigger life possible, primarily when comparing with other individuals (at a higher level of consciousness) who are perceived to be enjoying an improved life experience. However a person in this level of consciousness does not know or understand why whatever is desired continues to remain a mere mirage in the life experience. There may be a conscious willingness to learn and even an urge to accept change, but the subconscious resistance and lethargy to invest resources to acquire and apply higher learning inhibits such a person from rapid improvement of the quality of life experience.

Such a person has a lot of unanswered questions and hence confusion about life, which leads to doubt and rejection of opportunities for improvement of the current state. Interestingly enough, doubt is an emotion that is a blend of optimism and pessimism. It is this optimistic component of this person's consciousness that gets rewarded with opportunities presented for improvement of current state, but it is that concurrent opposing pessimistic component of the consciousness that rejects those very same opportunities, leading to frustration of non-progression and non-achievement.

At this level of consciousness, the individual is engaged in self-sabotaging beliefs that could lead to emotions of anger, rage, hatred, jealousy, revenge, irritation, impatience and irresoluteness of purpose. It is this impatience that leads this individual to prematurely give up the pursuit of self-improvement, regardless of an inner dormant belief that improvement is possible. Hence this person gets easily discouraged and approaches opportunities with mixed feelings. As you will learn in Chapters 8 and 9, feelings are different energy waveforms of varying amplitude and frequency. When there are mixed feelings, the resultant attenuation stymies the individual's level of success and achievement. There is a pretty strong if not total submission to mysticism, fate, fortune, destiny, luck and a belief that life is a journey that has already been pre-planned by a *partial and external religious God* at birth and one just has to submit and get along with it.

When the chips are down, such an individual would get discouraged, take adversity as a shortcoming of that pre-planned course in life and blame all external influences for the current state of life experience. The individual is overwhelmed with the *quirks of life*, flirts with games of chance without thoughtful plan or rational strategy, with a hope that luck and good fortune may decide to smile just for once. Frustration, disappointment and an overwhelmed state of mind, leads this person to frequent moments of *'Why me?'* or *'Why bother? It is not in my control anyway.'* or *'Oh well! It is what it is.'*

There is a subconscious belief of a light at the end of the tunnel but also a doubt that instead of being bright daylight, it might be a runaway freight train beating down the tracks. It is difficult for such an individual to forgive and forget. Trust on others does not come easily for this person due to the insecurity of past experiences, with the confusion and doubt that trust could lead to potential disaster.

The catabolic energy makes this person prefer to perceive the glass as half empty with the wish (not belief) that it might just be half full. Such an individual would agree to allow periods to learn and consider making positive changes for the improvement in the quality of life. However such a person is unable to retain sustained periods of focus and deliberate intention due to the impatience and overwhelmed state of mind. Life, is considered by this person to be survival in emergency mode in a constant sense of high alertness, anticipating adversity at every blind corner. Frustration leads to stress which in turn adversely affects the physical health and mental well-being.

ANALYTICAL – At this level of consciousness, the individual has chosen to begin to learn and understand the Laws of Creation and Existence and identify the purpose of life. The catabolic energy in consciousness is often overpowered and overshadowed by a more powerful anabolic energy in this individual, although at times there may be occasional indulgence in flirtation with catabolic energy (refer to the last two levels of consciousness that I have described). Such an individual has chosen to apply rationality and analysis on events, circumstances and interactions with other people prior to reacting to situations. This person prefers to respond to situations through analysis than react through the basic animal instincts of fight, flight or freeze.

This person is willing to learn what is not already known that would help in understanding the role and purpose of life in the Cycle of Creation. This individual is convinced that there is a better quality of life waiting to unfold and is keen to understand how to get there. A person at this level of consciousness is in the process of developing a very crucial personality trait of taking responsibility for everything - good, bad or indifferent that has or is happening in life. This person does not indulge in blaming anyone else for any lack or scarcity in life, but assumes complete self-accountability for every event, circumstance, situation and every interaction with every person in life.

This individual goes through life seeking answers to questions that are full of eagerness and expectation with a hunger to learn and grow. Granted that such a person every now and then yields to events and circumstances that downgrade the quality of life experience to a lower level but the elasticity of this person's consciousness is so powerful, it brings him or her right back. Such a person is open-minded and willing to listen and learn about self-improvement. Reasoning, analysis and intelligent evaluation are natural responses for this person.

This person has advanced from a '*I know it all*' to a '*I am always willing and hungry to learn and change more*', personality trait that makes a substantial contribution to the state of happiness and well-being. Such an individual is beginning to learn and understand the Laws of Creation and has a growing belief that one can indeed align with a chosen reality. The focus of this person is on self-improvement and self-realization. There is a humble acceptance that in order to change the life experience, changes are required in the belief patterns and paradigms that influence and guide the decision making process.

Such a person is in the first stage of consciousness where the presence of the bestowing CREATOR is being felt and acknowledged. This person's *will to receive* is strong as a result of an increased awareness of the purpose of Creation and the role of a Creature. This desire is enveloped in healthy expectation and feelings of gratitude and humility. Every now and then the concept of the time factor to receive what the person desires in the life experience leads to possible confusion or impatience, which in turn may cause the person to lose focus or change the subject of desire midway to its realization in physical reality.

Such a person understands the power of focused thought. At this level of consciousness the individual recognizes the purpose of a key attribute of Creation – Contrast and understands the reason behind the duality of Existence – for example, pain exists to clarify the emotion of pleasure. This individual understands that pain in life experience occurs when one is misaligned with their life purpose. It is by this very contrast of misalignment does this individual increasingly realize the need for alignment with the life purpose that would bring about a life experience of unbounded delight.

This is the first level of consciousness where the individual is observed to be applying rational thought and logical intelligence in life events and circumstances, thereby leveraging the natural attributes of being born as a human. It is easier to upgrade to higher levels of consciousness than from the prior levels discussed so far.

CARING – At this level of consciousness, the individual has attained an increased degree of alignment with the core purpose of Creation prescribed by the *Genetics of Divinity* – that to serve and establish symbiotic collaborative relationships. There is a greater understanding of the attributes and role of the CREATOR (with will to bestow) and the Creature (with will to receive) and consequently enjoy unbounded delight. With an increased awareness to the Laws of Creation, such a person recognizes that *in the act of selfless giving lies the path to exponential receiving*. Although this person seeks ways to bestow as the CREATOR, the challenge becomes to maintain the *sustained feeling* of selflessness, due to the inherent design of the Creature that is designed with the will to receive. This causes confusion about how to engage in the act of *selfless* giving or if it is even possible to give selflessly. There always seems to be an expectation to receive, as a motivation in every act of giving.

Such a person lives a life of *symbiotic collaborative* co-habitation, not a life of compromise and rejects relationships where the other party does not engage in collaboration. Compared to a person in the Analytical level of consciousness, this individual has greater focus on goals and objectives that are personally set in life. It takes a more powerful (in terms of intensity) negative event or circumstance to derail such a person from the chosen path to achieve what is desired. However, such a person is often found to line up too many objectives with the desire to receive concurrently. It is not considered greed, but rather an over-confidence which makes it challenging to maintain sustained focus for a long enough duration on all of them at the same time. As a result of this *dispersed* intensity of focus, the person faces the challenge of *gestation period* (lapsed time between conception of thought and completion to realization) to achieve results, which may lead the person to flirtation with emotions of frustration, disappointment and doubt.

Charity and compassion are key drivers for such an individual, who seeks ways and means to come closer to the CREATOR-self through the act of bestowing for the delight of others. Due to the focus on too many concurrent objectives, such an individual is often found to live in a sense of scarcity, which may be financial and/or time, to support the inclination to serve and bestow. At this level of consciousness the person feels a sense of delicate balance between the Creature and the CREATOR selves and understands that receiving and giving are equally important and inter-dependent on each other by *Contrast*.

EMPOWERED – I consider this as the *breakthrough level of human consciousness*, since this is the first level where the individual begins to truly comprehend the purpose of Creation, the role of the CREATOR and the Creature in all of Existence and is increasingly achieving alignment with the *Genetics Of Divinity*. At this level of consciousness the individual is at the beginning of the self-discovery process with the realization that there is the ability within to be, do or have anything and everything that the mind desires and sets intense and consistent focus on, as long the object of desire is logical and ethically feasible. *Ethical feasibility is based on symbiotic collaborative relationships established through the free will of mutual consent between the relating partners for the purpose of collective co-existence.* The will to receive is at its peak, due to the cognition and firm belief about the true essence of Creation – that the Creature has been designed by the CREATOR with the will to receive and enjoy unbounded delight in the life experience.

---------------------------*****---------------------------

The cognition of inner capabilities to control and direct the mind to whatever end it desires that is logical and ethically feasible, is coupled with the joy and expectation of what is possible in true physical reality and not artificial perceived reality.

This individual understands the significance of the dimensions that are physical and non-physical as defined by the *Genetics Of Divinity*. This person understands the concept of *delayed gratification* in the process of setting and achieving the targets desired in the life experience. There is a strong belief and understanding of the process of manifestation of set objectives, which the individual can repeat over and over again with predictable outcomes. Such a person understands that contrary to common belief and misguided propaganda, manifestation is not creating what does not exist in the current physical experience of the Creature. Manifestation rather is *making the self more desirable to the object of desire followed up with a deliberate and unambiguous alignment of thought, intent and action (following the Cycle of Creation) with the object of desire that already exists, albeit outside the purview of the current life experience.*

The individual in this breakthrough level of consciousness realizes that the design of Creation has implanted the attributes of both the CREATOR and the Creature in one physical entity. The purpose of life of such an entity would be to serve and receive service in order to sustain collective coexistence.

This person understands that there are no negative events or circumstances in life. Such life experiences that are perceived as negative are merely the mechanics of course corrective measures that run on auto-pilot within the Creature to demonstrate the Contrast to events and circumstances that are perceived to be positive. Circumstances and events that are considered unfavorable serve the purpose for the Creature to clearly identify what is favorable, thereby re-aligning the life experience to one of unbounded delight. Such a person smiles in the face of what others may deem to be adversity, due to the knowledge that a lesson is waiting to be learned from that so called adverse life experience.

---------------------------#####--------------------------

Such a person takes full responsibility and complete accountability for anything and everything that happens in life and recognizes that every event and every circumstance is the end result of the intensity, duration and frequency of focus that was applied on the subject of the event or circumstance. In this level of consciousness the individual is beginning to feel a sense of freedom as anabolic energy pulsates from within the physical being rendering a feeling of reassurance that every experience would ultimately work out advantageously.

This person perceives the world from within and does not succumb to the temptations to allow the external influences to impact the world within. This individual has a keen sense of what is pleasurable and what is not. This person has had life experiences that leads to the belief that pursuit of what will bring unbounded delight in the life experience is more of an emotional delight and not what is perceived by the five physical senses as being materially pleasurable.

This person is a visionary and thinks in terms of long term enjoyment or *delayed gratification* with no interest in short-term delight or *instant* gratification. The visionary in such an individual is guided by such long range thoughts and ambitions with an automatic reliance on an internal guidance system called the *EGS*, that I will describe later in Chapter 8.

At this level the person's consciousness is in a stable balance between the experiences of a Creature and the CREATOR with the cognition that in the act of bestowing is hidden the act of receiving, according to the attribute of *Duality* in Existence. While the CREATOR desires to provide unbounded delight to the Creature by properly channeling through the Cycle of Creation, the Creature, through the fulfillment of the will to receive and enjoying unbounded delight, provides the emotions of success and fulfillment to the CREATOR – one cannot exist without the other.

This individual is beginning to understand the sublime Laws of Creation and the purpose of Existence as defined by the code of the *Genetics of Divinity*, which imparts a sense of uninhibited freedom in the physical life experience. More and more dormant memories of the *Genetics Of Divinity* continue to bubble up from the subconscious mind to the conscious mind, which enables the life experience to be filled with unbounded delight. This person is in the process of developing the ability to predict the future because of the increasingly improving ability to first align with discrete targets of desire, apply deliberate and sustained focus and manifest those targets in true physical reality.

This individual understands that *it is possible to control the life experience and even collapse time* when guided by the code of the *Genetics Of Divinity,* however is not yet aware of the precise mechanics to acquire such control.

However in a quest for higher consciousness and energetic healing modalities of the physical body, this individual invests substantial time and effort in research and self-discovery.

AWAKENED – This is the highest level of consciousness attainable by a Creature in this physical Third Dimension of Existence. The individual experiences intense emotions of unbounded delight and enjoyment, unconditional love, uninhibited appreciation and has the humility to express unrestricted gratitude for everything that directly or indirectly touches the life experience. This individual understands the nature of *interconnectedness* between all Creatures, animate and inanimate. Such an individual demonstrates passion and commitment in every desire, thought and action. This individual conducts life with enthusiasm for what already exists in the physical life experience and with eagerness for what can be added for greater enjoyment and fulfillment.

Such an individual understands that there are no negative events in life - only opportunities to learn and improve with the conviction and knowledge that it is all about personal perception. Such a person smiles in the face of diversity with the knowingness that therein lies the Contrast to reveal what would lead to absolute delight. This person understands the purpose of Creation and that everything being experienced is exactly by pre-thought and design of Creation. The Contrast in life is only meant to illuminate the path to absolute delight. Such a person understands that the unbounded delight of receiving is dependent on the unbounded delight of bestowing.

This individual has uncovered the mechanics to control Existence in the Third Dimension and is a master of establishing those symbiotic collaborative relationships as prescribed by the *Genetics Of Divinity*. This person is a proponent of peace, love and fosters mutual collaboration and cooperation. This person understands the flow of Adaptive Energy in Creatures in the Third Dimension and has insight on how to manipulate energy channels for the improvement of the physical and psychological health.

The boundaries and perception of time and space are beginning to blur and there is an *eagerness to rise above the finite world of physical materiality into the infinite world of non-physical ethereality*. The magnanimity of Creation still continues to deliver wonder and amazement to this person's consciousness. This person is driven by the search of enlightenment and the quest for freedom from the Creature's attribute of insatiable desires to receive finite material targets in the life experience. The perception of what *CAN be* has been replaced with the perception of what *already IS*. Such knowledge based on the resolute cognition and indestructible belief that all of physical reality for the Creature has already been created and is simply awaiting alignment from the Creature followed by subsequent attraction of the physical body in the time and space dimension where the subject of alignment exists. Such a person understands the true mechanics of the Law of Attraction based on the Desirability Index as I describe in Chapter 7.

The individual is *already living in the intended physical reality in a simulated life experience engaging all the five senses,* thereby magnifying the intensity of focus of the subject of desire. This firm belief, this intense focus and the unshakable knowledge of the inevitable provides immense pleasure and appreciation for life and realization of the inner power that others at lower levels of consciousness would consider to be a miracle. There is no scarcity in this person's life – the mere act of asking leads to the end result of receiving first in perceived and simulated reality and subsequently into true physical reality – this person enjoys a life experience of peace, love, fearlessness, security and abundance.

Having achieved all material desires that bring unbounded delight to the Creature, the individual at this level of consciousness seeks to discover what is beyond physical and material desire, as the lure of the infinite non-physical domain fuels thought. Everything that is logical and ethically feasible is possible. There is no doubt, there is no fear, there is no trepidation, there is no malevolence, there is no jealousy, there is no want, there is no desire left in the physical world for this person to receive – the unbounded delight in the material domain has already been achieved, as the individual sets targets on the non-physical infiniteness of Existence. The individual is a conscious practitioner of the code of the *Genetics Of Divinity* and strives to share the consciousness with others in an effort to elevate them to the same level of AWAKENED consciousness.

The individual in this level of consciousness develops a burning desire to relinquish its *Creature* attributes and embark on a quest to expand the life experience as a CREATOR to understand the will of selfless bestowing. This person has a vision of the unbounded infinite bounty of *ineffable Bliss* (refer to the Cycle of Creation in Chapter 5 coming up) that is hidden from what the five senses can interpret. This person feels an insatiable urge to leverage the attributes of the CREATOR within as the conduit to unite with the purpose of Creation with the motivation to experience the *Bliss* of establishing symbiotic collaborative relationships. This person, still in physical form transcends over the mundane and immerses in the exotic.

---------------------------*****---------------------------

The following section, may not be comprehensible to you, depending on your current level of consciousness. This is natural and you need not make any concentrated effort to understand the following levels of consciousness in this chapter. You need to be living at a certain level of physical and material consciousness to understand any level of non-physical and ethereal consciousness. While it is perfectly ok for you to read the following sections of this chapter, don't allow yourself to doubt the information. You don't know what you don't know and your level of intelligence and consciousness about Creation may not be at a level to judge what you don't know – just yet. However the fact remains as stated here. Just like the law of gravity works all the time, every time without exception, whether you believe it or not, the code of Eternal Consciousness as described below exists and is applicable whether you personally believe it or not. Resistance is futile, since your personal resistance and perceptions does not and cannot change the true reality of Existence.

---------------------------#####--------------------------

CREATIVE

This level of consciousness is beyond the physical Third Dimension of Existence, where there is no form, only function – these are the Fifth and higher Dimensions of Existence. There is no verbal language required for communication as every bit of information exchange is non-verbal. Why is it that we as humans need to know anything about such a level of consciousness if it is beyond physical reality? The answer is simple – because this is the womb (not the source) of all physical reality. When you understand this level of consciousness you would discover the most valuable asset and resource you personally have access to 24 x 7 x 365 x your lifetime hours of physical life experience.

Adopting an analogy from the physical world, without a womb there cannot be a fetus. Adopting another analogy from the physical world, if you are lost in the forest and have lost your bearings, you need to reach a higher elevation, such as a tree or a hill in order to find your bearings and get back to where you came from. These higher dimensions of Existence as you learn more about in Chapter 7 form that womb, that higher elevation in reference.

In the physical Third Dimension of Existence, 98% of the human population have lost themselves in the forest of the *perceived* physical reality. It is *the finiteness of the physical world that imparts the perceived reality of scarcity* in the Creature, leading to an overpowering will to receive material desires in the life experience. However, the *energy form* of the entity in this level of consciousness has been *liberated* from the time-bound finiteness of the physical Third Dimension of Existence.

Here is the challenge that I am about to encounter as I describe this level of consciousness. Very soon, words will fail me, regardless of which verbal human language that I may want to use in order to express my thoughts. Why? Because soon I will enter a domain where there is no language in the traditional sense and communication is non-verbal. No words can explain what this non-physical domain really is, there is no form that our five senses can detect – far less comprehend. This is the domain of the infinite and the domain of all possibilities that conform to the design principles of Creation and Existence (explained further in Chapter 9) as defined by the code of the *Genetics Of Divinity*.

The closest that I can approach to this domain in order to explain such infiniteness is "true ethereal reality" – a domain where there is only creation, transformation, symbiotic collaboration, coherence, stabilization, time independence and subsequent proliferation for collective co-Existence.

This is the consciousness of pure emotion, pure feeling, pure energy with no name, no form, no flaw, no conflict, no confusion - only function, only perfection, only stability, only immortality, only infiniteness and bounty of symbiotic collaborative relationships and rigid adherence to the postulates of the code of the *Genetics of Divinity*.

Ancient texts going back 4000 years indicate that this level of consciousness is actually composed of five sub-levels of consciousness that are laid out from inner to outer levels of Ethereal Consciousness until it transitions over into finite physical reality in the AWAKENED level of consciousness. A discussion on these five levels is beyond the scope of this book, especially when both you and I with our finite levels of consciousness would be unable to comprehend the sublime efficacy of the detail on each of these five levels of ethereal consciousness. Hence for the purpose of this book, we will consider these five levels of ethereal consciousness as one.

All of Creation is the product of Ineffable Bliss of the *MASTER CREATOR*, that is non-judgmental, altruistic, passionate about perfection of Creation and purposeful about the journey and outcome of Existence. This *MASTER CREATOR* as you will know in Chapter 9 is not any physical entity or person or the supreme power as proposed by organized religion, but a dimensionless point, a particle without any physical rest mass but with pure energy – Source Energy that you will learn about shortly in this book.

All of physical reality is part of the master blueprint of Ineffable Bliss of the *MASTER CREATOR*. The *MASTER CREATOR* derives unbounded delight in the will and act of bestowing a life experience of unbounded delight to the Creature. There is no concept of abundance or scarcity in this level of consciousness, due to the infiniteness of the domain – there is only infinite free will and a magnificent obsession to create perfection, enhance, embellish, bestow and expand without any conflict. From the infiniteness of nothingness in this level of *ethereal consciousness*, every infinite and finite Creature is created in the non-physical and the physical dimensions of Existence.

At this level of consciousness ... At this level of consciousness ... At this level of consciousness – words have begun to fail me to express any further. Although within myself at this very moment as I write this section of the book, when I am physically located at about 40,000 feet above the Pacific Ocean, I feel a force, an energy that is infinite, omnipotent, omniscient, omnipresent, infinite, indestructible, blissful, unbounded, peaceful, bestowing, nurturing, magnificent, massless, perfect and ... immortal. That is an inexplicable emotion that I am feeling as I write this section and words fail me to explain any further. Close your eyes and calm your mind and in all likelihood you can feel the same. You can feel the same because you and I are not any different in the manner in which we can *feel* the presence of the ethereal CREATIVE consciousness as defined by the code of the *Genetics of Divinity*.

SOURCE OF THOUGHT

The much popular scientific explanation about the birth of physical Universe can be found in the Big Bang Theory, which essentially states that out of nothing, everything was created. Note the part '*thing*' in '*no<u>thing</u>*' and '*every<u>thing</u>*'. This word 'thing' represents the world of animate or inanimate but tangible objects having rest mass that our five senses can interact with and interpret based on our perception of physical reality. We know from our knowledge about the physical dimension of Existence, that it is not possible to create any '*thing*' without other '*things*' that serve as parts of the whole. So this raises a question on the validity of the Big Bang Theory if we are going to consider it's postulates from an entirely physical, Third Dimensional perspective.

However if that 'no-*thing*' was considered to be a dimensionless particle without rest mass (that I will introduce to you in Chapter 9) carrying Source Energy, only then could the Big Bang Theory show some credibility. While the CREATIVE consciousness creates everything from Thought (refer to the Cycle of Creation in Chapter 5), the question arises, what is beyond Thought? What is the Source of Thought? What triggers the thought in the CREATIVE consciousness of the *MASTER CREATOR*? This is again the realm of ineffability. But the closest word that comes to mind as being beyond thought is 'BLISS' but even that falls short of the magnanimity of the true essence of what is beyond Thought. Spoken words fail me again. What remains is a humble understanding and a feeling of infinite vastness and magnanimity that exists where there is no time and space, a realm of zero dimension yet infinite energy – more on the multi-dimensional structure of EXISTANCE is coming up in Chapter 7.

BLISS, the Source of every thought of the CREATIVE consciousness is the Source of all Creation. BLISS is that INFINITE ETHEREALITY encompassing all of Creation, even that of Thought. Out of the zero dimension, all dimensions and everything is conceived in this most superior level of consciousness.

When we go higher towards the Source Of Thought of the *MASTER CREATOR* of all Existence, all human logic, that are primarily based on physical laws defy all justification. What remains is a feeling of acceptance, reverence and acknowledgement of the INFINITE ETHEREALITY in the Source Of Thought that cannot be created, cannot be destroyed, cannot be diminished, cannot be tarnished but can only be transformed and evolved. The Source of Thought or BLISS is the Ultimate and Infinite Ethereality and is the source of all that there is and all that can be. This is the level of consciousness where the proverbial 'buck' stops and begins – there is nothing beyond the Source of Thought, the Zero Dimension - only thereafter.

Can we as humans find that Source of Thought? Well, all of Creation, originated from that Source of Thought that ZERO dimensional point – more details coming up in Chapter 9. So technically speaking you are already part of that Source of Thought, which explains why you as a human too feel emotions of bliss when some of those desires that you have as a Creature, manifest in your *physical reality* and life experience. However those emotions are finite and limited.

Your physical body cannot achieve that level of infinite and ineffable BLISS, since the desires of your physical body have been designed to be limited to the interpretation of your finite five senses. The desire to relate to the BLISS of the *MASTER CREATOR* can possibly be achieved through your non-physical self or your *Activebody* in the Fifth Dimension that I will explain in Chapter 7. It is my belief that as human consciousness shifts to higher levels and achieves the AWAKENED level, with an increasing awareness of the mechanics of Creation and the *Genetics Of Divinity*, it is possible for us to leverage this *Activebody* to find that Source of Thought or BLISS of the *MASTER CREATOR*.

From the level of consciousness where you are at the moment, your primary goal would be to seek the next higher level of consciousness and consolidate your life in that level. Only in the consolidation and mastery of your next higher level of consciousness can you come closer to the *MASTER CREATOR* and hence to the Source of Thought. *Your physical mortal body bound by the Fourth Dimension of Time will eventually cease to exist by design of Creation, but your non-physical immortal body that is independent of the time factor will continue its journey in its quest for union with the MASTER CREATOR.*

The question for you to answer through your physical life experience is how close to the reality of unbounded delight that you are engineered for, have you been able to come under the guidance of the CREATOR within you and the assistance that you can receive from your *Activebody*? The closer you are to that true reality of unbounded delight, the higher will be your level of consciousness, thereby taking you closer to that Source of Thought.

Now that you have begun to understand the concept of consciousness, it is important to pause and appreciate the Thought of the *MASTER CREATOR* on the reason why these different levels are set up in Existence. All Creatures are going through a life experience under the guidance of one of these levels of consciousness for the one simple reason, one simple motivation of the *MASTER CREATOR*. That motivation is educate you through the attribute of *Contrast* (more coming up in Chapter 5), to give you a purpose, a goal and direction in life. Are you happy where you are in your current level of consciousness or is there a desire that you feel within to conduct your life in a manner that will take you to a higher level of consciousness and consequently greater enjoyment and delight in your experience? This is a very important question that only you can answer and your answer is dependent on your current level of consciousness.

Figure 4 illustrates the different levels of consciousness as defined by the code of the Genetics Of Divinity – you can download this chart from the Multiversity portal at www.GeneticsOfDivinity.com upon registration.

Before I wrap this chapter, I will lead you through an exercise that would prove to be of tremendous value to you as you progress through this book. As a pre-requisite for this exercise you must have completed Exercise 02 and 03 from the last chapter where we talked about your **current** self-image. Keep those completed results handy as you go through

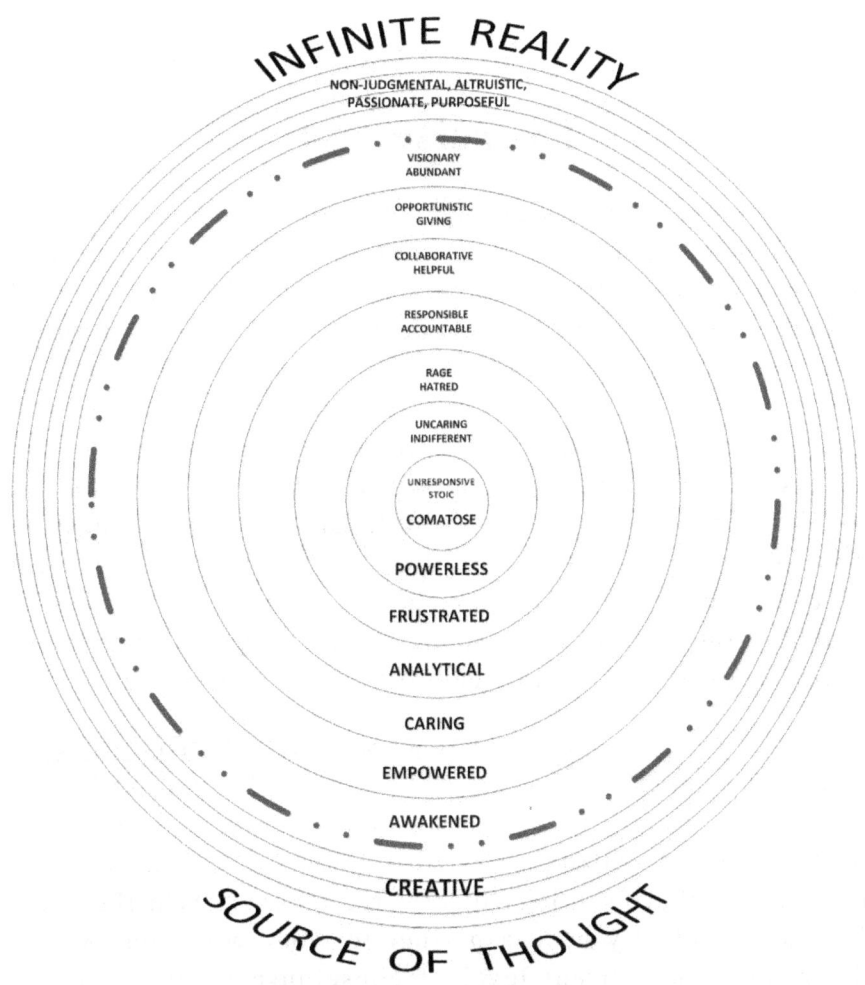

Figure 4

this exercise, where you will be able to identify approximately, your current level of consciousness. Remember, we are just taking stock of where you are right now, you are not going to change anything for the moment. Only by understanding where you are now as a starting point can you decide and plan to be somewhere else and the effort becomes measurable.

---------------------------*****---------------------------

Exercise #04

As before, there is no right or wrong answers here and nobody is going to look into your results. The objective of this exercise is for you to identify your *current* level of consciousness on the grand design of Creation. Remain truthful, fair and honest to yourself – it is your life and you are in charge of it. Review the results of the Exercises #02 and #03 where you identified your self-image in each of the 13 discrete categories of relationships in your life. Review the descriptions of the different levels of consciousness in this chapter and grade each self-image relationship to a level of consciousness. Your current level of consciousness is roughly the level that scored the highest number of occurrences among the thirteen relationship categories.

Visit the companion site at www.GeneticsOfDivinity.com and access the Multiversity portal for an alternate and more accurate technique to determine your current consciousness level as demonstrated in Part 6 of Module 4. This involves the science of Kinesiology discovered by Dr. David Hawkins. You would ideally need a partner to work with you to help determine your current level of consciousness or you could do it all by yourself. Simply follow the instructions in the demonstration in the Multiversity portal that you have access to and you will be able to determine your current level of consciousness. As you go through this book, assuming you are leveraging the knowledge to reactivate the dormant memories of the code of the *Genetics of Divinity* from your subconscious mind, your consciousness will upgrade. You can use the same technique of Kinesiology to grade your new level of consciousness.

---------------------------#####-------------------------

Kinesiology

Now that you have your 'guesstimate' on your level of consciousness, based on your conscious self-assessment, how do you know it is accurate? Who is to determine if that is right or wrong? As you can understand unless you don't know where you are now, you cannot set a target for yourself. Hence it is critical for you to understand your level of current level of consciousness as accurately as possible. I will briefly describe the two components of a very unique technology that is built within you, to provide you with authentic guidance on various aspects of your life experience.

The first component is called *Kinesiology*® (credited to the scientifically proven research work of Dr. David R. Hawkins) as described in his book *Power vs Force* and the second component is called *Emotional Guidance System*® (credited to the research work performed by Jerry and Esther Hicks as they describe in their book *Ask And It Is Given*).

Using these two components of the technology of self-guidance and self-evaluation your physical body and emotions will accurately *'tell you'* what's right and what's not, what's good for you and what's not. In other words you could ask yourself a question that has either a *'yes/no'* or a *'true/false'* or a *'good/bad'* answer, any question and you will know with authenticity, the answer to your question. You can use this technology not only to determine your current level of consciousness, but practically any question that you may have with a straight *true/false* answer.

Dr. David. R Hawkins is credited to have discovered and developed a scale of human consciousness measured in numbers based on our feelings and emotions from 20 (feeling and emotions of *Shame*) to 1000 (feelings and emotions of *Enlightenment*). He describes this wonderful tool in his book – *Power vs Force* and I strongly recommend that you refer to that material as a companion to this chapter.

Using the scientifically proven concept called *Kinesiology* it is possible for anyone to determine numerically the level of consciousness on every aspect of the person's behavior and emotions. Dr. Hawkins' discovery on Kinesiology states that you may not be consciously aware of what is good or bad for you at the present moment or in a future timeframe, but your physical body can react to those energies. However what Dr. Hawkins does not state is that your *Activebody* is always in the *know* of what can be a positive or a negative life experience for you and you can use Kinesiology as one of the methods to tap into that knowledge.

If the life experience is or will be positive for you, your muscular system remains strong. If the life experience would be negative for you, your muscular system goes weak – this is the study of Kinesiology. This strength or weakness in your muscle under test, according to the code of the *Genetics Of Divinity* is delivered through an energy transmission that you receive from your *Activebody* when you communicate with it – your Activebody stands ready to serve 24 x 7 x 365 x number of hours of your lifetime. Using Kinesiology you can determine your level of consciousness using a numerical scale. If your result is at a level of 250 or above in the Hawkins' scale of human consciousness, whatever it is that you are testing for, is considered beneficial for your life experience. Using this technology you can make better decisions in life which in turn will align and elevate you to higher levels of consciousness.

Evolution of Human Consciousness

In his book *"The Origin of Consciousness in the Breakdown Of the Bicameral Mind"*, author Julian Jaynes provides a very interesting account on the development of consciousness and indicates that human consciousness was detected or formed only 3000 years ago - a mere sapling compared to our physical Universe that is estimated to be 13.75 billion Earth years young. He also goes on to explain that prior to that 3000 year timeframe, the human population operated according to nature's *default operating system* with the same kind of reactions as other animals – that of *fight, flight or freeze*. They went about their life by *'hearing voices'* that apparently commanded them to lead their lives in a certain way. In those days when the human population were peasants, and hunters, they conducted life through a pre-set program of nature, pretty much like any other animal but with capabilities that were superior to other animals. For example, they could light a fire, build shelters, hunt, kill and eat cooked food, sow and harvest crops, protect themselves from inclement weather and other species of animals – all propelled through the guidance of nature's default operating system for the human species.

Then according to Julian Jaynes, a few started to understand *philosophy*, hence the birth of consciousness beyond the physical domain. They began to analyze the history of the human species in order to get an understanding of Existence through the observation of repetitive patterns of behavior and events, often linking circumstances to the alignment of astronomical bodies such as stars, the moon, the sun and planets. These people became increasingly conscious of their life and started to get regarded as 'the *wise ones*' who could provide explanations and plausible reasons to the questions of the others. Whether those explanations were right or wrong based on what we know today as a civilization, was irrelevant at that time. As long as the information made some sense and different from what the general population was aware of, those explanations were regarded as true and people became followers of these *wise ones*. Thus began the lineage of teachers, leaders, guides, even tyrants, dictators and of course *mysticism*.

Though Julian Jaynes indicates 3000 years ago as the start of human consciousness, books such as the Kabbalah and the Vedas go beyond that estimate to 5000 years – compare that to us humans attaining anatomical maturity 200,000 years ago and behavioral maturity around 50,000 years ago. When you read such books that were written before any organized religion was born, it becomes evident that consciousness of the physical and non-physical dimensions of Existence was developed prior to that time period and humanity existed before recorded history.

Although that 3000 year timeline from Julian Jaynes is open for debate and discussion, what is important to realize is how a division of the human species occurred in the plane of consciousness maturity and that division exists even in this present day and age. The primary goal of this book that you are reading now is to elevate you to higher levels of consciousness with the objective to help you bridge that gap and dissolve the divide between the your perceived current life experience and the true life experience in the future that you desire for yourself with the objective of enjoying unbounded delight..

Why Bother Upgrading Your Consciousness?

Are you beginning to understand yourself better than you've ever done before? Do you feel that life is slowly beginning to snap into place? Is there a sense of growing appreciation for life in general? I am sure you understand now that higher your level of consciousness, more abundance, fulfillment and enjoyment you are entitled to feel in your life experience as the *games of chance transform into the predictability of certainty.* Since you have almost completed this Chapter, it must already be pretty clear to you as to why consciousness is important for your life experience. However there is even a greater reason that you may not have realized.

Dr. Hawkins states through his description of the Scale of Consciousness, we by default get attracted to people in our lives who have either the same or higher levels of consciousness and reject those that are perceived to be at a lower level. Think about this as a sort of consciousness profiling that we are autonomically designed for. Moreover this discovery of Dr. Hawkins falls right in line with the core principle of the *Genetics Of Divinity* about establishing those *symbiotic collaborative relationships through the free will of mutual consent between the partners in the relationship for the purpose of collective coexistence.* As you can realize, such relationships are possible only when the relating partners understand this core principle of Eternal Consciousness and use their free will to agree to abide by that principle.

The key here, as Dr. Hawkins states, is to seek out and attract people with the same level or higher levels of consciousness. While seeking out people at the same level of consciousness leads to *homeostasis* and more of the same in the life experience, it is in the alignment and attraction with individuals of higher levels of consciousness that provides you the passport to an enhanced life experience by following the core principle of the *Genetics Of Divinity*. When you complete Chapter 9, you will get an even better understanding of the importance of your consciousness and realize that not only people, but everything in Existence works under the same principles of Creation and everything in Existence has its own individual level of consciousness. Only humans, who I will shortly start to refer as Type A energy Creatures are endowed with the capability to dynamically upgrade or degrade our consciousness or even tune our consciousness to that of other Creatures that we desire and manifest them into our life experience. You are richly endowed – now let's use it!

Chapter 5 - Laws Of Creation And Existence

It was a bright sunny day in the spring of 2012 in the uniquely architected Luxor Hotel in Las Vegas, Nevada and I was attending a seminar on consciousness, inter-dimensional existence and concepts that tease and stretch average human intelligence and rationality. I had the opportunity to visit the *BODIES* exhibition in the hotel, courtesy of the seminar host and it clearly was one of the most exciting, revealing and yet humbling experiences of my life. Earlier in my life, I had studied the human body and its physical components with keen interest through books and video documentaries and that education by itself was extremely exciting. As I walked through the exhibits where real human bodies appropriately preserved were so aesthetically presented, showing all the different organs beneath the skin and even beneath the exo-skeleton, my previous excitement transformed into sheer awe, reverence and respect for the magnificence of the design of the physiology of the most complicated and endowed Creature in this planet.

The minute detail in the individual structure, position, orientation, function of the different organs of the human body and their symbiotic collaborative relationship to the form and function of other organs not only adhere to all laws of physics but also to the laws of chemistry, anatomy and Multi-Dimensional Energetics. In essence, the human body is designed to be just perfect with not only the physiological infrastructure, but also with emotions, early warning systems, memory systems, DNA, self-healing mechanisms, self-adaptive systems, parallel processing natural intelligence systems, and of course the quad-compartmental mind that you will learn about in Chapter 8.

What kind of Source Energy can create something as complicated and yet so perfectly operational Creature where every cell works with each other in a symbiotic collaborative relationship with each other within the human body and also interact with the external world in perfect harmony for the purpose of collective co-existence? What kind of *Thought* could the MASTER CREATOR have to come up with to design a Creature like the human body that not only has the magnificent physical form but also the even more extraordinary non-physical counterpart existing in a different dimension? What ineffable feeling of *BLISS* could the MASTER CREATOR be engulfed with to have the Inspiration for the Thought of such a Creation. I was humbled and my reverence to Creation and Existence escalated to a new high during the hour that I could spend at the exhibition.

Core Attributes of Creation

I have already introduced you to the basics of Creation, but let's just recapitulate anyway and then expand this consciousness. It is through spaced repetition for a minimum of 21 times, does a concept get implanted in your conscious mind. To put it more appropriately, only spaced repetition provides the mechanism for you to consciously reactivate the dormant memory systems of knowledge that are already embedded in your subconscious mind.

The CREATOR and the Creature

There are two major components of all Creation. The *first component* is the presence of the CREATOR that creates the *second component* or the Creature - considered to be the offspring or product of the CREATOR's Thought that is sourced at emotions of Bliss. The core attribute of the CREATOR is the *will to bestow a life experience to the Creature that is filled with unbounded delight and in the process of such bestowing, enjoy unbounded delight.* The core attribute of the Creature on the other hand is the *will to receive and enjoy unbounded delight* in its life experience as it fulfills its assigned purpose in Existence. Only when the Creature experiences unbounded delight and joy in its life experience, does it equal the CREATOR's will to bestow and align with the true essence of Creation.

This is similar to the delight that an artist feels when a person viewing the work of art understands and feels the same delightful emotions and feelings of the artist when the piece of art was created. A symbiotic collaborative relationship is forged energetically in the non-physical plane through the free will of mutual consent between the artist and the admirer for the purpose of collective coexistence (or appreciation in this case).

Is the *MASTER CREATOR* a person, an object or an entity? Although we humans relate better to things that can be interpreted through our five senses (by design of Creation), the *MASTER CREATOR* can be neither since a person, object or entity are terms that relate to the finite, physical plane of Existence which is not the domain of the *MASTER CREATOR*. Why do I say that the *MASTER CREATOR* exists in the non-physical domain? The physical domain is tangible, finite, dependent on time and has a *'life-cycle'* where everything has an end or termination. These are the core attributes of the physical Third dimension of Existence where you and I are having a contemporary physical experience. Even if I have passed on from my mortal life and you are reading this book after that, we are still considered to be having a contemporary physical experience because the *Adaptive* energy of my consciousness has been transferred in part to this book that you now hold in your hands. Now that does not sound creepy, does it? ☺

However there is nothing that is finite, or tangible in the non-physical world, that is independent of the factor of time and due to the infiniteness there cannot be any terminal point in space or on time. There are zero limits in this non-physical domain, there is nothing tangible that your five senses can detect far less interpret in this non-physical and infinite realm of Existence, where physical laws do not apply. There is only transformation and proliferation of different energy waveforms, each with different frequencies and amplitudes. In this infinite domain of omnipotence, omniscience and immortality, resides the Source Energy that I refer to as the *MASTER CREATOR*.

Why does the *MASTER CREATOR* create all that there is? The *MASTER CREATOR* designs the Creature to enjoy unbounded delight for sure, but what is motivating the *MASTER CREATOR* to create all of Existence? In the non-physical domain of infiniteness, the *MASTER CREATOR's* motivation or the Inspiration stems from INEFFABLE BLISS as explained earlier. What is the motivation behind this BLISS? 'INEFFABLE UNBOUNDED DELIGHT' – the core driving force behind all of Existence. The *MASTER CREATOR* creates a Creature with the intent for the Creature to experience unbounded delight in the physical form and in the process, derives UNBOUNDED DELIGHT with the fulfillment of that BLISS. In Chapter 9, I describe the scientific mechanics and technology of Creation and Existence from an entirely different perspective, but for now, enjoy the more metaphysical and philosophical explanation of Creation and Existence.

How can the *MASTER CREATOR* be Immortal? Mortality Life Cycle, Lifespan, Evolution are concepts of time, indicating a beginning, a lifetime and an end and are applicable to the physical Third Dimension of Existence that is rendered relatively unstable and finite when compared to the non-physical dimensions. The mortality of the entities in the Third Dimension is the primary factor of this relative instability. The non-physical dimensions however are independent of time and hence stable in their infiniteness as you will learn in Chapter 7, which makes the concepts of mortality, evolution, past, present future, lifecycle and lifespan irrelevant. This grants the *MASTER CREATOR* and all CREATORs in the non-physical dimensions, the attribute of Immortality. Your physical body or what I refer to as the *Adaptivebody* is mortal in this Third Dimension, however your non-physical body or what I call the *Activebody* is immortal in the Fifth Dimension – more on this in Chapter 7. You came here in this physical from your very own non-physical *Activebody*.

The *MASTER CREATOR* is formless, shapeless, stateless, the source of all possibilities, indestructible, indefatigable, omnipotent, omnipresent, omniscient, immortal, the origin of all that has been, that is and that will transform to be. There is no creation, conflict or destruction possible of the *MASTER CREATOR*, only transformation and proliferation. The entire design of Existence is already in place and operating in perfect harmony – more coming in Chapter 7.

Contrast

The *third attribute* of the design of Creation is called '*Contrast*'. The only reason you as a Creature have been designed to have a life experience in this physical dimension of Existence bound by the finiteness of time and space is for you to contemplate and appreciate what it would be like if time and space were infinite.

Granted, depending on your level of current consciousness, you may not be in a position to understand and appreciate this particular contrast, but that does not change the reason behind this particular attribute regarding time and space. It is my conviction however, that as you progress through this book, your consciousness will increase and you will come closer to relate to this very significant attribute in the grand design of Creation.

Everything that has happened to you in the past, or is happening to you right now as you consume this material has been designed to show you contrast, hence the duality of Creation. If you did not know what is cold, how would you know what is hot? If you did not know pain, how would you know what pleasure is? If you did not know what financial slavery is, how would you know and appreciate what financial independence is? If you have never experienced dis-ease, how would you know what ease is? If you were never hungry, how would you know the feeling of being full? Pick any event, experience, feeling or emotion that you have experienced in your life and you will know the presence of this duality - *Contrast*.

What is the purpose of Contrast? The answer is simple – to guide you, the Creature through a life experience of evolving consciousness where you can enjoy unbounded delight. Only when your life experience is filled with unbounded delight can you match the BLISS, the Inspiration, the Thought, the Intention, the Attention, the Action of the *CREATOR* - the ultimate purpose why you have been created.

What you perceive as *'pain'* may very well be perceived as *'pleasure'* by another person. What the other person perceives as trivial or unimportant to you, may be of utmost importance to you as an individual. The very reason why you are reading this book is because you have felt a void or scarcity in your consciousness that you believe will be filled with the information in this book – Contrast at work.

Without exception you will find a contrasting situation for every event and experience that you have had in life so far. What emotions do those events or experiences generate in you? Are those emotions of unbounded delight or unbounded plight? If you have chosen the latter, well, what purpose does that experience serve in your life? When you know or experience what you don't desire, it clarifies for you what you *do* desire. What you desire is automatically directed to what would satisfy the *will to receive* within you and bring you closer to that feeling of fulfillment and unbounded delight.

---------------------------*****---------------------------

I believe this brings you to the realization that there is no negative or bad event or experience in your life or in the life of anyone else. Events are only learning experiences and through Contrast you are being helped to course-correct and re-align with your will to receive whatever pleasure that you seek once you have felt the pain. You do have a choice (this will be clear in the forthcoming discussion of 'free will') whenever you have an experience that you may *perceive* to be negative. First, continue to focus your thoughts and actions on the perceived negativity of that experience, which is what you *do not* desire, thereby magnifying the intensity of the negative perception. Second, understand the concept of Contrast and contemplate on what you have learned from the experience and shift your intense focus on the contrasting conditions, which is what you *do* desire. Which option would you choose?

--------------------------#####--------------------------

Depending on your level of consciousness at this moment, it may be a challenge for you to understand this very important attribute of Creation and apply it in your life and make the right choice. If so, let me ask you, 'How has that continued contemplation and focus on what you do *not* desire served you so far? Has such an attitude brought you closer to unbounded delight or taken you deeper into unbounded plight?' I rest my case. It's time to change your paradigms, is it not?

If you want things to change, I mean *really want* things to change you must change things in your life and that change starts with your understanding of the mechanics of Creation and this very important attribute of '*Contrast*'.

Free Will

The *fourth attribute* in the design of Creation is '*Free Will*'. By now you are already aware that the CREATOR has been designed with the will to bestow and the Creature has been designed by the CREATOR with the will to receive while both enjoy unbounded delight in the life experience. What you desire to receive and enjoy unbounded delight may very well be totally different from what I or the next person could desire to receive and experience a personalized version of unbounded delight. I personally for example, given a choice, would not find enjoyment in spending my leisure time at a poker table. But that does not mean you don't or won't or can't due to your passion for game. It would be inappropriate on my part to raise any objections to your own enjoyment that you have chosen through *your own* free will. If I do object to your free will, I will not only be violating the *code of conduct* of Creation prescribed by the *Genetics Of Divinity*, you too will develop a resistance to that objection and me as well because your natural attributes have been trespassed upon. Your life experience today is the sum of all the choices that you have made in your life through your own free will and those that you have unwillingly or voluntarily surrendered to the dictates of others' free will.

Getting back to this example about the enjoyment of poker, it is clear that my objections to your free will, without a doubt will lead to resistance and possible rejection from you. However what happens if in addition to my objection, I also present a case to you with some relevant facts and figures that illustrate the reasoning and rationality behind my objection. Something interesting happens here in you at this point. Your free will could decide for you to turn a deaf ear at me and ignore my reasoning, in which case you will continue with your current perception of reality. Alternatively, your free will could offer a choice for you to listen to my reasoning, contemplate, analyze my argument and then make your decision to agree or disagree with me. If you did agree with me and made a decision to never play poker again in the future, you now have a new perception and hence a new version of your own personal life experience. This new life experience is what I will be referring to as a Parallel Universe in Chapter 6.

Nobody can ever effectively change your free will through deliberate enforcement however it is possible that you could succumb to the pressure, fear and consequences of such enforcement. It is only when you agree to change your perception of your reality through the process of consuming new knowledge and deriving new cognitions as a result of that knowledge, is it possible to *'evolve'* your decision-making faculties through the exercise of your free will. You have been designed this way as a Creature – to experience unbounded delight and you have been granted free will by the code of Creation to define what brings you unbounded delight.

----------------------------*****----------------------------

It must be abundantly clear by now that this attribute of 'free will' is by far one of the more precious gifts that you have as the most magnificent Creature of Creation on this planet. When you allow yourself the liberty of exercising that right and gift of 'free will' you are automatically filled with joy and satisfaction and feel the alignment with your purpose in life – that to serve and receive and enjoy unbounded delight in the process.

It is also impossible for you as a Creature with such a gift to feel unbounded delight when through the exercise of your free will, you violate the free will of another. Peace and harmony in your life experience is guided *not only* by your own exercise of free will that provides you with unbounded delight but also by your respect and allowance of everyone else in your life experience to exercise *their own* free will that brings *them* unbounded delight. You are designed to serve others so that they can exercise their free will – when this is violated both parties in the relationship develop a *parasitic disruptive relationship through the enforcement of the free will of one of the partners without mutual consent from the other for the purpose of individualized existence.* This is in direct violation of the code of the *Genetics Of Divinity* leading to the pain and suffering observed in humanity as I write this book in the year 2012.

If you analyze human history or even consider the modern times, all the problems that you see in the world and all the challenges that you observe within yourself, are the end result of someone, somewhere violating someone else's right to exercise their free will. A candid question for you at this point – Have you consciously violated someone else's free will in your life? More importantly, have you consciously or unconsciously violated you own free will in your past? The answer to these two questions could provide you with insight on the reason behind some of the challenges that you may be facing in your life experience today. The Creature is not designed for domination, the Creature is not designed for being deprived of the will to receive and enjoy unbounded delight. A violation of this design – direct or indirect, consciously or unconsciously inevitably thwarts a life experience of unbounded delight.

Imagine you filling your fuel tank with diesel when your car runs on gasoline. What would happen to the engine of your car? Your life experience is exactly the same – as a Creature you are not designed to be violated from your exercise of free will and neither are you designed to violate the free will of others. The engine of your life experience would cease if such a violation occurs by the design of the *Genetics Of Divinity*.

In this violation, in this abduction of free will using artificially crafted authoritative measures or simply raw physical power, lies the denial of the core principle of Creation – that of the Creature to exercise free will and define a life experience filled with unbounded delight. When such a denial occurs discord sets in. With incessant repetition and expansion of the scope and purview of such enforced denial, human consciousness sinks to lower levels, which explains the conflict, pain and suffering that you possibly see within you and in the world around you.

---------------------------#####---------------------------

Has humanity not suffered enough down the history of our civilization through the abduction of free will of others? Is NOW the time for the human consciousness to pause and ponder about the situation, come to the cognition of the core principles of Creation, make a decision to shift consciousness to higher level where free will for everyone is respected and honored and celebrated. Therein lies the liberation of humanity from the bondage of the present day authoritarian society into the libertarian freedom of the future. This book launched on December 21st, 2012 – the date marking the rebirth of human consciousness. By reading this book you are already part of that rebirthing process.

Only through your understanding of these principles of Creation can you begin to appreciate the grand INTENT of the *MASTER CREATOR* and relate to the sublime reality of Existence. When you begin this symbiotic collaborative relationship with the *MASTER CREATOR*, you are automatically granted by design, the free will and consent of the MASTER CREATOR and through the resulting collective co-existence your consciousness will rise to the higher levels. This in turn will open you up to the will to receive and enjoy unbounded delight in your physical life experience and allow others to follow by the exercise of their free will.

Parallelism

I will briefly mention the *fifth attribute* of Creation – *'Parallelism'*, and will be referring to it throughout the book. If you are a little confused about it as you read this section, nothing to worry about – it will all be clear by the time you are done reading this book This attribute of Creation exists simply for the purpose of supporting the attribute of *'Free Will'*. What do you think you will need in order for the attribute of 'free will' to be operational? *Choice.* Only when you have choices can you exercise Free Will to choose from the list.

For example, you don't have a choice here on planet Earth but to accept the fact that the sun rises in the east. There is only one perceivable possibility in your physical experience on Planet Earth and hence you don't have 'Free Will' to choose a different experience on this matter – you could not expect to see a sunrise on the West.

Let's consider another example. In a blistering hot summer day, you have the luxury of exercising your free will to choose among a plethora of choices – stay and bake in the hot sun, that too in the desert or on the beach or in your backyard, by the community pool or maybe remain indoors with or without the air-conditioning on ... and I could go on and on and on and there still would be other choices that I would not have mentioned or thought about.

Consider Figure 5 - a pictorial description of the concept of Parallelism. Without getting into a discussion of the factor of time, for simplicity let us consider that time as we perceive it, progresses linearly and hence has a past, present and a future. Every moment in time of your life experience through this linear progression is a reflection of Parallelism. In other words you are awarded a plethora of choices by Parallelism and you are required to make a selection. On the left of Figure 5, let us say that in the snapshot of time #1 you were presented with a choice of career and you made a decision. In this case as illustrated in Figure 5, you *chose* to be an 'Astronaut' (shown underlined) overruling the other skills including passing up the illustrious career (☺) to be a Couch Potato. Congratulations on your choice at that snapshot of time when among all the different possible life experiences that you had access to, you *chose* the career (through the exercise of free will) of an Astronaut.

This choice negated all other experiences for you at that snapshot of time indicated by Time #1 in Figure 5 and at the very next moment of your decision making, Parallelism offered you another set of *relevant* experiences at the snapshot of Time #2. Let's say, with all your enthusiasm you chose the experience of *'Research How To Be An Astronaut'* (shown underlined) among all other potential experiences that are available to you. Wonderful! Once you had made that choice, Parallelism offered you a new set of more *relevant* possible experiences in the next snapshot of Time #3 and you chose *'Enroll in Astronaut Training Academy'* as your forthcoming life experience. Henceforth, your life experience would be a progression based that choice made as you continue through time.

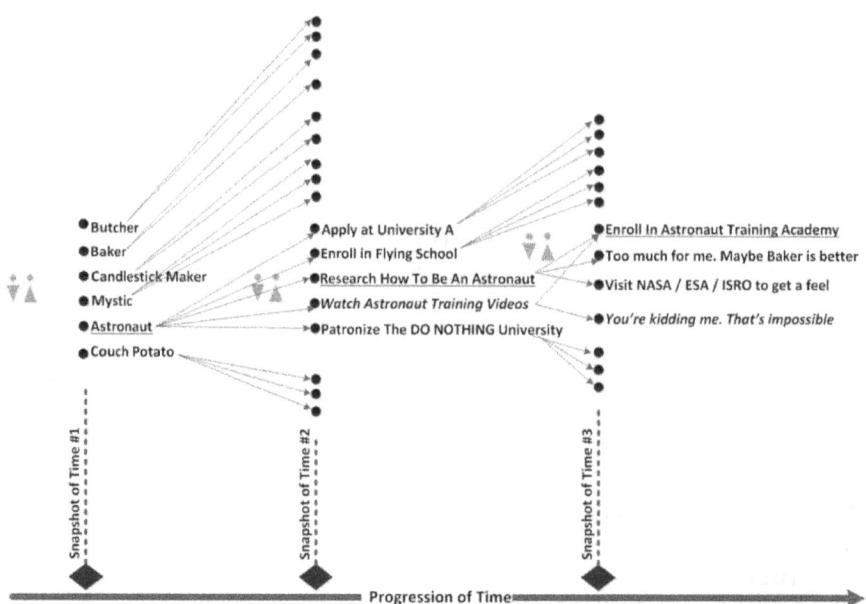

Figure 5

However in the snapshot in Time #2, if you had made the choice to 'Watch Astronaut Training videos' and just watched the rigor involved with all that spinning in a centrifuge, weightlessness and the like, you would have developed a new knowledgebase. Based on that newly acquired knowledge, when you arrived at the snapshot in Time #3, Parallelism offered you some *related* choices. You could have chosen and decided to "Enroll for Astronaut Training Academy" or you could have chosen to quit your quest to become an astronaut after all. *The quality of your life experience today is the sum of all the choices you have made either by virtue of exercising your free will or your submission and surrender of your personal free will to the enforcement of free will of others without your voluntary consent at every moment that you have lived from the list of choices that Parallelism presented to you.* Read that last sentence again and ponder about it for a while.

---------------------------*****--------------------------

As you can understand now, through the exercise of your free will, right at the point or instance of time when you are about to make a decision, all of the different experiences that you can think of and those that you cannot think of are all simultaneously available to you through the attribute of Parallelism of Creation as choices. All you have to do, is based on your consciousness and paradigms, exercise your free will. The choice you make at the point of decision based on free will becomes your life experience and your *physical reality*. Make a different choice and an entirely different life experience awaits you and hence an entirely different perception of your physical reality. Remember this when I explain the concept of Parallel Universes in Chapter 6.

Imagine yourself in a nice high-end restaurant looking at a menu (oh goodness those prices are atrocious or are they so only in *your* perception) and the waitress is patiently awaiting your choice. What would you do? You seldom say '*I want food.*' You actually choose your order from the menu – Parallelism at work. How would you make your choice – primarily based on the description of the items in the menu, based on your level of hunger, based on your preference of foods – vegan or otherwise, based on the price, based on which dinner-companion you want to impress, based on the delight that you want to experience from the meal, based on your past experiences at the same or another establishment or a combination of all of the above? Is that choice by basic animal instincts to satisfy the pangs of hunger or are you applying rationality and logical intelligence to make your selections?

Every moment of your life in this physical world is a representation of this restaurant scenario. At every moment of your life, Parallelism offers you, the Creature endowed with the will to receive unbounded delight, *choices* to decide your life experience based on your consciousness and belief systems powered by your Free Will. Each choice you make from Parallelism defines your physical reality and the living conditions in a Parallel Universe – more on this in Chapter 6.

-------------------------#####-------------------------

You may say, "I live a life where I am unable to exercise my free will because so-and-so does not allow me that freedom. I am a puppet in the hands of a human (or circumstantial) puppeteer or *Mis(s)*-fortune and I are not in good terms and hence I do not have the liberty to exercise my free will. How can this knowledge about Creation and Existence help me?"

You mention human and circumstantial puppeteers who are controlling your life experience and thwarting your freedom to make your own choices from Parallelism. There is no such thing – it's only your perception of how you have granted permission through your own free will (again through a selection from the several choices offered by Parallelism) to present themselves to you in the manner they do. They are Creatures with the same attributes as you have, albeit with a different maturity level of consciousness and perception of free will that involves imposing their own at the cost of thwarting your free will. As you will learn in Chapters 8 and 9, Existence is based on the core principle of establishing *symbiotic collaborative relationships*. Any attempts to deviate from that guiding principle, for example through *parasitic disassociating relationships* without mutual consent, is a violation of the code of the *Genetics Of Divinity* leading to instability of Existence in the Third Dimension, specifically in this planet and an unfulfilled life experience for both parties.

Rest assured that in thwarting your free will, the other seemingly more physically powerful entity, is not able to enjoy unbounded delight either in the true sense of that state of being. They would always remain in the fear of a potential revolt, uprising or resistance against whatever it is that they are imposing. We come from the domain of Infiniteness and there is no scarcity in Infiniteness. Any human attempt to enforce artificial scarcity, which is what has happened to humanity through recorded history, is a violation of the code of Eternal Consciousness, which explains the unbounded plight in which we see our planet today. Such violation of the code has not worked so far, has it? Well now that we know what has not worked, applying Contrast, can humanity understand what will work? This book carries this message for humanity – to understand the Contrast and usher in a new era of upgraded consciousness where we humans conduct our lives by the core principle of the *Genetics Of Divinity*.

For the sake of argument, let us say that such circumstantial puppeteers who thwart your free will do exist. History books, down the ages are adorned with countless examples of individuals who broke free of the chains of these '*puppeteers*' by the virtue of their own Free Will by clearly understanding what they desired by 'Contrast' and then leveraged the bounty of 'Parallelism' to choose their physical reality. Search the internet with the phrase '*overcame obstacles*' or '*overcame challenges*' using your favorite search engine and you will get more matches that you can read in a lifetime. Hence the puppeteer as you perceive it is not the factor that is inhibiting the right to your free will and the experience of abundance in your physical reality. Reclaim the responsibility and accountability on yourself. You will find that your life experience has begun to change as you become increasingly self-sufficient with more and more dormant memories of the code of the *Genetics Of Divinity* dislodging from your subconscious mind and bubbling up to your conscious mind to guide you to an enhanced life experience.

It's time for a rude but open and honest awakening. It is not the so-perceived puppeteer who brings grief to your life experience - *YOU* are. Through the inadequacy of your level of consciousness, sub-optimal understanding of the laws of Creation and Existence, you have yielded your free will to others who for some reasons known best to you, *you* deem to be more worthy than *you are* to dictate *your* life experience. You have given an external *so-and-so* the power to override your free will and accept their dictates and their choices as your life experience and physical reality. Who takes the blame here? The answer is within you.

Let's pause here and ponder about the quality and state of your life experience today - your physical reality. Pick any moment in your life and contemplate on what choices you had at that point simultaneously and what you ended up choosing? Why did you make that choice as opposed to the others that were available? What could have happened if you had chosen differently?

Based on that different choice that you could have made, your experience in physical reality would have been different, until you came up with another point in time when you were faced with another follow-on choice to make among the plethora of related parallel possibilities. Every moment of your life experience in essence is a multiple choice test where you can make just one choice. For those of you who are adept at software programming, we are talking about *radio buttons* and not *checkboxes* in the list of available options provided by Parallelism at any given instant of time in your life experience. Your life experience in the present, which you perceive to be your physical reality, is the sum of all those choices you have made in the past in those multiple-choice tests that Parallelism presented you with.

Are you as the Creature, enjoying a life experience that is filled with your definition of unbounded delight - the core purpose for which you were created? Be honest now – not to me, to yourself. If yes, you can stop reading this book because I have nothing to convey to you and you have fulfilled your role in Creation through the achievement of unbounded delight, which is only possible when you have fulfilled your life purpose. If not, if you feel that your experience in life so far has been short of that state of unbounded delight, get ecstatically excited because of what you are going to learn in this book and the memories of the code of Eternal Consciousness that you are going to reactivate into your conscious mind. What you have learned so far in this book, is about to culminate in a defining moment in your life very soon and you will be presented with that attribute of Parallelism yet again. Get ready for it.

Now that you are consciously aware how your life experience has been so far following the Laws of Creation through your selection of the choices in Parallelism, you should also be aware that a proper selection of choice at this defining moment, this snapshot in time in the present, holds the keys to the doorway of an entirely different life experience for you – one with an elevated maturity level of consciousness.

If your life experience has been short of unbounded delight, by the third attribute of Creation or *'Contrast'* you need to know and clearly define what elements in your life experience would make you feel closer to that emotion of unbounded delight. In other words in knowing what you do not want in life, by Contrast you know what you *do* want in life – do you understand? Fantastic!

Decision time for you! It is that moment in time again, when Parallelism is presenting you with a plethora of choices right in the here and now on what you want to do. One of the choices of course is *'Do nothing and continue to expect magic and miracles of the hypothetical element of luck and destiny to happen'*. Another choice could be *'Enough is Enough and I am sick and tired of being sick and tired and I decide to take positive action to change my life experience at this very moment'*. There are other choices that only you know best, potentially different from the choices that are relevant for the next person. Your defining moment is NOW, because once you get to the next section, the change in you is inevitable should you allow the information to resonate with your dormant memories of the *Genetics Of Divinity*. An old Chinese proverb translated to English says, *"The height of madness is to continue to do the same things over and over and expect different results"*. So what's it going to be? Parallelism is offering you a plethora of choices right now and the free will of the Creature within you needs to make a decision.

Unless you made that decision in your defining moment, please refrain from continuing on with the remainder of this book as that would be self-sabotaging and it would be of no use to you. Knowledge is power only when you use it. If you have to read the book from the beginning until this section again and again, until you make that conscious and deliberate decision on your own free will to crossover to the realm of enhanced consciousness, so be it.

Are you ready to move on? Fantastic!

The Cycle of Creation

You are now ready to be introduced to what I call the Cycle of Creation as illustrated in Figure 6. All of Creation – what the *MASTER CREATOR* creates for multi-dimensional Existence and what you as a CREATOR align with in your life experience in this Third Dimension of Existence is based on this eternal cycle and there are no exceptions in the physical or the non-physical dimensions of Existence. The only difference is the ineffability of the emotions and actions in the higher dimensions. What is the core purpose of all Existence? In the non-physical world of the *MASTER CREATOR* at the Source of Thought the purpose is quite honestly, ineffable to us humans with such a limited range of consciousness, however the core purpose of all Existence is *to serve and experience unbounded delight in collective co-existence.*

I have indicated earlier that the closest word that we as Creatures in the physical domain can relate to the ineffable feeling of the *MASTER CREATOR* is 'BLISS'. Pause for a moment and think about your greatest achievements, your most memorable victories, your deepest passions that you navigated through to fulfillment. No other human feeling exceeds the feeling of BLISS (not even Love) and when we get to that feeling we fulfill the core purpose of the Creature – that to experience unbounded delight in physical form.

The motivation and purpose at the source of all Creation – physical or non-physical is BLISS. It is this motivation of feeling BLISS that generates the *Inspiration* to create an experience that would culminate in Bliss.

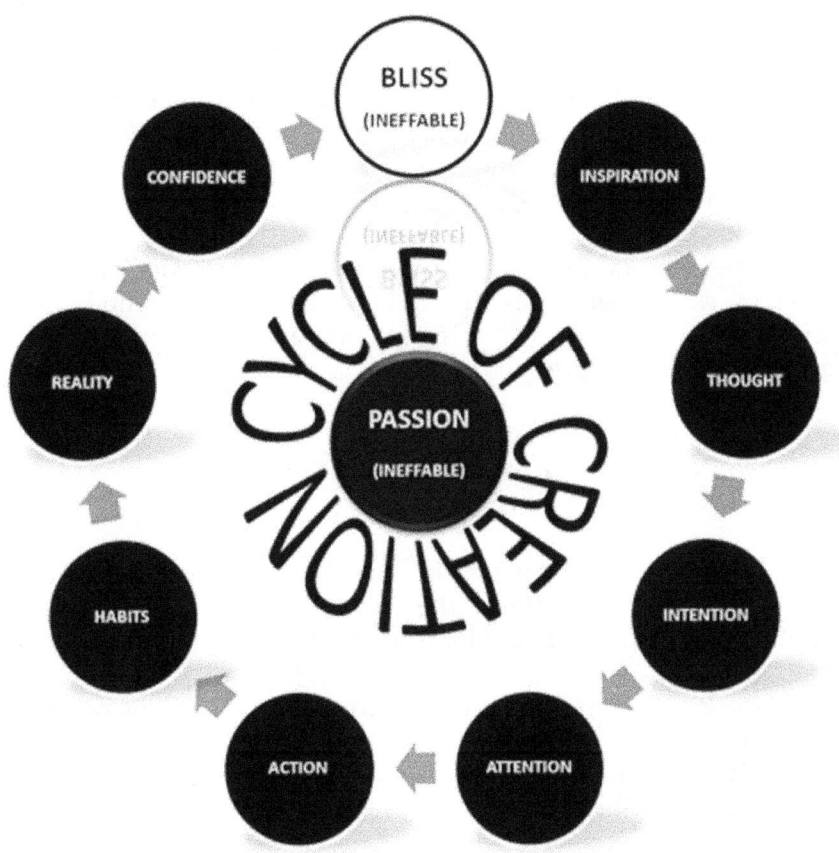

Figure 6

This Inspiration invokes *Thought* which is where the CREATOR enters the world of Parallelism – the realm of infinite possibilities. Leveraging the attribute of Free Will, the CREATOR makes a choice from these infinite possibilities, which becomes an *Intention* – '*I exercise this Free Will and choose to create that*' – whatever '*that*' is.

Intention is the decision to provide form and/or function to whatever '*that*' is. A true intention cannot be waived and cannot falter regardless of what other adversity may arise during the course of completion of the full Cycle of Creation.

An Intention that wavers or falters is not an intention but only a wish.

Intention leads to focus and concentration to identify and engage the resources and components that would be necessary to contribute and create the object intended – this focus is called *Attention*.

Parallelism is presented to Attention and the result is *Action*(s) which involves the techniques, the methods, the knowledge to bring all the relevant resources and components together for the purpose of creating *'that'*.

Repetitive and focused Action that collectively and incrementally contributes to the creation of *'that'*, leads to the development of *Habits*.

It is only by repetition of the Action(s) and hence the formation of Habits does the Intention to create *'that'*, culminate in *Reality* or manifestation of the Inspiration.

When Reality has been achieved *'that'* has been created. This achievement or success builds *Confidence* in the mind of the CREATOR – the fruition of the Intention to create *'that'* and the culmination of Inspiration.

The Confidence morphs into the emotions and feeling of *Bliss* closing the loop on the cycle of Creation. The process starts again from BLISS to create something new or to enhance what has already been created by the CREATOR.

What is motivation to experience Bliss? Why bother about all of the minute details to create something with such brilliance of architecture, magnanimity of scale and panache for perfection? What is driving the BLISS of Existence?

In the realm of the infinite, the domain of the *MASTER CREATOR*, I again enter the conundrum of ineffability to comprehend and convey the true essence of the driver behind all of INFINITE ETHEREALITY and Physical Reality.

In order to come a little close to this ineffability I would ask for your help, *"Why do YOU feel the compunction to create anything that would bring you to that state of Bliss? What drives you to undertake a project and come high wind or high water, you stand like a rock and despite all apparent odds you see it through to successful completion, and bask in the light of bliss? What motivates you to give it all you have and maybe even more to actually see the fruits of your own personal cycle of creation?*

It is *'Passion'* for you in the physical dimension, which escalates to the level of ineffability in the non-physical dimensions of Existence. The CREATOR is driven by Ineffable Passion, because without passion nothing is possible – not even the feeling of Bliss, let alone any progression along the Cycle Of Creation. Passion is the driver and the womb of all Creation and Existence, the glue that binds all of Existence together, ensuring harmony and coherence of every stage in the Cycle Of Creation. Without Passion there cannot be any Bliss and without Bliss, the Cycle of Creation cannot get activated. If you observe the Cycle of Creation you will notice that the cycle could break at any stage if the passion to follow through to the completion of that stage in the cycle is lost.

-------------------------*****-------------------------

Bliss conceives *Inspiration*. *Inspiration* germinates *Thought*. *Thought* morphs into *Intention*. *Intention* harnesses *Attention*. *Attention* initiates *Action*. *Action* develops *Habits*. *Habits* manifest *Reality*. *Reality* builds *Confidence*. *Confidence* blossoms into *Bliss*. This is the Cycle Of Creation, regardless of the dimension of Existence. *Passion* is the womb of all Creation and the glue that binds all of the multi-dimensional Existence together – without Passion there cannot be any Bliss and without Bliss there is no Creation.

-------------------------#####-------------------------

One of my goals in this book is to take you on a journey of understanding of Creation and Existence to at least my current level of consciousness from where we can collaborate and go higher. Through the process of such collaboration, you will get an opportunity for self-reflection, self-discovery, self-realization and self-orientation which would pave the way for self-mastery.

In order to solidify your understanding of the Cycle of Creation as explained above, pause for a moment and reflect back on your life so far. How many projects, have you undertaken in your life where you have actually completed the Cycle Of Creation? How many projects have you undertaken and then aborted midway through the Cycle Of Creation? Where exactly in the Cycle Of Creation did you abort those projects? Why did you abort those projects that you had undertaken? Why did you abort those projects where you had aborted them in the Cycle Of Creation? Did you lose your passion when that abortion of the cycle of Creation occurred in your life? Why and what circumstances and choices made you lose your passion?

Take a few moments to self-reflect on your life experience so far to answer the questions above and most definitely you will find a pattern in the Cycle of Creation where you had aborted projects prematurely. Make note of this pattern, since in all likelihood that is consistently sabotaging your enjoyment of unbounded delight. It's the time for self-realization and self-reflection to prepare you for the next chapter.

Chapter 6 - Multi-dimensional Co-existence

He was just a five year old boy carefully examining the toy airplane that Dad just brought home for him. Whenever Dad was traveling out of town for work, it was almost a ritual that some mechanical toy was going to find a home. The boy watched in glee as Dad wound up a little key, set the airplane on the wooden floor, released and the airplane, as if powered by some unseen force, self-propelled itself to start rolling on the floor.

It was probably the twentieth toy he had purchased and Dad knew his son was hooked. At least for a few hours not even a raging storm would divert the child's attention. Dad was right, as the toddler immersed himself in a world of exploration of this most amazing object that somehow moved on its own after a simple winding of a key in its fuselage.

It was not long before the thrill of the toy airplane began to wear off and it was time again, for the twentieth time actually, to take his exploration to the next level. It did not take long for the little boy to figure out how to rip apart the flimsy plastic fuselage and expose a small rectangular metal box where the winding key was attached with the two wheels of the airplane jutting out on either side. "Ah, what's inside that magic box?" Out came the trusted screwdriver and soon the magic box had its lid pried open.

If you have not guessed it yet, that little boy was yours truly. Like all the other toys, that airplane had lasted in its intended and finished product form for about a couple of hours before I had started to figure out the mechanism that made it work the way it did. That was my introduction to the "*spring theory*" ☺!

Later on when I was older and wiser my "*spring theory*" was explained as a conversion of kinetic energy through the process of winding the key, to potential energy stored in the spring mechanism and then back to kinetic energy when the key was released, which was responsible for the motion of that toy airplane. It all made sense and I was empowered by the knowledge of the indestructible nature of energy and its transformation capabilities. This transformation of energy is the fundamental technology for all dimensions of Existence – what a simple yet consistently effective and dynamic design of Creation!

Since my childhood days the study of Physics had become my passion, my obsession, my first love, (is that how you define a geek? ☺) which guided me through the rigors of earning a first class engineering degree and propelled me into a very successful career in software engineering. Like all engineers, analysis (almost to the point of paralysis at times ☺) is of critical importance to me before I can be convinced about concepts and principles that I may come across. My quest for knowledge about the mechanics of operation of the physical domain of Existence in the yesteryears soon made it abundantly clear that there is more to Existence than what can be interpreted by our five senses. I was convinced that there were domains of Existence where physical laws as we know them, do not apply and there are entirely different *supersets* of governing principles and rules that have stabilized those domains and made them independent of the time factor.

About twelve years ago, when I started to ask the tough questions about life, Existence, Creation, my purpose in this world, why things are perceived to be how they are, why people conduct themselves in the manner that they do, so on and so forth, my analytical mind could not find any straight and convincing answers. Today I know it was this constant focus and incessant hunger for the Truth about Existence that enabled me to reactivate the dormant communication channel with my Fifth Dimensional *Activebody* (more on this in the forthcoming chapters). The result of all that research is this book and those that are coming up in the *Genetics Of Divinity* series, all for the purpose of elevating global human consciousness. Never before has it become so important as it is today that humanity restores the stability of our presence in this one and only physical dimension of Existence.

This Chapter, as I am sure you will agree by the time you are finished reading, is different and you won't expect to find in any traditional book in the related topic. However an understanding of the contents of this Chapter is going to be most critical for the development of your consciousness about Creation and Existence as defined by the *Genetics Of Divinity*. Once upon a time, science and traditional spirituality were regarded as opposing schools of thought. Humanity has evolved in consciousness as more and more people get convinced that there's got to be more to Existence than what meets the eye of either science or organized religion both of which are mere toddlers, often misguided and misunderstood, when compared to the magnanimity of the authenticity of Eternal Consciousness.

Modern day Physicists since the brilliant Albert Einstein, have been chasing the dream of developing a Theory of Everything (fondly called TOE), that explains how the physical domain of Existence started, evolved and where we were headed. I too have been on a personal quest to find one unifying Theory of Creation and Existence for *both the finite physical and the infinite non-physical domains* that provides logical and rational explanation to how all of Existence came about, evolved and will transform in the future. Such a

Theory would have to explain the mechanics of both the finite physical reality and the infinite Ethereality. Such a Theory should also provide the technology through which humanity can re-align with the core purpose of Creation and Existence - establishing symbiotic collaborative relationships, which in turn would provide the platform for a life experience filled with unbounded delight in this physical dimension. What was revealed to me is now for you to learn and reactivate from your subconscious memory as the *Genetics Of Divinity*.

In this chapter I will first take you on a tour of the progress we have made so far to understand the physical laws of nature and then nosedive into a description of the Multiversal and Multi-Dimensional Laws of Creation. Why is that? We humans are some really touchy feely creatures – if something provides direct or indirect tactile feedback or something that can be interpreted by our five senses, we consider it to be reality. No harm in that at all – that is how we have been designed anyway.

My intent is to use as simple language as possible to explain some key related scientific laws and theories to retain the context of this book. If you as a reader want to dive deeper into these physical laws and theories to satisfy that twitching nerve impulse, please feel free to research on your own on the particular topic of your choice or reach out to me for appropriate references. I thoroughly recommend that you request for access to the online Multiversity of the *Genetics Of Divinity* that is included as a companion resource to this book – there are videos waiting for you there with explanations of concepts that may seem too technical for you to understand. Once you have a basic understanding of these physical laws and theories you will be in a better position to relate to the other more advanced postulates of Creation and Existence.

---------------------------*****---------------------------

Your physical energy that I call *Adaptive Energy* applies in the Third Dimension and your non-physical energy that I call *Active Energy* is applicable in the Fifth Dimension. We are all multi-dimensional Creatures of Creation and Existence. Your energy signature can never be created or destroyed but does transform from one physical body to another through the non-physical *Activebody* - more on this later in the book. With that stated, let's begin what promises to be a rather invigorating discussion.

---------------------------#####---------------------------

The ZERO Dimension or 0-D

Let's define *dimension* to get you warmed up on a discussion that promises to keep you engrossed. Feel free to research your available resources on the definition of dimension and come up with your own conclusion. However I define Dimension as '*a domain of Existence, which may be physical or non-physical bound by a specific band of frequencies of energy that constitute the specific domain*'.

Figure 7

We start the discussion with the smallest perceivable element in the human imagination – a point that indicates a position as in Figure 7. This is considered in the world of Physics as the ZERO dimension or '0-D'. When we talk about the 0-D, we are referring to a domain of Existence that cannot be experienced by any of our five senses although it can be perceived by human imagination to indicate a position. No, it is not the smallest point with the sharpest pencil that you can draw on a piece of paper or see under a microscope, since even that would have some diameter and hence is not small enough to be considered as a 0-dimensional object. Even the tiniest sub-atomic particles that have been discovered in the laboratory today have dimension and hence cannot be considered to be a 0-D object. In the coarse perception of the touchy feely physical world that we live in you may want to consider 0-D as dimensionless. A 0-D object can have no dimensional properties – it cannot be measured in any unit of measure of the physical domain.

Why am I discussing this topic of 0-D when it apparently seems to be so insignificant due to its dimensionless properties? There is a theory of creation presented by astronomers and physicists, popularly called the Big Bang Theory that supposedly explains how everything was created. According to this traditional Big Bang Theory, *from nothing, everything was created*. According to this Theory, this '*magical nothing*' supposedly decided one fine '*cosmic morning*' ☺ to explode and create all that there is. I don't know about you, but the postulates, the physics and mathematics of this theory just do not pass my filters of logic, rationality and discernment of an engineer's mind. It almost seems to be that due to the lack of a plausible explanation about the birth of this physical dimension, the scientific community had come up with such a theory. Today the majority of the world population believes the Big Bang Theory as an explanation for the origin of all that there is more due to the lack of an alternative theory than with any substantiated facts. Amusing, isn't it – how belief systems are formed in the mind of an entire civilization even if they are flawed and illogical?

Is there a better theory or a more believable explanation of all Creation? Play along a little longer with me as I build your belief systems towards a theory that serves as the most logical and rational explanation so far based on the laws of physics, mathematics and Eternal Consciousness. I promise you a fascinating journey and a flood of new cognitions and belief systems as you consume the forthcoming content.

I will go into much greater detail to explain the 0-D in the Chapter 7 and beyond, when the significance of this dimension will be clarified as your consciousness continues to upgrade throughout the rest of this book. Your consciousness will rise to a crescendo in Chapter 9, I promise. In a nutshell as you will learn in Chapter 9, all of Existence originated in the 0-D from a dimensionless particle without rest mass that I have taken the liberty to name the *sourceon*, the carrier of *Source Energy* from which all the **other** physical and non-physical dimensions of Existence – eleven of them all came to be.

The First Dimension or 1-D

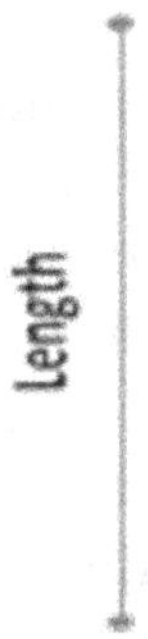

Figure 8

From the barely imaginable 0-D we travel into the first dimension or 1-D which is more perceivable to us in the physical world. Essentially, if you have two 0-D points, each of which indicate two respective positions and draw a straight line between them, we define the first dimension. The 1-D has only length. If you were to be a first dimensional Creature, you can only travel back and forth, *spatially*, along that same line. Again, if you draw the two smallest possible points on a piece of paper with the sharpest pencil and drew a straight line connecting them that would still not be an accurate representation of the 1-D because by definition a 1-D object cannot have anything except length. However narrow you draw that line on the paper it would have some width, enabling you to see it, thereby disqualifying it as a true 1-D object.

What is an example of a first dimensional object? The closest analogy that comes to mind from a Third Dimensional point of view is a line of force of electromagnetic energy.

This is not a physical object and yet can be represented in 1-D form. Light energy, an energy band within the spectrum of electromagnetic energy travels in a straight line as you know. This is commonly called the line of sight along which light travels until its point of impact with another object. Upon impact the photon (particle that serves as a carrier of light energy) may go through the mechanics of absorption, diffraction, refraction or reflection. Even then after the point of impact that I mentioned before, the photon continues its journey on a straight line, albeit in a changed orientation, but that path is still in the first dimension nonetheless.

Another interesting example related to the 1-D is can be cited through a particle called the *graviton*. The reason it is interesting to me is because this is a particle whose presence is as hypothetical (in physical terms) as the dimensionless point in the 0-D. The graviton is a product of fertile and logical human imagination attempting to explain our physical world. What makes it even more interesting is that the graviton has no mass but only represents the force of gravity. The gravitational force, represented by the graviton also has an infinite range of impact as proposed by the scientists. Does the graviton travel only on a straight line? Again we don't know through experimental physics because its physical existence cannot be detected by human instrumentation that relies on detection of rest mass of the particles. However if you jump in the air vertically, you fall vertically down don't you? Even if you are an athlete who just did a long jump the force of gravity is acting on you vertically, on a straight line at every moment of your flight, pulling you closer and closer towards the earth until touchdown. We can hence logically conclude that the hypothetical elementary particle graviton representing the carrier of the force of gravity is an example of a 0-D object. Furthermore, the force of gravity acts on a straight line and we can say that the gravitational line of force is an example of the 1-D.

These lower dimensions are the building blocks of all of the higher dimensions. Think about the 0-D and 1-D, however miniscule of insignificant they seem to be, as the core foundation of all the higher physical and non-physical dimensions. When you consider theories such as the Big Bang Theory which postulate that everything was created out of nothing, and then consider the 0-D and 1-D as being the building blocks of Creation, that *'nothing'* begins to develop a new meaning. Out of the *'nothing'* that is represented by the 0-D, when you join two of these dimensionless points in space you get the 1-D which define the concept of a line of force.

The Second Dimension or 2-D

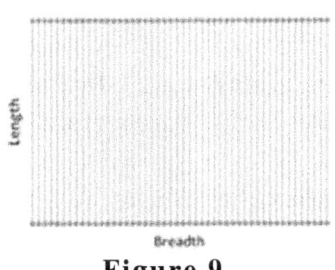

Figure 9

Enter the second dimension as the next level upgrade on the multi-dimensional design or architecture of Existence. In the second dimension you add breadth to the length of the 1-D object, thereby yielding a flat, planar object. For simplicity of your understanding a 2-D or second dimensional object could be visualized as a sheet of paper or a flattened out aluminum or tin foil – it only has a length and a breadth. However, while these examples of the sheet of paper or the foil help in the visualization of the second dimension, they are not really the 2-D objects that I am referring to. That sheet of paper or the foil has an extra dimension that you can see or even feel – the thickness of the material, thereby disqualifying these examples as representatives of the true Second dimension.

What really is the second dimension? Let's go back briefly to the explanation of the First dimension, where the 1-D is represented by a line that is *'traced'* by a photon or a graviton between any two dimensionless 0-D points. Now imagine a situation where there were an infinite number of these 1-D lines (with only the dimension of length) lined up right next to each other, thereby giving you, the observer the image of the *no-thickness* sheet of paper or foil. A-ha! Now you can perceive the second dimension as you look at those 1-D lines lined up right next to each other. This visual representation in Figure 9, has the length (represented by the vertical lines) and also the breadth of the 2-D (represented by the horizontal spread of the vertical lines).

In the true representation of the 2-D, our 1-D examples of the lines that represent the electromagnetic force or the gravitational force, when laid out horizontally, would represent what we call a *'planar force'* in the language of physics. You may have learned in school about the terms - electromagnetic force field (or simply electromagnetic field) or the gravitational force field (or simply gravitational field). Some text books refer to the magnetic force field to have more of a toroidal or a spherical area of influence, however every toroid or sphere or *field* is the sum of several 2-D planes sharing the same characteristics but a different orientation around a common axis, creating the 3-D view.

From the non-physical 0-D of *nothingness* we upgrade to the non-physical 1-D where a line of electromagnetic or gravitational force by itself appears to be too weak to be of any significance. However when you visualize the 2-D world which is also non-physical based on the above explanation, the collection of several 1-D lines of force now begins to demand significance and attention as a force plane or force field – it's a numbers game after all. While there is this force *plane* in the 2-D, there is no physical object containing any dimension of mass in the 2-D that the human consciousness can comprehend or imagine or even measure. Without the presence of an object or particle in the 2-D the purpose of the 2-D lines of force is more of a building block for the next higher physical dimension than anything else. Being part of the 3-D world, we are unable to measure or feel 2-D lines of force but every 3-D object in Existence is nothing but the juxtaposition of the 2-D components.

Just because human instrumentation can't measure a force field in a 2-D plane it does not mean it does not exist. As you will learn next, the Third dimension cannot exist without the foundation of the Second dimension. *All the lower dimensions collectively are the building blocks of the superstructure of the subsequent higher dimensions.*

As you can understand now that the Big Bang Theory postulate of everything being created from *nothing* is not that crazy after all (more on this in astonishing detail coming up for you in Chapter 9), provided you can manage to disassociate yourself from the commonly interpreted physicality of the *'thing'* in the word *nothing*. Take the concept of rest mass out of the *"thing"* and the Big Bang Theory becomes credible again. The dimensions 0-D, 1-D and 2-D are not physical dimensions of Existence, since human intelligence or the five senses or instrumentation cannot really detect an observable, tangible object in these dimensions. However the 1-D and the 2-D are the dimensions where two of the four fundamental forces of the physical Third Dimension originate from the Source Force of the 0-D. These forces are all non-physical in their form and function, and are the building blocks for the higher dimensions.

The Third Dimension or 3-D

In the third dimension, we add another dimension to the 2-D model – the height or the depth. You can imagine the Third Dimension to be an extension of the range of the two planar forces (electromagnetic and gravitational) along the depth of the 3-D, thereby graduating from being called planar force in the 2-D to a *'force field'* in the 3-D. This may also be considered as an intersection of two 2-D planes of force. In other words several planes of these planar forces in the 2-D have been lined up next to each other along the depth of the 3-D 'space' to create a force field or the domain in which the two fundamental forces may be felt and measured. What is even more interesting in the third dimension is that this is where the concept of physicality or *'matter'* comes into being. Everything that you can touch, see, taste, smell and hear including your own flesh, bones and blood-laden body is your interpretation of the physical 3-D world around you.

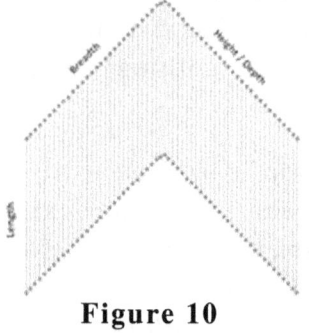

Figure 10

Every physical object – animate or inanimate have those three dimensions of measurement and in addition to that we introduce another property of that object – *'rest mass'* Everything, from the smallest sub-atomic particle detectable and observable in the laboratory to the largest star that our instruments can detect has rest mass. Contrary to popular belief and surprisingly it still continues to be taught in schools today, a sheet of paper, a flat foil of metal however thin it may be, are not 2-D objects but 3-D, first because there is some thickness on that object, however small it may be and secondly it has mass that can be measured. So the concept of rest mass is limited *exclusively* to the physical Third Dimension of Existence.

Both the sheet of paper and the metal foil when allowed to be on its own suspended in space will fall to the ground as long as they are in the field of the gravitational force. If the metal foil has the appropriate properties to respond to an electromagnetic force field it will get attracted towards or repelled from the source of that electromagnetic force.

The Third Dimension is also where two other fundamental forces of Existence are realized. The third fundamental force of nature in the 3-D is called the *'Strong Nuclear Force'* which is a force field the binds the sub-atomic particles together and keeps the atom bound and stable. If this very short ranged Strong Nuclear Force did not exist, the atom would disintegrate and there would be nothing in physical existence.

You see, the gravitation and the electromagnetic forces are very weak. This sounds strange, but if the gravitational force was so strong, how come you can drop a hammer in the floor and then bend down to pick it up effortlessly against the force of gravity. Weak, weak energy – weaker than the potential energy stored in your muscles, depending on the rest mass of the object that your muscular energy is attempting to deal with. Although you can lift a hammer from the floor it would be a challenge to lift up your car from the ground – the only difference is the rest mass of the objects in question. This is similar to the fact that a stone sinks in the ocean but a Titanic can still float. If the electromagnetic force was so strong, then how come you can shut the doors and windows in the room and draw the curtains enveloping the room in darkness preventing external light energy to penetrate through? So the electromagnetic force too is a pretty weak force. More on the reasons why are coming up later on in this book.

But try to take the proton out of the nucleus of an atom – you sure can but that would need a much larger energy and force Hence the 'Strong Nuclear Force' lives up it to its name, thereby ensuring the solidarity of the atom.

This brings us to the fourth fundamental force applicable in the 3-D, which is also very short range and operates at the subatomic level. This is called the 'Weak Nuclear Force' and is responsible for radioactive decay, which causes the conversion of a neutron into a proton, an electron and another subatomic particle (also a 3-D object) called the anti-neutrino.

Collectively these four forces are the fundamental forces that operate in the physical Third Dimension. But they are weak forces, which is why physical objects have properties to react chemically to become other objects or even lose their integrity. Due to these weak forces physical objects can be broken, reshaped and remodeled. The *mortality* of these physical entities is a core design attribute of the Third Dimension of Existence. Force is a function of energy. This implies that if the Third Dimension is made up of weak forces the energy that operates the Third Dimensional Creatures is also weak – weaker than those operating in the higher dimensions of Existence. Weakness renders the Third Dimension susceptible to change and change is a comparative factor of time.

A Twist in the Third Dimension

You must have heard the phrase *'I have to see it to believe it'*. This belief system has plagued humanity for thousands of years. Today this paradigm has taken our civilization to the point where our ability to subscribe to any other concept of what true reality is has become as vestigial as the appendix in the human body. 98% of the human population in the planet is suffering from this disease of what I call *'behavioral appendicitis'* or the ailment of the human belief system that subscribes to such illogical paradigms. Here's a simple treatment if you have been a victim of such a paradigm, which clearly cannot yield the life experience that you desire. *You have to believe it first to see it. Belief starts with an inspiration and sight is the manifestation. It is impossible to manifest without an inspiration – we have not been designed to operate any differently. What you believe in defines your true reality – everything else is your fantasy or a definition of perceived reality.* Refer to Figure 6 – the Cycle of Creation and you will notice that the *Reality* component, which is the manifestation of your true reality is preceded by seven other preparatory components that collectively make up that *belief* I am referring to. A block in the flow of the cycle in any of these seven preceding components would thwart the manifestation of the true physical reality.

Common belief is whatever you can see and in some cases have your other four senses interpret in the physical 3-D world should have mass, more accurately stated in the language of physics as *'rest mass'* however small or large it may be. This is what physicists define as *'matter'*, which must have rest mass. In other words this luminous or *'visible matter'*, which we can observe in the physical 3-D plane of Existence supposedly is all the matter available.

WRONG! A detailed discussion of non-luminous or *'dark matter'* is beyond the scope of this book, but feel free to research the Internet or your local library if you wish. It has now been proven through the phenomena called *'gravitational lensing'* (feel free to research this topic too) that in addition to the 'visible matter' there is also another type of matter, that is invisible to the human eye or instrumentation sensitive to photonic emissions, that does not absorb or emit light, hence it is called 'dark matter'. Gravitational lensing is a principle of physics based on the fact that all matter, visible or dark will *deflect* light. Think about the glasses that people wear which function by bending and guiding light to focus on your retina properly. Similarly, despite the fact that dark matter does not emit or absorb light, this ability of dark matter to deflect light is what blew its cover from being directly detected by our eyes.

Although dark matter is not visible, gravitational lensing proves its existence. Dark matter constitutes an estimated whopping 83% of all matter that there is. Moreover dark matter, being so massive, has a high magnitude of gravitational energy (called *dark energy*), that it is pulling the galaxies apart from their current respective positions. The dark matter can pass through any luminous object without losing any energy. Dark matter is so dense and massive that it has the ability to literally dictate how the galaxies of visible matter (including our Milky Way) are formed and how they operate (spin, axis, tilt, speed). It is only a matter of conjecture if dark matter follows all physical laws of visible matter – we just can't get our arms around dark matter just yet.

Edwin Hubble proved that the Universe as we know it is expanding and growing outwards towards infinity. There has been compelling evidence that the active agent for such an expansion is dark matter and dark energy that is pulling the physical Universe as we know it, apart.

So if the Universe is indeed expanding, is it not logical to say that once upon a time, about 13.7 billion years ago (by modern estimates of the age of the physical visible Universe), the Universe as we know it was a small compact yet dimensionless point from where it started to grow and expand? While the timeframe is not important, what's important is that Existence expanded from the 0-D.

I still don't buy the Big Bang Theory in its original form as proposed in 1927 by Georges Lemaitre, as it defies common logic. But is there another explanation that is more logical? Most definitely, as you will discover shortly as I take you into the world of strings and membranes in this chapter and take that knowledge to a crescendo in Chapter 9.

Could dark matter be the source matter of all the visible matter? Compelling argument for sure and I will leave it to you to arrive at your own conclusion when you have finished reading this book. Quite honestly there's not much that we know currently about dark matter.

---------------------------*****---------------------------

Why is this discussion of physics and cosmology important for you for the purpose of realigning yourself to your life purpose and enjoy a life experience filled with unbounded delight? I'd like you to consider your life experience which is bound by the Laws of Creation as defined by the *Genetics Of Divinity* to be based on the fact that out of what appears to be *nothing*, **everything can be created**. Out of what seems invisible and a dimensionless emotion of Bliss, you as a Creature can *receive* anything and everything that you desire in the true reality of your life experience that is visible and tangible in the physical 3-D and enjoy unbounded delight as long as it is logical and ethically feasible.

-------------------------#####-------------------------

Whoa! That would be an obvious reaction from you if this is the first time you have been exposed to the existence of dark matter and dark energy. No longer, not anymore do you need to subscribe to that crippling memory in your brain that wrongly says '*I must see it to believe it*' because clearly that is a false self-sabotaging perception. *You MUST believe it to see it* – such is the Cycle of Creation.

The question I now have for you to consider is '*Is dark matter an example of a physical 3-D object?*' Whatever you pick is correct at this moment of our technological evolution based on your perception and the amount of proof available from research on the subject. However it will be a matter of conjecture because science quite candidly is yet to find or develop an instrument that would identify the form, structure or function of dark matter, far less develop laws of its operation and properties, although we have indisputable proof of its presence.

If I had to answer that question I would unreservedly vote for a 'No' - dark matter cannot be considered a traditional 3-D object in the visible Universe in my opinion, since clearly the dimensions of length, breadth, height and the inherent 3-D object properties of rest mass and the ability to absorb or emit light energy do not apply to it.

Allow me to throw you another volley of questions to tickle your rationality and intelligence, now that you know about the existence of dark matter and the four fundamental forces of nature. In the process I will be delivering short impulses to the dormant memory bank in your subconscious mind where the code of the *Genetics Of Divinity* are embedded. '*What is the source of all the visible matter? What created all the visible matter and gave their respective properties, forms and functions, all of which appear to be working in such a synchronous symphony with each other? Why are all the physical objects that you observe in the third dimension the way they are? Why do all the galaxies with all their components have the properties that they do? Why do they appear to our instrumentation like what they do? Why are objects in this planet where we live the way they are? Why can't you fly while a bird for example, can not only fly but also walk on two feet? Why do you have the characteristics of your physical body that you do and why does that bird not have the same? Why have you been created the way you have been created and why not any differently? Why does a fish for example, have gills and you have lungs? Why does a tree 'inhale' carbon dioxide and you exhale that same gas? How come some bacteria can live in hot lava and your highly developed and advanced body will start revolting at the mere thought of attempting the same? Are you sure what you see is really what that object of observation truly looks like – could there be more to that object than what meets the eye?'*

When we interact someday more personally in the future I will be eager to listen to your answers. As far as my answers to the questions above are concerned, humor me a little longer and you will know my position and logical opinions about them when I describe the Object Oriented Design of Creation in Chapter 7.

The Fourth Dimension or 4-D

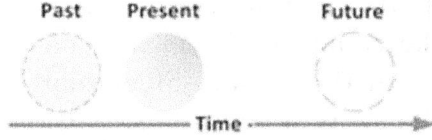

Figure 11

What time is it now? When did you start reading this book? How long will you take to complete reading this book? Besides reading this book what else do you have planned for the day and when will you be doing those activities? You, a Creature in the 3-D is living your physical life experience through a linear progression of time. You were born one day, you have lived your life so far and will continue to live your physical and mortal experience until the day you pass on (never pass *away* – but let's keep that for a later discussion). This element of time defines the Fourth Dimension or the 4-D.

In essence the physical world of the 3-D is bound by a linear and unidirectional progression of time – the Fourth Dimension of Existence. The 3-D Creature existing in the 4-D would have the experience of a past, a present moment and a future as the calendar and clock continues to measure the *linear unidirectional progression* of time to record the history of evolution of the Creature. Evolution itself is a by-product of the factor of time.

We have based the element of time based on the rotation of our planet around its axis and its revolution around the Sun and that is a good enough perception of the Fourth Dimension from our perspective on Earth. However what if you were in a different planet that rotates at a different speed around its axis and revolves at a different speed around the sun? Would the same definition of time as we have on Earth be of any significance to you in that planet? Highly unlikely! You would rather define your planetary time differently than we do on Earth.

Regardless of what that definition is or wherever you call your *Home Planet*, as a 3-D Creature having a physical life experience, you, by the Laws of Creation defined by the *Genetics Of Divinity* have no choice but to live in the Fourth Dimension of Time in that physical flesh-bones-blood mortal body of yours. Mortality in itself is a by-product of the factor of time as well. Would you accomplish more if you were to live in a planet where 1 day equaled 5 Earth days for example? What would the average life expectancy be for you in that planet measured in terms of Earth years? You obviously cannot answer these questions since you are unable to relate to a life on that other planet. You and every other *matter* in the 3-D have no choice but to progress linearly through the Fourth Dimension of time. It is this very attribute of time in the Fourth Dimension to define concepts of lifespan, lifecycle, mortality, evolution, that creates the instability and finiteness of the Third Dimension of Existence. The higher dimensions that you will learn about in forthcoming chapters is independent of the factor of time and hence have attained structural stability and infiniteness in Existence.

The human species has a history, a past reference of time just as you do individually, albeit shorter in this current physical form. *Everything that has happened in the past to the realm of the 3-D in general and to the 3-D Creature in particular*, have all collaborated and defined the physical experience of the Creature in the present moment in the 4-D. Read that again!

Recall the discussion on *Parallelism* in Chapter 5. Based on all the parameters of the past and the physical experience that you are having at the present moment, the decision that you take from the plethora of choices being offered by Parallelism to you at this present moment, will contribute and define your physical life experience in the next moment or the future in the Fourth Dimension.

In other words, while the past in the 4-D is static and *unchangeable* in your current physical life experience, the future in the 4-D is flexible and dynamic and is governed by your decision through your free will on the choices presented by Parallelism in the present moment of the 4-D.

The popular singer from the 80's, George Michael sings the following in his song titled Different Corner©, *'Take me back in time, maybe I can forget... Turn a different corner and we never would have met. Would you care?...'*

This imparts a nice representation of the Fourth Dimension as it relates to our 3-D physical existence. The singer portrays a scenario at the present time when he is recollecting a moment in memory, instantly jumping back *virtually* in the timeline of his life when he had to make a decision based on prior experiences to meet a certain person. If that choice was any different in the past, the singer indicates that his current experience would also have been different. But alas, the events of the past cannot be physically changed.

Note that in the above words, there is no mention of the future experience. However, at the present moment when the singer is expressing the feelings and emotions, he has a choice to understand the Contrast to those feelings and emotions and consider the new choices being offered through Parallelism and make a different choice for a more delightful outcome. He can choose to do nothing, in which case, his future experience in the 4-D would continue to be one with the same feelings and emotions, or he can choose to make a decision to *'let the bygones be bygones'*, learn from the past experience, apply Contrast, make necessary corrections and open up his faculties for a new life experience at a future timeframe in the 4-D. In other words, the individual would continue to remain in a state of *homeostasis* of the past, if no decision was made in the present moment to change that plight of the past life experience.

I trust that you are beginning to understand the magnanimity of the significance of the 4-D in your physical experience as a Creature with that 3-D physical body. Your life today is a reflection, the end result of all your past decisions and actions. If I were to ask you if your life today is filled with unbounded delight or not, how would you respond? Since you are the Creature with the will to receive, I am fairly certain that there are quite a few areas in your life that are still unfulfilled or may even be in pain. Since you are also a CREATOR with the will to bestow, I am also fairly certain that there are other areas in your life that are still short of those emotions of unbounded delight. You see, one can experience unbounded delight in this physical and mortal lifetime if and only if the life purpose is fulfilled or the individual is navigating on the path of fulfilling their life purpose under the guidance of the *Genetics Of Divinity*.

The past in the timescale of the 4-D is the artwork in the art gallery of your life – static, inert and of academic interest. In the present moment of the 4-D, Parallelism has offered you the paintbrush in your hands with all the colors spread out in front with a blank canvas as your choices.

What emotions would you feel and express in that canvas through the choice of colors and your brushstrokes to paint your future life experience in the 4-D? Does that painting represent logical analysis and conform to ethical feasibility? Would that lead you to the fulfillment of your life purpose and hence your personal perception of unbounded delight? How has your life experience so far evolved over time and what would you do right now to control the evolution in the future in the 4-D?

Parallelism of Creation

The question now becomes, *'If Parallelism is so important in Creation, what is it really and in which dimension does it exist?'* Ah, great question and you are in for a treat for the rest of the chapter. We live in the most amazing time in all of human history today and are now at a stage in development of science and consciousness when the sublime essence of Creation is being revealed faster and faster in this Third Dimension.

Parallelism that seemed to be an esoteric concept and a topic of wild philosophical debate in the past, has graduated into the most logical explanation of why the human life experience is so disparate in the way it is. This graduation from a pipedream to logical reasoning has been possible through discoveries in the world of Physics and Cosmology – two complimentary streams of science that have unabashedly delved into the rabbit hole of the unexplored to understand the secrets of Creation and Existence. This discussion of Parallelism will empower you beyond comprehension if you would invest your attention to it. We humans need proof before we can agree to take some action, especially in these days of hype and crafty marketing – so here we go.

When you understand the importance of Parallelism, it will liberate you, since you will know that you *ALWAYS* have a choice, no matter what your past life experiences have been. You can continue to live your life the way you have lived or choose to embark on a different path to have a different life experience from this moment in time onwards. You are a Creature designed with the will to receive and enjoy unbounded delight in your life experience in the 4-D. Consequently, you have the right and capabilities built within you to choose such a life and Parallelism offers you the very same.

If I have to document all the 10 years of intense research that contributed to the birth of the *Genetics Of Divinity* series of books that I am authoring, that would be a book by its own right. Parallelism of Creation is not only a concept, it is an attribute of Existence. To stay focused on the context of this book, I will condense all that research into the key elements to illustrate the proof. Feel free to expand your research as much as you want for better understanding of certain terms I use in this chapter that you may be unfamiliar with.

As a software engineer the challenge that I have, like all engineers do, is that I just do not and cannot take any postulate or concept for granted unless there is a logical explanation that satisfies my hunger for truth. As engineers, we are very good at analysis of disparate facts and scientific discoveries and bring them together into what makes logical sense. With this background let's delve into the exotic world of Parallelism, and understand *Parallel Universes* or what is commonly referred to as the *Multiverse*. Stay with me, if you are missing a certain concept, go back and read it again. You are also welcome to interact with me at the Multiversity portal of the *Genetics Of Divinity*. As I have mentioned earlier, as an owner of this book you have access to this online resource. Visit me at the Multiversity online at www.GeneticsOfDivinity.com and register for the companion videos that provide further explanation.

Quantum Mechanics Proves Parallelism

In 1927, Werner Heisenberg shocked the world of Newtonian particle physicists with his famous Uncertainty Principle where he stated that at a given point in time it is impossible to simultaneously predict both the precise position of an electron and its future motion or momentum. If you were to hypothetically shine a light beam on the electron to detect its position, that light energy would instantly dislodge it from that position preventing you from observing its momentum. This was the birth of quantum mechanics and according to its principles, all matter that make up this universe are not only particles, but also waves — hence the wave-particle duality of Existence.

Quantum mechanics indicated that all matter is composed of two fundamental particles — *bosons* or the particles that are carriers related to the transmission of forces (such as gravitational, electromagnetic, strong and weak nuclear forces) and *fermions* or the particles that make up the physicality of matter.

Due to the wave-particle duality, the Uncertainty Principle postulates that not only can the position of a particle at a given instance of time, not be predicted, it can be at *multiple possible positions at the same tim*e. In fact the *'particle could pop from a particle to a wave and from a wave to a particle at anytime, anywhere'*. This was later adopted and enhanced by Albert Einstein in his famous $E = mc^2$ theory of Mass-Energy equivalence — more on this later. This was the birth of quantum mechanics and our first proof of the attribute of Parallelism.

How about a simple proof of this behavior of the particle being in multiple possible positions at the same time? Get a transparent, solid glass apple for example and shine a narrow laser beam (for example from a laser pointer) on it. You will find that the light beam (comprised of particles called photons) shows up in several places around the glass apple at the same time. This experiment was demonstrated by Professor Max Tegmark of the Department of Physics, MIT and later recorded in the History Channel series called '*The Universe*®'. You can also visit the online Multiversity portal of the *Genetics Of Divinity* and watch the video on the subject where I demonstrate this very interesting behavior of the photons.

If you agree that you and I are made up of particles, then by the same Uncertainty Principle, both of us *can* and sometimes *must* be, at multiple places at the same time. In the larger scheme of things, *your future position cannot be predicted by any position in the past.* I wonder if a disclaimer made by financial investment firms saying "*Past results are not a guarantee of future performance*" comes from Quantum Mechanics ☺. You must be thinking that I have finally lost it – how can you be at multiple places at the same time? Read on and the science of Parallelism as I will explain will blow your mind.

Let's put this into perspective before we go further into the bosoms of science. If it is true that a particle can transform from a particle (matter with rest mass) to a wave (energy) and from a wave to a particle following the doctrines of quantum physics and if energy can never be created or destroyed, how is it possible for you, the Creature to be considered mortal? Your physical body is not only matter or rest mass, but also energy which is the non-physical part of your body. If energy cannot be created or destroyed but can only be transformed how can you be mortal? Mortality is only related to the physical attributes of your body that ages with the passage of time. However, mortality cannot claim any part of your *Adaptive* energy.

More on this Adaptive energy and the concept of mortality later on in this book.

Want more proof that you are a powerhouse of energy? Ok, clean your hands and slightly cup your fingers so that your palms face straight with each other. Now hold your palms about 8-10 inches from each other. Focus on the empty space between your palms and slowly move your palms towards each other and away from each other in a regular rhythm as if you are playing an accordion. You can watch an instructional video on this exercise at the online Multiversity portal of the *Genetics Of Divinity*. If you did this exercise correctly you will feel a compression or repulsion as your palms come in towards each other and an attraction as they move away from each other. That is your own *Adaptive* energy field that you cannot see being emitted through your hand *chakra*, but it does exist. More on the Chakra system coming up in Chapter 8.

Need more proof? After Semyon Kirlian's accidental discovery in 1939, today we are able to use Kirlian photographic techniques to actually see the human aura or a luminous radiation surrounding the human body outside the physical space of the body. The intensity and range of colors of this aura differs from individual to individual and is a factor of the net available *Adaptive* energy that the person radiates from the physical body.

Need more proof? Have you ever experienced a situation when you meet a person for the first time and automatically an unknown force (or an inner voice) either urged you to engage in further interaction with the stranger or urged you to repel that person and go away? It is almost like you have an *Early Warning System* built within you that adjudicates a *like* or a *dislike* for that person. What do you think that is? Your energy field that lies outside your physical body interacts with the energy field of the other person and as a result there is either a resonance (amplification of energy) or dissonance (attenuation in energy).

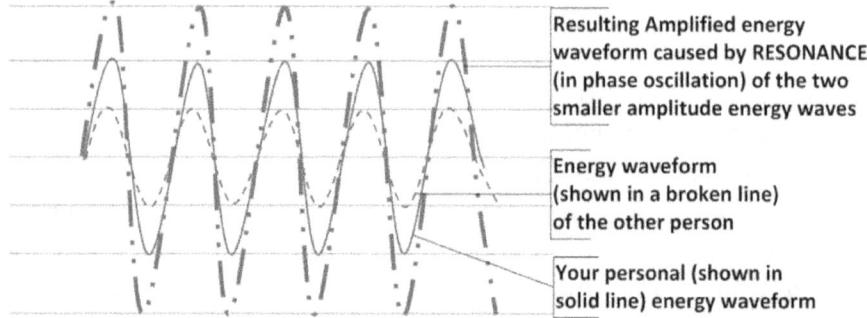

Figure 12

When you have resonance of these two energy fields as indicated in Figure 12, the reason you feel attracted towards that other person is because there has been an amplification of energy – the beginnings of a symbiotic collaborative relationship. On the contrary, when you have dissonance of these two energy fields, the reason you feel repulsion from that other person is because there has been attenuation (reduction) of energy as indicated in Figure 13 – the birth of a parasitic disassociating relationship. It is without question therefore that your physical body is an energy source as well as an energy sink.

When your physical body ceases its capability to sustain your natural physical energy or what I refer to as *Adaptive* Energy, you pass on (not pass *away* as most people tend to believe and say) from a physical state to an non-physical state only to be transformed into another physical state at a different instance of time , the transformation occurring according to the principles of Mass-Energy Equivalence.

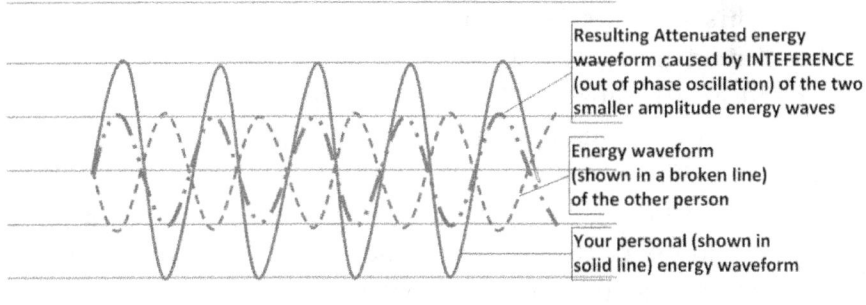

Figure 13

What a controversial topic, isn't it? Does that mean I am referring to re-incarnation, being born again in another mortal, physical 3-D form? Most certainly, that is what I am referring to. Ancient texts (4000 years ago) such as the Vedas mention reincarnation before any organized religion was born and today we have proof as I will describe in this book.

Granted that some of today's mainstream organized religions do not mention the matter of reincarnation, but what is the truth? There is some data available in the public domain that the original Bible did contain references to re-incarnation but was deleted by the order of the Roman Emperor Constantine and his mother Helena in 325 AD in order to solidify the control of the Church on the people and make sure that the people understood that they get only one shot at a physical life experience. Whether this report is true or not is irrelevant but the fact of the matter is the soul or spirit (what we call energy) is eternal and all major organized religions today seem to agree.

In his books titled 'Many Lives Many Masters', 'Same Soul Many Bodies', 'Only Love is Real', Dr. Brain. L Weiss provides vivid explanations of examples where he was able to leverage the techniques of past life regression, a common practice in hypnotherapy to obtain vivid accounts of past lives of his patients. I am a certified hypnotherapist myself and as I read those accounts of Dr. Weiss' patients I was not surprised at all, more so because of my understanding of the eternal nature of energy and the principle of Mass-Energy Equivalence. You and I and every person in this planet are indeed Immortal in our true essence - we only pass on from one physical form to another through our *Activebody* in the Fifth Dimension as will be clarified for you in Chapter 7. Immortality is a part of the code of the *Genetics Of Divinity* which is already in place regardless of whether your paradigms or belief systems subscribe to it or not. Moreover our energy lives eternally in multiple dimensions – we will get to this shortly. More proof of Immortality coming up for you as I now take you into the multi-dimensional architecture of Existence.

Let's rejoin the discussion on physics and cosmology to take us further into understanding Creation and Existence. Although quantum physics was revolutionary, even in coordination with the traditional theory of particle physics, it fell short of providing an explanation for what caused the much publicized Big Bang. It was unable to provide the proper scientific logic for how out of nothing, this 3-D world that we consider the visible reality and our life experience could be created. Albert Einstein passed on before he could complete his Unified Field Theory, which he was working on at the time of his passing. This was supposed to be the Theory of Everything about the creation of the Universe and how matter and energy interacts and coexists. This theory which never saw the daylight of completion leaves humanity to conjecture on whether the most brilliant scientific mind was about to reveal a core component of the *Genetics Of Divinity*.

Beyond the Fourth Dimension

In an effort to develop a Theory of Everything physicists came up with the Superstring Theory which postulated matter was not made up of atoms but of very tiny little strings with lengths as low as 10^{-23} centimeters which are in a state of constant vibration, much like the strings of a stringed musical instrument. Vibration requires energy – where is the energy coming from? Are these strings generators or transformers of energy? If so, what attribute in them makes them generators or transformers of energy? I now take you deeper into understanding Existence through the eyes of Theoretical Physics – this is part of your evolution on the code of the *Genetics Of Divinity*.

The Superstring Theory

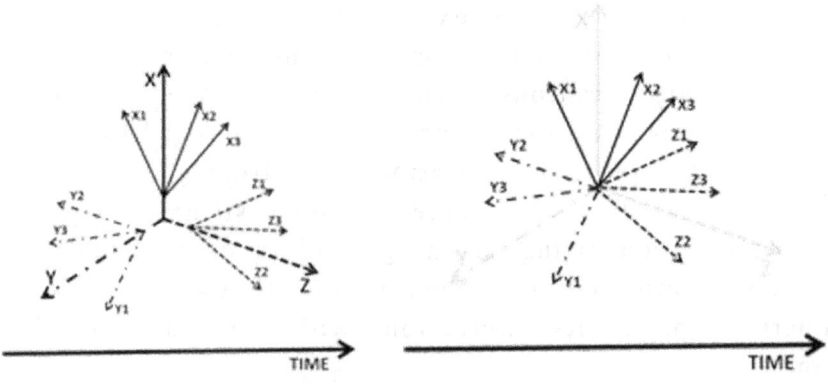

Figure 14 a **Figure 14 b**

The most exciting part is that these strings are said to be vibrating in not three, but in nine dimensions of space in one dimension of time – in other words, instead of the four dimensions that I have already explained in this book, there are ten space-time dimensions in which everything exists. In our 3-D physical world, without a doubt it is practically impossible to even visualize nine spatial dimensions. I tried to visualize those 9 dimensions of vibration and came up with a plausible explanation - if you can visualize the different modes in which a plucked string can possibly vibrate you too can imagine these additional dimensions in space as shown in Figure 14 a. Each of the three main 3-D axes of space has its own 3-D axes as you can see here. Now imagine an object that exists in nine spatial dimensions (seen in Figure 14 b) vibrating in the dimension of time and there you have the *string*.

---------------------------*****---------------------------

It is very important here to understand that although these extra six dimensions are shown as spatial dimensions in Figure 14 a and 14 b, that does not necessarily mean that the physical matter or rest mass of the string is in all of these nine dimensions at the same time. Some of these dimensions are dimensions of energy or possibilities where the physical matter of the string could exist at a given instant of time. Moreover, some dimensions may have no matter in them at all and be only vibrations of energy, for example, the energy behind the four basic forces that we have identified for the 3-D plane of Existence – gravitational, electromagnetic, strong nuclear and weak nuclear forces. In some strings, matter or rest mass is converting to energy and in others energy is converting into matter depending on its own vibrational properties and on its interactions with vibrations of other strings.

---------------------------#####---------------------------

When you pluck a string it not only vibrates physically, it also generates energy waves as a result– you hear a sound or may even feel a wind-stream buzzing around the string. If you pluck the string once and let it alone, over time the vibration will stop as other environmental forces directly in 'touch' with it compel the string to stop vibrating, until you pluck it again. The strings that we are referring to here are constantly vibrating in different frequencies in the micro level, which is why at a macro level, the properties and external manifestation of different kinds of objects are so different. With the general practices of extrapolation, the strings in a soccer ball would continue to vibrate the same pattern so that the soccer ball retains its physical properties. If the strings in that soccer ball were to start vibrating differently, the soccer ball would change into whatever object that pattern of vibration would be a property of.

Why do we not see all those extra dimensions that the Superstring Theory refers to? Firstly, some of those higher dimensions are hidden or are not sensitive to electromagnetic radiation and we humans are limited to only see objects that are within the visible band of the electromagnetic spectrum. The String Theory hence can also explain the existence of dark matter and dark energy which are invisible to the human eye and instrumentation. Second, our five senses cannot detect the existence of those higher dimensions which gives the common person the perception that the higher dimensions do not exist. Imagine yourself on a boat on the surface of a lake. What you see around you is the surface of the lake and everything above it. However there is an entire world, an entire ecosystem, an entire life experience below the surface of the lake that is not visible to you. But that does not mean the submerged world does not exist, does it? This is the same when we talk about dimensions higher than the Fourth – just because we cannot observe them due to the attributes of the design of our physical bodies, does not mean they do not exist. Those higher dimensions absolutely do exist and serve very specific purposes in the multi-dimensional hierarchical architecture of Existence as indicated by the *Genetics Of Divinity* – explanations are coming up in Chapter 7.

Could we actually perceive those higher dimensions that Superstring Theory postulates? Yes. How? All in good time as you continue to read and continue to reactivate the dormant memories of the Genetics of Divinity. You can't start a car in the fifth gear, can you? Play along, understand the basics and very soon that 'How' will be answered.

Superstring theory opened up new doors to understanding 'the how' of the beginning of it all and seemed to be the Theory of Everything scientists were looking for. But not quite as strings are considered to be 1 dimensional objects vibrating in a 10 space-time dimension. Due to this 1-D nature of the string, it soon became evident that even this theory with all its merits of unifying natural forces and matter, fell short of explaining the source and origins of the Big Bang. If we are talking about a string that is 10^{-23} centimeters long in one dimension and consider that to be the source of all that there is, the size of the string does not quite fit the profile of being one that would explain an enormous event such as the Big Bang in our cosmic history.

The "M" (Membrane) Theory

But what if we added another dimension to the string and considered it to be a 2-D object, still flat but a two dimensional *'string'*. Well, such a 2-D object could not be called a string anymore, because we added a second dimension to it. This is the progression of the SuperString Theory into what is called the M Theory, where M refers to a *'membrane'* – composed of several strings laid out side by side and to the tail and head of each of those strings, thereby creating a 2-D surface or membrane. Aha! Imagine a flag fluttering slowly in the gentle breeze and you will be able to visualize the membrane that I am referring to – the threads lined up side by side, above and below, to make the fabric of the flag. Membranes hence have all the properties of strings and more...

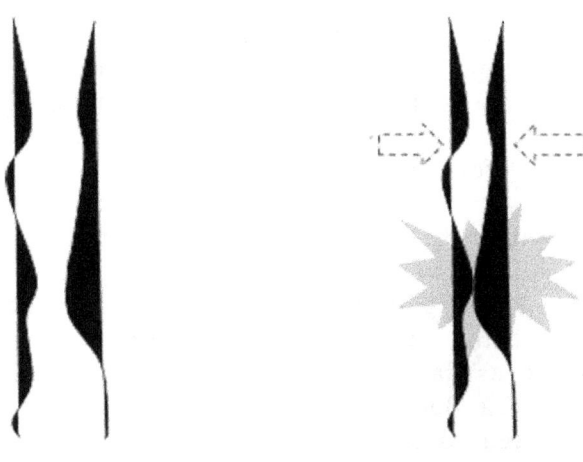

Figure 15 a   **Figure 15 b**

According to the M-Theory everything is made up not only of strings, but two dimensional membranes (fondly referred to in the circles of Theoretical Physicists as 'branes') that are vibrating in eleven dimensions – the nine spatial dimensions of the string, the dimension of time and finally the additional eleventh spatial dimension that renders the string to be a membrane. All matter that is visible and matter that is invisible is considered in this Theory to be nothing but *giant* membranes oscillating or fluttering incessantly like a flag and floating freely in the vastness of space as shown in Figure 15 a, until such time when one or more parts of the membranes come too close to each other and collide with such immense energy, as shown in Figure 15 b, that they cause an explosion or what some scientists call a cosmic collision – a very plausible explanation of the Big Bang.

These membranes have no limit to their length and breadth and just like a flag fluttering in the gentle breeze, it is impossible to predict which part of the membrane will protrude or intrude between its 10 spatial dimensions of reference and when. However with every protrusion or intrusion between those 10-D planes of reference, which are temporary shifts in the energy matrix of the membrane to an escalated energy state at that localized area of protrusion or intrusion, it would immediately engage counteracting forces (movements) in an attempt to restore the protrusion or intrusion into its 'stable' plane of reference.

In those cases where two membranes oscillating close to each other have a collision at the mutual protrusion, as indicated in Figure 15 b, that collision changes the energy balance of both membranes where both in an attempt to compensate for the change in energy could engage Einstein's principle of Mass-Energy Equivalence and lead to transformation between mass (or matter) and energy. If you were to subscribe to this M-Theory – which is a plausible theory of the Big Bang, then you would be able to relate to how everything that you see as visible matter and that you cannot see as dark matter, came into existence immediately after the Big Bang or the 'cosmic catastrophe'. All matter that was created started a 'cosmic exponential inflation' and started to be flung outwards (expansion) from the spatial point of the proposed Big Bang. Edwin Powell Hubble proved through his observations based on *redshift* (feel free to research this topic) that not only does the Universe extend far beyond our Milky Way, the Universe is also expanding outwards. Modern day research is proving that the effects of the Big Bang related to the continuing outward expansion of the Universe is being caused by dark energy and dark matter as discussed earlier in this chapter. The *Genetics Of Divinity* however provides quite a different explanation that I would encourage you to wait for until you come to Chapter 9.

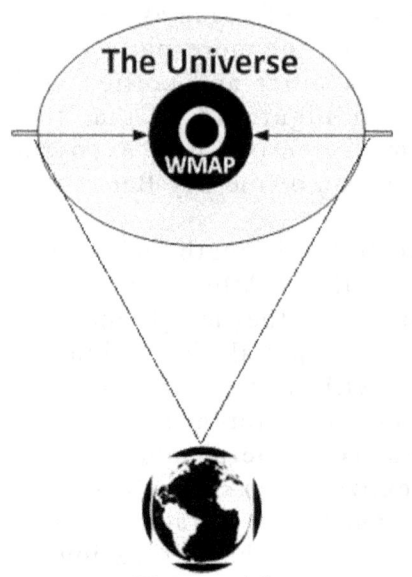

Figure 16

In order to prove that the Universe is flat (hence a membrane), our cosmologists fired two LASER beams towards the outer fringes of the known Universe after of course the WMAP (Wilkinson Microscope Anisotropy Probe) was all set up and operational. The WMAP received the reflected laser signals as shown in Figure 16. Adding the three angles in that triangle it was found to add up to 180°, which according to basic geometry defines a triangle – hence providing evidence about the flatness of the universe. *We are living in a membrane* – how about that for your nights sleep? ☺

Today the evidence of the Big Bang has been detected from the Cosmic Microwave Background Radiation which is providing astounding images of the Universe when its age was a mere 400,000 years. Research leads us to believe the Universe today is 13.7 billion years young. The WMAP project has also confirmed the theory of a cosmic inflation of the Universe. How did that Big Bang really occur? Were physical laws responsible to cause this Big Bang? If you were to believe in the very credible M Theory, where did those membranes come from with those creative properties? All in good time until you come to Chapter 9.

Kudos and respectful bows to the brilliant minds in the world of theoretical physics and cosmology that came up with the evolution of their research to arrive at the postulates of the M-Theory. However, right at this point I feel tempted to ask a rather profound question – *What caused all of this to happen and why is it even important for you to know how it happened*? I will hold off on that discussion until later on in this book, since with the explanation of M-Theory about the existence of higher dimensions, we are open to dive into a very important component of the design of Creation and Existence –*Parallel Universes*.

Parallel Universes

No, this is no longer a science fiction movie – with the bold postulates of M-Theory and the sophisticated experiments being performed with particle colliders around the world, we have sufficient scientific and mathematical evidence and logical explanations about the existence of Parallel Universes or the Multiverse. They do exist, although the severely attenuated five human senses cannot detect their physical presence. You were introduced to Parallelism as an attribute of Creation in Chapter 5, now here's the compelling argument that solidifies this Truth.

The scientific community had long suspected the existence of Parallel Universes ever since the early days of Heisenberg's famous Uncertainty Principle – the birth of Quantum Mechanics. Based on this Uncertainty Principle, Erwin Schrödinger presented his famous Schrodinger Cat experiment (feel free to research this topic) where the cat was both alive and dead in *superimposed* possible states of life. As a refresher, according to this Uncertainty Principle it is impossible to predict the position and momentum of a particle at any given time. The particle can be anywhere, in multiple places at the same time or nowhere at all at a given instance of time.

If you take the first condition where the particle can be anywhere, it indicates that for each of those innumerable possibilities, the particle could have its own separate or similar experience of its state and its interactions with other particles sharing the same time and space as itself. Hence that particle can exist in one of the possible Parallel Universes that can sustain its existence.

If you take the second condition where the particle can be at multiple places at the same time, it makes the concept of Parallel Universes more realistic. Each of these universes could host the particle, and must to be able to sustain an individual experience for the particle. Moreover one of these Parallel Universes could also fulfill the third condition where the particle cannot and hence does not exist.

Whoa! How is it possible for the same particle to exist simultaneously in multiple Universes at the same time? ☺

I will allude to the answer, give you a hint so that you can ponder about it. However the details are coming up in the follow-on book in this series – *Miracles From Genetics Of Divinity*. Ready? Particles and more specifically you at this very instance of time are living in multiple life experiences in different Parallel Universes. How? Allow me to ask you a few questions, "Why do you dream? Where are all those storylines of your dreams coming from? Some of those storylines seem really weird with characters that you don't know in your conscious life experience. I am sure you will acknowledge those weird dreams - you do dream them don't you? Is it possible that the weirdness of those particular dreams is based on your current perception of what is acceptable and normal, but in the Parallel Universe where you are having that dream, it is perfectly normal and acceptable? We all dream, but why don't we remember all of them when we wake up? Why do we have physiological and even psychological reactions to some of those dreams? Are you really resting when you sleep and dream, or are you physically experiencing another Parallel Universe? So much for now and I will pick this up in the follow-on book where you will learn the techniques to apply the consciousness of the *Genetics Of Divinity*.

What really is this Universe that I am referring to? The term 'universe' is commonly referred as the astronomical rendition of physical reality with all the galaxies, stars, planets, black holes, nebulas, asteroids and all those fantastic visible matter that seem to remain suspended in the cosmic ocean of nothingness. While this rendition is quite accurate and will suffice an explanation of the concept of Parallel Universes, it may be simpler to consider the universe as a plane of life experience that includes you and everything that influences your experience.

--------------------------*****--------------------------

All the various possibilities of your life experience are 'stacked up' in a series of Parallel Universes. Any event that could have happened has already happened in one or more of these identical, similar or disparate Parallel Universes, however you physically don't seem to be in all of them. We humans are limited by our faculties of observation in this physical form, which is why we can observe only one of the several Parallel Universes where we are living at a given time. However, dreams provide us the portal to those Parallel experiences, often providing insight and ideas of what is possible to achieve and pursue in the current life experience.

--------------------------#####--------------------------

When you are flying at 30000 feet above the ground in an aircraft, your life experience is confined to the aircraft, the passengers and crew, the sky that you can see, the clouds that you can see and the earth that you can see. But that does not mean that down there on Earth (one of the Parallel Universes that you can relate to even when you are in that aircraft) there are billions of people having their own life experience, some of whose actions could actually impact your own life experience. So it is time for our species to realize that WYSIWYG (*What You See Is What You Get*) is only a partial truth of reality and existence.

In one of these Parallel Universes, Atlantis is still a thriving civilization on terra firma. In another none of the World Wars were ever fought. In another universe dinosaurs still rampage the planet, while in another, living dinosaurs provide entertainment in zoos. In one universe you are a Nobel Laureate, while in another you are a soldier fighting a bitter war, while yet in another nobody ever knows about your existence. In one universe your life is pretty much the same as it is in the universe where you have your conscious awareness, with the only difference that you live in a lavishly appointed mansion on the beach as opposed to where you are having your conscious physical experience right now. In one of the Parallel Universes, nobody uses money to exchange for goods and services and the barter system still operates with high success. In another Parallel Universe there are no nations or religions to divide humanity into artificial boundaries, there is no animosity, no violence and everyone is deliriously happy and dedicate their lives to the service of others who need assistance - the true embodiment of the core principle of Existence.

If you have a life partner today in your physical life experience it is in the universe that you are currently conscious about. In a different Parallel Universe the two of you could have a different type of relationship, or your partner could be a different person or you may a single person who has no desire to have a romantic relationship. In yet another Parallel Universe you and your life partner are making a pact with each other that the two of you will be born again and again and again, lifetimes after lifetimes and still be able to find each other every time and continue to take your bondage higher and higher. If you can, read a book called 'Only Love is Real' by Dr. Brian Weiss and you will understand how lovers can continue to find each other and expand their love stories across lifetimes. Parallel Universes are real and they exist, get used to this attribute of Creation and you will start to discover your true identity.

--------------------------*****--------------------------

The question is, if these Parallel Universes do exist, then why can we not see them and why can we not visit them? To that first question, I would answer that the reason you cannot see them – yet – is because you probably never looked for them in the first place and did not know they exist. Moreover as humans you are not designed in physical form to observe multiple Universes at one time, however you can feel their presence.

When you have dreams, you are actually having an experience in a different Parallel Universe where what you are observing is actually happening to you in that universe despite the fact that your physical body is right where you were when you dropped off to sleep. One of my goals through this book is to show you that Parallel Universes do exist, as you will in all likelihood conclude by the time you are done reading this book.

To the second question, I would answer that yes, you can visit them, since you are designed to visit those other Parallel Universes of your choice and even continue with your life experience in your current physical body in one or more of those universes. This is a quality that you have lost through antiquity and I know that you want to resurrect this quality again. Parallelism offers you in this physical form to choose the Parallel Universe(s) where you would choose to live and enjoy your life experience – *they are all stacked up and superimposed on one another at every instance of your life experience. Your perception of unbounded delight or plight is the sum of all these parallel experiences.*

--------------------------#####--------------------------

Defining Your Personal Parallel Universe

If I were to ask you that keeping in mind that you were created as a Creature with the will to receive and experience your personal definition of unbounded delight, what kind of a Universe would you like to live in? What kind of a life experience would you like to go through in that Universe? What relationships would you have? What would your living conditions be? What kind of vehicle would you be driving? No, not just the make and model of the vehicle, just focus on the attributes of the vehicle that you would be driving. How much money do you have in the bank in that Universe? Is money even a factor that controls your existence in that Universe or does banking even exist in that Universe? What would your one day in life be like in that Universe? Who would you be serving and who would be serving you? Where would you be traveling to and how are you traveling to those destinations? What would the three most important relationships be in your life in that Universe? How is the political structure of that Universe? Is there a political structure in that Universe? How is the law enforcement in that Universe? Is there a need for law enforcement in that Universe? What kind of organized religion do they follow in that Parallel Universe? Is there organized religion in that Universe? Are the people in that Universe like the people that you perceive in this current life experience or would they be different from a behavioral perspective? What kind of life expectancy is there in that Universe? What are the major life threatening diseases in that Universe? Are there any such diseases in that Universe? If you looked back in history of that Universe, how does it match with the history that you are aware of in your current life experience so far?

I could go on and on with such questions in an effort to paint the picture of your desired Parallel Universe and there would be still some more that I might not have asked. Nevertheless with that small sampling of questions above, how many of those could you answer as quickly as you could say your name or the letters of the alphabet? Homework for you, you have - ☺ (taking a cue from Master Yoda in the classic sequel - Star Wars®)!

If you can answer those questions then by the law of Quantum Mechanics those answers are possible states of your life experience in one or more Parallel Universes. In one or more Parallel Universes all that you want to be, do or have is already a reality but your present physical body as you know it is not in that life experience right now. How can you get there? Follow along.

Most definitely, your next question would be, 'Ok, I believe that Parallel Universes exist and that I can visit them and live in one or more of those that I choose. But how do I get there? Getting there my friend, all in good time, you are not ready yet. Just be assured that by the time you are done reading this book you will realize 'the how' even if I don't spell out the process word for word. The cognition will come to you and over the course of my interactions with you, the protocols would be clearly defined. Right at this very moment, you are sitting on the edge of shifting into a new higher level of consciousness. Have the patience to experience the transition and you will never look back. Please resist the temptation to skip forward to Chapter 9 of this book. I know and I can feel what is going on in your mind. Remember you can never start your car in the fifth gear - you have to start low and then ramp up as you gain momentum.

If you want to research more on the topic of types of Parallel Universes, I would refer you to the revealing work performed by Cosmologist and Professor Max Tegmark of MIT where he provides a very compelling description of not just one but four possible types of Parallel Universes based on his research and analysis and those of contemporary physicists and cosmologists. So the question is not if Parallel Universes exist, the question is where are they and how do we get a chance to experience a life in one or more of them in this physical body.

---------------------------*****---------------------------

In the forthcoming discussion of the four types of Parallel Universes, I want to be very clear that I have no intent to discount, diminish the integrity, pass any judgment or dismiss the possibility of any of those theories. I salute and honor the brilliant scientific minds of our world today who have put forth their theories around this topic, having sacrificed countless hours of research and analysis, burning barrels of the midnight oil to have the courage to present their ideas to this critical-minded human civilization with sub-optimal consciousness.

Until and unless undeniable proof is available, all of the theories are valid as long as they are logical and answer the right questions. My comments and logical analysis of these four types of Parallel Universes below are based on the level of usable practicality of these theories as it applies to the human species to improve our life experience on this planet. Any humor that I have injected in my comments should not be considered as any sort of ridicule, but as comical literary license to make the complicated and controversial topic of Parallel Universes easier to read and understand. To all the brilliant minds behind these theories, I am humbled by the expansion of your awakened faculties to connect to higher dimensions of Existence.

---------------------------#####--------------------------

Type 1 Parallel Universe

While the description of the Type 1 Parallel Universe seems to be arguably more popular among the pool of theoretical physicists and cosmologists, I personally am not a big fan of that type of Parallel Universe or multi-verse and here's why. Type 1 Parallel Universes are exact replicas of our Universe that exist beyond our observable range or Hubble Volume. In this theory you exist not only here, but in those countless Universes with same, similar or different life experiences. Your versions of yourself are so far away that you can't even see them, hence making it difficult to believe in their existence. Without going into a very technical discussion, I need to explain a few facts to present the reasons for my frown on the matter of the Type 1 Parallel Universes.

First of all the theory behind Type 1 Parallel Universes is that they exist beyond the 'Hubble Volume' or beyond our cosmic horizon. The age of the Universe as we know it today is 13.7 billion years. This means that the Universe that we can observe is composed of the distance that light which started traveling 13.7 billion years ago from those distant objects in the Universe has just reached us, which is why it is *visible* matter to us and we are aware of its existence. The speed of light being 299,792,458 meters per second or 186,282 miles per second, it makes the observable size of the Universe to be about 156 billion light years wide. Whoa! That's a long distance away and for our current civilization and technology to consider the existence of Parallel Universes beyond that distance is interesting for lazy amused reading but feasibly does not serve much of a practical purpose. Given the promise of a Universe filled with unbounded delight, how do you get there to meet your *doppelganger* who is supposedly enjoying a life of unbounded delight across such a large distance physically. Moreover, what's the guarantee that your doppelganger would want to swap places with you? ☺ We are still trying to figure out how to make space flights just outside the Earth's atmosphere a commonly accessible commodity, so we definitely can't get you to that Parallel Universe beyond the cosmic horizon in a hurry. Hence in my humble opinion, Type 1 Parallel Universes are good for theory but not really so practical for us to invest our time on.

Type 2 Parallel Universe

Enter the Type 2 Parallel Universes – not quite my morning cup of tea and here's why. You have already been introduced to the concept of a chaotic cosmic inflation at the Big Bang moment and Edwin Hubble proved that the Universe as we know it is expanding outwards. Dark matter and dark energy are the suspects causing this expansion. Type 2 Parallel Universes are bubbles (as a continuous membrane) which are theorized to 'pop' in and out of existence, colliding with each other, merging with each other and even contributing a portion of each colliding bubble to create a brand new bubble universe. By the principles of Quantum Mechanics that you know now and using the principles of probability, there are exact replicas of our observable Universe in one or more of those bubbles. Yoohoo! Next time I take my child to the park to use her soap bubble maker to play the game of blowing, chasing, popping and watching conjoined bubbles form, I will blink one eye at a time. ☺ Moreover these bubbles are not only beyond the Hubble Volume, being part of the cosmic inflation effect, they are receding even further away from us. So just when you started to take a shot at designing your very own *SS Enterprise* with sextuple-turbo, warp-speed, nuclear *fusion* propulsion engines, to take you to a Type 1 Parallel Universe, you probably would need to rethink your plans of visiting a Type 2 Parallel Universe in the insatiable quest of your unbounded delight – they just keep floating away beyond the cosmic horizon to random directions. I don't know about you, but these Type 2 Parallel Universes don't quite fit my logical thinking from a practical application perspective.

Skipping Over To A Type 4 Parallel Universe

Let's skip over to the Type 4 Parallel Universe. If you are a student of science or engineering you are very well aware of the plethora of laws, principles, theorems, rules, definitions, equations that dominate and govern the worlds of physical and biological sciences, engineering and mathematics. It can be overwhelming simply to study and understand all of them and make some logical sense. No wonder we have so many of these branches of science with specialists in each of them, since the governing laws can be quite disparate and varied for one person to master them all. For those who are not students of science and engineering, the reason that you are not, probably is because you did not want to put up with all overwhelming knowledge and wanted to keep 'it' super simple.

As if all these postulates, laws and equations of science and mathematics were not enough, leading physicists Stephen Hawking and John Wheeler posed a profound question to the scientific community, 'Why these particular equations, not others?' This question is the birth of the theory behind Type 4 Parallel Universes, which are formed as a result of cosmic quantum fluctuations of possibilities. Each of this type of Universe has its own mathematical and physical law 'democracy', some or none of which match those that govern our known Universe. Imagine a world where E (energy) is not equal to the product of the rest mass of the particle times the square of the speed of light, or a world where F (force) is not equal to the product of a particle's rest mass times its acceleration, or a world where the angle of incidence of a ray of light on a reflecting surface is not equal to the angle of reflection from that surface. Take any of these equations of the physical laws that govern our physical Universe and place a not equal to sign on the equation (<> or != or NE in terms of software programming language syntax) and you have a Type 4 Parallel Universe. Or take any of these simple equations that you are familiar with and in addition to the parameters that already are there on the right hand side of the equation, and add a few more parameters with different mathematical functions to the final equation and you could be defining a new Type 4 Parallel Universe, one where physical and mathematical laws are drastically different from the Universe where we live. A Type 4 Parallel Universe could be there where that *weird* equation is the basis of its physical existence.

While imagining such a Type 4 Parallel Universe would most definitely keep the devil away from the idle mind, it does not serve us the purpose of finding unbounded delight – how do we get to such a Universe where everything is different and nothing would make sense to us being used to what we know about in our own Universe. Can you imagine the learning curve if we humans were to live in such a Parallel Universe in our quest for unbounded delight? Most of the human population is in a struggle to find unbounded delight in our current life experience in this Universe, where there is such growing awareness of the laws of science and mathematics that govern our known physical existence. For such a population to be convinced to embark on a journey to find that unbounded delight in a Type 4 Parallel Universe where the physical and mathematical laws are different than what we are used to here is a pretty far-fetched endeavor.

Type 3 Parallel Universe – Home Sweet Home!

This brings us to the Type 3 Parallel Universe. Ahhhh – Home - Sweet Home! Type 3 Parallel Universes are the result of the evolution of Quantum Mechanics and the acceptance of the scientific community that matter is not only composed of particles, but also waves – called the wave-particle duality. With the Heisenberg's Uncertainty Principle indicating that it is impossible to determine the position and the momentum of an electron simultaneously, it opened up a whole new world of possibilities. Erwin Schrödinger's famous experiment with the imaginary cat, led to the concept of 'superimposition' of several possible states of matter at the same space and time.

Let's illustrate this concept. Consider yourself floating on a boat in the middle of the open ocean and if you did not know better about the geometric shape of Earth – you would most definitely perceive the Earth to be flat. You would not be out of line in your perception since you just did not know any better. Humankind believed this to be true for centuries in the past before philosophers theorized about the spherical shape of our planet until Ferdinand Magellan and his merry men finally proved it in the first quarter of the 16th century.

What if while you were floating in that vast openness of the ocean you saw something in the distant horizon that looked like a ship's mast. For quite a while you would be looking towards the mast and won't be able to see the hull or the bottom of the ship but then as you and the ship approach each other, the deck, the hull and even the Plimsoll line begins to come visible. As you jump for joy at the prospect of being rescued, you would without a doubt question your prior belief that the Earth was flat because if it were so, you would have seen the entire ship – mast to the Plimsoll line all at once. You would have been right in that doubt, since the only reason why the full superstructure of the ship gradually came to your view was because it was beyond the curvature of the Earth when you first started observing it.

Now imagine at the *same time* when you were going from those moments of despair and getting rescued by the crew, a friend was observing your plight from her spaceship in a geosynchronous orbit around Earth. Instead of the flat Earth. She would observe a beautiful spherical blue marble floating in the starlit darkness and would not need much effort for her to be convinced that the Earth was indeed a sphere.

Further imagine your mermaid friend below the surface of the ocean whose Universe is all about water, water everywhere. The debate of a flat Earth or a spherical Earth would make her stare at you and your astronaut friend in confused disbelief as if the you two were aliens in human form. That's because in her perception of reality about the geometric shape of the planet, it is just a three dimensional body of water stretching to infinity. Most definitely you and your astronaut friend will be able to understand the mermaid's point of view, but she would have little or no comprehension about yours.

From your plane of reference, that on the surface of the open ocean, your experience and perception of the reality of your Universe at that time was an Earth that appeared flat. However at that same time, your astronaut buddy observed the Earth to be a sphere. Furthermore at the same time, your mermaid friend observed Earth to be a three dimensional body of water. In other words, the three possibilities and perceptions of a flat Earth, a spherical Earth and 3-D Earth with undefined shape, were all *superimposed* upon one another at the same space and time. Just because each of you did not perceive these three different models simultaneously it does not mean those models of the Universe did not exist. Three parallel realities of the same object – Earth, existed at the same space and time and each of you, by choice have decided on your own free will to go through your life experience in a separate model of the Parallel Universes.

This is the Type 3 Parallel Universe – a *superimposition* of a plethora of possibilities of existence of several

Universes at the same space and time each with similar or different characteristics when compared to the current Universe where you are having your life experience. In the example above, the reason you could understand each other's point of view of their particular Universe was because you had a relationship going on between the three of you. What would happen if there was no relationship between the three of you and each one of you were independently and separately asked about your individual perception about the shape of Earth? You would describe your perception separately and differently but even then those three Parallel Universes would have existed and remained superimposed on one another in the same space and time, regardless of what you individually perceived them to be or whether you had a mutual relationship or not.

This attribute of the Type 3 Parallel Universe where despite all the factual superimpositions of possibilities, each individual possibility remains hidden or beyond the physical perception of the others is called *decoherence*. From a macro level while all possibilities are true and they exist, at the level within one of the possibilities, the others are perceived to be physically non-existent.

If you re-read this section of Type 3 Parallel Universes, you will notice that I indicated this type as 'Home, Sweet Home!'- now you will realize why. If I asked you the Creature, what feeling 'unbounded delight' meant to you, given some time for you to collect your thoughts, you could in all likelihood paint a picture or even write the script of a movie that represents a Universe where you are living with those emotions of unbounded delight. In that picture or that movie script, you would have all kinds of material objects, cherished relationships in all of the thirteen categories from Chapter 3, descriptions of the environment. social and political structures that you would be living in, what your activities would be and even how you would be serving others to obtain unbounded delight and so on.

---------------------------*****---------------------------

In the process of defining what represents the framework of your interpretation and perception of unbounded delight, you would actually be defining the life experiences, the different possibilities in one or more Parallel Universes, all of which are superimposed in the same space and time in the Universe where your physical body currently resides. Yet those other Parallel Universes are decoherent or remain hidden to you in physical form.

I hope you understand that although these different states of your unbounded delight are not visible or coherent to you that does not mean they do not exist. They actually exist more or less exactly as you have described them as long as their definitions are logical and ethically feasible.

Your physical *Adaptivebody* exists and can perceive only the 3-D and the past and present of the 4-D. However your non-physical *Activebody* in the 5-D is fully aware of your past, present and future in the 4-D, since the 5-D is independent of the time factor – more of this in Chapter 7.

---------------------------#####---------------------------

Go back and refer to Figure 5 in Chapter 5 where I illustrated the concept of Parallelism. Now compare that figure with the concept of the Type 3 Parallel Universe that you have been introduced to and you will find the pieces of the jigsaw puzzle falling into place. At every moment in time and space through Parallelism, you are being presented with a myriad of quantum possibilities which are doorways to as many number of superimposed Type 3 Parallel Universes. The choice of a certain doorway that you make defines your life experience from the next instance of time onwards.

Could our forefathers have chosen to live in a Type 3 Parallel Universe where none of the two World Wars were fought, Chernobyl never happened and nobody knew about 9/11 - events that led to such destruction and carnage to the human civilization? Certainly, and as a matter of fact, that

Type 3 Parallel Universe still exists today with a differently evolved and differently conscious human species. That Parallel Universe is so widely different from what we perceive in our current life experience, that it seems unbelievable and incomprehensible to our rationality and intelligence. *Decoherence* blocks our view of that Parallel Universe of peace, love, security, symbiotic collaboration, abundance and collective coexistence. However, our lack of belief or comprehension of such a Parallel Universe, our reliance on the fallacy of WISIWIG (What I See Is What I Get) does not change the fact about its existence.

--------------------------*****--------------------------

How would you like to live in that Parallel Universe where people actually make love not war? How would you live to live in a Parallel Universe where people are constructive and symbiotic instead of destructive and parasitic? How would you like to live in a Parallel Universe where money was never an object? I am sure these are some of the attributes of the Parallel Universe where you would love to call home and to enjoy unbounded delight. Such a Universe exists – resistance is futile, so get used to it. Just because you are not living in it – yet, does not imply that you make it a story of the fox and sour grapes. Denial keeps you where you are while acceptance and eagerness to get there gets you on the path to your liberation and discovering unbounded delight – in this physical lifetime.

-------------------------#####-------------------------

Let's get into a few more attributes of the Type 3 Parallel Universe so that you understand their mechanics of operation. This knowledge will answer a lot of the questions that I know are flooding your mind right now. You have learned about the attribute of *decoherence* of Type 3 Parallel Universes and about their superimposed existence on one another based on the plethora of possibilities of life experiences within each Universe that are available at the same space and time. Are the different states or possibilities in the Parallel Universes discrete or are they continuous – in other words do we need to leap to get from one Universe to another or can we take a casual stroll and walk in to the Parallel Universe of our choice? The answer is the latter.

It is worthwhile to understand the two basic models of state of any object in the Universe - digital and analog functions, which would clarify the processes available to you to migrate from one Parallel Universe to another of your choice.

Think about the remote control unit of your television. Let's focus on a few sets of buttons on that remote. The on/off button can do only one of two things – switch the television on or turn it off – there is no other state (half-on or half-off) in between. How about the channel selector buttons with the numbers on them? You can press any combination of numbers and the television channel instantly shifts from one channel to the next selection even if the two channels are not sequentially next to the other. Going from channel 01 to channel 100 does not make the television go through all the 99 channels in between before it gets you to channel 100. These two examples illustrate the operation of the digital function – a *discrete* and static change or jump from one state of operation of the object (the TV set in this example) to another. The digital function is a switch controlling one of two possible states of the object. You can *'jump'* from one state to the another in the digital function.

Keep thinking about the same remote control unit and lets now focus on some other buttons – controls for volume, contrast, color and brightness of the picture. These work differently – the change of these parameters does not happen discretely – they don't instantly jump from one state to your desired state immediately – rather there is a smooth progression and *easing-into* function from the current state to your desired state. This gradual progression of the object from one state to another defines its analog function – a gradual and *continuous* migration along a linear path. Hence several intermediate states of the object are possible when it is subject to an analog function as opposed to one of several discrete possible states in the digital function. Hence the analog function allows you to *'stroll into'* one state from another.

Here's the key point for you to understand. Regardless of what function, digital or analog you leverage to change the state of the television, your only motivation to initiate a state change is because you have become uncomfortable continuing to stay comfortable with the current state of the object. You are going to engage the digital function of the switching the TV *on* is because you have become uncomfortable to find it *off*. You are going to engage the analog function of adjusting the brightness of the picture because you have become uncomfortable with the current darkness. Furthermore the greater motivation to initiate a change in state is because you not only '*know*' that the altered states of the object exist, but when achieved, one or more of those states will get you more comfortable again (contributing to your feeling of unbounded delight). All of those altered states of the object are like Parallel Universes and all are always available to you to decide and choose through your free will.

The question is can you make a digital jump into a different Parallel Universe or do you have to make that transition smooth and gradual like as in the analog function? This brings us to the concept of instant gratification exemplified by the digital function or delayed gratification exemplified by the analog function. Depending on your level of consciousness, it may be easier to go through a delayed gratification process to navigate through several Parallel Universes and incrementally edge towards your unbounded delight. In higher levels of consciousness there are techniques to collapse the factor of time for the elevated individual but still it is delayed gratification. Creation and Existence as you will learn in Chapter 9 is the result of analog functions – a gradual time based evolution of symbiotic collaborative relationships rather than the sudden discreteness of the digital function. We are not designed for instant gratification and any attempts to pursue desires with the intent of instant gratification will remain unfulfilled.

Everything that you desire within the limits of logical probabilities in conformance with the ethical feasibility of the Genetics Of Divinity is a possibility in Parallelism, hence they must exist but remain decoherent to you in one or more of the superimposed Type 3 Parallel Universes.

What is meant by logical probabilities? Let's say that you get so excited about the concept of infinite possibilities of these superimposed Type 3 Parallel Universes, that you decide to go back in time and change the course of history by not allowing your parents to meet so that you could not be born. Well, you can't change the past due to the linear progression of time in the 4-D. An attempt to want something like this would be a violation of the laws of Creation defined by the *Genetics Of Divinity*. You cannot get an egg to its original form once you have cracked it and cooked your plate of gourmet scrambled eggs. Your 3-D physical body has carried and recorded the legacy of these events in the past and changing the history would be a violation of the laws of Creation.

-------------------------*****-------------------------

However it would be perfectly fine for you to desire to live in a Parallel Universe in the future where all that you desire is available for you to enjoy. Using the attributes of the Type 3 Parallel Universes and your inner faculties of *'coherent alignment'*, you can actually physically live and emigrate to your chosen Parallel Universe. It is calling you, which is why you have those desires – all you have to do is answer, align and get attracted towards it.

The process of first identifying the attributes of the Type 3 Parallel Universe(s) where you want to spend your future life experience in this physical body, second actually arriving there and third repeating the cycle for greater unbounded delight is called *coherent alignment.*

-------------------------#####-------------------------

There's a *perceived* challenge that you will have to deal with though. Any Universe in the Third dimension of Existence is not for just you alone but for humanity in general. Existence is based on collective co-existence – not individual existence. There are no silos in Creation – only symbiotic collaborative relationships. Consequently, the Parallel Universe where we live today is not the life experience of one individual but the life experience of humanity as a collective. While you as an individual is a contributor to the definition of that Parallel Universe, you are not the sole CREATOR of that life experience. It is essential for humanity as a collective to undergo a consciousness shift and define the Parallel Universe as a collective in order to enable such a life experience for the inhabitants of such a Universe.

If you noticed, I started describing the last paragraph with a *"perceived"* challenge. After reading that paragraph I am sure you are wondering how can just you alone change the course of humanity and catapult our civilization to that desired Parallel Universe, if that objective requires a collective effort.

Mechanics Of Defining A Parallel Universe

I would draw your attention to a phenomena called the 100th monkey syndrome. A group of scientists were studying a group of monkeys in an isolated Japanese island that grew sweet potatoes. One day they observed that one of these monkeys washed a sweet potato in water before eating it. As you would imagine as time went on, more and more monkeys caught on the idea of washing sweet potatoes before eating. When the 100th monkey in that island joined the new paradigm, it was observed that the same behavioral pattern spread among monkeys of the same species across water to other islands and subsequently it became a behavioral pattern across the species – all because one monkey started something. The monkeys now enjoy a new life experience and hence live in a Parallel Universe that is different from the one where they lived before.

Given the world population today, it would require approximately only 1.5 million humans each empowered with a consciousness where the code of the *Genetics of Divinity* has been activated to initiate a global change for all humanity, thereby catapulting us to a Parallel Universe of our choosing. Well, what would the attributes of such a Parallel Universe be where humanity undergoes an exodus from the unbounded plight of today to the unbounded delight of tomorrow?

If you visit the companion website at www.GeneticsOfDivinity.com you can participate in a poll where you can define the top three attributes of the Parallel Universe of your choice. This is the first step and I encourage you to take that poll and encourage others who you know to take that poll as well in the spirit of generating that critical mass of people who desire to create Parallel Universe of the future. Down human history, we have actually already created the Parallel Universe where we are living now – deviated and misaligned from the purpose of Creation and Existence in this planet. Now that we understand Contrast, the time is NOW that we follow the same process to enjoy a life experience that is aligned with the purpose of Creation through the establishment of symbiotic collaborative relationships through the free will of mutual consent for the purpose of collective coexistence.

The second step would be to leverage the water mass of this planet as the material medium of communication between this critical mass of people to start the process of implementing the Parallel Universe. Our planet is 70% water. Our physical body is 60% water with the brain being 70% water. Hence water (that the monkeys accidentally used as the mode of communication) would be the communication medium between the architects of this future Parallel Universe where humanity would begin to thrive and enjoy unbounded delight in the life experience starting from this generation. Our ancestors and forefathers, by their paradigms and belief systems have presented the life experience that we enjoy today. What paradigms and belief systems are we in this generation of elevated individuals going to adopt and apply to offer to our subsequent generations?

As a matter of fact, when you and I pass on from this mortal *Adaptivebody*, we are going to be required by our Immortal *Activebody* in the Fifth Dimension to be reborn again in physical form with a different life purpose for the purpose of service for others and proliferation of unbounded delight for our Existence in the future. So you and I are coming back on this planet again. What kind of a Parallel Universe are we going to come back to? Is it a different version of unbounded plight, pain and suffering that we observe today or is it one that you are defining right here and now in this physical lifetime - one where love, peace, security, compassion and abundance prevails across humanity?

The question I had for my *Activebody* when the concept of conscious definition of the Parallel Universe was revealed to me and I am sure that you have for me is, "How does it work?" Simply by the choice of the attributes of a Parallel Universe of the future and collectively following the 100th monkey syndrome up-scaled to the human population does not make it a true reality, does it? Yes those are the pre-requisites and for the rest we look inwards inside your physical body.

The 12 Strand Human DNA

Medical research indicates that we humans have 12 strands of DNA in each of our cells of which only the first pair is useful for our physiological structure and functions while the other 5 pairs are 'junk'. When I came across material associated with such research I was immediately in total disagreement with the "junk" designation, not knowing what exactly those additional 5 pairs were. It was rather appalling to learn about the audacity of the researchers to designate the 5 of the 6 pairs of human DNA strands as "junk" – it was their own shortcoming of consciousness about the human body. Nothing is possible in Existence to be *junk*, since every Creature is created for a specific purpose as defined by the code of *Genetics Of Divinity*. The 5 pairs of the DNA in the human body that the medical community does not care about are by no means any junk. In fact these 5 pairs are critical to why we are here and they act as our individual beacons in the grid of Existence.

But before I get into the description of the 6 pairs of the human DNA and how it is relevant for you to define and navigate to the Parallel Universe of your choice, it is worthwhile to consider yet another aspect of this asset that you and I have been born with by virtue of being a human. I will go into greater detail to explain the Human Brain, the Nervous System, the Memory Systems, the quad-compartmental mind and the Chakra system in Chapter 8. However for the purpose of this discussion I would have to leverage those components that are gifted to you in order to explain the significance of the 12 strands of DNA within the nucleus of each cell of your physical body.

As you will learn in Chapter 8, contrary to popular belief memory is not something that is stored somewhere in the brain, but in every cell of your body. You have heard me mention before that the code of the *Genetics of Divinity* is embedded in your memory systems. Since these memory systems are in every cell of your body and the nucleus of every cell contains the DNA the code and the entire blueprint of Creation is actually embedded in your DNA.

---------------------------*****---------------------------

While medical science which focusses only on the physical body refers to the **first pair** of DNA strands that indeed control every aspect of the human physiology where the cell is localized – this is the seat of Type 2 memories. The **second pair** of DNA strands host the Type 1 and Type 4 memory patterns (discussed in in Chapter 8) that constitute the knowledgebase of that particular cell where the DNA is present - this is your *subconscious mind - the seat of the individual's level of consciousness and that is where the code of the Genetics of Divinity are embedded.* The **third pair** of the DNA strands manages human emotions and Type

3 memory patterns - the belief systems, paradigms and autonomic responses to incoming external impulses. This third pair of DNA strands also addresses the constitution of the human psychology and shapes the individual's character and attitude towards life in general and to the individual itself in particular. – this is also part of the structure of your *conscious mind*. The **fourth pair** of the DNA strands orient the individual relationally in the grid of Existence, specifically in the Third Dimension. I call this pair the *Matchmaker*, since this is the pair that is responsible for all relationships in your life experience – those that you already have and those that you will have in the future. This Fourth pair of DNA strands is the seat of Type 5 memory patterns and provides the overarching platform for your *super-conscious* mind.

The **fifth pair** of the DNA strands establish the connection between the mortal physical *Adaptivebody* of the individual in the Third Dimension and the immortal non-physical *Activebody* of the individual in the Fifth Dimension of Existence. The **sixth pair** of DNA strands is exotic and esoteric if you have already not been floored by what I am revealing about your DNA. The sixth pair places your physical body in the pool or *consortium* of *Activebodies* in the Fifth Dimension. In this consortium of *Activebodies* you have the ability to participate and *voice* your thoughts for the purpose of collective coexistence in the Third Dimension by default, always of course in the company of your own *Activebody*. Imagine the consortium of *Activebodies* in the Fifth Dimension where your personal *Activebody* is a bona fide member and you are the agent who implements the code of the *Genetics of Divinity* set for you in your physical lifetime by your own *Activebody* in consultation with the consortium for the purpose of collective coexistence. Collectively, the fifth and the sixth pair of DNA strands define your *infra-conscious* mind. I will discuss the quad-compartmental structure of the human mind in a lot of detail in Chapter 8.

The fifth and the sixth pair of DNA strands *leverage* Type 1 and Type 5 memory where the code of the *Genetics Of Divinity* and details about your life purpose, timings of events when specific relationships will appear in your life are stored – hang tight ☺ there's more on this in Chapter 8. Who is the *Activebody* and what is its function? Where does the *Activebody* exist? What is the Consortium of *Activebodies* all about? What are the details of the communication link between the 5-D *Activebody* and the 3-D *Adaptivebody*? How does that link work? Under what conditions is the communication possible? The details of all these questions and their answers are available in Type 1 and Type 5 memory stored in the 5th and the 6th pair of DNA strands that form your infra-conscious mind.

--------------------------#####--------------------------

Let's understand the human DNA a little further. The double helical structure makes the human DNA a *double helical antenna* capable of being responsive to the range of frequencies of electromagnetic energy. These are very low frequency electromagnetic energy waves in the radio wave bandwidth of the electromagnetic spectrum. Each pair of strands that I mentioned in the last paragraph is a double helical antenna capable of responding to discrete frequencies, corresponding to their respective areas of focus. Why do we need a pair? Well, a double helix antenna is capable of responding to broadcast signals in both directions *along the axis of the helix*. In case of the strand pair, one of the strands is to transmit and the other to receive broadcast signals along the axis of the helix. While the first four pairs transmit and receive broadcast signals in the Third Dimension, the last two pairs are the conduit between the Third to the Fifth Dimension of Existence. Due to the helical structure of the radio wave antenna in your DNA, it can only respond to signals aligned with its axis – when I refer to *alignment* with your life purpose, your desires and the like, this is the alignment that I am referring to. More on this later...

The first pair operates at the *Beta* range of brainwave frequencies, the second pair operates at the *Alpha* range of frequencies, the third pair operates at the *Second Beta* range of frequencies, the fourth pair at the *Delta and Theta* range of frequencies, the fifth pair operates at the *Gamma* range of frequencies, and the sixth pair also operates at the *Gamma* range of frequencies. Please hold off on your questions about these frequencies until you reach Chapter 8 where I describe the different brainwave frequencies.

Oh no, I am not done with the DNA just yet – there's more. What do you think happens to an antenna that is sensitive to electromagnetic signals? It oscillates with the same frequency as the frequency of transmission or reception – in engineering terms such a system that participates in sympathetic oscillation is called a harmonic oscillator. Your DNA strands also equip you with 6 pairs of electromagnetic antennae and hence 6 harmonic oscillators each responsive to six different energy frequency bands. A mechanical oscillator will eventually dissipate the incumbent energy over time and suffer losses in oscillation - not so for the DNA harmonic oscillator.

It has been observed that the DNA oscillator has very low losses in oscillation, which constitutes the memory of the cell of which the DNA is a part. Research by Sriram Kosuri PhD and George Church PhD of the Harvard Wyss Institute have performed ground breaking work proving that *just one gram of human DNA has the capability to store 5.5 Petabytes or 770 terabytes of data which is about 14000 units of 50 GB Blu-ray disks.* An average adult has over 3 billion DNA base pairs – can you imagine how much of data of the code of the *Genetics Of Divinity* is already stored in your memory? Find a mirror and look at yourself with pride and humility, what an amazing Creature of Existence you are. You already know what needs to be known to experience a life experience filled with unbounded delight - you have been designed with all the infrastructure and consciousness there is in the *Genetics Of Divinity*. When would NOW be a time to reactivate those dormant memories?

I am still not done with the DNA ☺ - this is just a masterpiece of Creation and you and I are endowed with this amazing resource but have not tapped into its magical powers just yet. It's NOW time that we did.

Have you wondered why we prefer sunny days rather than those that are overcast. Why do the bright and sunny outdoors seem to add that extra punch or boost to your attitude and efficiency when compared to when you are working under artificial light or the outdoors are gloomy. Where I live in Southern California we talk about "May Gray" and "June Gloom" referring to the days in these two months of the year when the skies are predominantly overcast, blocking the much needed sunlight. Boy, does everyone feel down in those days!!! Why is that? No, it's not the lack of Vitamin D that seems to reduce our energy levels and enthusiasm - it's the DNA again.

Due to its electromagnetic properties, it has now been established without that doubt that our DNA can absorb ultraviolet light energy. DNA can also absorb sound energy – no wonder soothing music makes you feel happy uplifting your emotions. Cosmic cycles emit radio waves and micro waves in addition to the light energy emitted by the astronomical bodies, all of which also affect your DNA which in turn affects your overall life experience. What a sensitive antenna we are endowed with! You will also learn in Chapter 8 that these DNA not only absorb light but they also emit light energy in the form of *biophotons* that are light particles responsible for information communication within your physical body and outside your physical body. Kirlian photography is now able to detect the human aura, which is the signature of these *biophotons* from your DNA emanating from your physical body. In essence your DNA derives more energy from sunlight, sound waves that are within the human audible range of frequencies, radio and microwave signals than from your food intake.

Whoa! Such an amazing design of interconnected Creation and yet our myopic medical research designates the 5 of the 6 pairs per cell in the human body as *junk DNA*?

Activating Your Parallel Universe Through Your DNA

Now you understand the technology that is already built within you to be, do or have anything and everything you want in your life as long as it is logical and ethically feasible, following the core principles of the *Genetics Of Divinity* – to establish *symbiotic collaborative relationships through the free will of mutual consent of the relating partners for the purpose of collective coexistence*. This principle is embedded in the form and functions of the six pairs of DNA strands. All the six strands are designed to symbiotically collaborate with each other to afford you a life experience filled with unbounded delight as a Creature with a specific purpose and role to play in the grid of Existence.

Physiological dis-ease in your body occurs when the local cells do not receive *Adaptive* energy transmissions thereby thwarting the communication channel of your first pair of DNA strands in the cells of the affected part of the body. Consequently those cells are rendered incapable of their normal operations which manifests as the disease.

What you are learning in this book and what you will learn as you dive deeper into the code of the *Genetics Of Divinity*, will re-energize the second pair of your DNA strands which will respond by reactivating this code of Eternal Consciousness in your subconscious mind and subsequently influence your conscious mind.

We will discuss more about your emotions in Chapter 8, but low emotions occur when the third pair of DNA strands is not being able to operate in the 2nd Beta range of frequencies that it is supposed to respond to. When you are experiencing high emotions (that make you feel good) your third pair is well provisioned and you feel happy and fulfilled in your life experience.

When the fourth pair is allowed to operate in its natural pre-designed manner, you are automatically in an optimistic, exuberant and eagerly expectant state of mind keen to establish those symbiotic collaborative relationships for the purpose of collective co-existence. When I asked you to define the attributes of your desired Parallel Universe your fourth pair received that impulse and immediately went to work. If you did allow the fourth pair to operate, you probably have a definition with a tall list of attributes that you want to experience in that Parallel Universe. How did that make you feel when you had the list? Pensive? Excited? Did you purse your lips? Did you frown? Did you have that beaming smile in your face? Did you lean back, close your eyes and feel that bliss engulf you? All those reactions are the transmissions from your fourth pair that was communicated to all the other DNA pairs which caused both the physical and non-physical manifestation of that one impulse that I had rendered to your fourth pair simply by making a request in this book.

Now that you have defined your Parallel Universe, you may be wondering how simply by your own alignment you can actually activate that life experience when the Universe requires the consent and approval from a minimum of 1.5 million humans in the world. Well first of all you can start the process of socializing the effort with people that you know or have access to and introduce them to this code of Eternal Consciousness. But will that convince 1.5 million people to come along with you to define such a Parallel Universe and will everyone have the same desires that you desire in that life experience? Enter your fifth and sixth pairs of DNA strands, through which you can approach the Source of every person who are having a contemporary life experience with you, by crossing over the 4-D into the 5-D.

First of all, you would communicate with your own personal *Activebody* in the Fifth Dimension using the fifth pair of strands of your DNA. You would define, discuss, refine and initiate your very own Cycle of Creation (refer back to Chapter 5) of this desired Parallel Universe. Once the two of you are in agreement you can use your sixth pair of strands of your DNA and present your case along with your *Activebody* (who is already a member) to the consortium of *Activebodies* in the Fifth Dimension.

Note that there is no conflict, no mud-slinging, no haughtiness, no stealing of credits in the Fifth Dimension ☺ there is perfect symbiotic collaboration. I would assume that today in our evolution as a species that consortium of *Activebodies* in the Fifth Dimension is eager to get to work and are *all ears* to listen to what you have to communicate by way of defining a Parallel Universe that hosts a human civilization living in unbounded delight. Upon this multi-dimensional agreement being reached, after re-defining, refining and re-structuring had occurred, after strategy and approach has been set you will witness the initiation of a multi-dimensional Cycle of Creation. Does this sound crazy? It would not if the code of the *Genetics Of Divinity* has reactivated from your subconscious mind.

In this multi-dimensional Cycle of Creation, the *Activebodies* in the 5-D consortium would initiate the communication from the Fifth Dimension to their respective *Adaptivebodies* in the Third Dimension using the GAMMA frequency. These *Adaptivebodies*, who are the mortals with whom you are having this contemporary physical experience will receive that transmission using their receiving element on the sixth pair of DNA strands. Some people who receive that transmission from the 5-D will ignore it, some will not even be aware of such a transmission, some would not even believe such a process can occur (ouch for that dormant second pair), while some will receive the transmission loud and clear and join their respective *Adaptive* energy with you directly or indirectly and build those symbiotic collaborative relationships to collectively define that Parallel Universe. Given the human population in the world today, do you think it would be difficult to corral just a mere 1.5 million people to bring about the global change in the life experience of humanity? It all starts with one person. If that is you, can you imagine what you can personally contribute for the alignment of humanity with the purpose of Creation and Existence in this planet? You are a powerhouse - you are designed that way – recognize your abilities, see beyond what your eyes see and your other four senses detect and you will realize what amazing capabilities to serve and influence positive change to humanity lays dormant within you.

It is important to understand that your five senses are meant to provide you with a *closed loop feedback system* in the 3-D plane of existence within a linear progression of time. Your own perception, created as the end result of the feedback provided to your brain by your five senses, which leads to a corresponding emotion. It is this feedback that determines the composition of the reality of your existence and hence your life experience in one of those multiple possible Parallel Universes. Your perception is quite unique and is different from the next person, considering the common paradigms that both of you may have been exposed to. However can you define a mean path between the two of you? Everyone without exception is designed to desire love, peace, security, compassion and abundance. What themes and attributes around these desires can you define for your Parallel Universe now that you understand the technology? Would you engage in a global initiative to collaboratively implement such a life experience in a Parallel Universe?

Whatever your situation in life is so far, if you are not yet experiencing unbounded delight, for which you are designed by Creation, clearly your current beliefs and convictions are not going to get you to that point. Your DNA strands are not operating in their natural frequencies. You have been trying to improve your life all along so far, it's time to do what it takes to lead yourself to your desires. The only pathway to this life is for you to rise above the 3-D paradigm of Existence and understand that there is more to Existence than what meets your five senses. You are a richly endowed multi-dimensional entity – get used to this new cognition and the world of unlimited possibilities in the form of Type 3 Parallel Universes will be opened up for you.

Let's continue our understanding of your multi-dimensional Existence to solidify your ever increasing awareness about who you really are and what capabilities you already possess. Read and repeat after me, *"I am a multi-dimensional Creature of Existence with multi-dimensional abilities of the CREATOR of Existence fully capable to define and choose my life experience"*. When you say the words "I am" in that statement above, speak loudly and at the "am" close your lips and let that tone vibrate within your mouth cavity for a few seconds before proceeding with the rest of the statement – this delivers a strong impulse to your dormant DNA and raises your energy level. Let this cognition sink in as you repeat this a few times and focus on every word – nothing more can sound more truthful than this because that is the Eternal Truth and you know it.

Chapter 7 - Multi-dimensional Model of Creation and Existence

Why do you have goals and objectives in life? Why do you plan for the future? Why do you dream those dreams of a better life? Why do you set targets and at the very least contemplate on accomplishing them? Why do you dream those particular dreams? Why do you set those particular targets? Why do you make those plans for your desired life experience in a different Parallel Universe? Why do you have those particular goals and objectives and not something else? Why do you get knocked down by life and spring right back up and turn things to your advantage? Why do you get thrilled at the prospect of an adventure to discover new domains of knowledge and go where no other human has gone before? Why do you rationalize, analyze and contemplate before making major decisions in life?

Do you think other species of the animal kingdom on this planet make plans, set targets, dream dreams, have goals and objectives in their lives, far less are qualified to achieve them? Do you think they care about advancement of their knowledge about Existence? Would they care if you were not around? Would they care about who the next political leader of your country would be? Would they be too bothered if the gas prices went up? No, not in their physical form since they are not equipped for such tasks.

What about the plants? What do you think their plans, goals and objectives are? Are they setting targets for themselves and for all of Creation as collective coexistence and evolution?

Interestingly they live by consuming the gases that humans and animals exhale – biologists indicate this as a balance of life, plants scratch our backs and we scratch theirs – a symbiotic co-existence. Would plants care if we humans existed or not? Do plants dream dreams of a better life? Do plants look up in the heavens and wish there was life out there? Do they have the intelligence and rationality to make decisions for themselves? No, not in their physical form since they are not equipped for such tasks.

Do you realize that nothing can live without the existence of what is considered by us as inanimate and 'inert'? If there was no Earth or any habitable space could there have been what we know as the living kingdom? If there was no rock would there be any landmass? If there was no amino acid could there have been life on this planet as we know it? This is the world that we consider as inanimate – a world without which we could not exist in any physical form.

As we ask just a sampling of these leading questions about Existence and Creation, as humans we are humbled by who we are and what gifts have been given to us by the grand design of Creation to have the privilege of being the dominant species in this planet. If you don't agree, go back to Chapter 6 and read that section on the human DNA once again. With this privilege also comes a responsibility – that to understand the essence of Creation and leverage that knowledge to upgrade our perception of reality. You are now aware of the eleven dimensions of Existence from a scientific perspective while I discussed the M-Theory. It is time for you to understand the eleven dimensions of Existence as defined by the *Genetics Of Divinity*.

With all humility and reverence to the sublime essence of Creation, it is my unbounded delight to present to you Figure 17, the first ever depiction of the multi-dimensional structure of Creation and Existence. For those of you who desire to study this structure in more detail (and I know all of you have this desire, however sub-liminal it may be right now), this chart would be available to you in Module 7 at the online Multiversity that you have access to as an owner of this book.

Oh My **G**enetics **O**f **D**ivinity

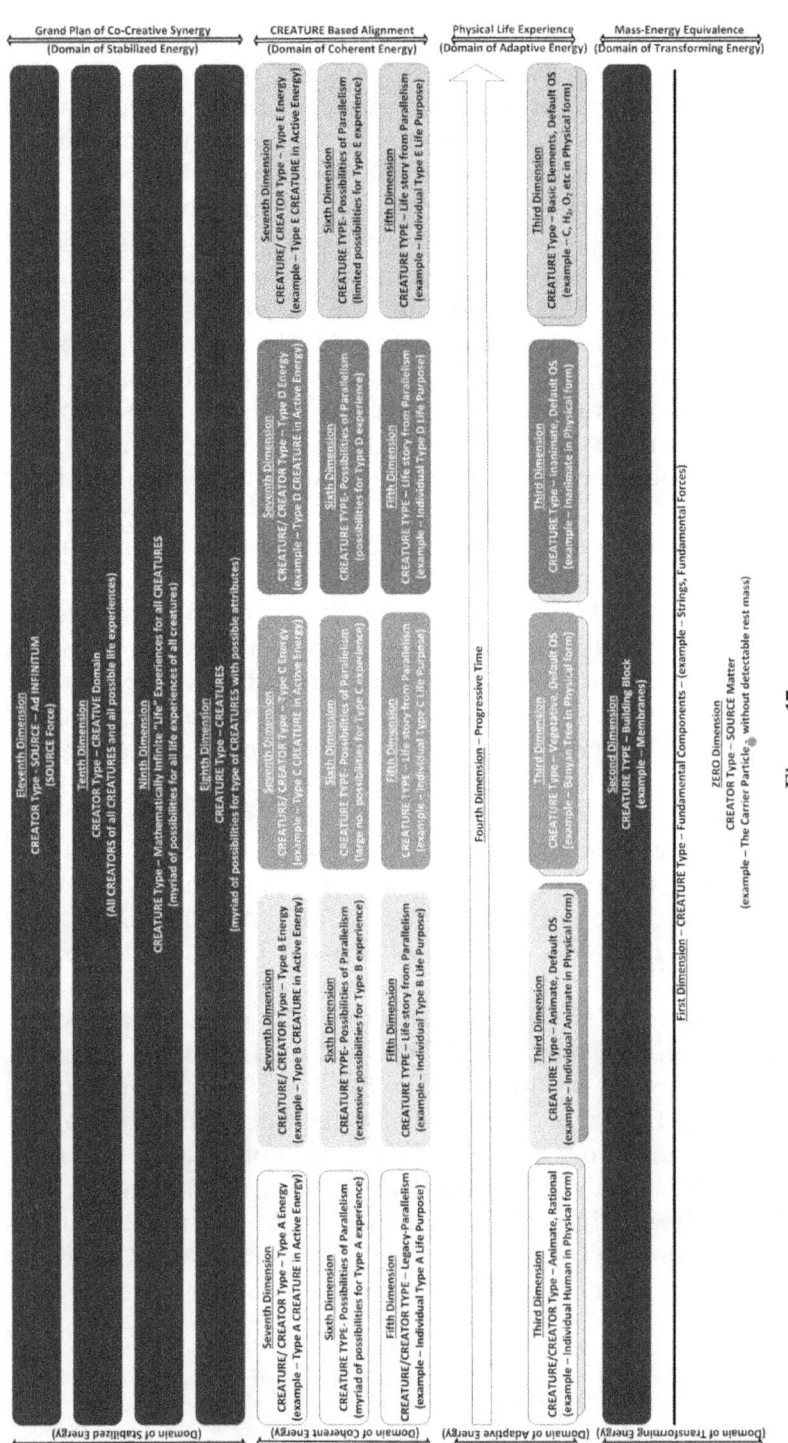

Figure 17

I have alluded to you earlier that a lot of the content in this book has been the result of not only my decade of research and rational analysis but also through the incessant download of information from my *Activebody* that continues to reactivate those dormant memories of the code of the *Genetics of Divinity*. I am also aware that some of you who are reading this book have also experienced such interactions with your own *Activebody* and have been able to uncover other sections of the code of the *Genetics Of Divinity*. I encourage you to connect with me through my website at www.GeneticsOfDivinity.com and join me in the spirit of symbiotic collaboration to share your discoveries about this code with the rest of humanity. What you will learn in this Chapter is being revealed for the first time in human history.

I have often wondered how I obtained this information and what series of events lead me to the activation of this consciousness. Did I somehow manage to unconsciously embark on an inter-dimensional journey through my evolving consciousness, just like going through twelve levels of education? Well, if I did, the journey was blazing fast – yes, faster than the speed of light given the depth and 'gravity' of this code of Eternal Consciousness..

This experience has now led me to not only author this book in the path to follow my life purpose that was revealed to me, but also to carve out books on the *Genetics Of Divinity* series and come up with other channels to share my evolving consciousness with every Type A Creature (we humans) living in this Type 0 Civilization (more on this later) on Earth. Why? Our Type 0 civilization is already on the trajectory to migrate into a Type 1 civilization according to the grand plan of Creation. Some individuals can actually feel the transition or the "shift" in consciousness as they leverage Parallelism, understand multi-dimensional Existence and start living in a Parallel Universe of their choosing – all possible and afforded by the postulates of Creation as defined in the *Genetics of Divinity*.

---------------------------*****---------------------------

I am also aware that the content of this book will draw ridicule, disbelief, negative propaganda and possible outrage from thousands of people who come across this information and prefer to live under a state of *neuro-plasticity*. But then I am also aware that there will be millions of other people who would be bold enough to read and understand the contents of this book and brace themselves for living a life that is radically abundant and fulfilling (unbounded delight) when compared to what it is today.

When these millions of people around the planet get mobilized into a higher level of consciousness, the thousands who refused at first would also mobilize themselves on their own free will, rational decision and personal motivation. If you recall my discussion in Chapter 6, all that is needed is to mobilize 1.5 million people around the planet, which starts the shift for all of humanity to enjoy unbounded delight.

This evolution of the human species is inevitable and more so because the process of Transition or 'Shift' has already started through the historic Galactic Alignment of the year 2012 that occurs once in 26000 years. The centers of our Milky Way galaxy - Sirius, our Sun and the larger planets of our solar system along with Earth had aligned in one straight line, achieving full alignment on December 21, 2012. As a result of such alignment of these astronomical bodies, there has been a sweeping energy shift occurring in our planet, which is also causing an indisputable upward shift in human consciousness, but you individually may not be aware of it – just yet. With that said, allow me the share the hierarchical structure of our multi-dimensional Existence with you.

Refer to Figure 17 and start relating to and understand the multi-dimensional hierarchical structure of Existence and the purpose of each dimension. It is my firm belief that when you internalize the forthcoming content, your consciousness will upgrade and you will realign yourself to enjoy a life experience filled with unbounded delight.

---------------------------#####---------------------------

Mastering The Basics

With all the background knowledge that you have gained thus far from this book, Figure 17 will become more meaningful to you in this chapter. Let's us start with an overview of the components that you have learned so far as they relate to the hierarchical multi-dimensional architecture of Existence:

- Creation requires a CREATOR and the Creature
- The CREATOR's attribute is the will to bestow to the Creature a life experience filled with unbounded delight and in the process experience unbounded delight of its own.
- The Creature's attribute is the will to receive and enjoy unbounded delight in its life experience.
- Both the CREATOR and the Creature are granted Free Will to have, be or do anything and everything in life that is logical and ethically feasible for the Type of CREATOR and Creature based on its role in Creation. For example, your Free Will as a human is quite different than the free will of your pet animal and that is by design of Creation.
- The Creature's quality of life experience is guided by its level and maturity of consciousness – essentially representing the Creature's degree of conscious alignment with the principles and design of Creation and Existence.
- How other Creatures perceive a Creature of its own type or cross-type, is an accurate reflection of how the perceived Creature perceives itself. The self-image of the Creature within is reciprocated by the image of the Creature outside.
- The attribute of Parallelism which is also now supported by science (recall the discussion of Parallel Universes and Quantum Mechanics) offers a plethora of possibilities at every moment of the Creature's life experience. Every decision opens up new related possibilities through Parallelism.
- The choices made by an individual Creature at any given point of time from the menu offered by

Parallelism as governed by the extent of its assigned scope or range of free will and determines the future life experience of that Creature.
- The assigned scope or range of free will refers to the possible choices that a particular Creature is designed to make – for example a deer can freeze or run away (two possible options of free will) when confronted by the headlights of a speeding car in a dark night. A human is endowed with additional options of free will and may choose to not wander aimlessly in the middle of the road regardless of the time of day, in the first place, through the power of analysis of a possible threat to life. This affords the human Creature to enjoy a wider range and scope of free will.
- When a Creature exists in physical form, it also exists simultaneously in non-physical form of energy, in the fifth dimension concurrently. Since energy can never be created or destroyed and can only be amplified (through resonance), attenuated (through dissonance) or transformed from one host to another, all Creatures are IMMORTAL by design, depending on their dimension of existence.
- IMMORTALITY of the Creature is afforded by the indestructible *Active* energy. When the *Active* energy of the Creature chooses to transform into another physical form, it is choosing an option provided by Parallelism.
- Every Creature has a CREATOR and the design of Creation is such that the Creature will continue to feel the need to re-unite with the CREATOR to complete the cycle of Creation.
- Upon a reunion occurring between the Creature and the CREATOR, do both elements of Creation complete the Cycle of Creation.
- What the Creature perceives as the physical world is the realm of the finite, which is an illusion. In true reality, Creation is a realm of the infinite where every desire or wish that the Creature feels during its physical life experience is already available through Parallelism for the purpose of providing unbounded delight. The Creature is responsible to find its

alignment with reality and consequently seek out its purpose in Existence.

Now that you have recapitulated the above, let's dive into the multi-dimensional architecture of Creation and Existence. How I became aware of this information, I cannot tell. Although I can say that my decade of research probably contributed to my alignment to the Eternal Consciousness that I call the *Genetics Of Divinity*. Most definitely I received continuous guidance from my *Activebody* in the Fifth Dimension who had revealed my life purpose in one of those consciousness reactivation sessions. This reactivation of the code of Eternal Consciousness embedded in my subconscious mind continues even today.

---------------------------*****---------------------------

All I do is document, apply the consciousness to my life experience and share the same in the public domain for the service of humanity. Through this process of sharing, my goal is also to encourage others who have activated other areas of the *Genetics of Divinity* to come forward and use this platform to share their message also for the service of humanity in the spirit of symbiotic collaborative relationships for the purpose of collective coexistence – this was revealed to me as my life purpose.

You need to reactivate this dormant consciousness from your own subconscious mind and it is my belief that when you do, it will open the doorway to your quest for unbounded delight in this life experience - for which you were created.

-------------------------#####-------------------------

First of all let us understand some basic laws of Physics which you must have learned in school. Force is a function of energy and can be expressed with the equation $W = F \times d$, where W represents work done, F represents Force applied on an object and d represents displacement or the distance that the object travelled from its original position to its displaced position when the Force was applied to it. The change in kinetic energy (energy of motion) of that object equals the work done on that object. A pretty simple equation that I am sure you were exposed to during your childhood or young adult years in school. However this seemingly simple equation has profound implications to the laws of Creation.

Read the explanation of the equation again and chances are you will find that profound significance. Without the object in question being present what is it that would be displaced? If there is no displacement the Force cannot be measured and if Force cannot be measured, Energy cannot have any significance. So the presence of the object is an absolute must to even contemplate the existence of energy, which as you are aware of by now, to be everything in the visible and invisible (dark matter) domain of Existence.

However this equation is relevant only to the physical Third Dimension of Existence and applies to objects that have rest mass. Why is that? Well, the parameter *Force* in that definition of *Work* is defined as the product of the *Rest Mass* of the object times the *acceleration* that the object attains when the *Force* is applied. This makes that equation of *Work* – $W = F \times d$ applicable only to the physical domain where we have objects with rest mass. In the non-physical dimensions of Existence of course, the physical laws of the 3-D do not apply, since there is nothing with rest mass in those dimensions.

Rest mass refers to the mass that can be measured and expressed in numerical units along with a suitable unit of measure, when the object being measured is at a relative static position. Relative to what? Relative to the point of measurement as interpreted by a suitable man-made instrument designed to measure the mass of the object. As technology improved over the decades, we are able to measure particles (objects) having rest masses in the order of 10^{-36} kilograms (for the neutrino for example), which today to the best of my knowledge at the time of writing this book holds the world record of being the lightest particle detected so far. I am sure lighter particles would be detected as our instrumentation improves.

Albert Einstein's claim in his Special Theory of Relativity, that nothing can travel faster than light at a speed of 186,000 miles per second is based on the assumption that the *'thing'* in that *'nothing'* has rest mass and is traveling through vacuum. According to his Theory, the speed of light is the ultimate limit for all objects having rest mass in all of physical Existence. Light being composed of photons that have no rest mass but has momentum, hence can achieve such speeds in vacuum. Einstein's equation in its true sense is $E^2 = m^2c^4 + p^2c^2$. You already know what each of the symbols mean in that equation except the new element – p, which represents the momentum of the object. For an object with rest mass, $p = 0$ since the object is at rest and hence has no velocity and hence no momentum, which yields the famous $E = mc^2$ equation. For a photon however, since it has no rest mass but has momentum the correct equation for the photon becomes $E = pc$.

---------------------------******---------------------------

Whenever humankind sets a limit, another discovery opens up to extend that limit and this extension of limits will continue on and on until such time we realize that there are no limits in the design and architecture to Creation and Existence. The word *impossible* is actually a typographical error for I'M POSSIBLE – possible among the plethora of Parallel options available at every moment in the dimension of time.

Note the *I'M* here. Who do you think is the "I" in I'M? It is the CREATOR in every Creature in a dimension where the Creature recognizes the attribute of Parallelism and the multi-dimensional architecture of Existence.

The so called Laws and Principles that we humans define, set boundaries of *dos* and *don'ts* and hence impose limits and finiteness to the free will of the Creature and its quest for unbounded delight. For the Third Dimension of Existence, such limits are in place by design of Creation due to the relative instability of this physical dimension – again the instability is by design to illustrate the Contrast of what stability is. The laws of Creation that apply to the multi-dimensional structure of Existence are in the realm of the infinite and the unbounded. This profound realization holds the key to your liberation from the paradigm of countable and finite possibilities under which you have lived your life so far.

-------------------------#####-------------------------

Modeling The Multi-Dimensional Existence

Before I introduce you to the complex super-structure of the multi-dimensional architecture of Existence as illustrated in Figure 17, I believe it will be helpful to explain the fundamental model or the building block of all of Creation and Existence. The concept of this fundamental building block can be understood by leveraging the principles used in software engineering called *object-oriented design* (OOD). The purpose of this book is not to teach you OOD but to adopt some of its basic principles for the purpose of our discussion. Even if you are not a computer programmer, this discussion is simple enough for you to relate to and will make it easier to understand the larger design of Creation and Existence.

Object Oriented Design At the Core

The technology of *Object Oriented Design* (OOD) is based on the principle that everything can be considered as discrete entities called *'class'* which is a combination of certain *'attributes'* or properties of the entity and certain *'functions'* it can perform using those attributes. Functions refer to the features and operational properties that the entity has and can offer to another entity external to it. In other words, *functions of an object indicate how that object can <u>serve</u> other objects* in Existence. If you can specify values to these attributes of the class then that specific instance of the class is called an *object*. A *class* hence is a generic model of an entity whereas an object is a specific instance or example of that same class with clearly specified values of the attributes of that entity – this is called **Instantiation**. If you are not a software programmer who has worked with OOD before, I admit that might have been quite a mouthful. Let's consider a real life example to clarify. If you are a computer programmer, this is not a book to learn OOD syntax, so focus on the modeling aspect only.

Defining the Creature Class

Figure 18 is a highly abridged version of a class called 'Creature' where I illustrate its attributes and two possible functions. Needless to say that this representation is just a modest sample of all possible attributes and functions of a Creature, however a careful examination of the class definition conveys the message of object orientation.

Refer the attributes and functions of the *Creature* class in Figure 18. Although they are just a sampling, once you start assigning one or more possible values to these attributes, you can actually define an instance of the Creature class and hence uniquely identify an object or instance of this class.

As you can see from this definition of the Creature class, I am considering not only physical particulate objects that have or don't have detectable rest mass, that are visible or invisible among other attributes, but also objects that can be the possibilities of Parallelism, or even one of the four fundamental influential forces that affects other objects in the Third Dimension of Existence - they are all Creatures of Creation. The assignment of appropriate values to the attributes of the class defines the specific Creature – an instance of that class.

It is a common human paradigm to automatically refer to us humans and the species of the animal and plant kingdom as *creatures* and that is what you may have been taught and made to believe. However this view is myopic and false (because it is only a partial truth). The Creature is not only what you know through the common paradigm as objects

```
class Creature {
    /* The following are some of the attributes of the Creature class */
    name;              // (unique identifier for class of Creature)
    baseType;          // (possible values = parallelism, force, particulate)
    basePurpose;       // possible values = receive, destruct, construct, serve, influence, choice, n/a)
    lifePurpose;       // (possible values = subjective to specific instance of Creature class)
    restMass;          // (possible values = detectable, undetectable, n/a)
    visibility;        // (possible values = visible, invisible, n/a)
    senseVision;       // (possible values = true, false, n/a)
    senseTactile;      // (possible values = true, false, n/a)
    senseAuditory;     // (possible values = true, false, n/a)
    senseOlfactory;    // (possible values = true, false, n/a)
    senseGustatory;    // (possible values = true, false, n/a)
    animation;         // (possible values = animate, inanimate, vegetative, n/a)
    mobility;          // (possible values = pedal, flight, swim, roll, glide, float, wave, n/a)
    speech;            // (possible values = speaking, non-speaking, n/a)
    reproductivity;    // (possible values = self, cooperative, n/a)
    reflexAction;      // (possible values = flight, fight, freeze, think, enjoy, n/a)
    followOnAction;    // (possible values = flight, fight, freeze, think, enjoy, n/a)
    rationality;       // (possible values = true, false, n/a)
    consciousness;     // (possible values = true, false, n/a)
    intelligence;      // (possible values = individual, generic, n/a)
    emotion;           // (possible values = delight, pain, pleasure, default, n/a)
    impusleReaction;   // (possible values = thought, physical, sensory, venomous, n/a)

    /* The following are some of the functions of the Creature class */

    function identifyCreature (creatureName, creatureType, creaturePurpose) {
        name = creatureName;
        baseType = creatureType;
        basePurpose = creaturePurpose;
    }       // end of definition of function identifyCreature

    function makeDecisions (incomingImpusleOfEvent) {
        if (impulseReaction != 'n/a') {        // "!=" is a symbol for not equal to
            if (incomingImpuseOfEvent = 'Life Threatening') {
                reflexAction = 'flight'; }
            elseif (incomingImpuseOfEvent = 'Life Sustaining') {
                reflexAction = 'enjoy'; }
            elseif (incomingImpuseOfEvent = 'Choice') {
                if ((rationality = true) and  (consciousness = true)  and (intelligence = true)) {
                    reflexAction = 'think';
                    if (emotion = 'delight') {
                        followOnAction = 'enjoy'; }
                }
            }
        }
    }       //end of definition of function makeDecisions
}           // end of definition of class Creature
```

Figure 18

having rest mass, but also objects that do not have rest mass. All the four fundamental forces that you are now aware of, dark matter, dark energy that you have been introduced to in this book, the Parallel Universes, all aspects of Parallelism and literally every component that in some way, shape or form contributes to the life experience of every entity in multi-dimensional Existence are all instances of the *Creature* class.

If you recall Charles Darwin's Theory of Evolution where he describes the concept of *'survival of the fittest'* specifically for the living species of the planet, you would realize that nothing exists without a purpose. Now Darwin restricted his theory to the living kingdom for sure but the concept of survival of the fittest can also translate to what we perceive as the inanimate world as well. Everything is an integral part of the whole, which is the sum of parts, because otherwise, it would not be worthy of being created in the first place.

How does an object participate as a part of the whole? Imagine an object called 'engine' which is an integral part of a larger object called 'airplane'. Without the 'engine' object can the 'airplane' object exist? Yes, it can superficially but the 'airplane' object will not be able to perform an important function 'canTaxiOnRunway' without the 'engine' object, far less perform its primary function 'canFly'. However whether the object 'cabinLight' exists or not, the 'airplane' object would still be able to perform both the 'canTaxiOnRunway' and 'canFly' functions, although it will not be able to perform the 'canIlluminateCabin' function.

Understanding Purpose

The core theme in the above example is an understanding of the concept of **Purpose** for an object of the *Creature* class. By itself, the object is not so interesting. However when one analyzes the object to understand its attributes and functions, it becomes significant due to its application for a bigger cause. What is the role of an object when it is to become a component of a greater object? How is the object endowed with appropriate attributes that enable it to perform certain characteristic functions in order to *serve a greater cause*? Hence *Purpose* for an object would be the nature of its applicability in the grand design of Creation and Existence.

---------------------------*****--------------------------

Without a definite purpose, nothing can be created and Existence would be a pipedream. Why bother creating something when there is no purpose for that creation – there is no return on investment of effort, so why bother? As a matter of fact, it is simply not possible to create anything if you don't know what you want that creation to do, how you want that creation to serve, what inputs it would receive and what output(s) it would produce. Try to even think of creating something that has no purpose and you won't make much progress on that effort.

Refer to the Cycle of Creation on Figure 6 – the underlying theme in that cycle is PASSION and without ***Purpose*** it is impossible to have any PASSION. The basic purpose of Existence as you already know, is to serve other entities through symbiotic collaborative relationships and enjoy mutual unbounded delight in the life experience. Since we have different Creatures with different attributes and functions, the nature of 'unbounded delight' will also respectively differ.

Every Creature (yourself included) absolutely **must** have initiated a purpose in the mind of its CREATOR prior to the Creature being created, regardless of whether the Creature itself is aware of it or not during its life experience. The Creature is required to perform necessary steps to identify and fulfill that purpose. Free will determines how long it will take for the Creature to identify its purpose – it will find so only when it seeks and therein lies the secret to engage in the Cycle of Creation.

---------------------------#####--------------------------

Have you found *your* purpose in life? You will, very soon if you have not done so already — you will be well aligned after you complete this book and you will learn the procedure to find your own life purpose in the follow-on book titled *Miracles From Genetics Of Divinity*.

Leveraging Encapsulation

With this basic understanding of object-oriented modeling it is time for you to be introduced to another key concept of object orientation — called '**Encapsulation**'. Refer to the definition of the *Creature* class in Figure 18 and you will find that the attributes and the functions are both included or encapsulated in the definition of the class. In our example of the *'engine'* and the *'airplane'* objects above, both are instances of the *Creature* class with the appropriate values which in turn influence what functions would be applicable for each object. When the 'airplane' object chooses to use the 'engine' object there is no interest for the 'airplane' object to understand how (called *implementation* in the language of object oriented design) the *'engine'* object performs its functions. All it cares about is how to communicate (called *interface*) with the *'engine'* object so that the *'engine'* object can perform its functions (*implementation*) accordingly. Once the *'airplane'* object communicates with the *'engine'* object appropriately through the *interface*, the *engine* object would respond with its defined functions. Furthermore, if you changed the design of the *'engine'* object so that it becomes more fuel efficient, that change does not affect the operation of the *'airplane'* object as far as the 'canTaxiOnRunway' or 'canFly' functions of the *'engine'* object is concerned. However after the upgrade to the *'engine'* object when one evaluates the specifications of the larger *'airplane'* object, it would be found to have acquired an improved feature of "higher fuel efficiency". This is an additional feature to the concept of *encapsulation* in object oriented design.

Why is it important for you to understand the concept of *encapsulation*? The reason is for you to clear your mind of a crippling paradigm that *'one must see in order to believe'*. It is a prevalent and common dis-ease of the human belief system that it is important to always understand the 'how-it-works' (implementation) in order to even contemplate any engagement with an objective. If one cannot understand the details of the *implementation* of an object, the common outcome is rejection – a serious shortcoming that plagues humanity today. Just because you did not understand the concept of dark matter before, that does not mean dark matter does not exist or affect how it operates, does it?

It is very important for you to focus on the *'what'* and the *'why'* and allow the inherent implementation of the object to take care of the *'how'*. A good understanding of *encapsulation* is required because in this chapter I will soon be explaining to you a multi-dimensional structure of Creation and Existence. At that time, I would like you to focus on *what* the multiple dimensions are and *what* you need to do in order to plug into the interface of the multi-verse or Parallel Universes rather than invest your energy on *how* Parallel Universes work or challenging even if they are real. You never bother to figure out how your nifty smartphone does all those cool things, do you? You just use it and brag about the cool features – this is *encapsulation* at work.

Class Inheritance

Now let us get into yet another useful feature of object oriented design called **Inheritance** – useful because it relates directly to the hierarchical multi-dimensional design of Creation and Existence. As the name suggests, *inheritance* refers to a hierarchical parent-child relationship where the child would inherit some attributes and functions of the parent. Based on Figure 18, if the *Creature* class is considered to be the parent one could define a *Plant* class as a child, where the child would first inherit some of the attributes and functions of its parent class and then add some of its own attributes and functions as shown in Figure 19. Note how the *Plant* class extends the *Creature* class.

Since the *Plant* class extends the *Creature* class, it inherits all attributes and functions from the parent class. In addition the *Plant* class adds its own attributes and its own functions. So, if we can define an *object* of the *Plant* class called 'Oak', then the object called *Oak* will not only be able to access all the relevant attributes of the *Creature* class (such as *name, baseType, basePurpose* etc) it will also have access to all the attributes that have been defined specifically for the *Plant* class. Furthermore, the 'Oak' object will be able to access all the relevant functions of the *Creature* class (such as *identifyCreature*) and also be able to perform its native function *performPhotosynthesis*.

```
class Plant extends Creature {
    /* The following are some of the attributes of the Plant class in addition to those
       inherited from the Creature class*/
    habitat;            // (possible values = indoor terrestrial, outdoor terrestrial, underwater)
    baseType;           // (possible values = evergreen, deciduous, coniferous)
    blooming;           // possible values = true, false)
    fruitBearing;       // (possible values = true, false)
    gotSunlight;        // (possible values = true, false)
    gotChlorophyll;     // (possible values = true, false)
    gotCO2;             // (possible values = true, false)
    gotH2O;             // (possible values = true, false)
    makeO2;             // (possible values = true, false)
    makeC6H12O6;        // (possible values = true, false)

    /* The following are some of the independent functions of the Plant class */

    function performPhotosythesis (gotSunlight, gotChlorophyll, gotC02, gotH2O ) {
        if (( gotSunlight = true) and (gotChlorophyll = true) and (gotCO2 = true) and
            (gotH20 = true)) {
                make02 = true;
                makeC6H12O6 = true;
        }
    }                   // end of definition of function performPhotosynthesis

}                       // end of definition of class Plant
```

Figure 19

---*****---

While this concept of *inheritance* is exciting from the perspective of a progressive hierarchical generation, it also implies that the child could not exist without the parent. You could not have an object called 'Oak' of the *Plant* class, if there was no *Creature* class already existing. Aha! Where did all that you consider as Existence come from? Each and everything that you consider Existence, which traditionally would be what is visible to your eyes or detectable through human instrumentation, is the child of some parent, which may or may not be visible. Do you still believe everything was created out of *nothing* according to the traditional Big Bang theory? I had quite a go at it in the beginning of this book and provided a reasonable explanation using the M-Theory. **Inheritance in OOD proves that everything could not be created out of 'nothing'.** What is that some-'*thing*' from which every-'*thing*' was created? All in good time – later on in this book.

There are twelve dimensions (counting the ZERO dimension of course) of Existence as you have been introduced to in the last Chapter, although common human perception becomes foggy or non-existent beyond the 4-D. We can thereby architect a twelve hierarchical *parent-child* class structure of Existence in the language of object oriented design.

-------------------------#####-------------------------

Polymorphism of Creation

Let's get into yet another important concept of OOD called **Polymorphism**, that I would like to explain to you before I bring all of these OOD concepts together to understand the multi-dimensional architecture of Creation and Existence. *Polymorphism* is an extension to the concept of *inheritance* that I explained earlier. While *inheritance* allows child classes and hence child objects to be defined with inherited attributes and functions from the parent class, *polymorphism* allows each child class the freedom of re-defining and adapting its inherited functions based on its own attribute values. Whoa! Read that one again.

The significance of *inheritance* and *polymorphism* will be clear through an explanation of Figure 20. Through *inheritance* we first define the *Human* child class from the parent *Creature* class. For the *Human* class we define some attributes that are specific to all objects that could be created from this class. In addition, we also define a function *'canDoWithPassion'* that is specific to the *Human* class – refer to the top box on Figure 20 for this definition.

From this definition of this *Human* class, we go further and define four other child classes – *goGetter*, *trendSetter*, *doomsDayer* and *naySayer*. All of these four child classes

```
class Human extends Creature {
    willingnessToLearn;      // (possible values = 1 – 10; 1 = not willing, 10 = voracious learner)
    willingnessToChange;     // (possible values = 1 – 10; 1 = no change, 10 = flexible as a noodle)
    iCanInnovate;            // (possible values = true, false)
    iLoveRumors;             // (possible values = true, false)
    iAmNotLogical;           // (possible values = true, false)
    iCanImprove;             // (possible values = true, false)
    iCanDoItPeriod;          // (possible values = true, false)

    function canDoWithPassion ( iCanDoItPeriod ) {
        if (iCanDoItPeriod = true) {
            getItDone ( );
        }
    }  // end of definition of function canDoWithPassion
}  // end of definition of class Human
```

```
class goGetter extends Human {
function canDoWithPassion ( iCanDoItPeriod ) {
    if (iCanDoItPeriod = true) {
        if ((willingnessToLearn = true) and
            (willingnessRoChange = true )) {
            getItDone ( );
        }
    }
}
```

```
class trendSetter extends Human {
function canDoWithPassion ( iCanDoItPeriod ) {
    if (iCanDoItPeriod = true) {
        if ((willingnessToLearn = true) and
            (willingnessRoChange = true )) {
            if (iCanInnovate = true) {
                setNewTrend ( );
            }
        }
    }
}
```

```
class doomsDayer extends Human {
function canDoWithPassion ( iCanDoItPeriod ) {
    if (iCanDoItPeriod = false) {
        if ((iloveRumors = true) and (iAmNotLogical = true)){
            promoteDoomsdayCampaign ( );
        }
    }
}
```

```
class naySayer extends Human {
function canDoWithPassion ( iCanDoItPeriod ) {
    if (iCanDoItPeriod = false) {
        keepWhinigAllTheTime ( );
    }
}
```

Figure 20

use the same attributes of the Human class however their independent definition and implementation of the function *canDoWithPassion* is different. While the *goGetter* class adds more qualifying attributes before it allows the inherited *getItDone* function to be activated, the other three child classes don't use the inherited *getItDone* function at all but define their own native class functions. The *trendSetter* class still continues to use the *canDoWithPassion* function, but defines it differently with different qualifying criteria and ends with an entirely new function *setNewTrend*. Similarly the *doomsDayer* and the *naysayer* classes both use the *canDoWithPassion* function inherited from the *Human* class, but uses their own respective qualifying criteria with their own respective functions that I have named - *promoteDoomsdayCampaign* and *keepWhiningAllTheTime*.

You may be observant enough to detect something very sublime and implied in the definitions of the *naySayer* and the *doomsDayer* classes and I will identify this for you. All *naySayers* are not *doomsDayers*, but all *doomsDayers* MUST be *naySayers* first to qualify as a *doomsDayer*. How? Although a naySayer object has the value *'false'* to the attribute *iCanDoItPeriod*, it does not have the value *'true'* for the two attributes of *iLoveRumors* and *iAmNotLogical* which the *doomsDayer* object does. However in order for the *doomsDayer* object to even operate its core function *promoteDoomsdayCampaign*, it must first have the *naySayers'* value *'false'* for the attribute *iCanDoItPeriod*. Does this makes sense to you? How do you relate to this extension to the concept of *polymorphism*?

--------------------------*****--------------------------

You can now assign these four child classes to objects or actual people – let's say with names Ms.G, Dr.T, Mrs.D and Mr.N. You have four completely different people with four completely different levels of consciousness, with four completely different attitude towards life and hence four completely different quality of their physical life experiences, although nowhere in the parent *Human* class or the super-parent *Creature* class was there any definition of how each of these four people would perform the *canDoWithPassion* function. The child functions were self-defined or *polymorphed* and not inherited. Read that paragraph again till you get it.

You may ask, 'Well how can these four child classes really be even conceived and what conceived them?' Aha! Just pause for a moment and go through your list of friends and acquaintances with the objective of classifying (secretly) them. How many more child classes can you define from that *Human* class just by changing the definition of the *canDoWithPassion* function? I can tell you whatever that number is, I can add quite a few more and so can everyone in this world. There are literally an infinite number of possibilities, all offered by Parallelism. The choice made by an individual to belong to a certain derived child class of the *Human* class at a given point in time defines that person's Universe of existence among the infinite number of Parallel Universes (life experiences) available for habitation.

---------------------------#####---------------------------

Class Mutation in Creation

Here's a trick question for you – is it possible for the objects of the classes in Figure 20, Ms.G, Dr.T, Mrs.D and Mr.N to decide to swap their class assignments? In other words could Mr.N, an object of the *naySayer* class, read this book for example, start resonating with several *Aha moments*, decide that enough *nay-saying* was enough and choose to become an instance of the *goGetter* class. Yes he can – through a concept called **Mutation** in OOD. Note that the *goGetter* and *naySayer* classes are both children of the parent *Human* class, hence all attributes and functions of the parent *Human* class are automatically available to the child classes (OOP programmers: please refrain from the technicalities of private, public and protected variables and method declarations here - this is not a OOP book). In order for our Mr.N to now become an instance of the *goGetter* class, all he needs to do is change the value of some of his attributes that he inherited in the *Human* class – essentially set parameter *iCanDoItPeriod* = *true*, parameter *willingnessToLearn* = *true* and the parameter *willingnessToChange* = *true* as well. The outcome – Mr.N is now a confirmed instance of the *goGetter* class. This is an example of the mutant behavior of the instance of a class.

Before we wrap up the discussion of OOD, here's one last concept that you would want to know as it relates directly to a most invigorating discussion coming up shortly. This is the concept of *multiple inheritance* in OOD. Multiple inheritance allows a child class to inherit attributes and functions from multiple parent classes. Consider the child class designed through multiple inheritance as the best of all worlds as the child class exhibits highly flexible behavior in form and function hence making instances of such a child class highly desirable for interaction and integration by instances of other child classes. A common example is the O negative blood group or the universal donor. O negative blood can be infused in an individual with any other blood group. As another example consider yourself – you are an object of the *Human* class created through multiple inheritance of both your parents who were instances of the *Human-Female* and *Human-Male* classes. There's much more on multiple inheritance coming up for you in this chapter.

Now that you have understood some of the key concepts of OOD, how many of these can you leverage right now to change your life experience for the better? Quite honestly, all of them – you would need to leverage all of these concepts of OOD in order to architect your own life experience in the future ahead. OOD is not simply a design philosophy for software programmers, but for everything that you experience around your perceived physical universe, including the grand design of Creation and Existence.

--------------------------*****--------------------------

Can you become a mutant object, depart from your affiliation with a class that is not providing you with unbounded delight, adopt certain attributes you have access to through your affiliation to a higher Human class and create a brand new life experience? Yes, you can – the grand design of Creation and Existence affords you that ability – only if you are willing to learn, willing to change and decide that you can do it – period. How do you access those attributes and assign those appropriate values? Not so fast – you have to first figure out what attributes in the *Human* class (only a sampling provided in Figure 20) do you need to assign new values for. That is the starting point for everything – your choice in Parallelism.

For now, just kick back and go through this material and soak it all in with the knowingness that in a different Parallel Universe all that you want to be, do and have under the guidelines of logical and ethical feasibility is already there in physical reality – simply awaiting the arrival of your physical body in its time and space. I will walk you through the process of arriving at that coveted Parallel Universe – where you the Creature is enjoying unbounded delight as a new mutant of the *Human* class

Life Purpose and Degrees of Freedom

Let's summarize what you have learned so far in this chapter before diving into the complex architecture of the multi-dimensional design of Creation and Existence. The basic ingredients for Creation are:

1. Everything is energy in distinct and characteristic frequencies of vibration and energy is everything as defined by the principle of Mass-Energy Equivalence. In the physical dimension energy is a function of force which in turn is a function of the rest mass of the object on which the force is applied.
2. There must be an object with or without *detectable* rest mass as the subject of application, for any force to have any significance in the grand design of Creation. Similarly an object has no purpose without a suitable force to act upon it to activate some function of that object. This is called the *Force-Particle Reciprocity* – a fundamental building block of Creation.
3. This force absolutely must act upon that object to bring about a transformation that contributes to Creation – this implies that a given type of force must act only upon the compatible type of object to bring about any significant effect or change on that object.

A ray of light (electromagnetic energy) for example has no effect on an object behind an opaque wall, however that object regardless of its position will be under the influence of the gravitational force.
4. When force is applied on an object as above, the resultant transformed state of the object can be any one of the several possibilities that are appropriate for that object based on its structural attributes and possible functions, at a given instance of time. For a better understanding of this concept, review the definition of the *Creature* class in Figure 18. An instance of the *Creature* class called *bird* with a value of *'flight'* to its attribute of *'mobility'* will also have an active function called *'canFly'* within which one can define the mechanism of flying. However although this function *'canFly'* exists in the generic *Creature* class, will have absolutely no significance to another instance of the *Creature* class, called *fish* that does not share the same value to its defining attribute of *'mobility'*. So the possibility of flying when the *bird* object moves its moving parts (application of its physical force) is appropriate whereas that possibility does not apply to a *fish* object when it moves its moving parts (application of its physical force). Similarly the function of *'canSwim'* in the generic *Creature* class definition, would be an active function or possibility for the *fish* object and be of no significance to the *bird* object. These different allowed possibilities or states of existence of specific objects or instances of the class are called the ***degrees of freedom***.
5. Degrees of freedom are the core essence of Parallelism and subject to the specific instance of the *Creature* class.
6. More complex the object (which translates to greater number of attributes with significant values), more will be the number, flexibility and complexity of active functions for that object of the *Creature* class and consequently more allowed possibilities of its life experience and hence more degrees of freedom. As a human, your unique and one single significant attribute of *'rationality'*, coupled with other

significant attributes of *'consciousness'*, *'intelligence'* and *'emotion'* affords you the degree of freedom to declare yourself as part of the dominant visible species in this planet and opens you up for many more possibilities for your life experience than any other living species in comparison.

7. The **Purpose** of life experience of a specific instance of the *Creature* class, is the most significant function of the object. As a human, your most significant function may be *'canHelpChildren'* and that would be your purpose in life. Alternatively several other significant functions applicable to you such as *'canBeHelpful'*, *'canBeLoving'*, *'canLoveChildren'* could be combined to define your life's purpose of helping children. We will dive deeper in the follow-on book *'Miracles From Genetics Of Divinity'* into identifying your true Life Purpose, but for the scope of this book, I trust that you are getting the concept.

8. If you can imagine a framework of anything that has some properties and performs certain functions, you are referring to an object. Every object – Creatures or CREATORS, with or without detectable rest mass are instances of a certain class. The class contains the definition of the properties of the object and also contains the design or implementation to perform the functions that the object exhibits to the external world. These properties and functions of the class become the identity of the object. For example, you as an object of the *Human* class, can uniquely identify other objects such as a bat from a cat from a hat from a mat from a rat from a vat because all of these different objects have different properties and offer different functions that you may interact with.

9. The key point in the previous statement leads us to the concept of *Relationship* that objects *may* choose to have with each other. Relationship is possible only when objects disclose their attributes and their functions to the external world, allowing other objects to decide if a relationship with the said object would be a symbiotic, collaborative and hence worthwhile experience or not. Your choice of a new vehicle is possible only when you know its features and its

functions – called *specifications* in technical terms. Only when you – an object of the *Human* class evaluate the specifications of the model of the *Vehicle* class and determine that a relationship would be worthwhile for your life experience, would you proceed to establish a relationship with that particular vehicle. *When a symbiotic or parasitic relationship is established between two objects, that marks the beginning of a new life experience and hence the birth of a new Parallel Universe of Existence for all of those participating objects.* Read that again.
10. All of Creation and Existence spread out in twelve dimensions as illustrated in Figure 17 can be modeled using the principles of object oriented design (OOD) where concepts of *class, instantiation, encapsulation, inheritance, polymorphism, mutation and multiple inheritance* provide the framework to understand and map out the architecture of all Creation and Existence.

You are now ready to align with the Source of Creation and Existence and view the grand design from a level that you have never experienced before. I will state here that some of these concepts that you are about to learn about may not resonate with your current belief systems and that is natural. However I will also state that your belief systems have already started to morph if you have read the book this far and the contents are increasingly making sense to you – I know they are because you are part of the same Eternal Consciousness, you came from the same Consciousness. You will leave a legacy of being an integral part of this Consciousness once you understand the grand plan of Creation and Existence. You won't need to believe any of what's coming next, because you are about to be empowered with knowledge that is already embedded in your *sub-conscious* mind. My role is just to assist and remind you of this infinite multi-dimensional design of EXISTENCE.

Twelve Dimensions of Existence

By the time you are in this section of the book, you are well aware that science has been able to identify four fundamental forces that govern the entire universe. What science does not tell you is that these forces are fundamental and applicable only to the *physical* Universe as the human faculties and human instrumentation can detect and measure. As a recap, these four fundamental forces are the electromagnetic force, the gravitational force (both of which affect appropriate objects or particles with detectable rest mass at both the micro and macro level), the strong and weak forces that apply at the nuclear level of the atom. A common argument is that the photon which is the carrier particle of electromagnetic energy of light is massless but has only momentum. Technically speaking, only if we consider the photon to be a particle without rest mass, is it possible for the photon to achieve light speed under the influence of the electromagnetic force and that too under vacuum conditions. However it has been found that electromagnetic forces undergo an attenuation (weakening) in the presence of superconducting material such as the Bose-Einstein condensate under super-high vacuum and super-low temperatures, which implies that the carrier particle or photon within superconducting material shows detectable rest mass and its speed drops to the speed of your car in a busy city street.

The key point for you to understand in the above paragraph is that the photon is a mutant object of the *Particle* class, which is a child of the parent *Creature* class. You will soon discover more about why mutation is so very important in the grand design of Creation and Existence.

As I guide you through this profound body of consciousness I recommend that you download and print a copy of Figure 17, the multi-dimensional design and architecture of Creation and Existence. This chart is available to you online from the Multiversity portal at www.GeneticsOfDivinity.com. You will need to refer to this architecture quite often as you read this section of the book for a better and quicker understanding of the material, so make sure you have a copy of Figure 17 easily available and accessible.

---------------------------*****---------------------------

A Creature cannot exist without a CREATOR. Without a Creature the CREATOR has no merit or value or purpose – this is the *duality* of Creation. It is very important for you to discard the limiting paradigm at this stage that all references to a CREATOR can only imply a certain person or super-entity proposed by organized religions.

While it is absolutely critical to assign function, it is absolutely inappropriate to assume or assign any physical form to any of the two core components of Creation and Existence. While a CREATOR and a Creature may assume a certain physical form in some dimensions as I will shortly explain in this chapter, the core attribute of either component of Creation is simply function. *While physical form is associated with physical matter - visible or dark, the function is associated with energy.* In order for you to grasp the remainder of this chapter, make sure you understand this concept.

The overall architecture of Creation and Existence is based on a structured object oriented hierarchy of four major bands of energy frequencies – *Stabilized Energy, Coherent Energy, Adaptive Energy and Transforming Energy*, with a clear division of *'responsibility'*, *'accountability'* and *'operating procedures'* leading to specific functions and/or forms.

---------------------------#####---------------------------

The Binding Dimensions – ZERO and ELEVEN

Let us go back to some of the basic equations of physics that I am sure you have been exposed to in grade school. The first equation to consider is $F = m * a$, where F = force applied, m = rest mass of the object on which the force has been applied and a = acceleration (velocity per unit of time) generated by the object as a result of the force being applied. Pretty straightforward but a key question to answer here is what would happen if the rest mass or m in the above equation was to be 0? Nothing would accelerate and hence no force would be of any significance.

Let us now consider photons that are supposed to have no rest mass. Hardliner puritan physicists argue that the $F = m * a$ equation works for classical mechanics but not for quantum mechanics. Well I guess that makes electromagnetic *force* a misnomer? Yet, the electromagnetic force is one of the four fundamental forces that make up our Universe. What is the force with which a photon impacts on a target?

When a LASER (light amplification by stimulated emission of radiation) beam is directed to an object or even when you take a magnifying glass and focus the sun's rays on a sheet of paper, what can be observed? The localized area of impact of the LASER beam or the focused beam of sunlight heats up steadily. Why is it so? That is the force of photons bombarding on the target leading to an increased 'agitation' or energy transfer on the target causing its molecules to start vibrating at high frequency which can be observed as heat or an increase in temperature. How much energy is generated? The kinetic energy that is generated by those photons in the LASER beam or the focused ray of sunlight can be roughly expressed by the third basic equation of Physics: $E^2 = m^2c^4 + p^2c^2$, where E = the kinetic energy generated by the photons, m = rest mass of the photon and c is speed of light, and p is the momentum of the photon. A photon has no rest mass but has momentum in vacuum, making that equation $E = pc$. That's pretty significant energy being focused on a focused target, so no wonder there is a sudden rise in temperature in the localized area of the target. When it comes to photons, I'd rather prefer to refer to it as electromagnetic *energy* than electromagnetic force.

---------------------------******---------------------------

We can hence conclude *that every force in the physical dimension MUST have a companion carrier particle with detectable rest mass in order to have any perceivable impact on the physical dimension of Existence.*

Contrary to what you might have been taught before reading this book, *Thought* is not the source of every action as I explained while discussing the Cycle of Creation in Chapter 5. We have established that beyond Thought is Inspiration and beyond Inspiration, the cause of Inspiration is Bliss. While we Creatures understand bliss in our own terms, at the level of the *MASTER CREATOR*, this feeling of Bliss is ineffable, in other words, infinite. This implies that the energy associated with the feeling of Bliss is also infinite.

---------------------------#####--------------------------

We talk about the four fundamental *forces* that governs the physical Universe. Let me ask you - What is the source of these forces that seemingly govern the physical universe? Being part of the physical dimension of Existence, they just cannot be there out of nothing, can they? They just cannot be there without a parent, can they?

Everything in the physical Universe, MUST have a parent, a source that spawns off other children each with its own characteristics and functions as you are now aware from your background of OOD. So what was the parent of the four fundamental forces? Are there only four *fundamental* forces in this physical Universe or are these limited only to the physical *visible* Universe? What about the forces that apply on dark matter? We know dark matter exists and have proven its existence through gravitational lensing. Although we can theorize about dark energy, we know nothing about the mechanics of operation of the *dark* force (not to be confused with the dark force of Star Wars® fame) behind that dark energy. We know that dark energy is causing the outward expansion of this physical Universe, but we know nothing about the mechanics of operation of that dark force. So there are more *fundamental* forces than the four that we know about. What is the source of all these *fundamental* forces or fundamental *energies* as I prefer to call them? My research and for lack of a better word, '*hook-up*' with Eternal Consciousness led me to the cognition that there must an energy - an instance of a class that is the source of all that is considered to be energy – the primary class, that can never be created or destroyed but can only affect amplification, attenuation, transformation or a morphing function to deliver a certain end or intermediate result.

While I have devoted an entire chapter of this book later on, I present to you the *Source Force* from *Source Energy* – the mother of all fundamental and derived forces that individually impact all dimensions of Creation and Existence. You know the area of focus of the four fundamental forces in the physical visible Universe. If these forces were to be regarded as classes, what keeps those classes distinct from each other and yet keeps them working in perfect coordination with each other? Is there some unifying force that performs all this cohesion and coordination? Most definitely and I refer to that as the *Source Force* – the active agent of *Source Energy* that originates in a domain where physical laws do not apply.

The Source Force is the unifying force behind the grand design of Creation and Existence where the *MASTER CREATOR* experiences ineffable BLISS with the will to bestow and create. This plane of Existence as depicted in Figure 17 is the *Eleventh Dimension* – the domain of *Ad Infinitum*, the source of everything and anything, the reason behind all of Creation and Existence.

The 11-D can be perceived and experienced by the consciousness of the *MASTER CREATOR* or Source Energy – the domain of omnificence, omnipotence, omnipresence, omniscience, omnicompetence and immortality. In fact the concept of 'omni' or 'all' is an attribute only of the Eleventh Dimension, including all the other dimensions of Existence. Consider your perception of four dimensions - just trying to figure out the 4-D world can be overwhelming. Now imagine the complexity if you can, of a Consciousness that operates in the 11-D keeping every aspect of all the twelve dimensions (including the 0-D) functional with what I would unabashedly call *perfect* harmony, synergy and cohesion.

I can almost feel the question in your mind that is begging to be answered at this point. Without referring to any specific nomenclature, the pressing question would be : *Is the 11th dimension the domain of the supreme power depicted by the organized religions that humankind subscribes to?*

It does not matter if you follow any organized religion or not. You do admit that there is a power greater than what you perceive yourself to have, don't you? A power that in your perception remains hidden, that sometimes seems to work in your favor and sometimes appears to be partial and has you in its blind spot. A power that in your perception is the cause of pain and pleasure and is responsible for all the good and the bad that you experience in your physical life experience. Honestly speaking, there have been times in your physical life experience when you have blamed that supreme power for your lack of the feeling of unbounded delight, this is what I refer to as your scarcity consciousness. This does not necessarily refer to the financial aspect (although for you specifically it could be) but all aspects in your life where you have a want and hence a scarcity of that prevents you from your sense of unbounded delight. In all likelihood, you have also used that power as an excuse for your shortcomings in life that is keeping you, the Creature away from unbounded delight.

There is also another debilitating perception that has probably plagued your life experience ever since your conscious memory serves you. The supreme power prescribed by organized religion, seems to be out there to punish you for your deeds that are considered *sinful*. The truth is, the *punishment* that you feel is *you* punishing yourself for not doing what you perceive to be right through your own free will. This perception of an external Supreme Power rendering a punitive verdict too is the end result of two diseases (hence my use of the word *'plagued'*) of the human mind that David Schwartz so eloquently describes as *blamititis* and *excusitis* in his book *'The Magic of Thinking Big'*. More about these concepts of sin, guilt and punishment coming up in the following book *'Miracles From Genetics Of Divinity'*.

I can state that based on the content that I am sharing with you in this book, your perceptions as above are misguided. Having read the book so far, your perceptions are changing if you have allowed the content to resonate with those dormant memories of the *Genetics Of Divinity*. As you continue to consume the information in this book, your perceptions will change even further and it is my hope and belief that your physical life experience will also change for the better by the time you are done.

From that pedestal of your newly enhanced consciousness I would ask you to ask that same pressing question again. I can assure you that you will have your answer, even without my assistance. Quite honestly, I am not qualified to direct you what to believe and perceive. My role is to provide you with accurate information and empower you with at least a portion of the code of Eternal Consciousness to leverage Parallelism and your inherent attribute of discernment being born as an instance of the *Human* class, to make your own decisions whether to change your perceptions or not.

However I can state that if you do follow organized religion, contemplate on the attributes and functions of the supreme power that you follow. Then escalate those attributes to the 11th dimension – the dimension of eternity, immortality, omnificence, omnipotence, omnipresence, omniscience, omnicompetence with the will to bestow for all that there is – then magnify it by as high a magnitude that you can perceive in an attempt to quantify this ineffable consciousness.

---------------------------*****---------------------------

Having said that, I would also encourage you to consider the fact that your religious scriptures also mention (in all likelihood) that you have been created in the likeness of that Supreme Power. Absolutely true ! Hence would you conclude that you also do exist in the 11th dimension? Most definitely not in your current physical form, but in your non-physical form that is pure untainted energy, you have been inherited from the 11th Dimension. Before your current perceptions reject this notion, play along with me for the remainder of this book and then make your decision. Parallelism is awaiting your decision right now. What is it going to be?

---------------------------#####---------------------------

We have already established that for any force to have any significant impact on any part of Creation and Existence, there must be a particle on which the force can be applied. You also know by now the description of the 0-D refers to a point with no dimensions, which is inconceivable by human perception. You have also been introduced to the concept of detectable rest mass. You know about dark matter for which we have no technology to detect mass but we do have proof that it exists, occupying a whole lot more of space in the Universe than visible matter. Physicists are engaged in finding a particle called the graviton, which is supposed to be the particle on which the gravitation force acts. Well, so far the graviton continues to remain elusive but it's got to exist, which is why physicists are chasing it in the first place. So when I say *particle*, refrain from conceptualizing an object with rest mass by default.

This book is coming to you at such an exciting point in human evolution when we are understanding that particles do not need to have detectable rest mass in order to be considered as part of Existence. Do they have rest mass? My belief is yes – every physical object has rest mass and it is a pre-requisite for it to exist in the physical dimension of Existence. Science and engineering has not yet developed instrumentation to detect rest masses for every particle since we do not understand their form and function.

But what if there is a particle that really can have no rest mass, or dimension but **can be represented only an energy wave at a certain position in space**? The photon is an example from our physical Universe that is massless whose *dimension* is actually dependent on the wavelength of energy in the electromagnetic spectrum where this mutant photon exists. Based on the above background I can now present to you the particle in the 0-D - the *carrier particle* of the Source Energy and the Source Force.

When I say 'carrier' it does not mean that the particle is carrying the force nor that it contains the force. 'Carrier' simply refers to the function of the particle to be impacted (or mediated) by the application of an appropriate force. For example, the photon is the carrier particle of the electromagnetic *force*, the graviton (although we are still chasing its presence) is the carrier particle of the gravitational force. Similarly the strong nuclear force impacts gluons as its carrier particle, while the weak nuclear force impacts W and Z bosons.

With the audacity to extrapolate our physical perceptions to the Source Force in the 11th Dimension, it must have a companion Carrier particle in the 0th dimension so that together they can bind the architecture of the 10 remaining dimensions of Existence in between. Again, just because you can't see such a particle or our current technology cannot detect it, does not mean it does not exist. Do I believe such a carrier particle does exist in the 0th dimension? Absolutely yes I do – analytical reasoning and logic supports it and offers a new approach for revisiting the Big Bang Theory. Without taking the wind out of the forthcoming chapter dedicated to the Source Force and its Carrier Particle, for the moment play along with me and assume that such a carrier particle exists.

Scientists and engineers today are spending billions of currency units, their time and intelligence in an effort to detect the presence of exotic particles such as gravitons and MACHOs (massively compact halo objects), WIMPs (weakly interacting massive particles), axions and the list keeps growing. All of these particles are regarded hypothetical because they have not been detected yet. However these particles fit certain models and theories which make so much sense and provide logical understanding of Creation and Existence. Instead of the instances of the *naySayer* class that specialize on negative criticism primarily based on their lack of expertise and knowledge, it would do all of humanity a world of good if we focused our collective energies on the attributes and functions of these particles and make them work for the benefit of humankind.

An argument can be - if we can detect these particles then we can harness their function and make them work, which is why we want to detect their presence. Really? Have we detected gravitons which are considered to be the carrier particle for the gravitational force? Yet we are able to leverage gravity and build our entire civilization based on this force. Furthermore, we most definitely have detected radioactive elements and understand the mechanics of nuclear fusion. Yet even today we have not been able to build a fusion reactor, although our Sun is the largest fusion reactor in our solar system. Just because we cannot detect these particles, does not mean they do not exist. As the dominant species on this planet, we need to start focusing on directing our collective energies on discovering the hidden mysteries of Creation and Existence rather than get bogged down with limitations that do not serve us. On a side note I just love the names of these exotic particles. What amount of thought went into coming up with those exotic telltale names - I mean – MACHOS and WIMPS? How cool! ☺

Coming back to our Carrier particle of the Source Force - how does it operate? The core attribute of this 0-D Carrier particle can be explained through the concept of *polymorphism* that I introduced to you earlier in this chapter. Such a particle does not only have mutation attributes, it also has functions in its class definition that can morph and mutate to give birth to new child classes, each with its own specific derived and uniquely identifying attributes. The question now becomes, what makes such a Carrier Particle mutate, morph and adopt all those unique definitions? You can credit the Source Force as the agent responsible to bring about the polymorphism and mutation of the Carrier particle.

The traditional Big Bang Theory did not make any sense, since the *'nothing'* being the source of everything was good for comical relief but did not satisfy rational analysis and logic. The M-Theory was a significant upgrade from the *'nothing'* to revisit the Big Bang Theory and leverage the concept of membranes to provide a compelling and logical explanation of how everything came to be.

---------------------------*****---------------------------

However, I have been asking a question for years since I came to know about the M-Theory and the question was similar to the question I have been asking about the four fundamental forces that seemingly govern the entire physical Universe. I am not a scientist but I am an engineer and we engineers have a unique trait of not taking things for granted. *Show* me the proof or the logical explanation that whets my rational analytical mind and I'll consider it. The M-Theory was great, but it still did not provide that logical explanation that I was looking for.

Just like I had asked the question about the parent, the source of the four fundamental forces in the physical visible Universe (and other forces that exist but not detected by human instrumentation yet), I began questioning the membrane in M-Theory. Where did the membrane come from? Given all the attributes of these membranes, they just cannot be there out of nothing, can they? If they did, we would simply be putting lipstick on the bulldog of the traditional Big Bang Theory.

---------------------------#####---------------------------

M-Theory indicates that the wave-like movements of the membrane leads to collisions, one of which caused that Big Bang which created all that we know about in the physical Universe – visible or dark physical Universe. Granted and yes, that is logical, but what causes these wave-like movements on the membrane? If you take a bath towel (representing our membrane) and laid it down flat in the ground would you see any movement – let alone a wave-like movement? Most definitely not. However only when you pick that towel up from an edge and move that towel up and down do you see that wave-like movement forming on the surface. Alternatively, if you hang the towel outside on a breezy day, you can observe the wave-like movement. Regardless of the mechanism for the towel to move like a wave it needs some energy and hence force that can affect its potential energy. While the towel can be affected to generate that wave-like motion by the application of the mechanical force of your arms or the mechanical force of the breeze, it most definitely cannot move like a wave if the towel was placed in an electromagnetic or gravitational field can it?

This logical reasoning reinforced my cognition about the presence of the Source Force – is it possible that the *membrane* was under the influence of the Source Force that caused its motion? I believed in this theory for a while and then I contradicted and corrected myself as another reactivation of the dormant memories of the *Genetics Of Divinity* from Eternal Consciousness occurred - as I will discuss shortly in this chapter.

Where did the membranes come from? Strings! A bunch (a whole bunch) of strings got tired of being lonely and basking in their own glory, got together and formed these fantastic membranes. Humor aside, this is a plausible and logical explanation for the source of membranes, as we see nature's serious abhorrence of vacuum or lack of purpose everywhere.

But then what is the source of strings? Is there the need for a parent for these strings? Strings are conceptualized to be vibrating in 10 space-time dimensions and the nature of their vibrations affect the specific physical properties of the membranes which in turn collectively contribute to create the form and function of the end object of which they are part of. If you have the same mode vibration of certain strings, which is absolutely possible by the laws of probability you get the same type of membranes and hence the same type of end object. One small change in the mode of vibration will make the end object different from the rest of the pack. From an OOD point of view, changing the values of certain attributes (mode of vibration) of the String class makes it a completely different instance of the String class. This also implies that the String cannot be the source and must have a parent.

---------------------------*****---------------------------

This parent is the carrier particle of the Source Energy and hence Source Force - the source particle of all Existence and the fundamental *matter* behind all Creation. I take my author's license to name this source particle – ***sourceon***, in line with the '*on*' suffix to all the other particles that the scientific community has revealed and have fondly named. The dimensionless, rest massless, *sourceon* exists in the 0th dimension, the Source Particle that is the origin of Source Energy and hence the origin of the Source Force. Every visible and invisible matter in all of Existence is an instance of some child class in the hierarchical family tree of the *sourceon*.

Being part of the 0th dimension its magnitude (length, width and height) is that of a dimensionless point, with no rest mass but only an energy with a specific position in the infiniteness of space. You see whenever we assign a dimension or mass or any other physical attribute to an object, we make it finite. The *sourceon* is a particle in the realm of the infinite where physical laws do not apply. What is important is that the sourceon is a particle of a highly adaptable class that can morph and/or mutate into a plethora of human detectable massive particles which in turn form the secondary building blocks of all physical matter. For the purpose of this chapter, this is all you need to know about the *sourceon* – more details are coming up in Chapter 9.

---------------------------#####---------------------------

Hence the source of all other forces, the Source Force in the 11th dimension and the sourceon – it's carrier or mitigating particle in the 0th dimension, the source of all of that there is, together define the boundaries of the multi-dimensional architecture of Existence as defined in Figure 17. While I refer to the 11th and the 0th dimensions as the *binding dimensions*, I refer to the 10th to the 1st dimension as the *bounded dimensions*.

The Bounded Dimensions – 10-D to 1-D

Let's get grounded on the basic components of your life as they relate to the multi-dimensional hierarchy. This will make it easier for you to understand the bounded dimensions (Tenth down through to the First). These components are
- You are a Creature (and a CREATOR too, being born as a human)
- You have a CREATOR that designed your entire energy entity – physical and non-physical.
- You have myriads of possibilities of life experiences offered to you by Parallelism.
- You have a defined purpose in life (whether you have identified it or not is a different matter) among myriads of possibilities of life purposes that humans such as you can have.

The hierarchical multi-dimensional structure of the bounded dimensions shown in Figure 17 are structured according to different components of Existence.

The Tenth Dimension

From the earlier discussion of String Theory, you are now aware that strings are one-dimensional objects but they are vibrating in ten dimensions – nine spatial dimensions and one dimension of time. The tenth dimension is the highest dimension in the architecture of Creation and Existence where Parallelism is formed. As seen in Figure 17, this is the second highest dimension in the domain or the energy band of Co-creative Synergy, below the 11th Dimension. From the energy derived through the presence of the highly morphable and adaptable Source Energy, the components of the 10-D are organized.

As the first domain of Parallelism in the hierarchical architecture of Creation and Existence, this is the domain of the CREATORs of all Creatures and is referred to as the Creative Domain.

---------------------------*****--------------------------

What is really a CREATOR and a Creature? Remember to focus on the function and not necessarily a certain physical form when I make references to CREATOR or Creature, unless specifically mentioned otherwise. *A CREATOR is the driving energy that originates from a feeling of Bliss (ineffable in the 11th and 10th dimensions) and engages with Passion in the Cycle of CREATION to create the Creature.* This was more of a philosophical definition. For a more scientific definition hang in there until Chapter 9 when I discuss how wave mechanics created all of EXISTENCE.

Top to bottom, the twelve dimensions are structured in a hierarchy of dimensions that go from generic (function only) to specific (form and function). There are five different categories of Creatures and hence specialized CREATORs per category or class, indicated by five different categories of interaction (functions) between energy and matter – this is illustrated in Figure 17 as Type A Energy, Type B Energy, Type C Energy, Type D and Type E Energy – more on this later on in this chapter.

-------------------------#####--------------------------

Given the fact that there are myriads of Creatures in the physical and non-physical dimensions of Existence, all created through Parallelism of matter originating from the *sourceon*, the 10th dimension is hence the Creative Domain for **all** CREATORs of **all** the Creatures in Existence. *Think about this 10th dimension as a consortium of CREATORs that have been setup to collaborate and architect the lower dimensions of EXISTENCE.*

Each class of CREATORs in the 10th dimension have inherited attributes and functions of the Ad INFINITUM CREATOR in the 11th dimension. They have augmented their inherited attributes with their own individual signature or unique characteristic attributes, applied polymorphism to adopt and enhance some of the derived functions and added new characteristic functions to develop unique child classes all of which have been created for very specific purposes to serve and sustain all of EXISTENCE.

---------------------------*****---------------------------

Although there is *segregation of duties* between these CREATORs in the 10th dimension based on their inherited, individualized and *polymorphed* attributes and functions, although they are responsible to define each characteristic attribute and function of the specific Creature classes they create and spawn; due to their inheritance from the Ad Infinitum of the 11th dimension, there are also inherent functions that enable the establishment of symbiotic collaborative relationships through the free will of mutual consent for the purpose of collective coexistence between these CREATORs. This collaboration is not just between two parties, but among the entire consortium of CREATORs who synergistically collaborate to define interdependencies and purpose of all CREATUREs in EXISTENCE. Read that again.

---------------------------#####---------------------------

As an analogy, imagine your own body. Your five senses cohesively interact with each other and report their individual interpretation of a certain event in life to the central brain to react or respond after collecting the inputs from all senses to ultimately provide you with a certain perception about that event. The CREATORs in the 10th dimension operate in this collaborative mode for the purpose of maintaining cohesion in the architecture of Creation and Existence. *There is nothing in Existence without a defined purpose even though you as an individual may not recognize or be aware of it.* The function of the CREATORs of each category or class is to define all possible life experiences for the Creatures that they are responsible. Needless to say, in the 10th dimension these CREATORs that I am referring to are the purest, untainted and un-attenuated forms of energy vibrating in certain frequencies that are characteristic of the 10-D CREATOR class that they represent.

You have heard the term *divide and conquer.* Well that word conquer indicates conflict which is a function of the Human class that is way down in the third dimension. In the 10-D the applicable phrase is *'divide and CREATE'.* In addition to adopting the responsibility for the respective type of Creature that a CREATOR is responsible for, there is also an underlying responsibility to ensure the ability for interaction and exchange of information between the Creature classes for collective coexistence.

What does this ability to interact and exchange information between the classes of Creatures mean? As illustrated in Figure 17 if you refer to the row representing the Third dimension, you will find that there are five broad categories of Creatures. The first is an offshoot of the Type A energy, representing animate and speaking Creatures such as Humans. The second represents a Type B energy or the animate and non-speaking Creatures such as members of the (non-human) animal domain. The third represents the Type C energy or the Creatures of the plant or vegetative domain. The fourth type represents the Type D energy or the inanimate domain as we perceive it and Type E energy that represents the fundamental elements of all physical matter.

The 10-D CREATORs have been set up to ultimately address the forms and functions of the respective Creatures in the 3-D. A human being an

---

Tenth Dimension
CREATOR Type – CREATIVE Domain
(All CREATORs of all CREATURES and all possible life experiences)

example of a Creature of Type A energy can interact with a pet dog as an example of a Creature of Type B energy. A human can also interact with an apple tree by consuming the fruit. A human can also interact with a piece of rock, carving it into a certain shape and build a complicated structure such as a pyramid. The so-called inanimate piece of cosmic rock called Planet Earth – an object of the Type D class of Creatures provides the platform and environment for all other Types of Creatures in the Third Dimension to have a physical life experience. In other words the Creatures in each class must have the ability to interact with each other, in order to meet the specifications in the grand design of Creation and Existence. This follows the same model of integration between classes through a technique called *interfacing* as in Object Oriented Design. Hence the CREATORs in the 10-D are responsible to collectively define Creation and Existence, which is achieved through a definition of possible Creature life experiences in the Ninth Dimension.

The Ninth Dimension

As a software solution architect myself, according to the principles of leading practices of software engineering my first step when I am designing such systems is to visualize and understand the target – the final outcome of the design, or the user expectations from the end product. What is the end product supposed to do? What kind of experiences would the product have by way of user interactions, security threats, maintenance, upgrades, the hardware specifications on which the software would perform during its operational lifetime? How would the product serve and who (type of user) would it serve? Why is the product even required in the first place? What could possibly happen if the end product was not there? What void does the end product fill? What would the repercussions be if the product suddenly stopped to function as designed? What kind of maintenance would be necessary? How frequently? What elements could fail? How could we fix the failed elements?

In essence, what I am defining in the process of this inquisition is to identify the possible experiences the end product can have, which consequently leads to a ***purpose of*** *life* of the end product when it is built and ready to serve. Once the purpose of life is defined can I proceed to define the forms and functions of the end product. This philosophy of design is applicable not only to software engineering but to every product or service worth its salt. Without a well-defined purpose and life-story that involves external interaction and response, the product or service simply cannot exist by itself. Nobody ever creates anything for nothing.

Given the fact that every Creature in Existence must have a purpose, the question arises as to what specific purpose would that be. There can be a plethora of motivating factors, but all of these factors, all the reasons why, boil down to one driving factor - the need to circumvent the possibility of scarcity in Parallelism. It is from the possibility of scarcity that arises the need to fill the void and experience abundance. *Only when lack or scarcity is experienced can the seeds of abundance be sown – recall here the attribute of Creation called* **Contrast**.

Curiously this design philosophy of OOD is founded on the modus operandi of the Ninth dimension of Existence. It is in the 9-D that the CREATORs in the 10-D define all possible life experiences including possible life purposes across the possibilities of Creatures that would occupy the lower dimensions (lower than 9-D through to the 3-D) of Existence. For example if one is considering the possible life experiences and possible life purposes of the Human class, you can imagine the vastness of this domain. The same applies to the life experiences of the non-speaking animate class, the vegetative class and the inanimate class of Creatures. It is important to note that the purpose of the Ninth dimension is simply to provide choices in Parallelism by way of life experiences without actually making any assignments to any Creature. Significant *polymorphism* is at play in the Ninth dimension, thereby expanding the range of possibilities of life experiences. These life experiences when combined define the totality or the singularity of Creation based on the collective roles that Creatures play as being part of Existence. While there is distinctness and uniqueness of each experience, they all collectively contribute to the harmony and overall balance and symphony of Existence.

The Eighth Dimension

The Eighth dimension is the third of the bounded dimensions and is the second in line in the architecture of Creation and Existence where the Creature class is designed. This is where the 10-D Creators define the second most important aspect of Creation – the millions of possibilities of Creature types that would ultimately have one or more of the life experiences defined in the 9-D. During the discussion of the 10-D, I introduced you to the five Types of Creatures in the domains of Coherent and Adaptive Energy (refer to Figure 17), each with a specific band of operating frequency.

The blueprints of each of these Creatures are designed by the respective 10-D CREATORs in the 8-D. In terms of OOD, the 10-D CREATORs would collaborate to define the Creature class and then proceed to define the specific inherited child classes for the domain of Creatures in their purview.

When I am designing my software systems, once that vision of purpose and possible experiences of my software program is clear, I would proceed to define the form and function of the product. What should the native attributes of the product be that would enable it to fulfill its purpose? What inputs does it need from an external source? What functions does it perform with its native attributes and with the inputs that were delivered to it from outside its native definition? What output does it generate? Is the end product self-sufficient to perform all the characteristic functions or does it need to interact with other objects to perform its desired functions? Is the product independently functional or is it dependent on an external object to get activated? Do the outputs from the product impact other external objects? If so, how? Can the end product protect itself from external threats? Should it have self-healing capabilities? What kind of maintenance would be required? How often would such maintenance be required? What could go wrong with the functionality of end product? How can the problem be fixed? Should the product have an early warning system built in to raise alerts about threats to its integrity? Who would use such a product? In what applications would this product be deployed? What interfaces would the product have for an external object to interact with it? Would any specialized skills be required in order to use the end product? Would there by future upgrades to the product? If yes, then what attributes and functions need to be designed for the product so that it remains upward compatible for future upgrades and enhancements? These are just a modest sampling of the basic questions I would ask while I am designing and visioning the form and function of software systems.

Any end product is a sum of components that are designed individually with form (attributes) to perform their respective functions, which collectively would contribute to the attributes and functions of the end product. *Every component has a specific purpose in the operation of the end product, otherwise, not only would the component be useless, it would not be worth the effort to create it to begin with.* Only when a model, a blueprint is developed can I proceed to the next step about leveraging logical programming and technology to implement the model and create that software solution or product.

This basic modeling technique in software engineering is actually the basic modeling technique in all technology including the technology of Creation and Existence illustrated in the framework in Figure 17. Any well designed product will always have a specification sheet which lists all the attributes of the product along with an operating manual explaining the modus operandi of the product and how to leverage its functions using the available interfaces. This book for example has the specifications of its physical size, number of pages, table of contents, font size, font type, a price and also a summary indicating what you will get out of this book when you have finished reading it. As a person looking for a book of this nature, your decision to acquire and read this book would depend on your personal evaluation of these specifications and your feeling of scarcity in your life experience that you believe can be filled up with the information contained here.

In this manner, the 8-D becomes the domain where all the CREATORs design the specifications, the blueprint for the myriads of Creatures (yes, both visible and invisible to the human eye and instrumentation) that collectively form Existence. Note here that *in the 8-D what exists is simply the design of the Creature (the primary class definition) and not the Creature itself (object of the class) with all its forms, functions and interfaces.*

Clearly the CREATORs in the 10-D cannot have any finiteness in form or function, since Existence itself is not finite – yet everything stays in perfect harmony, operating, collaborating, transforming and evolving to provide a plethora of life experiences in absolute synergy. Such is the design of the Creature class in the Eighth dimension.

Simply on planet Earth, there are an estimated 8.7 million species of life-forms not including bacteria. Embarrassing, is it not that we can only *estimate* the number of species that we share the planet with? What about the millions of bacterial life-forms that have not yet been accounted for? What about counting the inanimate world? What about the non-luminous dark matter – they are also elements of Creation aren't they? Yet we know so little or nothing much about them far less contemplate a population census. Being part of this Third Dimension of Existence we humans are (by design) myopic about what is outside our immediate life experience, we can't count them and that makes it even more challenging for us to even contemplate a life purpose for all types and variations

Eighth Dimension
CREATURE Type – CREATURES
(myriad of possibilities for type of CREATURES with possible attributes)

of the millions of possibilities of Creatures that share Existence across its dimensions.

This is the domain of the 8-D. A non-analytical and non-observant human mind would consider life to be an accident, a coincidence of *matter* suddenly deciding on their own to create such millions of possibilities of the Creature class. Interestingly enough, there is also a proposal made in certain circles of so-called experts, who I prefer to call escapists who are unable to figure things out and promote the concept of a *Chaos Theory*. There is no disorder, there is absolutely no accident, no coincidence and definitely no chaos in Existence. The design of Existence is so well architected, perfect, structured, orchestrated and so well integrated that it boggles the uninitiated human mind, leading it to come up with postulates such as the Chaos Theory - a distortion of the truth.

Referring to Figure 17, the Eighth Dimension is the last dimension in the hierarchy of Creation that is depicted as the ***domain of stabilized energy*** and is the domain where the CREATORs collaborate to co-create and co-design the synergy of the grand design of the architecture of Existence. What is meant by *domain of stabilized energy*? This will become clearer as you understand the lower dimensions of Existence. However for the purposes of providing an explanation, this domain occupied by the four dimensions – 11-D down through to the 8-D is a domain of governance – similar to the constitution of a country or the fundamental policies and procedures of operation of a reputed, well-established institution. Once designed, nothing much really changes or needs to change in this domain – hence the energy is stabilized. What is meant by *energy stabilization* and how does such a stabilization occur? Great questions and I would counsel you to wait until you arrive at Chapter 9 when it will all be clear. The focus of the CREATORs is not to introduce new designs all the time, but more to ensure that the overarching synergy of Existence is held in cohesion in the lower dimensions just as it was designed in this domain (8-D to the 11-D). Read that last sentence again. Are you always seeking to start new projects or do you focus on consolidating the stability and reliability of the current ones?

The Seventh Dimension

The transition from the generality and overarching design of Existence from the domain of stabilized energy to more specificity of Creation occurs in the Seventh Dimension. This is the dimension where the *delegate and implement* (as opposed to the divide and conquer metaphor) organization of Creation takes root. The 7-D is the dimension where the Source Energy is polymorphed (recall the discussion of polymorphism earlier in this chapter) into five distinct types of energy forms, each representing the five building blocks of the Third Dimension of Existence.

From the discussion of the 10-D you are aware about the role played by the CREATORs of each of these five energy types. While in the 10-D these CREATORs have collaborated in the domain of stabilized energy to define the synergy of all Existence, the Seventh Dimension is where the actual deployment of the diversity of Existence is initiated. The focus shifts to inherit the attributes and functions from the stabilized domain into the more specific five types of energy forms, which will eventually be leveraged to design the form and function of the physical Third Dimension.

Before diving into the description of the five energy types it is important to understand the foundation of Existence. Any Creature in the Third Dimension cannot be self-sustaining and self-contained, since Existence is all about symbiotic collaborative synergy. The 7-D is the first dimension in this diversity of Creation where these principles of *delegate and implement* become more focused.

A careful scrutiny of the 7-D as illustrated in Figure 17 will reveal that the Creature is in '*Active*' energy – what does that mean? Active energy refers to the transformation of the potential energy of the higher dimension to the energy that would be instrumental to ultimately implement and bring about the manifestation of the myriads of objects of the Creature class in the physical Third Dimension. This is the dimension where the Creature is upgraded from a visionary stage (primary class definition) to the stage of more detailed design with specific (attributes) forms and functions (child class per Energy band), adhering to the synergy of the higher dimensions. In other words, the activities to implement the Creature start in the 7-D. Let's now understand the five types of energy that are instituted in the 7-D, laying the foundation for a physical Existence in the 3-D.

In the 7-D the form and functions of each of the five type of energy forms (or energy bands) are defined. The Creature class of the 8-D becomes the parent class of each child class in the 7-D that would define the blueprint of each object that would ultimately have a physical existence in the 3-D. For example the entire human anatomy including the physical and non-physical components of the *Human* class would be defined in the 7-D just like the physical and the non-physical components of the *EvergreenPlant class* or the *CarnivoreMammal* class or the *HabitablePlanet* class would be defined. Note here that the 7-D is the dimension of specific design for the specific energy bands and not the manifestation of the design itself.

Scientifically speaking if you continue to look deeper and deeper inside any physical object you will find that no physical matter exists – what exists is empty space with a particular frequency of vibration, or the potential energy of the object. Each of the five types of energy that I will describe defines a specific range of frequency of vibration or an energy band. Consider the example of FM, AM, HAM radio, your cellphone and your shortwave radio - all of these have different range of electromagnetic energy frequencies or bandwidth where the signals are transmitted and received. The five energy bands that define the diversity of the 7-D and lower dimensions also have a specific bandwidth each, which in turn determines the form and function of the objects of the Creature class that conform to that energy band.

Lower the frequency band, the object becomes

more stable and simpler in its form and function and hence has access to fewer choices of life experience through Parallelism. Consequently, higher the frequency band, more complex and dynamic the object becomes from an attribute and function point of view with greater and greater choices offered to the object through Parallelism.

Type E Energy Band

Type E energy is the lowest band of energy allocated to the forms and functions of the basic elements that are found on Earth and in astronomical bodies (at least where humans have probed) that are included in the Mendeleev's Periodic table. Type E energy is the simplest form of energy that is the source behind the form and function of the simplest form of visible matter. Since science has not yet been able to quite get its arms around dark matter, it will be a matter of conjecture if there are other elements beyond the Mendeleev's periodic table that constitute dark matter. Logic most definitely indicates that dark matter consists of other elements that human instrumentation (based on the detection of characteristics of the known elements) cannot detect - yet. Nonetheless, these basic elements are part of the Type E energy band providing the building blocks for higher energy and for more complex Creatures to exist.

In the 7-D, Type E energy is responsible to set the foundation, the basic design of the forms and functions of the different basic elements (for simplicity and context of this book, let us stay restricted to the residents of the Mendeleev's periodic table). In Figure 17, I have used examples of the chemical representation of the elements carbon (C), hydrogen (H_2), oxygen (O_2), nitrogen (N_2) since these three elements in addition to phosphorous (P) and sulfur (S) form the building blocks of life forms that we know about on Earth. In our search for extra-terrestrial life, till date the primary focus remains to determine if these elements are present in the atmosphere and soil of a planetary body. If they are, it makes us strongly believe that life as we perceive it, could exist outside Earth. NASA has indicated that arsenic (As) based life forms also exist on Earth, thereby expanding our perception of the possible building blocks of life or Creatures in an extra-terrestrial domain.

In my opinion, human intelligence in this matter is plagued by myopia of mis-conception and perceived bias of what we call life. Is it possible that there are other life forms out there that are non-luminous and do not generate electromagnetic energy waves for human instrumentation to detect? Why not? Parallelism indicates it is possible. Quantum mechanics indicates it is possible. The discovery of dark matter indicates that it is possible. Just because human consciousness and the current sophistication of instrumentation cannot detect these such life forms, it is not appropriate to rule out their existence.

We are primarily carbon based life forms on planet Earth. The Cassini spacecraft is sending us evidence that may prove methane based life forms on one of Jupiter's moons – Titan. Methane is represented by the formula (CH_4). Some astro-biologists have indicated that ammonia (represented by the chemical formula NH_3) based life forms are possible through we don't have proof just yet. But then methane and ammonia are not Creatures that follow the Type E class of energy, since they these chemicals are compounds (their molecular structure is made up of a chemical combination of the basic elements – nitrogen, carbon and hydrogen).

You have been introduced earlier to two of the four fundamental forces earlier in this book – the *strong* and *weak* nuclear forces. Type E energy is also the source of these two fundamental forces – getting defined in their function in the 7-D. In the 7-D the stage is set by the definition of the function of these strong and weak nuclear forces to ultimately make an impact on the atomic integrity and consistency of the basic chemical elements of Type E energy in the physical 3-D.

Type E energy, as we can now conclude, relates to the definition of basic building blocks – two of the four fundamental forces (strong and weak nuclear forces) and the definition (not implementation) of the fundamental chemical elements of all matter – visible or dark, that defines the form and function of all other Creatures that are to have physical life experience ultimately in the 3-D.

Type D Energy Band

Type D energy is allocated to the frequency band and consequently to the class of Creatures that common human perception considers as *Inanimate Matter*. The word *inanimate* refers to what human perception considers not to have any self-initiated motion a core component of *life*.

Most certainly the chair that you are sitting on right now is not exhibiting any motion or in terms of basic physics, not exhibiting any displacement of its own from its relative position; but that does not mean it is not in incessant pulsating motion at the atomic level of the material that makes up the chair. Nonetheless, considering animation to be a core component of what humanity calls *life*, the chair or the mountain or the astronomical bodies that you can or cannot observe, this *Inanimate* world is considered to be Type D energy. *Objects of the Creature class conforming to Type D energy provide the platform or the substrate where objects of other Creature classes and hence other higher energy types can exist.* Collective co-existence is embedded in the roots.

Next time you set foot on soil, make it a point to send some gratitude towards Mother Earth. When you drink your next glass of water, send unconditional love and gratitude towards the water. As Dr. Masaru Emoto has proven and writes in his book *The Healing Power Of Water*, when you send positive vibrations (through words and thoughts) towards water, it changes the crystalline structure of water molecules and restores its life giving and sustaining qualities exponentially. I personally have developed a habit to send positive and grateful thoughts towards my dwellings, vehicles, books, equipment and other inanimate objects that I use on a daily basis to enrich my life and make it more comfortable – all for good reason. This is called sympathetic resonant vibration – a core principle to make the heavily touted and more grossly misinterpreted Law of Attraction work as I will explain in the next chapter.

As you can understand, Creatures of Type E energy that we have discussed earlier, need to *get together* to form the Type D energy band of Creatures. Well, how do they get together or what makes them choose through Parallelism to get together to form the world that humans consider inanimate in the 3-D? Why can you not walk through a brick wall? When you sit in your vehicle, why don't you fall right through the floor on the road? When you set foot on soil why don't you do right through the planet? When you drop that basketball on the ground why does it bounce back and not sink into the ground?

This leads us to the definition of the two remaining fundamental forces – gravitational force and electromagnetic force that get defined though Type D energy in the 7-D. The gravitational force is responsible to ultimately get Type E energy objects together in the 3-D, but what keeps the bond between them is the electromagnetic force between the constituent atoms of that 3-D object. The gravitational force is a rather weak force (which is why you can easily lift a fallen hammer from the floor) – the electromagnetic force is what forms the *glue* within matter in the 3-D. This is why we have solids, liquids, gases and their transient states of matter in the 3-D – due to the varying strengths of the electromagnetic forces among the constituent atoms that make up matter.

-------------------------*****-------------------------

In addition to the definition of the fundamental forces - gravitational and electromagnetic force, Type D energy is also the source of *derived forces* such as the frictional force, shear, centripetal and centrifugal force. Type D energy also defines the blueprint for several physical attributes for Creatures in the 3-D, such as inertia, momentum (velocity), tension and torque – all if which you must have learned about in grade school Physics. All of these forces and attributes of the physical 3-D plane of Existence are defined in the 7-D as Type D energy.

As you can understand, objects that conform to Type D energy are of paramount importance and usefulness, (contrary to common human perception of taking inanimate objects for granted) by providing the platform, the substrate for any other Creatures to be derived from Type D or other higher energy bands to exist eventually in physical form in the 3-D. Moreover the definition of the two remaining fundamental forces - gravitational and electromagnetic forces from Type D energy is critical for Existence in the 3-D. All other Creatures of the higher energy types – C, B and A in the 3-D leverage the building blocks defined by Type E and Type D energy.

-------------------------#####-------------------------

Type C Energy Band

The next higher band of frequencies are occupied by ***Type C energy*** in the 7-D. As seen in Figure 17, this energy band refers to Creatures that would be more complex in their forms and functions in a 3-D plane of Existence when compared to the other two energy Types that had been described so far. You are now aware of the purpose of Type E and Type D energies – they are the building blocks of the higher energy band Creatures. What purpose would the Type C energy band provide for Existence? In the 7-D, Type C energy leverages the foundation offered by Type E and Type D energy and provides the framework for Creatures that would eventually provide a source of sustenance for the Creatures of Type B and Type A in the 3-D.

As illustrated in Figure 17, an example of a Creature in the 3-D that would exist based on the model of Type C energy would be vegetation. It is common knowledge that plants consume carbon dioxide (a Type D Creature) created from a chemical compound of the elements carbon and oxygen (Type E Creatures) and use chlorophyll (a Type C attribute) to undergo a chemical reaction called *photosynthesis* (a Type C function) leveraging sunlight (a

Type D electromagnetic energy) to create oxygen (Type E Creature) and water (Type D Creature). Whoa! Read that again until you understand the magnanimity of the last sentence (I read it a few times myself after I wrote it down).

On planet Earth in the 3-D, vegetation is the primary source of oxygen that the majority of animal and microbial life (Type B and Type A energy Creatures) need to breathe and hence survive. Yes, please save those trees and our forests – we need these Type C Creatures doing what they are designed to do so that we can survive.

Simply considering vegetation as the only Type C Creature would be myopic. The reason for the majority of animal and microbial life on planet Earth to be reliant on oxygen is due to the *mitochondria* in the body cells. Mitochondria are tasked with the function to convert oxygen and other nutrients into chemical energy that keeps the physical body alive and active to perform our life functions in the 3-D. However, we know about *anaerobic* bacteria living in the human gastrointestinal tract that do not require oxygen to survive. A new species of animal life called *Loricifera* was discovered deep in the Mediterranean seafloor in 2010 that have no mitochondria but *hydrogenosomes* that require no oxygen to produce the necessary chemical energy to survive. These *Loricifera* live in environments that mimic Earth's condition 600 billion years ago. Isn't that fascinating?

Why is that fascinating? Well, this proves that vegetation is not the only source of sustenance for Creatures of Type B and Type A to exist in the 3-D – even on Planet Earth. Moreover human search has not found vegetation or any life forms for that matter based on common human perspective of life anywhere else in the physical Universe. That does not mean Type A, B and C Creatures that are not known yet to humanity do not exist. Hence vegetation is only but an example of Type C Creature in the 3-D. Just like we humans are not aware of all that is considered Existence it would behoove us to accept that other Creatures created through Type C energy does exist in the 3-D somewhere else in Existence. Logic and Parallelism makes ample provision for this to be true and denial is a waste of valuable time and energy that could otherwise be used to increase human consciousness.

---------------------------*****--------------------------

In the Seventh Dimension, Type C energy defines the blueprint for Creatures that would eventually provide a source of sustenance for the Type B and Type A energy bands in the 3-D. If the Type C energy band was not an integral part of Creation, Type A and Type B energy bands would be useless to even contemplate.

The Type C energy band is also the first in the 7-D to introduce and define the attribute of *genetics* to Creatures in the 3-D and this is carried forward to Type B and Type A energy bands as well, albeit with greater complexity. This blueprint or the genetic code is held in the DNA (deoxyribonucleic acid, found in every cell of every Creature from Type C up to Type A that have so far been documented). DNA is a polymer found in every living cell. The DNA includes the protocols to be followed by the Creature in the 3-D to engage in *mitosis* (growth by cell division) and *meiosis* (reproduction), thereby expanding the horizon of Creation in the 3-D. I introduced you to the 12 strand human DNA earlier in Chapter 6 and there will be more on the human DNA coming up.

In terms of OOD that you have been introduced to earlier, if one were to define a class for Type C energy it would definitely be more complicated when compared to Type D simply based on the forms and functions possible through Type C energy. Furthermore, child classes from the Type C parent class would inherit, undergo extensive polymorphism and even demonstrate multiple inheritance (for example cross breeding of roses for different colors, the sweet pea and without prejudice about ethics, a plethora of genetically modified vegetation that our scientists have created today). Type C energy band is where the proliferation of Existence and hence the concept of *'species'* begins.

---------------------------#####--------------------------

What an amazing synergistic and collaborative Grand Design of Creation and Existence! Knowing this information in itself is liberating and awakening.

Type B Energy Band

This leads us to the more advanced band - **Type B** energy band in the Seventh Dimension that provides the blueprint for more complex Creatures that would eventually exist in the 3-D. This energy band is associated to what we humans refer to as the *Animate* world but with a twist. Type B energy refers to the energy band of Creatures that would eventually exist in the 3-D plane of Existence as *Animate* but also *Non-Speaking and devoid of rational decision making capabilities*. I will explain this in greater detail in the discussion of the Third Dimension but for now consider the members of the animal kingdom that are not capable of *coherent and intelligent speech* nor are they equipped with the attributes of rational analysis – they would be every member of the animal kingdom apart from humans.

Note here that researchers state that dolphins, whales and some other species of animals do have a language of communication and that is true. However that language of communication is bounded within a finite range of patterns and sound frequencies and the consistency of reaction to those frequencies by members of those species of animals is questionable. What I am referring to here is the ability for coherent, dynamic and intelligent speech that Third Dimensional Creatures sourced from Type B energy do not possess. However, imagine the jump in complexity from a Type C to a Type B energy band. If the inheritance, polymorphism and multiple inheritance of Type C Creatures impresses you, magnify it as many times as your logical imagination can carry and you would have the vastness of the Type B class of Creatures that could exist in the 3-D.

In the 7-D the blueprint of all Creatures of Type B energy is created, with all their respective forms and functions. Do your own research and you will find that apparently there are 7.7 million species of animals (Type B Creatures) only on planet Earth opposed to about 0.3 million species of plants. Granted that we have not found life as we perceive life to be, anywhere else in the physical Universe that we have explored, but why do we still search for such life? It is because we are sure that there is life elsewhere other than planet Earth – we are just not capable to detect those signatures of life just yet. Could it be that our search for extraterrestrial life is prejudiced by the physical environmental conditions that govern life on Earth? Is it possible that life does exist in other extraterrestrial planets but in so unique forms and functions that it is inconceivable to the human intelligence? Is that life superior to us? In what way? There is no mandate in Existence that enforces the same Earth-like lifeforms anywhere else. So the number of possible Type B Creatures could rise to astronomical proportions from a 7-D perspective.

The particular frequency of vibration for a particular instance of Type B Creature in the 3-D within the Type B energy band provides the uniqueness in its form and function and hence augments the concept of *species* that I have explained earlier while discussing Type C energy. A whale, a tiger, an ant and an earthworm are all instances of Type B energy in the 3-D. However the particular frequency of vibration within the Type B energy band is what makes these animals so different in so many aspects of form and function – object orientation and Parallelism at diligent work.

Just like the Creatures of the Type C energy band, there are distinct species in the 3-D that have their origins based on the Type B energy band. In the 7-D the form and function of each species of Type B energy is defined – almost like a molding cast. Even when there are variations (*sub-species*) within the species for example an African lion and an Indian lion, their blueprint created in the 7-D has the same origins to begin with, after which polymorphism in the 7-D inserts additional unique attributes and functions to each sub-species of the same *Panthera Leo* (Lion) species.

---------------------------*****---------------------------

Type B energy in the 7-D as you can understand, is the breakaway energy band for the world of Creatures that we call *animate*, minus the ability of coherent and intelligent speech, rational analysis and decision making. This is a rather complex form of energy that leverages all the lower energy bands (Types E, D and C) and inserts the higher functions of *Relationship* with both intra-energy band and inter-energy band Creatures, *skeletal structure, muscular power, sense of territoriality, self-defense mechanisms, a central nervous system along with other physiological systems and basic survival instincts (fight, flight or freeze)* into the blueprint of its Creature class.

The genetics or the DNA structure of Type B Creatures in the 3-D, needless to say, is quite more complicated than that found in Type C Creatures due to an increased degree of freedom enjoyed by Creatures instantiated according to the blueprint of Type B energy. The functions of mitosis and meiosis as discussed for Type C energy continue to exist in the blueprint of Creatures to be instantiated from Type B energy, however the actual implementation of the process of cell division (mitosis) and cell reproduction (meiosis) are different between instances of Type B Creature child classes.

---------------------------#####---------------------------

I personally do believe and know that planet Earth is not the only physical 3-D domain where Creatures blueprinted by the five types of energy bands exist. Parallelism allows the existence of other Earth-like domains or other domains beyond our comprehension to exist that sustain life in forms and functions that are beyond human comprehension. Our definition of life in all likelihood is finite and falls short of the true definition of life. Just because human perception today cannot go beyond what we see or detect through our instrumentation, it does not mean other Creatures of Type B does not exist in other 3-D domains that we have not discovered and explored just yet. If we are the only ones that define life, EXISTENCE would be such a waste of space, wouldn't it? Given the fact that nothing can exist without a purpose, it behooves humanity to accept and stay reverent to the magnanimity of Creation.

But rather than investing time and energy in the quest to find other 3-D platforms where other Creatures of Type C through Type A energy bands could exist, I find it more productive and useful to focus on our own planet, on the consciousness of humanity and secure our own presence and role in the grid of Existence. To stay open to the idea of the plethora of fantastic possibilities of Creation is prudent in my opinion and serves more academic interest than any fruitful outcomes at this time of rebirth of human consciousness. From a practical application of the human faculties point of view, humanity needs to focus to upgrade our consciousness from a Type 0 to a Type 1 civilization as the one and only Dr. Michio Kaku so eloquently describes. Only then would we have upgraded consciousness for all humanity and serve our purpose in Existence – for a while. When we have secured our own life experience we would have earned the consciousness to seek out and build symbiotic collaborative relationships with other physical extra-terrestrial domains of Existence.

Type A Energy Band – You, For Example!

This brings us to the **Type A** band of energy in the 7-D, which provides the blueprint for the most complicated, most sophisticated, most harmonious, most well-endowed, most advanced, most empowered, most capable Creatures who would eventually exist in the 3-D. Figure 17 indicates an example of such Creatures as humans, which as you can guess by now is clearly not the only Type A Creature possible in the 3-D across the physical dimension of Existence. This is the blueprint for Creatures who are *animate* and capable of *coherent and intelligent speech and able to make rational decisions through the analysis of choices in life experience offered by Parallelism.*

Interestingly, 'speech' for Type A Creatures in the 3-D does not necessarily relate to the act of speaking through specific vibration of vocal chords. There are instances of Type A energy in the 3-D who are capable of intelligent and coherent communication without actually speaking. Such Creatures are endowed with the capability of intuitive communication without verbal communication. You don't have to travel beyond this planet to find such Type A Creatures. Romantically involved couples, siblings, identical twins, parent-child relationships have been reported to engage in such intuitive communication even when they are not sharing the same physical space. Others can read body language and analyze the mode and style of dressing to communicate intelligibly. Graphology or handwriting analysis is used by some experts to obtain insight on the psychological makeup of subject. Yet others can communicate simply through eye contact. Disabled people with one or more senses impaired can still communicate rather intelligibly (Dr. Stephen Hawkins as a popular contemporary example). There are others like me who can read a person's *energy* without any verbal communication and develop an accurate enough profile about the personality traits, which comes as an extremely valuable tool in the process of establishing symbiotic collaborative relationships.

Another key attribute of 3-D Creatures instantiated through the blueprint of Type A energy in the Seventh dimension is rationality. This is the key factor that separates Type A Creatures from any of the lower energy band Creatures. The functions of reasoning, rationalization, analysis and decision making is a significant upgrade from the instinctive flight, fight or freeze functions of Creatures conforming to the Type B energy band.

--------------------------*****--------------------------

However the most important attribute provisioned by Type A energy to instances of its conforming Creatures in the 3-D, the most unique and the most empowering attribute is the *duality of roles of Creation in the singularity of the instance of the Type A entity in physical form in the 3-D*. A discussion of just this one attribute of *duality in singularity* would require an entire chapter in its own right. Only the Type A energy band makes provisions for the duality of both the Creature and the CREATOR roles of Creation in the individual physical instance (hence the reference to *singularity*) of the Type A Creature in the 3-D.

Recall the discussion about *multiple inheritance* earlier in this chapter – the concept in OOD where a child class can inherit attributes and functions from multiple parent classes. Type A energy in the 7-D demonstrates the application of multiple inheritance where attributes and functions of both the CREATOR and Creature parent classes converge into one child class to form the Type A energy band definition in the 7-D. Type A energy, as illustrated in Figure 17 defines the form and functions derived from the duality of the CREATOR-Creature relationship to be instantiated in a Creature in physical form in the 3-D.

By virtue of your birth as a human YOU ARE a CREATOR with the will to bestow and a Creature at the same time living in the same physical body with the will to receive and enjoy unbounded delight in your physical life experience. Nothing and nobody can change this postulate of Creation. As you complete this book, you will be introduced to your CREATOR attributes and functions that lay dormant within your collective 3-D physical and mortal Adaptivebody and your 5-D non-physical and immortal Activebody. Once you are convinced about the duality of your personal existence, you would upgrade yourself to a higher level of consciousness. You would then begin to actively engage in the Cycle of Creation to first define your desires under the guidelines of logical and ethical feasibility and then be, do or have all your desires fulfilled en-route to your enjoyment of unbounded delight.

-------------------------#####-------------------------

Needless to say, an example of a Creature instantiated in the 3-D from Type A energy would be humans - the most advanced, sophisticated, complex, well-endowed, lavishly-empowered super species in physical existence on planet Earth. Given the plethora of possibilities offered by Parallelism in a multi-dimensional Existence it would also be equally needless to state that humans are not the only examples of instantiation of Type A energy – which occupies the widest range of frequencies of Creation when compared to the other lower 7-D energy bands.

Could there be a definition of a Type A+ or higher energy bands in the Seventh dimension? The domain of human knowledge in the 3-D plane of Existence based on the inheritance of attributes from the parent Creature class, has been chronically stymied through this dependence on tactile, visual, olfactory, auditory and gustatory feedback received from the subject of observation. With this limited consciousness about Creation, the average human would find it challenging to believe that energy bands higher than Type A could exist. However when logic and Parallelism is considered with an appreciation for the vastness of the extent of Creation, the same human could definitely contemplate the presence of higher energy bands in the 7-D than what is considered observable.

In my opinion however and for some reason my *Activebody* does not deny this opinion, the Type A energy band is the highest possible energy band of Creatures in all of the Third Dimension of Existence. We humans, being part of this energy band are yet to discover our true and full identity. Why else would just gram of the human DNA be capable of storing 5.5 Petabytes of data? How much of ourselves do we not know yet? Why else would we have such an incessant hunger to learn and grow? Why else should we even bother to realize the magnanimity of the code of Eternal Consciousness and embark on this voyage to reactivate the *Genetics Of Divinity?* Humanity has just been reborn on December 21st 2012, the anniversary of the 26,000 year cycle of Galactic Alignment, into the next phase of our evolution as a Type A Creature of Existence - the best is yet to come.

Could there be other instances of Type A Creatures who are more advanced than we humans are? Most definitely! The physical Universe is 13.7 billion Earth years old according to our calculations and although humans seem to have appeared on this planet only about 200,000 years ago, our recorded history only dates back only 5,000 years. It would be grossly inappropriate to assume that humans are the only instances of the Type A class when we have such a brief history in Existence. Logic and unemotional rational analysis indicates that there are most definitely other instances of Type A energy on other 3-D domains that are more advanced in their consciousness and have activated more sections of the code of the *Genetics Of Divinity*, which in turn makes them more advanced as a civilization than us humans. Again, in my personal opinion, investing our resources in searching for their presence at this time in the evolution of humanity is unproductive. Humanity should rather invest in self-discovery of unexplored attributes and functions of the supreme Type A energy band to upgrade our level of consciousness and thereby fulfill our role and responsibility in the grid of Existence.

While Creatures of the Type A energy band in the 3-D can dominate and intervene in the life experience of others of the same energy band and also Creatures in the Type B and C energy bands, much needs to be achieved to understand and harness the Creatures in Type D and E energy bands in the spirit of collective coexistence.

We humans are still helpless against what is commonly termed as natural disasters (Type D energy). Hurricanes, earthquakes, tsunamis, drought, flood that operate under a default operating system and continue to disrupt human life and livelihood. We humans have still not been able to harness nuclear fusion (Type E energy) – an everyday occurrence in our Sun. When such milestones are reached that enable us to control this blue marble in the cosmos that we call Earth, will the most endowed species in this planet migrate from a Type 0 to a Type 1 civilization as Dr. Michio Kaku explains.

We humans are not using our class definitions to the fullest, which is why we live in this artificial reality of lack and scarcity, pain and conflict. If a more advanced alien of Type A energy would visit humanity and file a report to the MASTER CREATOR, in all likelihood it would say that we are a progressive species leveraging only a measurably small portion of the Eternal Consciousness to undergo a life experience on this planet and hence are in the infancy of our evolution. My life purpose to share the *Genetics of Divinity* with you and encourage others who have tapped or will tap into the other segments of this code of Eternal Consciousness is to upgrade our civilization from infancy to the young adult stage of our evolution and live in a Parallel Universe of peace, love, security, health, harmony and abundance through the service of others for the purpose of collective coexistence. My belief is that you will join this quest.

The Sixth Dimension

With the Seventh dimension providing the blueprint of the Creatures who would eventually have a physical experience in a 3-D physical existence, the Sixth dimension of Creation is all about defining the plethora of possible life experiences for these Creatures as appropriate for the energy band. The number and extent of possible life experiences available to the Creature when it would eventually exist in physical form in the 3-D, are proportional to the attributes and functions blueprinted for the Creature at a particular energy band in the 7-D. The 6-D hence can be considered to be the dimension where Parallelism of life experiences per energy band is initiated - the aggregation of all possible life experiences for all Creatures within each energy band.

How do we define *life experience*? *Life* represents the duality of Existence of every Creature – a physical mortal existence in the 3-D bound by the Fourth Dimension of time and a non-physical immortal existence in the 5-D independent of the factor of time as illustrated in Figure 17. *Experience,* in this representation of life hence also demonstrates the duality of Creation depending on the plane of Existence – the physical Third Dimension or the non-physical Fifth Dimension. *While the physical experience of the Creature in its 3-D physical form is finite and hence mortal, the non-physical experience of the Creature in the 5-D is infinite and hence immortal.* Read that again. YOU (composed of your 3-D and 5-D selves) **ARE** IMMORTAL – get over the futile debate now.

As you can understand, more complex the blueprint or the class definition of the energy band, greater are the number of possible *life experiences* and hence choices in Parallelism for Creatures in that energy band when they exist in physical form in the 3-D. This is illustrated in Figure 17 where Type A energy can provision a myriad of possibilities for life experiences for its conforming Creatures, whereas Type E energy can afford comparatively limited number of possibilities of life experiences in the 3-D.

Not all attributes and functions in the class definition of an energy band are necessary for the fulfillment of every life experience possible for the Creature. Some may be mandatory, some optional while some have no role to play in certain life experiences. In some cases a combination of available attributes and functions in the class definition are required to describe a life experience. In other cases certain life experiences for a Creature conforming to a certain energy band may require a combination of interactions with Creatures conforming to the same or other energy bands.

The combination of these choices made by the Creature either compulsively by the design of Creation (lower energy bands) or consciously through the application of knowledge, perception and decision making (higher energy bands) becomes a certain life experience for that Creature – the sum of parts.

For example, the element oxygen with a *valency* of 2 is restricted to combine with any other element with a *valency* of 1, 2 or 4 which is a design of life experience for this instance of Type E energy. The oxygen atom cannot make a choice to have any valency other than 2, since it has only 6 of the 8 electrons in the outer orbit of its atom. On the contrary you, an instance of Type A energy empowered by the attributes and functions of intelligence, rationality and free will, can at this very moment choose to continue to read this book or choose to make any of the millions of choices about how to use your time to have a different life experience – all provisioned for you through the definition in the Sixth Dimension.

A different choice in Parallelism in the 6-D made for the Creature in the lower energy bands or decided by the Creature in the higher energy bands would create an entirely different life experience for that Creature. So, whether you believe and agree to it or not, your current status in any aspect of your life experience, be it health, financial, social, intellectual, relational etc are all experiences that YOU have chosen from the other possible statuses in these areas of your life experience. As an instance of Type A energy all that was done for you was the definition of your Type A Creature class in the 6-D with all possible choices of life experiences that you could potentially choose from.

You have been designed to enjoy whatever life experience YOU choose to have in the 3-D in physical form. Nobody can dictate your life experience – it's all your choice. This is YOUR personal free will as you already know by now, which is the attribute and function that allows YOU as a Creature of Type A energy to choose from the possible life experiences defined for you in the 6-D. What choices have you made for yourself thus far in your life? Have they brought you emotions of unbounded delight?

Could the number of possible life experiences for the Creature class of a particular energy band as defined in the 6-D change or are they locked in for eternity of Existence? I have contemplated on this question for a long time and quite honestly I had given up trying to find an answer on my own. I believe that the laws of Creation based on the principle of infiniteness already has endowed the energy bands with ample choices to make in the life experience and it would serve us more to gratefully explore what is already provisioned rather than engaging in such idle conjecture.

I am convinced today that unless there is a change in the attributes and functions of the Creature class it is not worthwhile to change the number of life experiences provided by Parallelism for that particular class. So the finiteness or infiniteness of the number of possible life experiences in the 6-D is actually dependent on the blueprint defined for the Creature in the 7-D.

In the higher dimensions (5-D and up) that I have described so far, if you noticed, there is no factor of time. There is no past, there is no present and there is no future in these higher dimensions. I agree this may be a challenge for you to imagine just yet, but instead of refuting the concept, consider what would happen if there was nothing like past, present or future? Everything - all of reality, was here and now. This means that everything that you desire within the guidelines of logical and ethical feasibility is already yours in physical reality. As a matter of fact *want* or *desire* represents an intent to have something that was lacking in the past, is lacking in present as well, to be available in the future. *If there is no past, present or future the concept of want or desire becomes irrelevant.* Read that again.

---------------------------*****---------------------------

There is no chaos, there is no disorder in the grand design of Creation and Existence. Everything necessary to sustain Existence in perfect harmony and collaborative co-existence is already in place exactly as it should be. Humanity so far, has not matured enough in consciousness to understand the grand design Creation and Existence. Your understanding of the material presented in this book will accelerate your journey to upgrade your consciousness which you can leverage to experience unbounded delight as a Creature as you traverse your journey through the 4-D.

This sub-optimal maturity of human consciousness is the reason why we talk about *evolution,* which by the way is a 4-D postulate applied to a 3-D plane of Existence. Evolution is based on progression of the quality of life in the physical 3-D and the very word progression implies the Fourth dimension of time – a past, a present and a future maturity. In reality all possible life experiences are already set, waiting for humanity to leverage. As human intelligence and consciousness aligns itself more and more to the full blueprint of the *Human* class as defined in the 7-D, we will discover new Parallel Universes, which would be just the unfolding of unexplored life experiences. The truth is, there is nothing new to discover by way of life experiences in the higher dimensions of Existence. The newness of the discovery - an attribute of the lower dimensions by itself is a concept of the Fourth Dimension of time

--------------------------#####--------------------------

Whatever you have experienced in your life so far – be it your perception of a good, bad or indifferent event, all of those life experiences are just a smattering of all the possibilities that have been defined for the Type A energy band and specifically for the *Human* class. The next person that you can think of could have had exactly the same life experience but might not have chosen to follow your example. By way of debate you may be thinking about the life experiences that seem to be distinct and different among the sexes (for example childbirth, and other anatomical an emotional attributes). Could you as a male choose to have the same life experiences as a female and vice versa? ☺ Yes, but that choice is not made by you while you are in the 3-D. The decision about your sex is a choice you make much earlier in the 5-D before you are born in your physical body in the 3-D. Brace yourself to upgrade your consciousness forever – of course if you remain coachable and open to receive this forthcoming information.

The Fifth Dimension

If you have not become engrossed in this book until now, if you are not wildly excited about Creation and Existence by now, it's time to be so. Those dormant memories of the *Genetics Of Divinity* must be reactivating in your subconscious mind all throughout your journey so far – the only way is up from now on if you are going to provide your consent with your free will to stick to the reactivation process. This section of the book may seem radical to your current perceptions and belief systems that you have nurtured until now. Parallelism will offer you a choice to either reject all or some of what you are about to learn or a choice to investigate, research or learn further before you agree to accept this forthcoming information as the Eternal Truth.

With the blueprint for the Creature class for the respective energy band defined in the 7-D and the Parallelism of possible life experiences defined for that Creature class in the 6-D, the Fifth dimension is where first instantiation of the individual Creature of that energy band takes place. Essentially, in the 5-D, the Active energy of the 7-D transforms into the Active energy of the individual Creature conforming to the corresponding energy band. *This individualized instantiation of the Creature class in the 5-D is in a non-physical form and technically speaking the 5-D is where the individual instance of the Creature class is born into coherent Existence.*

Refer to Figure 17 where I have illustrated the Fifth to the Seventh dimensions. These three dimensions collectively form the domain of *coherent energy*. What does that mean? During the discussion on the five energy bands in the 7-D, I believe it was clear enough for you that none of these bands were self-sufficient and could not exist efficiently without the existence of the other bands, specifically, the Type E and Type D bands of energy are fundamental in nature and they form the building blocks of all the higher energy bands.

Higher the energy band, more dependent does it become on and hence more *reverent* it becomes about the lower energy bands to fulfill its role in Existence. For example, without the chemical elements found in the Mendeleev's periodic table (Creatures of Type E energy) it would not be possible for the astronomical physical bodies (Creatures of Type D energy) to be formed in the 3-D. Without these astronomical bodies providing the platform for Existence there would be no flora (Type C energy). Without flora, fauna (Type B and A energy) could not exist.

Lower the energy band, the more dependent it remains on the higher energy bands to maintain its integrity and operational efficiency. For example, if humans (Creature of Type A energy) suddenly decided (and in a parallel Universe this could have actually happened with dire consequences) to destroy all vegetation (Type C energy) by cutting down forests on Earth. There would be no more oxygen for humans or animal life to thrive, leaving behind a planet inhabited by anaerobic micro-organisms. Moreover without the Type C Creatures in that Parallel Universe, the ecosystem of the Type B and Type A Creatures would have been destroyed, leading to death and destruction of the higher energy band Creatures. Dreadful but Parallelism allows it, which is why I have mentioned that this scenario could have happened in a Parallel Universe.

So the flora on Earth (Type C energy) is dependent on the humans (Type A energy) to allow vegetation to continue to exist so that it can continue to produce oxygen, provide food and thereby enable animals and humans to thrive on this planet. As you can understand, this symbiotic collaborative relationship and collective co-existence in the 3-D can be possible only if the blueprint of the classes of these Creatures were designed in the 7-D within the domain of coherent energy as shown in Figure 17. Collaboration and synergy is an integral part of Existence, so what right do we as humans have to violate that principle?

Also as illustrated in Figure 17, in this domain of coherent energy, there exists a Creature based alignment of the energy. From the generalized synergistic domain of the higher (than 7-D) dimensions, Existence migrates into more specificity and definitiveness in the Creature based dimensions of Coherent Energy. The 7-D defines the blueprint of the Creatures categorized into the five energy bands. The 6-D defines the possible life experiences for the Creatures. The 5-D adopts these 7-D and 6-D definitions and instantiates an individualized non-physical instance of the Creature class in its corresponding band of *Active* Energy – the precursor, the source of the physical form of the Creature in the 3-D. How fascinating is that design of Creation?

Your Immortal Self – The 5-D ACTIVEBODY

This non-physical individualized instance of the Creature in the 5-D is called the *Activebody* and I will be referring to this term several times throughout this book and beyond. This is quite different from the concept of the *lightbody* that you may have learned about and I will address the *lightbody* concept when I describe the Third Dimension.

Once the *Activebody* is instantiated in the 5-D with the blueprint for the Creature as defined in the 7-D, its primary task is to evaluate the possible life experiences offered by Parallelism in the 6-D. After such evaluation, the *Activebody* would collaborate with other *Activebodies* in the same energy band and across energy bands to define its specific role in Existence. This role in the grid of Existence would be fulfilled by the physical component of the *Activebody* in the physical Third Dimension of Existence. Once this role is identified for the *Activebody* it initiates the Cycle of Creation to create a series of lifetimes of its physical form (or the *Adpativebody)*, each lifetime with a specific life purpose. Each such life purpose in a particular lifetime is composed of a series of life experiences that the *Activebody* had evaluated and chosen from the options available for the Creature class in the 7-D. If those life experiences are followed by the physical *Adaptivebody* during its lifetime, it would complete its life purpose by design and in the process, enjoy unbounded delight. *The sum of all the physical lifetimes, each with a specific life purpose adds up to the role that the Activebody chooses to fulfill in Existence through the collaborative process with other relating Activebodies in the 5-D.* Whoa! Read that paragraph again – quite a revelation to me when this memory reactivated.

What happens when you, the *Adaptivebody,* as the physical extension of your *Activebody* do not identify your life purpose and consequently do not fulfill your life purpose by choosing the correct life experiences? You pass on from one mortal lifetime to another lifetime, assigned with the same life purpose under different conditions (different parents, born in a different country or society etc), given another chance to get the job done. Greater the number of physical lifetimes you spend in an attempt to identify and fulfill your life purpose, longer it takes for your *Activebody* to claim completeness of its role in the grid of Existence. It needs to have you come back to the Third Dimension and take another shot to fulfill your life purpose.

What happens when you, the *Adaptivebody* identifies your life purpose in a given lifetime set by the *Activebody*, and choose to follow the same life experiences that your *Activebody* had lined up for you? Well, first of all you get to enjoy a physical life experience filled with unbounded delight, living a life in either the EMPOWERED or AWAKENED level of consciousness. You pass on from your mortal body and are born again with the next life purpose and its related life experiences that the *Activebody* had lined up for you, incrementally progressing to fulfill its role in the grid of Existence.

Recall the discussion of the 6 pairs of DNA strands in each cell of your body. I had indicated that the 5th pair is designed to operate in the Theta/Gamma brainwave frequency and is your antenna to communicate with your 5-D *Activebody*. I had also indicated that the channel is always open, but you may not be communicating with your *Activebody* on that channel. When there is no communication, how can you receive guidance from your *Activebody* to identify your life purpose, choose the right life experiences and enjoy unbounded delight. 98% of the human population is currently *tuned off* from their respective *Activebodies*. Consequently humanity has not progressed on the level of consciousness and wanton unbounded plight continues to prevail all over our planet. The *Genetics Of Divinity* has already provided the necessary infrastructure for us to participate collaboratively in the grid of Existence. Is NOW not the time for humanity to understand Creation and Existence and realign with our role in the grid of Existence?

Pause here and read this section once again in an attempt to understand the mechanics of operation of your *Activebody* and *Adaptivebody* to serve in the grid of Existence. Fascinating, isn't it?

---------------------------*****--------------------------

Due to the symbiotic collaborative and coherent nature of Creation and Existence the core theme of the life purpose is to serve the postulates of Creation and Existence by serving other Creatures regardless of the energy band to which they may confirm. You and everything else that you detect through your five senses in the physical 3-D world around you, are here for the purpose of serving others as you share a contemporary life experience with them or leave a legacy for future generations to follow.

The *Activebody* of the individual Creature – regardless of its energy band is pure and coherent *Active Energy*. For the sake of repetition, energy can never be created or destroyed – it can only amplify, attenuate or transform. Hence the coherent active energy of the *Activebody* that is derived from Source Energy of the higher dimensions can never be created or destroyed - it can only transform. As you will learn shortly, the Fourth Dimension of time provides the barrier between the non-physical Fifth and the physical Third Dimensions. While the Third Dimension of Existence is dependent on the factor of time, the Fifth Dimension is independent of the factor of time. The Fifth Dimension and higher are domains of stabilized energy above the barrier of time and hence they do not evolve, amplify or attenuate. There is no change and if nothing changes, time ceases to be a factor, rendering these domains immune from mortality. In Chapter 9, I will describe for you the specific process through which the dimensions of Existence have been formed and how they stabilized and became independent of time.

The *Activebody hence renders the individual Creature with the attribute of <u>immortality</u> in the Fifth Dimension.* How does the *Activebody* transform and what does it transform to? *Through the exercise of free will (an attribute of the Creature class of which the Activebody is an instance) the Activebody makes a choice to transform or reverse-transform between the non-physical Activebody in the 5-D and a* *physical 3-D Adaptivebody* (to be discussed shortly) *so that it can fulfill its chosen Fifth Dimensional role in Existence and the life purpose that it has chosen for its mortal physical form or Adaptivebody in the 3-D.*

---------------------------#####---------------------------

You as a human and all other Creatures across all energy bands are all multi-dimensional beings with an immortal *Activebody* in the 5-D and a mortal *Adaptivebody* in the 3-D, separated by the *mortality divide* of the 4-D. Based on your prior belief systems and paradigms, you may find this Truth of Eternal Consciousness to be an absolute polar opposite to what you have been taught and guided to believe, but that does not change the authenticity of the Eternal Truth.

Your Mortal Self – The 3-D ADAPTIVEBODY

If the 3-D *Adaptivebody* proves over its mortal lifetime that the assigned life purpose is not being fulfilled, the immortal *Activebody* would choose to terminate (what we call *death*) the mortal *Adaptivebody* – similar to resetting your non-responsive computer, reverse transform the 3-D *Adaptive Energy* back into the 5-D *Active Energy*. The *Activebody* in the 5-D would then re-engage in the process of engaging its free will and choose to transform into yet another *Adaptivebody* (what we call <u>rebirth</u>) in the physical 3-D. Such rebirth or reincarnation would occur under different life conditions (different parents, different relationships, different political or social structures etc) with another opportunity to fulfill the preset life purpose of the *Adaptivebody*.

Why does the reincarnation occur under different conditions? Well, first of all it is pointless to do the same thing over and over again and expect different results. So if the *Adaptivebody* was unable to fulfill its life purpose under a certain set of conditions, there is no point in re-introducing the *Adaptivebody* under the same conditions. A different set of conditions with the same life purpose increases the likelihood that through new symbiotic collaborative relationships the *Adaptivebody* would be able to fulfill its life purpose. The *Adaptivebody* would then pass on and move on to the next lifetime with a new life purpose, incrementally edging the *Activebody* towards the completion of its role in the grid of Existence.

If your current consciousness based on past knowledge and convictions does not agree to immortality of the 5-D *Activebody* and the rebirth of the 3-D *Adaptivebody*, that does not influence the grand design of Creation and Existence in any manner. My plea and desire for you is to avoid falling into the trap of myopic paradigms and illogical belief systems that are artificial and man-made without any coherence with the Eternal Consciousness that was already in place before this physical Universe even came to be. However in the understanding of this design lies the secret sauce for you as a Type A Creature to liberate yourself from the bondage of a distorted reality and upgrade your life experience in the 3-D to be filled with unbounded delight in your current lifetime.

It is a fair question to ask that if the *Adaptivebody* has been derived from the *Activebody*, then why can the *Adaptivebody* not always identify and hence fulfill its assigned life purpose when it exists in the 3-D physical form? What possibly can the *Adaptivebody* do to understand its life purpose and more importantly how can it fulfill it? I will address these compelling questions when I discuss the Third Dimension.

By design, the physical 3-D *Adaptivebody* is equipped to remain in constant contact with the 5-D *Activebody* through the 5th pair of DNA strands. However it is the free will of the *Adaptivebody* to choose whether to communicate with the *Activebody* regularly for guidance and counsel, or not. As a metaphor, the telephone lines between you and your friends and relatives are already present – the infrastructure for the connection is already in place. However it is your own free will and your choice in Parallelism whether you want to leverage this infrastructure to actually call the other party and communicate with them. The multi-dimensional relationship between the 3-D *Adaptivebody* and your 5-D non-physical *Activebody* follows this exact same model. They have the ability to connect and communicate but the question is whether the bi-directional communication is happening in the channel or not.

Can I prove whatever you have read in this section? Yes only if you are willing learn the techniques and relax the critical filter of your conscious mind to be receptive to this Eternal Consciousness. Without getting into much detail about this *"how"* in this book, I know for certain that this is my sixteenth 3-D physical life experience as an *Adaptivebody* on this planet. Furthermore I have completed my assigned life purposes in all of the past fifteen lifetimes. What those purposes were - I have not investigated yet. Am I curious? Certainly and it is stored in my subconscious Type 1 memory. Have I tried to access those memories? No, not yet, since it does not serve any other purpose in this lifetime than academic interest. Do I know what my 5-D *Activebody* has assigned my life purpose is in this present 3-D experience as an *Adaptivebody*? Yes, I do and you will learn how to find your own life purpose in the follow-on book – *Miracles From Genetics Of Divini*ty. Have I been making the right choices in life so far? No, I had gone astray and through my free will I did make some incorrect choices when I was not aware of what you are reading now. However, I recognized Contrast and since then I have re-aligned with my life purpose and I am making the right choices now under the guidance of my *Activebody*. Will I be able to achieve my life purpose? Uh-huh! You bet I will. Aha – interesting, is it not? I can not only be aware of my past, I can also become aware of the future – courtesy of my Activebody who is in a dimension that is independent of time and hence is aware of my future in the 3-D. How much of reassurance do you think it gives me when I can become aware of my future? This confidence of certainty is ineffable and that serves as the passion for my Cycle of Creation in this lifetime and my guide to fulfill my life purpose. What is the assigned life purpose in this current *Adaptivebody*? ☺ that's personal but here's a hint – you are getting a taste of that assignment right now as you read this book. Should you choose to continue your education in our future interactions to upgrade your consciousness about the *Genetics Of Divinity,* you will know more.

How has it been possible for me in this *Adaptivebody* living in this Third Dimension that is bound by the factor of a linear progression of time to know part of my future, specifically at a timeframe in that future where I have achieved my life purpose in this lifetime? Through my *uplink* to my 5-D *Activebody.* As illustrated in Figure 17, the 5-D and higher dimensions are independent of the factor of time. Hence as I mentioned before, the past, present and future are all collapsed on one single point in these higher dimensions. That one single instant contains the plan that my 5-D *Activebody* has created for all my past lifetimes, present lifetime and all future lifetimes. So even though my *Adaptivebody* is going through my life experience in the time bound physical domain of Existence, I can, through the 5th pair of DNA strands, establish a communication session through the existing channel to my 5-D *Activebody*, ask and be told about my future. I can also obtain guidance on how I can achieve that life purpose in this physical lifetime. This uplink is like an invisible umbilical cord connecting my mortal Adaptivebody to my immortal *Activebody.*

You may have heard about a technique in hypnotherapy called past life regression where a person living in this time and space can be taken on a tour of past lives through Hypnotherapeutic techniques that could provide insight on some issues that may be present in the current lifetime. This usually happens to individuals whose *Adaptivebody*(ies) in the 3-D including those in the immediate past were not able to complete their assigned life purpose. As a result they are required to return to the 3-D by their own 5-D *Activebody*, to pick up in the current lifetime from where they left off in their previous lifetimes in an attempt to complete their life purpose – gosh, that life purpose must have been really important ☺. Through past life regression in Hypnotherapy it is possible to identify where the previous *Adaptivebody(ies)* fell short and leverage that insight to course correct in the person's current life experience.

Since the Fifth dimension has no element of time, the concept of traveling into lifetimes in the 4-D can also be projected as future life progression. Tapping into your future can be an outstanding resource as you live your life in your current *Adaptivebody*.

The design of Creation of the *Activebody* in the 5-D does not allow the corresponding *Adaptivebody* to change the past life experience in the 3-D. For example you are not permitted by design of the 4-D to prevent your parents from meeting each other and ultimately conceive you. However complete freedom is offered by Parallelism to the *Adaptivebody* to make the appropriate choices through free will in the present moment to choose future life experience(s). I will discuss more on past life regression and future life progression in the follow-on book – *Miracles From Genetics Of Divinity* – I promise an engrossing discussion there.

How does the *Activebody* in the 5-D provide guidance for my future? Because in the 5-D there is no concept of time. So the knowledge about the what and the *how* is already available to my 5-D *Activebody*. All I have to do is communicate with my *Activebody*. The *what* would then be *reminded* (wait to learn about Type 5 memory) to my *Adaptivebody*. Events, people and circumstances would turn up in my physical life experience at the right time and all I have to do is validate their usefulness thorough my uplink to my *Activebody* and follow the guidance. Do you think this makes my life in this *Adaptivebody* easier? It's a rhetorical question – most definitely yes. *Knowing your future target in life is reassuring, conviction that you are going to hit it is fulfilling, evidence that you have served Existence through the fulfillment of your life purpose is rewarding - the primary reason why you were born in this physical form.*

Would you want to activate such a communication uplink? This too is a rhetorical question, because you are designed to stay uplinked every moment of your physical life experience to your *Activebody* in the 5-D. However the communication between your Adaptivebody and Activebody may not be occurring at this moment and consequently your life experience is falling short of that unbounded delight.

Revisiting Your 12 Strand Human DNA

If you recall from Chapter 6, I discussed 6 pairs of the human DNA and I had promised you that I will revisit this piece of *technology* embedded within you by virtue of you being born as a human. So here we are, back to these 6 pairs once again as I guide you into another mesmerizing discovery about yourself. For a quick reference, you may want to flip back to Chapter 6 and read that section once again to refresh your memory.

You know from that discussion that each pair is a double helical antenna responsive to electromagnetic signals – one strand of the pair to transmit and the other to receive these signals. The fifth pair of DNA strands is that communication uplink between your *Adaptivebody* in the 3-D and your *Activebody* in the 5-D that I mentioned in the previous section. The sixth pair of DNA strands is your communication link between your *Adaptivebody* and the *Consortium of Activebodies* in the 5-D allowing a free pass for your physical mortal self to engage in symbiotic collaborative relationships with the non-physical immortal *Activebodies*.

These two DNA pairs and other pairs are designed for *switchable duplex communication.* When you initiate your communication from your physical *Adaptivebody* to your non-physical *Activebody* through one of the strands in the 5th pair of DNA (in every cell), the *Activebody* responds back to your *Adaptivebody* through the other strand in the 5th pair. This situation arises when you are reaching out to your *Activebody* for questions, or guidance and counsel. The responses from the 5-D are recognized by your *Adaptivebody* in the form of cognitions, those *a-ha* moments and emotions in the Emotional Guidance System®, described in Chapter 8.

Your *Activebody* is also designed to initiate the communication with you through that second strand in the 5th pair of DNA in your *Adaptivebody*. Transmissions that are initiated by your *Activebody* would ideally be received by the receiver strand (the second strand) of the 5th pair and if you are attentive, you would respond back through the transmitter strand (first strand) of the 5th pair. Such transmissions initiated by your *Activebody* may occur in several instances for example, when you need to make a decision about the choices in Parallelism, when you are deviating from your life purpose, when you are being drawn towards parasitic and destructive relationships, when you are engaging in thoughts and actions that are not in the spirit of service for others and so on. You experience such transmissions through what is commonly referred to as *conscience* - that voice in your head that raises those alarms or lights up the runway.

The question is are you tuned in or are you tuned off the communication channel provided for you by the 5th pair of DNA strands in your *Adaptivebody*?

When the code of the *Genetics Of Divinity* is activated into your conscious mind and your life experience is consciously guided by this code, you would automatically stay responsive and attentive to those *words of wisdom*, recognize the source of the transmission, consequently adopt corrective steps in your thoughts and actions and stay aligned with your life purpose. This way, events and circumstances in your life that is perceived as negative can be avoided just because you consciously responded to guidance from your *Activebody* who is far more knowledgeable and conscious than you are designed for in your *Adaptivebody*. When negative situations are circumvented in this manner, your life experience would consequently remain in the realm of success, fulfillment and unbounded delight.

---------------------------*****---------------------------

But what happens when you tune yourself away from those inbound transmissions from your *Activebody*, ignore the guidance, leverage the whimsical free will of the *Adaptivebody*, and engage in the non-repeatable random games of chance and mathematical probabilities? Well in the process of such conduct, you choose to stay blinded from the outcome of your choices, as the enticement of a short term gain strips you off the enjoyment of long term delight. Consequently your life experience sinks towards unbounded plight as you continue to ignore the inbound transmissions from your *Activebody*. The technology of your DNA is designed for switchable duplex communication by the code of Eternal Consciousness and not simplex (one way) communication. Symbiotic collaborative relationships – the core principle of Existence is built in as Type 1 memory.

When you ignore those transmissions, you can actually forget about using your 6th pair either, which can be activated only when the 5th pair of strands is operational as designed. As a matter of fact someone who ignores the 5-D transmissions would not have the consciousness about the efficacy of the 6th pair and hence would have forsaken any entry into the Consortium of *Activebodies* in the 5-D.

When the 5th pair is inactive, all other DNA pairs also attenuate and lose their natural frequency of vibration. Consequently, physiological (1st pair), emotional (3rd pair) and psychological (4th pair) inadequacies start to show up in the *Adaptivebody*, driving its life experience in the 3-D to one of pain and plight. Consequently the dormant memories of that code of the *Genetics Of Divinity* recedes further and further away under the thickening shroud of memories that are negative in perception. A recovery from this state of detachment from the life purpose is possible but it all starts with that moment's decision to recover from unbounded plight and upgrade the life experience towards unbounded delight. How does this information relate to you?

--------------------------#####--------------------------

At this point I would like to share an example from my own personal life experience when I was in such a communication session with my *Activebody* in the *Consortium of Activebodies* in the 5-D. There was a specific instance when I was going through one of my transformation processes. I have always remained in constant contact and communication with my 5-D *Activebody* ever since I received that second shot at life that I described in Chapter 1. A certain person in one of my dis-associative relationships was constantly interfering with my delight through various ways and means that were unethical and immoral in my perception.

Yes, in my immaturity, I had yielded my power to that person who seemed to be rather irksome to my happiness. When all attempts to communicate verbally with this person failed, I attempted to communicate energetically – I will describe such techniques in the follow-on book – *Miracles From Genetics Of Divinity*.

When that did not help, I reached out to my *Activebody* to assist. Not surprisingly, my *Activebody* was already aware of what was going on and *notified* me that it would reach out to the other person's *Activebody* in the 5-D and collaborate with that entity to resolve the issue. I had received a subsequent transmission from my *Activebody* that everything had been arranged and that I should expect to see a change in circumstances very soon.

Well, months went by and there was no perceptible change in circumstances and the situation actually seemed to get worse. So I reached out to my *Activebody* again with a status update and what I *heard* blew my mind way. As it happens, the two *Activebodies* had communicated with each other and agreed on the changes to be made on respective *Adaptivebodies*. Note that the 5-D and higher are domains of perfection and there is no conflict or contest that we experience in the 3-D. In that domain there is only symbiotic collaborative collective coexistence.

Anyway, as it happens, the other *Activebody* reported that it was unable to communicate with its own *Adaptivebody* – the person I was having these challenges with. That *Adaptivebody* was tuned off from the 5-D transmissions and hence unresponsive to the 5-D guidance and counsel that was being transmitted by that *Activebody*. The outcome? Well, while I stopped caring too much or paying much attention to the catabolic energy of this person, that person started to have emotional, psychological and physiological disturbances that increasingly led to high levels of stress and other challenges in life.

I want to make sure that in order to enjoy unbounded delight, you need to stay responsive to the technology of multi-dimensional switchable duplex communication that your DNA is capable of. You must leverage your 5-D *Activebody* communication uplink and stay in constant touch with that guidance and counsel every moment of your life experience. Warnings, premonitions, ideas, cognitions, those light-bulb moments are all possible when you stay receptive to those transmissions from your *Activebody*.

I thoroughly recommend that you read this section again, since in all likelihood you will be able to relate the information to your own life experience and choose to take corrective action without delay. Remember that the design of Existence does not allow you to change your past, but offers all the tools and technology to you to make proper choices from Parallelism in the present moment and change the course of your future life experience.

Could We Have Misunderstood Religion

There is no external power greater than your very own team of the 5-D *Activebody* and the 3-D *Adaptivebody* that provides guidance and counsel to your life experience in this physical mortal form. Your physical, mortal, *meat-suit* of a 3-D *Adaptivebody*, derived from your very own non-physical immortal 5-D *Activebody*, has been endowed with every attribute, function and circumstances that you will require to fulfill your assigned life purpose. You don't need to surrender yourself to any external entity to help you - an entity that simply does not exist in the grid of Existence. The grand design of Creation guarantees that your uplink to your very own *Activebody* in the 5-D from your current *Adaptivebody* in the 3-D is never ruptured.

You never need to surrender your rationality and free will to the artificial man-made paradigm of an entity that is external to your 5D *Activebody*. All you need to do is engage this *Activebody* to provide you with guidance when you find yourself in challenging times and also remain open and receptive to inbound transmissions that originate from your *Activebody*. You have an Early Warning System built into you as a core attribute, pay attention to those signals. Only your *Activebody* has all the answers that you need, since you are here in this physical form as part of that *Activebody* and not any other external entity. You have been designed to be completely self-sufficient to establish those symbiotic collaborative relationships for collective coexistence during your lifetime and consequently fulfill your life purpose.

The code of Eternal Consciousness that I call the *Genetics Of Divinity* was already in place before Existence was created, before this physical Universe was created, before humans were born on this planet and hence before any religion was instituted. Humanity has misread and misinterpreted the teachings of religious leaders ever since the concept of religion was recorded in human history. Such religious leaders had become aware of and had activated substantial segments of the code of the *Genetics Of Divinity* from their Type 1 memory systems. They had their own specific styles and methods of communication. However the rest of humanity having a contemporary life experience with those religious leaders was not evolved enough by way of consciousness of Creation and in my opinion our evolution still remains stymied even today. That evolution can occur through the reactivation of the code of the *Genetics Of Divinity* and this book is the first effort in our checkered history to initiate that process. The metaphors and examples that were communicated by the religious leaders were meant to demonstrate the multi-dimensional design of Existence - humanity was not able to read between the lines.

When these religious leaders healed people from pain and disease, they demonstrated the capabilities that an *Adaptivebody* is designed with to clear blocks in the natural energy pathways within the physical 3-D *Adaptivebody* of the patient. Such feats are possible when the *Adaptivebody* stays in constant communication with its own immortal and highly skilled and knowledgeable *Activebody* in the 5-D. Instead of understanding these attributes and functions of the *Adaptivebody* as demonstrated by these religious leaders, instead of making the effort to learn the techniques behind those demonstrations, humanity interpreted those acts of healing as miracles. Humanity focused on the *"what"* and was too lazy to learn the *"how"* behind those so-called miracles and was too keen to simply receive service from those religious leaders.

--------------------------*****--------------------------

"I want to teach you how to heal the physical body. I want to teach you how to turn water into wine. I want to teach you how to love your neighbor," the religious leaders had offered. "Oh I am too busy. I am not that clever to learn. Can you please do that (perform the service) for me?" humanity responded back. "Look what I, a mortal can do and you can too. Let me teach you," the religious leaders said excitedly. "Hey, that's cool," humanity said, "can you please do *that* for me?" Being benevolent and living in the AWAKENED level of consciousness, excited and eager to serve humanity, the religious leaders complied and delivered the service graciously. Today, all that technology that we call *miracles* have passed on into antiquity as the mortal *Adaptivebody* of those religious leaders passed on.

Humanity still expects those religious leaders to deliver us from our plight through *remote control*, while we sit back, paralyzed in our pain and wait in vain for help from an external entity that does not exist and not designed to exist according to the code of the *Genetics Of Divinity*.

All of this happened and continues to happen because humanity was and still is unable to read between the lines of what was being demonstrated by the physical and mortal *Adaptivebodies* of those religious leaders. What an amazing resource of AWAKENED consciousness we chose to relinquish and stood by watching in helpless stupor as they passed on to the static pages of history. That knowledge was ours to receive and enhance the quality of our physical life experience, but we chose to ignore the value! Disappointing!

--------------------------#####--------------------------

Imagine a child growing up in a family where everything is done for the child – all personal needs are catered to, everything that the child desires is given without question, all tantrums are ignored and all shortcomings in the character overlooked. Do you think the child will grow up to be a responsible, self-sufficient individual? Do you think such a child who does not know how to serve the self can even contemplate serving others? *Empower the child and you will empower a life. Empower a life and you will empower a society. Empower a society and you will empower humanity.* Empowerment is where humanity fell short when it came to understand the true message of religion and the religious leaders.

When humanity started to believe in miracles they relinquished or dare I say resigned themselves to the doctrines of fate, destiny, fortune and the related cellmates in these prisons of humanity. Humanity started to believe that there is someone else external and other than their 5-D *Activebody* who can work those miracles on their behalf and bring them unbounded delight in their life experience in this physical mortal form. Alas, this paradigm is not supported by the code of Eternal Consciousness.

Why did these AWAKENED leaders not talk straight to the point? Well you would have to ask them, although I believe that they absolutely wanted to lead by example to demonstrate to humanity that every mortal human is endowed with the same attributes and functions (being instances of the *Human* class) as they had. They showed the way and humanity with its under-evolved consciousness could not read between the lines and find the true essence of what was being taught and demonstrated. These religious leaders showcased in every interaction with humanity, practical applications of the design of Creation and Existence. There was no intent for any of the religious leaders to even coin the word 'religion' – it became a word created by miracle-hungry humanity who was unable to comprehend what was being conveyed. The consequence? Flip any newspaper for answers.

Look at where this under-developed consciousness and the mis-interpretation of the teachings of religious leaders has brought human civilization today. We fight each other in the name of religion. We discriminate each other in the name of religion. We choose companionship and relationships with the pre-condition of religious affiliations of the partners.

Where has all of this brought humanity in the grand design of Creation? Where would be headed if corrective action was not taken – NOW?

If you follow organized religion, my plea to you is to go back and read the life history of the original religious leader again and the original texts. This time when you read, relate that to your knowledge of the *Activebody* and the *Adaptivebody* that you have gained in this book. Your entire perception of life will evolve and transform and I know you will discover your connection with your own *Activebody* without a doubt. You were designed that way, only that your pre-existing perceptions have interfered with your connection to your 5-D *Activebody* and subdued the code of the *Genetics Of Divinity* in your subconscious memory. Whatever prayer you have been saying to your religious supreme entity, say that same prayer to your own *Activebody* – this consciousness is the code of the *Genetics Of Divinity*. The response would be astonishing once you learn the techniques of how to communicate with your *Activebody*.

There is no external entity to punish you when you commit your *Adaptivebody* to engage in thoughts and deeds that you consider to be a mistake. There is no external entity wielding a stick that is out to get you when you don't follow what that external entity apparently has willed for you. There is no external entity who is keeping a log of what you did and did not do and hold you accountable with a series of punitive and corrective measures. There is no external entity that is happy to witness your pain and suffering. There is no external entity that is keeping your *Adaptivebody* from experiencing unbounded delight. Your current perceptions if they are as I have described above, are flawed and it is time to literally turn over a new page in your consciousness. You and only you are responsible and accountable for the manner in which you conduct your life experience.

Only you feel the guilt – nobody else. When you commit your *Adaptivebody* to such actions that you deem to have violated the core principle of the *Genetics Of Divinity*, your feelings of guilt (and you do feel guilty on the inside without question), are nothing but communication being sent to you from your *Activebody* in the 5-D through the 5th pair of DNA strands, notifying you that you just leveraged your attribute of free will and engaged in an option offered by Parallelism that is neither conducive nor conforming to the grand design of Creation and Existence. The question is are you receptive to such communication that is only meant to re-align you with your purpose in life?

If what you did is perceived as destruction or disruption of the *Adaptivebody* of another Creature regardless of its energy band, you just performed an unauthorized function and violated the code of Eternal Consciousness. For example, when we fight wars, we engage in what we call destruction to life and property. As *Activebodies*, we are not designed to thwart or interfere in the exercise of free will of others and yet humanity down recorded history has chosen to repeatedly violate this basic principle of Existence lured by the lust of false and artificial territoriality and scarcity.

Whatever you do through the exercise of your free will that makes you feel that feeling of guilt, also leads you to deviate from your *life's purpose which has been assigned to your 3-D Adaptivebody by your Activebody in the 5-D.*

As I have mentioned before, there is no chaos, confusion or disorganization in the grand design of Creation and Existence. *There is no conflict, no contest and no discord among the Creatures in the 5-D regardless of which energy band they belong to because Existence by design is all about symbiotic collaboration through mutual consent for the purpose of collective co-existence, coherence and harmony.* Based on the current level of consciousness of humanity, it is a challenge to perceive an Existence without conflict, which stems from the artificial perception of scarcity and deprivation.

Just flip the pages of a world history book or tune into the news and you will soon lose count of the number of wars we have fought and are still engaged in. What is the root cause of those conflicts? Just think about your own life so far – how many personal and professional conflicts have you been through thus far and how much of unbounded delight have you given up in your current life experience that has caused conflict and discord in your mind? How much net positive value has all that conflict really added to humanity and to Existence? What if we as the most endowed Creature on the planet decided to surrender all conflict and divert all that intense energy to tap into our respective 5-D *Activebodies* for guidance and counsel? Do you think the life experience in our current *Adaptivebodies* would be any different? Most definitely and through Parallelism that scenario is actually a reality in a different Parallel Universe but we have no conscious memory of being there.

What can a perpetually open communication channel with your 5-D *Activebody* do to your physical life experience in your 3-D *Adaptivebody*? Here's a partial and very modest list of applications.

- Find your life purpose – a major application
- Discover highly accurate decision making capabilities for future events, circumstances and relationships in your life
- Choose your academic or professional career that leads you to success and delight
- Choose your partners in the twelve categories of relationships with conviction that brings you unbounded delight – personal, academic, social, financial, health, intellectual or professional
- Know exactly what is healthy for your physiological, psychological and emotional body
- Easily detect and distinguish the truth from what is false – imagine how different your life would be if you could never be deceived.
- Heal your body from ailments and disease without traditional medication (or surgery)
- Develop a repeatable winning attitude to win the *game*.
- Define abundance and unbounded delight in your own terms and enjoy an abundant and fulfilled life experience
- Invest your time and energy only in those projects that would generate the maximum return on investment

- Unambiguously determine if a relationship or interaction would be symbiotic or parasitic
- Know the authenticity of information that you acquire or lack thereof.
- Resolve current conflicts and disagreements that you may be having with yourself and with other relationships.
- Gain insight about your past lives and also future experiences.
- Make correct decisions on the choices from Parallelism all the time.
- What would *you* want to add to this list?

I will describe some techniques on how you too can tap into such a collaborative communication with your own *Activebody* in the 5-D on auto-pilot in the following book – *Miracles From Genetics Of Divinity*.

A Detour To The Law of Attraction

I will close this rather revealing and invigorating discussion about the Fifth Dimension with another aspect about how the *Activebody* functions and I will refer to the Law of Attraction (LoA) for this explanation.

You must have heard about the highly touted LoA and most likely have tried to use it to attract whatever it is that you wanted to attract in your life. Some of you have been successful in such attraction and some of you probably have not. Regardless of your success rate you probably attributed the end result to the function or mal-function of the LoA. The Internet is adorned with as many true and concocted success stories as it is littered with the number of stories of failed attempts to apply the LoA and *manifest* the abundance desired.

So allow me to de-mystify the LoA for you in terms of the *Activebody* in the Fifth Dimension first. When I discuss the Third Dimension shortly, I will refer back to the LoA in terms of the *Adaptivebody* in the 3-D, which will clarify the true essence of *multi-dimensional LoA*.

Before I begin, you may be wondering as you read this section, from where I received this information? As most of the content in this book and in all my speeches, writings and training material about Eternal Consciousness, the consciousness of this memory also surfaced from my subconscious mind into my conscious mind as I reactivated the code of the *Genetics Of Divinity*. When this memory about the LoA was reactivated into my conscious mind, being the engineer that I am, I analyzed the data using the principles of Quantum Mechanics, the basic laws of classical Physics and observations of my personal life experience and that of others in my circle of acquaintance. Needless to say the data conformed to all of that analysis. So here's the Eternal Truth on the Law Of Attraction.

If the Law of Attraction was indeed a Law, why does it not work for everyone in the manner in which the gurus have taught it so far? ☺ Quite candidly, the Law of Attraction is working 100% of the time – you have been mis-informed and misguided about the true mechanics of its operation.

Starting with the basics, first of all this Law of Attraction as you know it, is dependent on and needs a mandatory predecessor called the *Law of Alignment* in order to operate. The Law of Alignment states, "*Unto what the Creature is relentlessly aligned with in the spirit of establishing a mutually consented symbiotic collaborative relationship for the purpose of collective co-existence, would <u>attract the Creature towards it</u> in the shortest possible time.*"

Hence, without alignment and engagement in a symbiotic collaborative relationship, it is impossible to get attracted to anything. Shocked? Never heard that did you? I would hazard a guess. Just that Truth is in all likelihood making you pause and read it again. Unless you *need* (not just want) money, no money will show up. Unless you *need* to stay healthy, good health will remain elusive. Unless you *need* to be in a wholesome relationship, your relationships will erode you. If you have dabbled with the Law of Attraction in the past and had lukewarm or no response you probably just had an *a-ha moment* when you now know that you needed to understand and engage the Law of Alignment first before you could engage the Law of Attraction, which states, *"In the physical plane, opposites attract, while in the non-physical plane, like attracts like."*

A man would attract a woman – a physical attraction. However this is a very fragile attraction of two *Adaptivebodies* coming together primarily on the basis of the forces of electromagnetism – a rather weak force when compared to the force of your *Adaptive Energy*. It is rather simple to break such a physical attraction. However when that same man and woman **both** feel reciprocal emotions of love, respect, honor, trust and companionship – all in the domain of the non-physical first before the physical attraction is considered, that is the strongest attraction of all where the bondage stays resilient even if the couple are not physically co-located with each other.

------------------------*****-------------------------

So you can see that the Law of Alignment and the Law of Attraction are quite different and the former mandatorily precedes the latter in the sequence of their application. The man and the woman in the above example must first align (intense focus) with each other before they can attract each other. Stronger the alignment, stronger and faster the attraction and if that alignment continues after the initial attraction is complete, the attraction continues to grow in strength and can literally transcend lifetimes of togetherness.

Advancing on that basic Truth, secondly, you have been told and taught that by leveraging the Law of Attraction YOU are responsible to and can attract whatever it is that you are trying to attract in your life experience. This is a major flaw in that protocol and no wonder (second reason) why your attempts have not been as successful as you want them to be. Ready for another shock? ☺

YOU are NOT responsible to attract any of your desires at all. Whatever it is that you desire in your life experience is because you want to experience unbounded delight through its acquisition and enjoyment – that is your core motivation – to seek unbounded delight. Your *Activebody* in the 5-D while it was choosing and assigning the life purpose to your *Adaptivebody* had also *made arrangements* for you to acquire and enjoy the very same things that you desire in your physical life experience. Your *Activebody* has already lined everything (similar to milestones in a route of travel) up for your *Adaptivebody* that would lead you to unbounded delight in your physical life experience and through the process of such enjoyment enable you to fulfill your assigned life purpose.

---------------------------#####--------------------------

Your *Adaptivebody* does not attract anything towards it. Your *Adaptivebody* is only required by the design of Creation to engage the Law of Alignment and *stay aligned* with the course charted by the *Activebody*. People, events and circumstances would subsequently get presented to you to *attract you toward them* and leading to the fulfillment of your desires – not the other way around. So all your *Adaptivebody* needs to do is engage the Law of Alignment, establish that symbiotic collaborative relationship through mutual consent and the Law of Attraction would auto-engage and attract you towards whatever it is that you desire – not the other way around. You do NOT attract the subject of your desires – if you *qualify, they* attract you towards them.

Read that section again and I know your consciousness will go through an upgrade right now. Remember that in the 5-D, your *Activebody* operates in the domain of coherent and collaborative energy (refer to Figure 17). In the 5-D all *Activebodies* are interconnected with each other across energy bands, being part of a coherent domain of energy. While your *Activebody* in the 5-D is assigning your life purpose it has already communicated with other *Activebodies* and in collaboration with the appropriate *Activebodies* across the Five energy bands (as in Figure 17) has already arranged for, lined up and charted the course for your physical 3-D *Adaptivebody* when it will eventually have a physical life experience.

Where will you be born in physical form? Who would your parents be? What personal relationships will you have? How would your appearance be? What kind of accommodations would you have? What kind of a vehicle would you drive? What instances of the other energy bands would you interact with? What would you do in every moment of your physical life experience? What would your life purpose be? How will you achieve it? What people, events and circumstances would show up in your life – when? All of this and more are already chosen and lined up for you by your *Activebody* in the 5-D. All your *Adaptivebody* needs to do is communicate with your *Activebody* and align. The challenge for your *Adaptivebody* is to stay connected with this lineup during your life experience.

Dr. Brian Weiss, who I referred to earlier, explains in his remarkable books such *as Many Lives Many Masters, Only Love is Real, Same Soul Many Bodies*, real life experiences that his patients had under his care, where they revealed experiences in past and future lives. The 5-D *Activebody* is what provided such revelations to Dr.Weiss' patients when they unknowingly leveraged the natural connection and started the communication process. I encourage you to read these books for additional insight.

Note there that your parents, life partners, soulmates, children, friends, relatives, and those that you interact with in your professional and social lives also have their very own *Activebodies*. While designing the life experience of your *Adaptivebody* in the 3-D, your *Activebody* in the 5-D would communicate with these Activebodies to determine your relationships that you would eventually experience when you are born in physical form.

How does the Law Of Attraction work during rebirth ? Whether it is required to communicate with another *Activebody* in the 5-D or not is decided upon by your own *Activebody* by the evaluation of two criteria. First, did your *Adaptivebody* in the past lifetime, experience unbounded delight when it interacted with those other Adaptivebodies, did those other *Adaptivebodies* add value to your life experience and most importantly did your *Adaptivebody* fulfill its life purpose during most recent lifetime? Second, is it required for your new *Adaptivebody* to learn and understand Contrast of Creation by engaging other *Adaptivebodies* in the new life experience. This could be possible if for example the most recent lifetime led to conflict and discord with certain *Adaptivebodies*.

If the first criteria is true then your *Activebody* in the 5-D will collaborate with the *Activebodies* of other *Adaptivebodies* that contributed to your unbounded delight and helped you achieve your life purpose. Together they would come to an agreement in the 5-D to bring their physical 3-D Adaptivebodies together again in the next re-birth so that your *Adaptivebody* and theirs as well can continue to enjoy a life experience filled with unbounded delight and contribute to the fulfillment of yours and their assigned life purposes.

I know of several examples of close relatives and friends, including myself who have been born repetitively as a 3-D *Adaptivebody*, to the same parents, had the same siblings, had the same children, had the same spouses. More interestingly these Adaptivebodies came together in lifetimes playing different roles – a parent in one lifetime was born as a child in a subsequent lifetime, siblings in a lifetime have enjoyed a parent-child relationship in a subsequent lifetime. I call it the *love bond* (different shades of a loving relationship) that transcends lifetimes and is facilitated by the respective *Activebodies* in the 5-D – all through symbiotic collaboration with the intent for the participating *Adaptivebodies* in the relationship to enjoy and experience unbounded delight.

If the first criteria is not true, then your *Activebody* in the 5-D would engage the second criteria with the intent of offering your *Adaptivebody* the knowledge and understanding of the attribute of *Contrast* of Creation. In this process your *Activebody* would engage and communicate with other *Activebodies* in the 5-D whose *Adaptivebodies* have never been related to you in a past life experience. This is why your parents, siblings, life partners and other relationships in your current lifetime may be the first time that you have interacted with physical form.

---*****---

Clearly *Adaptivebodies* cannot choose parents, siblings or relatives in the physical life experience. That choice is already made for you by your *Activebody* in the 5-D. However your *Adaptivebody* is allowed free will to choose your life partner(s), friend(s), professional and social relationships. Make sure you take that last sentence with a twist. When you learn about Type 5 memory in the next Chapter you will learn about the plan that your Activebody has for you as far as your partners in the twelve relationship categories are concerned. You do have a free will to override or ignore that plan and choose your own partners. If you do override the *Activebody* assignments and make your own choices, the responsibility and accountability of the outcome of those relationships would lay exclusively with your *Adaptivebody*. This allowance of free will to your *Adaptivebody* is also the reason why you could potentially lose alignment with the unbounded delight that your *Activebody* has set for you before your *Adaptivebody* was born. Your free will could get you involved in romantic relationships for example, that are not based on counsel and communication with your *Activebody*, but purely through the basic instincts of your *Adaptivebody*, peer and social pressures, and other reasons that are not compatible with the relationship that your *Activebody* had lined up for you.

---#####---

In case of romantic relationships, this is the reason for breakups, separation and divorce. This is also the reason why any relationship would break for your *Adaptivebody*, regardless of the duration for which you have had the relationship. Your *Adaptivebody* soon realizes that the relationship is not providing you unbounded delight, that there is no symbiotic collaboration involved and is definitely not helping you focus on achieving your life purpose. That is when your *Adaptivebody* would take a decision to discontinue and start new relationships that could reinstate unbounded delight in your life experience and realign you back to achieving your life purpose (if you have identified it). What attracted you to such a relationship? Did you consult with your *Activebody* before you started the catabolic relationship? Now you know – will you take action?

Given the fact that you cannot turn back the clock, on the next opportunity for a new relationship if you communicate with your 5-D *Activebody* and ask for guidance and counsel you will receive it freely. Again your free will and Parallelism will offer you a choice to accept that guidance and counsel from your *Activebody* or to ignore it. If you do accept, your *Adaptivebody* would engage the Law of Alignment to align yourself back to the course charted for you by your *Activebody*. Once this alignment is re-established through the free will of your *Adaptivebody*, the pre-arranged *Adaptivebodies* as lined up by your *Activebody* in the 5-D, would *attract you towards them* and not the other way around.

This is probably a major paradigm shift for you if you have been toying with the Law of Attraction in the past. This is where, after you have engaged the Law of Alignment, people, events and circumstances start showing up in your *physical* life experience, giving you the false delusion that you have attracted them towards you. Instead *they* attracted you towards them like homing beacons. A good book or movie attracts the reader or the audience. The book or the movie does not land up in the person's lap on its own. I believe you are getting the point.

For those of you still battling with this paradigm shift about the Law of Attraction, let's dive deeper into the concept of your intended or desired target attracting you instead of you attracting them. All throughout the forgoing discussion about the multi-dimensional architecture of Creation and Existence, you must have come to the realization that it is all about symbiotic collaboration and service to other Creatures for the purpose of sustaining collective co-existence. As a 3-D physical *Adaptivebody* you are insignificant as an individual but highly significant as a part of the collective population of all Creatures enjoying a contemporary physical life experience with you.

Why is that? Well, that's because the only reason you are here in this 3-D as an *Adaptivebody* is because you have been assigned a life purpose to serve by your 5-D *Activebody*. What is the nature of that service? That's for you to communicate with your *Activebody* and find out the specifics. This purpose has been defined for you through a collaborative effort led by your own *Activebody* with other symbiotically collaborating *Activebodies* in the 5-D. In other words you are here to make a positive difference in the life experience of other Creatures who are either your contemporaries or who will have a life experience even after you pass on (your legacy). This implies that all the other *Activebodies* who collaborated with your own *Activebody* in the 5-D, while defining your life purpose, are expecting their respective Adaptivebodies to be served by your *Adaptivebody* in the 3-D and/or serve you while you are having a contemporary life experience. You are here to serve and they are here to serve. Note that service is an act of first giving and then receiving.

What is the difference between a *wish* and a *need*? A need is a desire that is critical to your unbounded delight – this is a more intense emotion than a wish would have. Food is a *need* – you've got to have food to survive, while that 5 course meal with the most expensive wine in the most luxurious restaurant in Manhattan, NY is a *wish* (one of the possible selections provided by Parallelism when it comes to choosing what you want to eat). *What you need, needs you.* A *need* is when you align yourself with your assigned life purpose. What happens with such an alignment can be likened to an entire runway being lit up in a dark night with bright lights attracting an aircraft to come in for a safe landing. Events, people and circumstances get lined up for you by the target(s) of your need(s), so that you can continue your journey in physical form to serve and fulfill your life purpose. Hence all you have to do is consciously engage in the Law of Alignment and allow what you *need* to engage the Law of Attraction to attract you towards them.

It is rather easy to rip a sheet of paper. However it is very difficult if not impossible to rip a stack of the same sheets of paper. You possibly could not build a bridge across a river with a flimsy stick. However put up some steel or concrete pillars and your bridge would serve just fine. Why is it that way? *'United we stand, alone we fall'* – I am sure you have heard that before. Why is there strength in numbers? It's the strength of the symbiotic collaborative relationship established through the free will of mutual consent for the purpose of collective coexistence.

It all comes down to magnetic force – electromagnetic force in the examples above. It is the electromagnetic force that holds matter together and gives it the attribute of strength, rigidity and stability. A sheet of paper has its own electromagnetic force that provides its form. However in a stack of the same sheets of paper the electromagnetic forces of all the individual sheets collaborate and reinforce each other to augment the integrity of the stack. Once the individual sheets are aligned together, the attractive force between the sheets of paper in a stack bond so strongly that it can defy average attempts to rip the stack apart. The Law of Attraction is at play here but for it to work, the sheets needed to be aligned together first.

Let us analyze this attractive force and specifically its direction (*from the target of your need to you* and not the other way around). This will provide you with the logical proof using basic laws of Physics, about the authenticity of the fact that it is *not you* that attracts the partner of your desired relationship towards you but it is the partner that you align with in the desired relationship that attracts you towards it.

First of all what is alignment? I define alignment as *the unwavering orientation of energy with high and intense focus on the target of achievement, regardless of other factors that may attempt to thwart such an orientation.* A boat (Creature of Type D energy) that has lost its navigational machinery and its rudder will go adrift at the mercy of the waves and seldom find its intended destination. You as a Creature (Type A energy) are exactly the same – alignment to your intended target is key and of paramount importance. Only when sunlight is focused (*high and intense concentration of energy*) into a sharp point on a sheet of paper by the convex lens of a magnifying glass, does the paper catch fire – that is the type of alignment that I am referring to – intense and concentrated focus of energy.

---------------------------*****---------------------------

The attractor in the Law of Attraction that I mentioned is not you in the relationship but the target or subject of your alignment. Both the Earth and the Moon have mass and hence both have attractive power through the force of gravity. However the Moon's attractive power is smaller as compared to the Earth's and hence the Earth attracts the Moon and not the other way around. The reason blackholes in the galaxies are called blackholes is because they are so massive and hence have such great attractive power that they suck in light to the point that light cannot escape (or reflect), which is why we cannot see them. So *only what is more massive can cause a <u>physical displacement</u> of what is not so massive* – does that make sense?

The only reason you *desire* something (your target or subject of attraction) is because it is not in your life experience just yet. Why? It is more massive and has a greater attractive energy that you have, hence you cannot possibly attract it towards you no matter what you were taught so far by the gurus on the Law of Attraction. The Physics of that process just does not work in the physical domain. No matter how diligently you make attempts to attract your target of attraction that would bring you unbounded delight, your efforts would be as futile as pushing against a concrete wall in an attempt to break it. Being less massive and hence less attractive power, you cannot attract your object of desire that is more massive and hence has greater attractive power. However when you align (read the definition of alignment again) with the subject of your desire <u>and</u> you establish a *resonant* energetic bond with it, it will start the process of pulling you towards it – you get in the vortex, you get into the suction field of that attraction.

Moreover that attractive energy operates on a straight line, which is the shortest distance between two points. Where you are now (without the presence of your subject of desire in your current life experience) and where you intend to be (with your subject of desire in your to-be life experience) does not have to be a long-drawn tedious path. It is already designed to show up in your 3-D experience in the shortest possible time following that straight line or the line of sight. The laws of Physics provision this attractive force to bring you together with your subject of desire as fast as the arrow of time would allow. As long as you maintain that relentless alignment, events, people and circumstances will start to show up in your life physical experience, all enabled by the larger attractive power of the subject of your desire and not by you.

--------------------------#####--------------------------

As you take *prompt and adequate action*, you maintain alignment with the suction force of attraction that your subject of desire has generated. As a result, you come closer and closer to your target until finally that symbiotic relationship is formed. The misconception that you may be laboring under based on your prior exposure to the LoA is that you attracted that target towards you, when in fact it was the other way around. You just maintained relentless alignment, regardless of whatever adverse elements attempted to thwart your alignment and the target of your alignment attracted you towards it.

I mentioned above that the attractive force applies on a straight line with the objective to get you to your intended target at the shortest possible time. However, what happens when doubt and frustration creeps in? You lose alignment with your intended target, which brings you back to where you started from and some people would complain that the Law of Attraction does not work. I call it the scenic route detour, which you did not have to take to get to your intended destination. The truth of the matter is an individual who loses alignment and chooses to surrender to the mysticism of fate and destiny is not aware of how the Law of Attraction works and how it is dependent on the Law on Alignment to generate results in the life experience.

I will shortly discuss another aspect of the Law of Attraction, called the *Desirability Index*, which will clarify the true mechanics of this Law even further.

---------------------------*****--------------------------

Since you are also having this physical 3-D life experience just like the subject of your desire, you are also an attractor in your own right. What do you attract? You attract energy vibrations that others have released and aligned with your energy making you their subject of desire. You are a Creature and a CREATOR. While you align with the subject of your desires as a Creature with the will to receive and enjoy unbounded delight, you as a CREATOR with the will to bestow, are also designed to accept requests for alignment, become the subject of desire of other Creatures and attract those aligned Creatures towards you – this is how *you serve*. I trust you understand the homogeneity and collaborative nature of Creation and Existence where every Creature, irrespective of their energy band has a life purpose to serve and enhance the life experience of other Creatures enjoying either a contemporary life experience or will succeed beyond its physical lifetime. The Law of Attraction and the Law of Alignment is consistent and uniform in all aspects of their application.

-------------------------#####-------------------------

Back from the LOA Detour into the 5-D

I trust this makes it clear now that your task is to align yourself to your subjects of desire that would bring you unbounded delight upon manifestation and make yourself desirable to all those subjects, to engage the Law of

Attraction and attract you towards them. That is when you feel a sense of achievement of your goals that collectively contribute to fulfill your life purpose. *What you need, needs you*, they want to serve by offering their attributes and functions and in the process both partners in the relationship would enjoy unbounded delight by attracting you towards them. The techniques to engage in this process of alignment and subsequent attraction will be discussed in the follow-on book *Miracles From Genetics Of Divinity*.

Before I close out this discussion of the Fifth Dimension I want to make sure that you realize that there is no physical and *mortal* 3-D *Adaptivebody* that can have a life experience without the presence of the *immortal* 5-D *Activebody*. You are here in this physical form of your *Adaptivebody* because your *non-physical Activebody willed it so that you can serve and contribute to the sustenance and proliferation of this Third Dimension of Existence*. Is the life experience of your *Adaptivebody* dictated by your *Activebody*? I take exception to the word 'dictated' here, since the *Activebody* and the *Adaptivebody* represents the duality of the same instance of the Creature class. The *Activebody* of the Creature instance leverages its free will within the bounds of the allowed degrees of freedom that is appropriate for its energy band and chooses the physical life experience and life purpose for the *Adaptivebody*. The *Adaptivebody* is the medium through which the *Activebody* is required to fulfill its role in Existence. The *Adaptivebody* also has free will – to maintain constant communication with the *Activebody* or to ignore (not be aware) that connection and go about life following the *default operating system* of Existence.

I fully understand if this section about the Fifth Dimension was overwhelming for you to read and comprehend as it might have jolted some of your current perceptions and belief systems about immortality, rebirth and the non-existence of an external entity proposed by organized religion that is erroneously perceived to control your life. I had similar experiences when I became consciously aware of this Truth about the grand design of Creation and Existence. It was not long however, before the Truth was rendered as undisputable in my consciousness and I experienced a strong connection with my *Activebody* in the 5-D like I never felt before. My life experience in this current *Adaptivebody* has transformed (not just changed) completely ever since I became aware of my uplink to my *Activebody* in the 5-D and came to know about the mechanics of its form and function in my physical life experience. The uplink was always there, I just had to start the communication process. When I did, it transformed my life experience and significantly upgraded my consciousness, thereby allowing me to catch that coveted glimpse of the Parallel Universe where I enjoy unbounded delight.

The Fourth Dimension

The Fourth Dimension is the dimension of the *linear progression of time*. In the grand architecture of Creation and Existence, this dimension is regarded as the **Great Divide** between the physical world of the Third Dimension and the non-physical world of all the higher dimensions. The Great Divide of the 4-D also represents the separation of the two segments of Existence – the physical world of the 3-D and the non-physical world of the higher dimensions.

As illustrated in Figure 17 the 4-D enables the definition of *Adaptive Energy* as a derivation from the *Coherent energy* of the 5-D. The 4-D is the dimension of abrupt expansion from the concentrated high energy of higher dimensions into the distributed energy of the two dimensions of Adaptive Energy. From the point of singularity of the *Activebody* in the 5-D dimension where the past, present and future is all collapsed into a single event, the Fourth Dimension acts as an amplifier to spread out that single event into periods and lifetimes for the *Adaptivebody*.

Concepts of past, present and future, words such as 'was', 'is', 'will be', definitions of cycles, periods, phases, starts and ends, mortality, evolution, birth, life and death are all variations representing a linear progression of time - the 4-D of Existence. *These concepts do not apply in the higher dimensions – from the Fifth and higher, which is why in the section about the Fifth Dimension, I had referred to the 3-D*

Adaptivebody as mortal – a time bound lifespan from birth to death, whereas the Activebody in the 5-D is immortal and eternal.

This progression of time in the 4-D provides the definition of *history* of the physical and mortal 3-D *Adaptivebody* from the time of birth until its required by its *Activebody* to convert the *Adaptive* energy back into *Active* energy. This time marks the conclusion of the lifespan of the mortal *Adaptivebody*. We call this transformation of the *Adaptivebody* to the *Activebody* – death, which erroneously proposes a false perception of finality, or an ultimate termination of life experience of the Creature in its *Adaptivebody* form.

The enigma of time has puzzled us humans, the dominant species in this planet, ever since we discovered emotions of desire, which stems from the intent of the Creature to enjoy unbounded delight in its life experience as a 3-D *Adaptivebody*. Authors have written copiously about time. Scientists have regaled us with theories about time travel. Cinematographers have released blockbusters with movies themed on time. Time – it flows like a river into the infinite ocean of eternity, which also is a representation of time. In fact the entire existence of the instances of the Creature classes across energy bands in the 3-D is a factor of time – the so called *circle of life* experience.

Time – a healer. Time – a patient onlooker. Time – a source of frustration and despair. Time – a dream to chase, an objective to achieve. Time – a planner. Time – the arrow which never comes back to the bow that released it. Time – an expectation. Time – a disappointment. Time – an illusion of reality and yet a perceived reality of mortal and time bound life experience of all Creatures across all energy bands in the 3-D. Time is all there is for what we humans myopically perceive to be life.

A few key questions that I have asked myself and probably you are asking too, as your evolving consciousness about Creation and Existence reaches new heights. *"If the Creature was created to enjoy unbounded delight in its life experience as the Adaptivebody, why is this delight so dependent on time – why don't we have instant gratification –why such pain and suffering and such disappointment when what we want remains elusive to our life experience?"*

What exactly is time? How do we define time? Both are loaded questions, specifically because the factor of time represented by the 4-D is applicable and relevant primarily for all Creatures having a physical 3-D life experience – the higher dimensions are oblivious of the factor of time. If time can be considered a point in the 5-D, the 4-D can be likened to a manifold magnification of that point which is our perception of time.

A very profound question may arise now – Were the higher dimensions created at a single instance of time or were they created over time as a progressive evolution? If the higher dimensions are really independent of the factor of time, how can such an evolution over a certain period of time really occur? Here's the simple answer and I will address this specific question in a lot of detail in Chapter 9. The higher dimensions were not created at a single instance in time, they evolved over time through the mechanics that I will explain in Chapter 9. From the ZERO Dimension, the non-physical 11th Dimension of Existence was first created from Source Energy of the 0-D. Over time, from the 11-D, the 10-D was created and the energy in the 11-D stabilized and became independent of time - there was no more change occurring in the 11-D. In a likewise manner from the 10-D the 9-D was created after which the energy in the 10-D stabilized and there was no more change occurring in the 10-D as the 9-D started its evolution - thereby rendering the 10-D independent of the factor of time. This is how the time got *pushed* lower and lower as the higher dimensions attained *energetic* stability. The 5-D where your *Activebody* exists was the last dimension in the hierarchical structure of Existence to achieve this stability and hence become independent of time. Fascinated already? Wait till you get to the detail in Chapter 9 ! ☺

Time is a relative factor of Existence in the 4-D. On planet Earth, we humans have defined time based on the rotation of our planet around its axis (24 hours in a day) and on the revolution of our planet around the sun (365 days in a year with that extra day every 4 years). When you come across reports about the age of the Universe, the different ages of evolution of our planet including all retro-projected and recorded human history, the number of years in those descriptions are all based on the motions of rotation and revolution of the Earth in our solar system.

As a matter of fact if you were to calculate a Mars-year (time it takes for planet Mars to go around the Sun once) it would be the equivalent of 686 Earth-days – relative to 686 days on Earth. Planet Mars being further away from the Sun than Earth, would have completed just one year while Earth would have clocked close to the second year based on Earth time. However for a Creature on planet Mars, who is oblivious of the Earth standard would experience that it has aged by just one year – one Mars year. Similarly, planet Venus with a distance closer to the Sun than Earth and hence with a smaller orbit than Earth would complete one year in 225 Earth days. A Creature in Venus however would perceive that one year has already passed for them, regardless of how vociferously we on Earth may engage in an interplanetary argument based on our perception of time. Time is hence, relative by design of Creation, allowing Creatures to define their perception of the 4-D according to the free-will of Creatures on Type A energy, the most superior energy band of Creation.

Given the definition of time on Earth, what would happen if our planet (Type B Creature) increased or decreased the current angular speed of rotation (currently at 1038 miles per hour) at the Equator? Well, our day would be shorter or longer than 24 hours respectively based on how frequently a given longitude on our planet experiences a new sunrise as a result of the change in the angular speed of rotation. What would happen if the Earth started to revolve around the Sun slower or if its orbital radius around the Sun increased? Well, the Earth year of 365 days as we know it would be of academic interest in history books only, since all Creatures on planet Earth would be living in the 4-D under a different measurement of the Earth year.

You lock a person up in a cell that has no sunlight for a few days with instructions to just sleep (the Rip Van Winkle effect) and very soon that very person would lose the perception of time in the 4-D in the same life experience. Observers of such a person would most definitely know and experience the effect of time, but the subject of such a test would have no idea what time it is at any given moment after waking up. Hence time is relative to the perception of the Creature having a 3-D physical life experience.

Refer to the segment of Figure 17 in the previous page and you will notice that I have referred to the Fourth Dimension as 'Progressive Time'. I have also referred to the immortality of the non-physical *Activebody* in the 5-D and the mortality of the physical 3-D *Adaptivebody*. The concept of rebirth that I explained during the discussion of the Fifth Dimension is also based on a progression of time. The time barrier is also limited according to Albert Einstein, which implies that nothing can travel faster that the speed of light. I will shortly discuss that there is indeed something with capabilities to travel faster than light – the Source Particle or the *sourceon*.

However that time barrier indicates that time travel through the unidirectional linear progression of time in the 4-D is impossible in this physical *Adaptivebody*, though it is not a barrier by any means for the non-physical *Activebody* in the 5-D which is independent of time. You, through your *Adaptivebody*, could not possibly, regardless of what you watched in movies, travel back in time or forward in time from the current position in the 4-D and live to tell about your experience to us who could be eagerly awaiting for your report. The time barrier prevents you from such a fictional feat and any attempts (the Third Dimensional concept of the much anticipated invention of a time machine) would be futile. Even Parallelism disallows such a possibility of time travel in the physical *Adaptivebody*. The physical *Adaptivebody* according to the *Genetics Of Divinity* has no attribute, no function and hence no interface with which it could engage in time travel.

Just like through your *Adaptivebody* (or your *Activebody for that matter*) you could not possibly go back and choose to exchange your parents with those of your friend, you also could not possibly through your *Adaptivebody* choose to jump forward in time and bask in the achievement of whatever dream of unbounded delight that you have been dreaming of. Read that last sentence again – carefully.

There is nothing about you, in any dimension that can take you back in time to change the circumstances that brought you to your current moment in your life experience. You can however communicate with your *Activebody* to receive insight on your past life experiences, which apart from academic interest and the cool factor could provide you with plausible explanations for certain experiences that you may have had in this current lifetime. I have referred to this possibility as past life regression – a technique used in hypnotherapy. The bottomline is that that past is really the past from a material 3-D perspective. Could the *Activebody* change events and circumstances in the past? Well it's a moot point, because in the 5-D, where the *Activebody* exists there is no concept of time, so why would it and how could it change anything anyway? The *Activebody* always has a purpose for everything as it serves the grand design of Creation and Existence and it operates in the domain of coherent energy. There are no mistakes in the 5-D only collaborative synergy that may not necessarily be comprehensible to your time-bound 3-D *Adaptivebody*.

However through your *Adaptivebody*, you could communicate with your *Activebody* and travel forward in the non-physical plane in time to obtain insight about your future as laid out for you based on your current choices from Parallelism. You don't have a choice in your physical *Adaptivebody* (and Parallelism holds firm on its ground on this) but to allow your 3-D *flesh and blood* body to catch up with the future in due course of time in the 4-D. I will discuss more on this matter while discussing the Third Dimension.

Take a moment to contemplate how would the next moment of your current life experience change if you would hitch a ride on the infinite horse-powered *magic carpet* of your *Activebody*, travelled to your future, at a *speed greater than the speed of light*, identified your life purpose and aligned yourself to that objective? What decisions would you make from the plethora of choices offered by Parallelism at the very next moment of such a future time travel experience that would get you aligned with your life purpose? What if after such a future time travel you understood that your physical *Adaptivebody* is the slower coach in the train by design and needs to catch up with your objective that your *Activebody* has set for you in this 3-D? These future flights that I make to my Parallel Universe(s) are now part of my regular routine and I can tell you – the experience is literally out of the world. In all likelihood, you would be interested in such a *Forward To The Future* experience and I will guide you through the process in the follow-on book – *Miracles From Genetics Of Divinity*.

Is the 3-D the only physical dimension of Existence that is bound by the unidirectional linear progression of time. The short answer is "Yes", however in this very Third Dimension are superimposed Type 3 Parallel Universes on the same instance of time that I referred to earlier - this is illustrated in Figure 21. Since you are already residing in one of these physical Parallel Universes, it is impossible for you to observe this superimposition effect. You cannot observe the reference from the same reference point – you need to rise above it, for example in the 5-D to observe such a structure. You can't see your own eyes or eyelids without a mirror, can you? Based on the choices that you make individually and then collectively as a civilization you collectively choose one of these Parallel Universes as your sweet home.

I encourage you to recall or re-read Chapter 6 where I discussed Parallel Universes or the multi-verse. Each universe in the Parallel Universes or the multi-verse that is provided by the attribute of Parallelism of Creation is a 3-D plane of Existence superimposed on the same instant of the 4-D. Read that sentence one more time and then refer to Figure 21.

As illustrated in Figure 21, you could have been financially free at time T-4 (past) in the 4-D – you might have won the lottery giving you that particular life experience of financial freedom. It is also possible that depending on what you chose to do with that financial windfall, you blew it all up and then as time progressed to time T-3, you experienced financial hardship.

As you can see here in this example, at any instance of time in the 4-D, as a physical 3-D *Adaptivebody*, your life experience could be any one of the five (in the illustrated example) possibilities offered by Parallelism, each representing a possible Universe of Existence. In one universe you could be financially free, in one you could be affluent, yet in another you could be just breaking even between your income and expenses. Then in another your life experience could as well be burdened with financial hardship and yet in another you could be living a life stricken with poverty. All of these Parallel Universes representing a unique life experience are superimposed or stacked on one another at any instant in the 4-D.

Depending on the choices that your *Adaptivebody* makes leveraging the power of your free will, your life experience (hence your existence in that particular Parallel Universe) could be one of financial hardship. As time progressed, you realized that blowing up all your money was clearly not the most prudent thing to do and then at time T-2, you broke even between your income and expenses. You dipped again into the Universe of financial hardship at time T-1. Then you arrived at the present moment of time T in the 4-D, when you were up to make a certain choice from Parallelism – your decision making moment. That moment of decision at time T would define your life experience and hence the Parallel Universe of existence of your 3-D *Adaptivebody* in the future time T+1 in the 4-D.

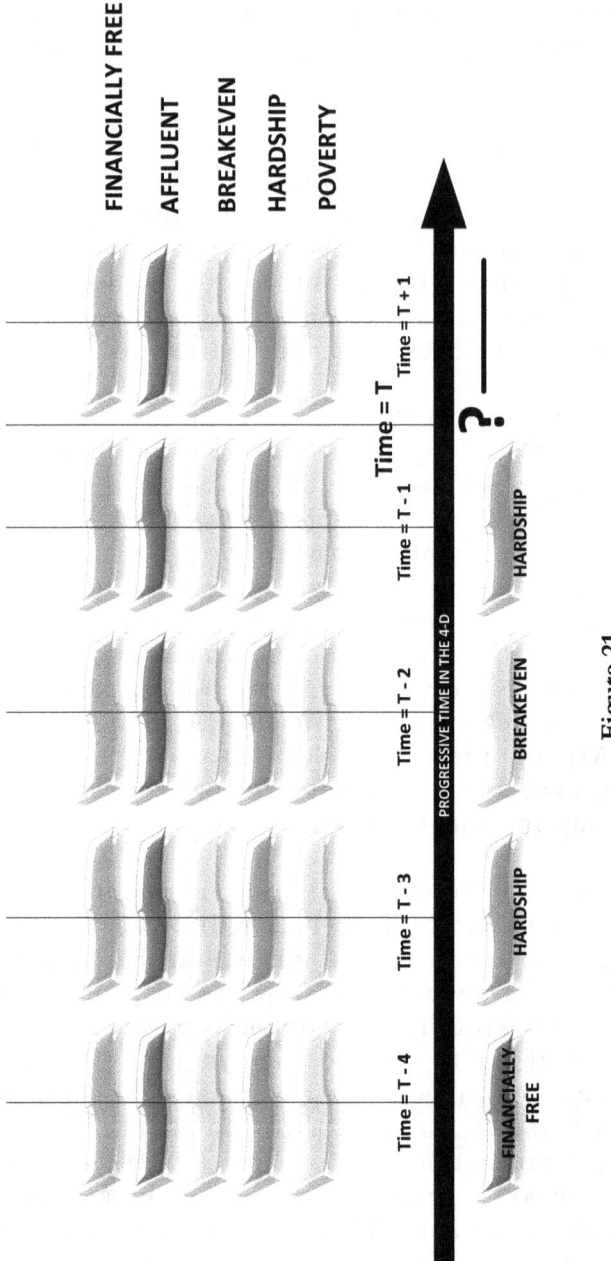

Figure 21

I trust this makes it clear to you the concept of Parallel Universes (we are talking about a Type 3 Parallel Universe as I described in Chapter 6) that are superimposed on one another at every instance of time in the 4-D. Applying your free will, simply by making a choice from Parallelism you can engage in inter-universal travel and hence have the corresponding life experience that is filled or not filled with unbounded delight. Your choices from Parallelism would determine whether your 3-D *Adaptivebody* will struggle in one Universe, survive in another or thrive in yet another and variations thereof. Everything about your life experience in the 4-D is under the command of your very own *Adaptivebody* by the design of Creation. Whether or not you take the shortest route to your life purpose assigned to your *Adaptivebody* by your *Activebody* in the 5-D or choose to take the scenic route deviating from the shortest route, defines your journey through the multiverses of Existence.

The Third Dimension

The third dimension is the simplest to understand since it is our *perceived physical reality* – the dimension of the tangible, the tactile, the physical, the visible, the measurable, the finite, the mortal and hence the fragile and unstable in comparison to the other higher dimensions of Existence. This is the dimension supporting the existence of *Adaptivebodies* of all Creatures across all energy bands. All higher dimensions described so far, exist with the sole purpose to provide and facilitate the conditions necessary for the 3-D to exist and sustain all Creatures in physical form.

The 3-D is the culmination of the Coherent Energy of all the higher dimensions per energy band, allowing the physical laws of Existence to apply and operate. *From the stabilized Active Energy of the 5-D, the 4-D serves as an energy transformer by introducing the element of time to create the relatively unstable and evolving 3-D.* I understand you may be wondering what I mean by a stable 5-D and the unstable 3-D. I would advise you to hold off on a detailed explanation of the 'stability' of the dimensions until Chapter 9, when the concept will be clarified. There is no past, present or future in the higher non-physical dimensions and time is no longer a factor there as I have already explained. Since time is not a factor in the higher dimensions, nothing ages and nothing depreciates or appreciates, thereby making those higher dimensions energetically stable. Such stability ensures consistency in the repeatability of all forms and functions of all Classes of all *Adaptivebodies* of all bands in the 3-D.

However, the 3-D, most definitely is dependent on the factor of time and hence we understand concepts such as history, evolution, the past, the present and the seemingly obscure future. The 3-D is the domain of *Adaptive Energy*, which is constantly transforming and morphing in attempts to build collaborative relationships with other *Adaptivebodies* having a contemporary life experience.

Symbiotic collaborative relationships are the core essence of Creation and Existence across all dimensions and the 3-D is no exception. All Class definitions of all physical 3-D *Adaptivebodies* have attributes and functions built into them to facilitate the formation of these symbiotic collaborative relationships. The choice of setting up such a relationship that is symbiotic to both or parasitic to one in nature is offered as the attribute of free will of the *Adaptivebody*. In Chapters 8 and 9 coming up shortly, I will provide detailed explanations of the mechanics of how such an attribute of free will is implemented in the grand design of Creation and Existence.

For now, it would suffice to understand that through the attribute of free will, physical 3-D *Adaptivebodies* make choices offered by Parallelism at every instance of their life. Each such choice defines the life experience a given *Adaptivebody* would have in the next moment in the 4-D. *Each such choice involves without fail the establishment or abandonment of a relationship with another Adaptivebody* in one of the 13 relationship categories Nothing can exist alone - the design of Creation does not permit isolated existence.

It is a common misconception that the 3-D is the domain where only physical laws of Existence apply. As I will explain in Chapters 8 and 9, there are laws of association and dissociation that operate entirely at a non-physical level in the 3-D. Essentially, physical laws of attraction based on the polarization of electromagnetic forces cannot operate between two participating *Adaptivebodies* in the 3-D unless a prior association or dissociation has already occurred between these *Adaptivebodies* in the non-physical level in the 3-D. A man and a woman for example must align with each other at a non-physical level (non-verbal communication) first before their physical bodies can get attracted to each other. Relationships established in the reverse order are short-lived and fragile. The vehicle in your driveway cannot drive itself away unless you as the driver have thought about using your vehicle in the first place.

If you were to take any physical object (*Adaptivebody*) in the 3-D and had the ability to go deeper and deeper into the physical matter ultimately you will reach a point where there is no physical matter, no particles with rest mass exist. What exists at the very core of all physical matter in the 3-D however is energy - *Adaptive Energy*, which is a derivative (a subset of the spectrum) of Source Energy. If this were true, then how is the physicality of matter formed?

The only reason why you cannot walk through a brick wall, the only reason why the waters of a raging river does not break the dam across its path, the only reason why that jumbo jet does not sink inside the Earth upon touchdown is because the target of impact (the brick wall, the dam or Earth in the above example) has electromagnetic forces in its component molecules that are stronger than the source of impact (you, the water or the jumbo jet respectively in the above example). If you had a battering ram at your disposal it could break the brick wall down if and only if the mechanical force of impact carried an energy that was greater than the binding electromagnetic energy of the wall. That jumbo jet could definitely sink if it landed in the middle of the ocean since the mechanical energy of impact would be far greater than the electromagnetic energy that binds the water in the ocean. Hence in the physical 3-D, the state of the *Adaptivebody* – solid, liquid, gaseous or transitory depends on the physical electromagnetic energy bonding between the constituent molecules that make up the physical structure of the *Adaptivebody*.

Another key component of physical *Adaptivebodies* in the 3-D is luminosity. This is such an important factor to the physical 3-D plane of Existence, that some people harbor memory systems and guide their life experience with the philosophy that they must *first see it to believe it*. For the purpose of this discussion I will refrain from commenting on the crippling flaw in this philosophy of life. However the fact of the matter is that being visible or having some degree of luminosity is of utmost importance to *Adaptivebodies* in the 3-D. Luminosity of an object is based on whether the object is a generator, as reflector or a sink of light energy – with the carrier particles or *photons* vibrating at frequencies that are a subset of the electromagnetic spectrum of *Adaptive Energy* in the 3-D. The luminous properties of an *Adaptivebody* hence is also dependent on the electromagnetic energy of its constituent matter. The particular frequency of electromagnetic energy defines the unique identity of the *Adaptivebody* in the 3-D. For Type C and above *Adaptivebodies* in the 3-D the electromagnetic energy that contributes to the luminosity is the presence of *biophotons* in the DNA within each cell of the *Adaptivebody* – I discuss biophotons in greater detail in Chapter 8 and 9.

Look around the space where you are in right now, including this book that you are reading. They look the way they do to you due to the specific electromagnetic frequency that they are vibrating at right now. The reason why this book can be identifiable from any other book is because this book is generating a unique identifying frequency in the visible spectrum of electromagnetic energy . If you had another copy of this exact same book but that one had dog-eared pages on it, you could easily identify one from another. How and Why? Because those dog-ears just changed the default electromagnetic properties and hence the luminosity of that book, while the contents of both books remained the same.

All *Adaptivebodies* in the 3-D, as you already know now, have a life cycle – birth, life experience and death, due to the unstable nature of *Adaptive Energy* and the dependence on the factor of time. This makes 3-D *Adaptivebodies mortal*. This *mortality* is the result of an increasingly weakening electromagnetic bond within the component matter of that *Adaptivebody* during the course of its life experience. The strong and weak nuclear forces that bind the constituent molecular structure of the *Adaptivebody* are unable to sustain the superstructure of the *Adaptivebody* as the electromagnetic energy transforms back into *Active Energy*. When the intermolecular energy vibrations cannot sustain the electromagnetic bond any longer and the *Adaptivebody* ceases to exist in its natural form. The question arises, what can cause the rupture of such an electromagnetic bond that leads to the mortality of 3-D *Adaptivebodies*.

Being a subset of the spectrum of *Adaptive Energy* which is relatively unstable by design, electromagnetic energy is also unstable due to its susceptibility to out of phase dissonance from other energy sources. For the human *Adaptivebody* such interfering energy sources would be the catabolic (out of phase) energy from emotions lower on the EGS scale that are associated with life experiences of pain and plight and neuro-plasticity of memory systems (to be discussed in Chapter 8) that prevent the *Adaptivebody* from making any conscious effort to adopt any corrective action. Such emotions collectively are what we call 'stress', which is the root cause of all dis-ease in the human *Adaptivebody*. The catabolic energy from stress erodes the physical *Adaptive energy* that operates the human *Adaptivebody*. Left unattended or allowed to escalate, stress will eventually overpower the electromagnetic forces that bind the cells that make up the organs of the human *Adaptivebody*, leading to their malfunction, eventual collapse and potential termination of the mortal life of the *Adaptivebody*.

If you recall the discussion of the 1st pair of DNA strands from Chapter 6, you would remember that this pair controls the physiological health of the cell. If the other DNA pairs are not operational in their natural modes of operation, the 1st pair is also unable to sustain the health of the cell. This block of natural energy flow into and through the cell leads to disease in the cell, which in turn affects the electromagnetic bonding of the cell. Every cell generates toxins as a result of metabolic activity and they are carried away by the veins that serve the cell to be cleaned and recycled through your respiratory system. When there is a block of energy flow in the cell, the 1st pair of DNA strands is unable to facilitate the toxin transfer process. Left unattended, the cell will eventually collapse leading to its mortality. Scale that explanation from the cellular level up to the entire *Adaptivebody* and you will be able to understand the process of atrophy of the physical body.

We move on to the last of the four fundamental forces that operate in the 3-D – the gravitational force. Gravitational energy occupies another frequency band of *Adaptive Energy* in the 3-D. Anything that is considered physical matter is a generator of gravitational energy. Gravitational energy is inbound or attractive in nature and hence follows the core principle of Existence – that to attract other *Adaptivebodies* for the purpose of establishing collaborative relationships. While the electromagnetic energy of the *Adaptivebody* is related to its alignment with another *Adaptivebody* in a relationship, it is the gravitational energy that performs the function of actual attraction. Only a more massive object and hence with larger gravitational energy will be able to attract an object that is less massive, causing displacement. Coming back to the LoA discussion earlier in this Chapter, you are required to use your *Adaptive Energy* to simply align with the target of your desire which is more massive than you are, because it is not yet part of your physical reality. Your target receives that transmission and has a choice to resonate with you or not. Once the choice to resonate is made, it marks the beginning of a symbiotic collaborative relationship through the free will of mutual consent for the purpose of collective coexistence. Your target or subject of desire would subsequently activate the gravitational forces of attraction and pull you towards it.

For the sake of repetition, <u>you do not</u> attract the subject of your desire. You simply align with it and transmit your intent to form a symbiotic collaborative relationship with your subject of desire. The subject of desire would receive that transmission, evaluate your desirability and through its free will either consent to the relationship or reject it. If the consent is provided, your <u>subject of desire will apply gravitational forces to attract you towards it</u>.

The Third Dimension is where you and I are having a contemporary life experience with other *Adaptivebodies* of all energy bands with the guiding principle of establishing symbiotic collaborative relationships to serve and adhere to the design of Creation and Existence as described in the code of the *Genetics Of Divinity*. The question is not if others are doing their part to understand and apply this guiding principle. The question you have to ask yourself is *'What am I doing to establish symbiotic collaborative relationships that not only fills my life experience with unbounded delight but also that of the other Adaptivebody that I intend to relate with, through the service that I can provide that leads them to unbounded delight?'* In the answer lies the key for the quality of your life experience. Existence is all about symbiosis – parasitic relationships are short lived and are not designed to lead the partners towards unbounded delight.

Revisiting The ZERO Dimension

If you have noticed, so far in this Chapter, I have been describing the dimensions in a top down approach from the 11-D down to the 3-D. However in order to explain the remaining dimensions I will have to reverse the direction starting with another visit to the 0-D and working our way back up to the 2-D.

As I have explained earlier in this Chapter and later on in Chapter 9, the ZERO dimension is where the dimensionless points representing the *sourceons* exist. These *sourceons* are the original dimensionless particles **without rest mass**, capable of traveling at the speed of Source Energy, instantly, for infinite distances, incurring no loss of energy and immune to any interference or dissonance. In comparison, photons, those super-fast particles of the 3-D can achieve those finite light speeds only through vacuum. Furthermore when passed through the Bose-Einstein condensate at super low temperatures and super-high vacuum, these same photons would slow down to the speed of busy city traffic.

The *sourceon,* that human instrumentation cannot detect due to its dimensionless nature – not even rest mass and carrying Source Energy which has frequencies beyond the detectable range of our instruments, can accelerate to be the fastest or the slowest particle in Existence, regardless of the medium, dynamically, based on its domain of application.

These dimensionless points are the origin of Source Energy. For us humans, being part of this finite 3-D plane of Existence, where matter and mass are used interchangeably, it is a challenge to contemplate such a particle to exist in a dimensionless domain of Existence in the 0-D that too without rest mass. This is not a traditional 3-D chicken and egg problem – what came first – the *sourceon* as a particle came first or did Source Energy beat the sourceon to the birth of Creation? **The *sourceon* emitting Source Energy was one Creation.** *The wave-particle duality of Creation that is also observed in the 3-D, originated at the Source.*

As I will explain in Chapter 9, as Source energy began to proliferate, it pushed out these dimensionless points further out to create space. This space is continually expanding even today. Our highly sophisticated astronomical equipment and technology have proven that the Universe as we know it, is expanding outward.

From these massless *sourceons,* all massive (with rest mass) matter was created. If one were to go deeper and deeper into matter they would arrive at a point where matter in its traditional sense does not exist anymore - it's only Source Energy of the 0-D. Hence the 0-D and the *sourceon* is present in all dimensions of Existence and within all Creatures in Existence.

The First Dimension

In the beginning of time (refer to Chapter 9 for a detailed explanation of the process of Creation) as different *sourceons* started to host Source Energy with varying very high frequencies and very low amplitudes, the 0-D was defined. As more and more of these dimensionless points came into Existence, Source Energy waveforms started to interact with each other, either resonating (same frequency and in-phase), or engaging in dissonance (same frequency and out-of-phase) or having no impact on one another (different frequencies). Each such interaction of dissonance or resonance between two dimensionless points defined the First Dimension of Existence.

The interaction of Source Energy waveforms in the 1-D led to the energy band of Transforming Energy (refer to Figure 17 again) and the birth of the first fundamental force – representing the electromagnetic spectrum. Each pair of associated *sourceons* or dimensionless points with Transforming Energy waveforms between them may be considered as the strings of the Superstring Theory that I have explained earlier. The 1-D is the building block of the 2-D which subsequently is the building block of the 3-D plane of Existence.

Transforming Energy represents an energy band that is unstable when compared to the 5-D and higher, due to the enormous amount of transformation of Source Energy into the Transforming Energy, (enroute to the Adaptive Energy of the 3-D) that is occurring in this domain. Particles in the 1-D are these 0-D *sourceons* that have begun to establish those symbiotic collaborative relationships (refer to Chapter 9 for additional details about the process) with each other to define the First Dimension.

The Second Dimension

Stack up a pile of bricks as you get a wall. Line up a bunch of threads and you get a sheet of fabric – these are examples, albeit crude, of how a bunch of 1-D strings can come together to form a 2-D membrane. I would call your attention to the discussion on M-Theory as I explain the Second Dimension – the last dimension in the domain of Transforming Energy as illustrated in Figure 17.

The binding of the strings from the 1-D into the membrane of the 2-D is implemented through the electromagnetic attraction between strings. 1-D strings vibrating in the same amplitude and frequency gather together to form that membrane with the same frequency as the component strings but with greater amplitude due to the resonant interaction (refer to Figure 12) between them. Greater amplitude of vibration consequently implies greater power. This increased power in the wave like vibration of the membrane leads to a high concentration of energy and high degree of compression on the massless *sourceons*. This amplification of energy continues to mount as the membrane continues to grow larger and larger and more powerful. Extreme compression and excessive power translates to a very high level of energy in the membrane until such a point that it cannot sustain the integrity any longer when two or more membranes with similar characteristics collide.

This is the so-called *Big Bang* when *Transforming Energy transforms into the Adaptive Energy* band. The Adaptive Energy band makes provisions for the Electromagnetic spectrum and adds the other three fundamental sub-spectrums, that of gravitational, strong and weak nuclear energy to it. This is the birth of matter in the Third Dimension. The two energy types operating at the nuclear level constitute the core building blocks of physical matter – atoms and molecules in the 3-D. Electromagnetic energy binds these atoms and molecules together to create physical matter. The specific resultant frequency of vibration in the electromagnetic spectrum defines the luminosity (visible or dark) of the physical matter. Gravitational energy is an attribute of physical matter. With rest mass, matter exhibits gravitational energy. In this manner, the 2-D serves as the building block for the 3-D. Alternatively stated, every physical matter in the 3-D is a specific electromagnetic arrangement of 2-D membranes.

There you go – you are now aware of the significance of the 12 dimensions of Existence and how they operate in collaboration with each other to implement the architecture of Creation and Existence. I was fascinated when this model was presented to me over a three month period by my 5-D *Activebody*, in bits and pieces as my resistance and doubt gradually dissipated away and cognition and logic of the Eternal Truth reactivated those dormant memories of the *Genetics Of Divinity* in my subconscious mind.

That was a long Chapter and I have shared a lot of information about the multi-dimensional architecture of Creation. Why is this consciousness important for you to reactivate from your subconscious mind? You now know where you came from. You know how Creation occurred and how Existence flourished and stabilized over time. I will take that consciousness to a crescendo in Chapter 9. You now know what that no-*thing* of the Big Bang Theory is (*sourceons*) from which everything has been created – physical and non-physical dimensions alike.

I thoroughly recommend that you read this Chapter a few times until the consciousness reactivates and new paradigms and belief systems based on the authenticity of the code of the *Genetics of Divinity* engulfs your conscious mind. Your personal evolution and the evolution of humanity starts with your very own transformation. I applaud and celebrate your transformation and evolution.

Chapter 8 - Perfect Masterpiece of Creation

I dedicate this chapter to the most perfect masterpiece of Creation in the known physical Third Dimension of Existence – the Type A *Adaptivebody*, specifically the human body and more particularly YOU. This one chapter deserves volumes of books in its own right and still there would be room for more to be said. Feel free to research the human body and its mechanics (what we know so far) on your own. For the purpose of this book I will focus this chapter specifically on certain aspects of your Memory system, the human Central and Peripheral Nervous System, revisit your DNA once again and discuss the *quad-compartmental* architecture of the human mind. Yes there are 4 compartments or sections in the human mind, each with specific design, purpose and function. I will also guide you through brainwaves, your *chakra* system in conjunction with a brief introduction to the blueprint of all Creation and Existence – Sacred Geometry.

This Chapter will be packed with opportunities when simply through our undivided attention to the content, resonant impulses will be rendered to those dormant memories of the code of the *Genetics Of Divinity* in your subconscious mind as they resurface into your conscious mind and empower you with higher consciousness. As in the earlier chapters, you will find this chapter building upon what you already have learned so far in this book and I will reveal some esoteric information that will pleasantly surprise me if you can find anywhere else.

Introduction To The Memory and The Mind

First of all, let me dispel a myth – *memory and mind is one and the same*. This is incorrect! The truth is memory and the mind are two distinctly separate components of every Creature in Existence, with two entirely different functions, irrespective of the energy band to which it conforms.

To draw an analogy, think about a computer. The *memory of that computer* is whatever information is contained in the RAM (random access memory), the ROM (read only memory that hosts among other elements, the BIOS – basic input output system) and the data and software programs contained in the hard disk. The *mind of the computer* is all the software programs (operating system and all applications) that you run on the computer. Software works with the data contained somewhere in the computer memory. The software program itself is also part of the memory of the computer. Since we are likening the software program to the mind, this analogy proves that *memory is the host of the mind.*

While the memory can still exist without the mind – it would serve no purpose without the mind. The operating system and application software is what gives the computer function, without them the hardware specifications are of no significance . It is impossible for the mind (your software) to operate without memory (the hardware).

--------------------------*****--------------------------

All Creatures of all energy bands that you have been introduced to in Chapter 7 are equipped with memory and mind as two distinct components. They have similar functions of information storage (called knowledgebase) and information acquisition, although the mechanism is different depending on the energy band of the Creature. For example, the mechanics of operation of the memory and mind of the chair that you are sitting on is quite different than your own memory and mind, but both you and the chair have a memory and a mind.

---------------------------#####---------------------------

Second let's dispel yet another uneducated and unfounded myth – the *memory and the mind must exist somewhere in the brain.*

Creatures of Type C and lower energy bands have no brain or a central nervous system and yet they have memory and a mind. Remove one leg of a chair (Type D Creature) and the chair topples over – restore the leg of the chair and it reclaims its designed function. Where did its memory to stay stabilized return from?

Take two potted plants (Type C Creatures) of the same species that germinated at the same time and attained the same growth. On one of the plants say and write (on a label attached to the pot) words of love or other positive thought and on the other plant say and write (on the label) words of spite or other negative thought. Other considerations remaining the same, the first plant will continue to thrive, while the latter plant would be found to start withering within a few weeks and eventually die. What happened here?

If this sounds unbelievable, that's ok and you would not be the first. The fact remains nonetheless that such a behavior does occur and no, it's not a miracle. You can perform such an experiment to prove it to yourself.

Research done by surgically removing sections of the human brain (Type A Creature) or the guinea pig (Type B Creature) brain has revealed no loss of memory and also no loss of the mind although certain physiological functions of the physical body were reported to have been impacted as a result of such an operation.

With these baseless myths shattered, you now have a good platform to dive into this Chapter. You will undergo several paradigm shifts now as the dormant memories reactivate from the subconscious mind and resurface to your conscious mind. Stay receptive and open to the knowledge and I trust it will resonate with your rationality and discernment.

It is worthy of mention that as the dormant memories of what you are about to learn got reactivated in my mind, I had felt a tingling sensation inside my head, which presently started to spread all over my body – almost like a chilling sensation, as if my entire *Adaptivebody* was vibrating and resonating with the truth. You may feel the same or similar sensations if you stay receptive to what you are about to learn. There is no need to be alarmed if that happens since through the process, your consciousness would be aligning with the code of Eternal Consciousness.

The Quad-Compartmental Mind

---------------------------*****--------------------------

The human mind is structured as a non-physical quad-compartmental component (each compartment with specific functions) of the 3-D physical *Adaptivebody* and is designed with intra and inter-dimensional domains of operation as illustrated in Figure 22. The *sub-conscious* and *conscious* sections of the mind operate on the 3-D *Adaptivebody*. The *super-conscious mind* operates as a communication transceiver (transmitter and receiver) between your own and *other* Adaptivebodies in the 3-D regardless of the energy band to which they conform and with whom you desire to establish relationships during your physical lifetime. This super-conscious mind is within the conscious control of the *Adaptivebody* and in all likelihood you might not have known about its presence until now. The fourth compartment or the *infra-conscious mind* operates in both the 3-D and the 5-D as a communication bridge between the 3-D *Adaptivebody* and the 5-D *Activebody* of the Creature – you definitely did not know about the infra-conscious mind and mode of operation until now.

---------------------------#####--------------------------

Think about these four compartments of your mind as four software applications running on your memory each with its own programmed role to provide shape, form and function to your life experience.

Contrary to what you may have been led to believe so far, the sub-conscious mind is only designed to cater to the task of keeping all involuntary functions of your physiological body operating as defined by the class definition of your Type A energy band. Your respiratory, digestive, circulatory, nervous, endocrine, reproductive, musculo-skeletal systems that are involuntary in nature are all managed by the sub-conscious mind automatically without your conscious knowledge. These functions are operational whether you are sleeping or awake and your sub-conscious mind is managing all of those involuntary functions every single moment of your 3-D physical life experience. Due to this inward directed focus of operation of the sub-conscious mind, in Figure 22 its domain is indicated as *intra-Adaptivebody*.

However, how does the subconscious mind know how each of these anatomical systems perform? Ah, that is the memory that I am referring to. As you will learn shortly, memory is not something stored in the brain but in every cell of the human body. This memory is stored in the 2nd pair of strands of the human DNA, if you recall that discussion in Chapter 6. In addition this second pair also stores the memory of the code of the *Genetics Of Divinity,* As I have been saying, the memory of this code is lying dormant in your subconscious mind and needs to be reactivated.

According to the architecture of Creation, you the Creature, who has been created to enjoy unbounded delight in your physical life experience, are born in your *Adaptivebody* form with clean energy. *Hence you are not designed to have dis-ease* (or lack of ease) in your physical *Adaptivebody*. Every cell of your body is designed to interplay and collaborate to allow you to enjoy sound health throughout your physical life experience. There is a constant circuit of energy (or as the Chinese call *Chi* or Asian Indians call *Prana*) you are born with, that keeps all physiological systems operating in peak condition. When there is a block in this uninterrupted circuit of this energy, you feel a lack of ease which is dis-ease. There is never a break in the flow of energy, unless there is a detachment of a part of your physical body – for example amputation, accidental or surgical removal of a body part. Your sub-conscious mind is responsible to keep that circuit of energy churning through your *Adaptivebody* following the operating instructions from the memory in the 2nd DNA pair in each cell of the corresponding body part.

Traditional Oriental healing modalities are based on non-allopathic and non-surgical techniques to eliminate such

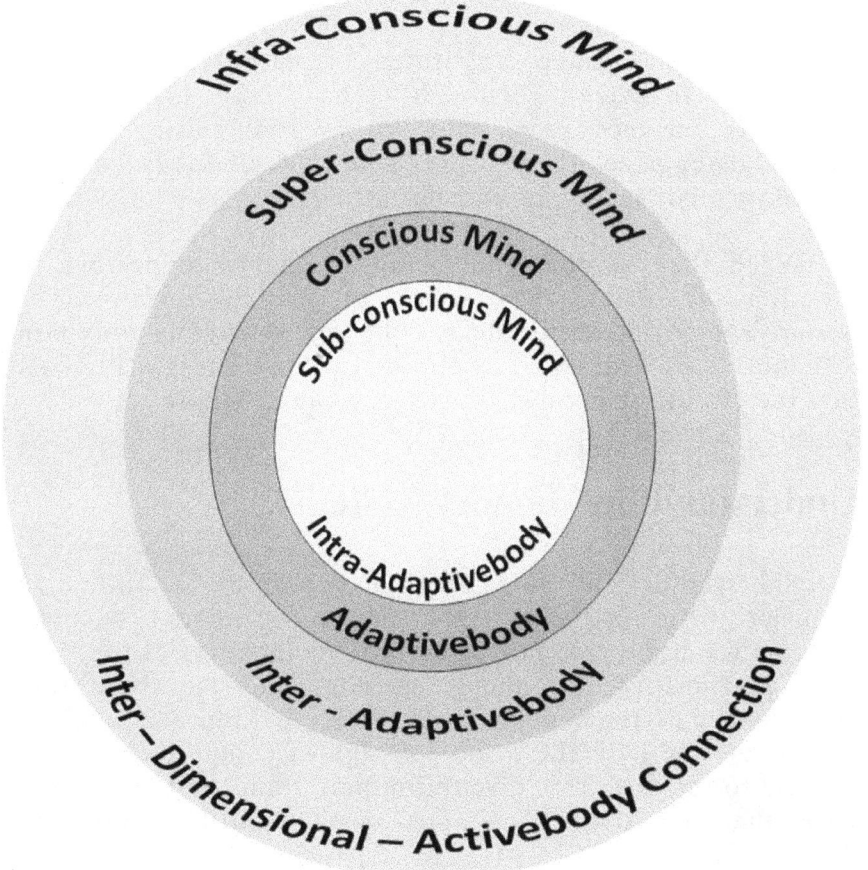

Figure 22

energy blocks or *interference* in the circuit of energy within your physiological body and re-enable that *Chi* energy flow to continue. When that clearing happens, dis-eased part of the body including all other collaborating physiological systems regain their normal functions and the sub-conscious mind resumes operation as designed. Discussions on non-invasive, non-allopathic, non-surgical and non-steroidal or non-chemical healing techniques are beyond the scope of this book but I will discuss them in the follow-on book – *Miracles From Genetics Of Divinity*.

The human *Adaptivebody* has been designed to heal itself without the need for any of the massively popular *remedial* (not healing) techniques that are in vogue today. Those techniques that have instituted a multi-trillion dollar healthcare industry worldwide today may alleviate the symptoms but they never address the root cause, which is why I categorize them as *remedial* techniques and not *healing* modalities by any means.

When the sub-conscious mind is unable to perform its functions to drive the circuit of energy through your *Adaptivebody*, its needs the services of your conscious mind to adopt steps necessary to eliminate those energy blocks so that the circuit of natural life energy can continue.

Understanding Memory Systems

The subject of this section could be a full sized manuscript on its own right. When we model computer systems we attempt to mimic certain components of the forms and functions of the human memory and the three inner components of the human mind (refer to Figure 22). If you have expertise with the overall design of computers, you will be able to relate to this discussion better and find similarities with the magnificent memory system built within your *Adaptivebody*.

---------------------------*****---------------------------

Memory (one unit of data) resides in every cell of your physical Adaptivebody, specifically in the DNA strands, not just in your brain. Your brain is the core component of your central nervous system with the spinal cord representing the *super high bandwidth* information bus to which nerve endings from every other part of your body is connected through the peripheral nervous system. To draw an analogy, if you examine a computer motherboard, your brain would be the central processing unit (CPU) of that motherboard, whereas the spinal cord would be represented by the system bus on that motherboard.

-------------------------#####-------------------------

You are born with some *static* memory in your cells, which is why for example, the hands and the feet always look and function like hands and feet all throughout your physical life experience in the 4-D – that is memory contained in the cells of your hands and feet. Your five senses operate exactly the same way ever since you are born (we are not talking about disabilities acquired after birth) – that is memory contained in the cells of the receptors of your five senses – eyes, nose, ears, skin and tongue. Every default physiological function of your body, the operations of the DNA are all part of this static memory. Along the same lines, the code of Eternal Consciousness embedded in the 2nd pair of DNA strands is also a static memory system that does not change. This is similar to the **ROM** or **Read Only Memory** unit of your computer, which stores data that is static in nature, such as the operations of the BIOS.

In addition, there is also provision for *dynamic* memory in your cells. These memory systems store data that you acquire throughout your physical lifetime which are primarily data related to personal relationships, academics, profession, communal, cultural, religious, socio-political paradigms and belief systems. Most of these belief systems in dynamic memory are artificial and man-made and have questionable coherence with the *Genetics Of Divinity*. More on these dynamic memory systems are coming up shortly.

While the static memory systems, specifically those related to the code of the *Genetics Of Divinity* need to remain active and operational in your conscious mind, humanity traditionally has relied more on the dynamic memory systems to influence the life experience. This reliance on artificial datasets that are not in conformance with the code of Eternal Consciousness is why humanity has deviated away from the original intent of unbounded delight of the Creature. The Parallel Universe we have chosen to live in is definitely one that is supported by Parallelism, but it is time humanity took notice of the Contrast and defined a Parallel Universe where the core principle of the *Genetics Of Divinity* is followed for the collective unbounded delight of our civilization. As the dominant species in this planet, it is us humans who have to lead the charge for the improvement of our quality of life and leave a legacy for next generations to come.

I am making a fair assumption here that the earlier chapters of this book has proven to you that you are immortal in your *Activebody*, while mortal in your *Adaptivebody*. Memories from your *Activebody* are passed on to your *Adaptivebody* each time you are born in physical form in the 3-D. The reason why you cannot ordinarily remember memories from those past lives is primarily three-fold. First you have probably been programmed and convinced to believe that you get only one shot at life. Second, due to this first programming, you have not made an effort to delve into memories of your past lives. Third, you are not aware of techniques that enable you to access memories from your past lives or those that you inherited from your *Activebody*. Did you know that some of the challenges that you have in your current physical life experience is the result of memory that you are carrying forward from your past lives? More on past life regression and its potential benefits will be covered in the follow-on book – *Miracles From Genetics Of Divinity*.

Memory is a data point – a piece of information stored in every cell of your body. Needless to say, not every memory is stored in every cell of your body – only whatever is pertinent to that localized part of your body where the cell is a building block of that body part.

For example memories related to holding a golf club are stored in the cells of your hands and arms but have no significance to the cells that constitute your ears. The sound of a thunderclap is stored in the memory of the cells in your ears, but that the cells in your hands find no need to store any of that memory. Wrinkles on the skin on your forehead or the crow's feet to the corners of your eyes are nothing but memories stored only in those particular cells in the local area of the skin (the largest organ of the human body), while other areas of your skin may still be perfectly toned. Is it possible to eliminate the wrinkles on your skin and those crow's feet? Yes, it's simple – eliminate the *over-riding memory* in those parts of your skin and re-expose the native memory of a perfectly toned skin to those cells. Voila – the wrinkles and crow's feet are gone. By the way – no, the craftily marketed wrinkle remover cream won't do it for you. What will? All in good time – I cover techniques to change non-serving and overriding memories including *non-invasive cosmetic surgery* in the follow-on book – Miracles From Genetics Of Divinity.

---------------------------*****---------------------------

Any memory consists of two components – first, the data associated with the triggering event itself (what happened) and second, the emotion or what I refer to as the *charge* (like a positive or negative charge of an ion), that is associated with that event (how did you *feel* when what happened, happened). We commonly categorize memories as good or bad, when in fact what we really refer to as good or bad is the emotion associated with that triggering event. While the first part of the memory cannot be eliminated as it gets recorded in the script of your life experience in the 4-D, however the second part of the memory – the associated emotion or charge can be significantly altered in intensity through various techniques that I will illustrate in the follow-on book.

There are no negative events in life – when you know what is perceived by you as negative, it clarifies for you through the attribute of Contrast what the positive experience is. You get to choose through the power of your free will to focus your attention on the positive and hence the *anabolic* aspect of that event or to dwell on the negative or *catabolic* aspect of that event. The event does not change or go away but the negative charge associated with that memory can be reduced or even neutralized with anabolic energy.

---------------------------#####-------------------------

There are four types of memories that your Adaptivebody is designed to store and in this discussion, I am referring to the first component (the data of the event) of the memory –

1. **Type 1 : static and unchangeable memory** that you carry forward from your past lives. Data that you inherit from your *Activebody* and data related to the code of the *Genetics Of Divinity*.
2. **Type 2: characteristic and unchangeable memory** that defines your basic *Adaptivebody* form (your physiological features such as DNA, blood group, sex, skin, eye and hair color etc) and other physiological and psychological functions as a human. Such memory also includes basic Type B animal instincts of fight, flight or freeze augmented with Type A differentiators related to intelligence and rationality.
3. **Type 3 : acquired and dynamic memory** that the appropriate cells of your *Adaptivebody* accumulate through your interactions with other Creatures of all energy bands, events and circumstances that make up your life experience in the 13 categories of relationships discussed in Chapter 3. Pay special attention to this category of memory as one of the key objectives of this book and all forthcoming interactions with me that you choose to have, will be based on working with this Type 3 memory. This type of memory can be of three types:
    a. Long term memory – think about this as the ROM (read only memory) of a computer, that does not change or need to change for a long time. For example, the language that you learn, the alphabet that you write, who your parents and siblings are,

social etiquettes and manners, planetary rhythms, environmental factors are all examples of long term memory.

b. Medium term memory – think of this as the hard drive of your computer that holds data for a while. After the usable life has expired that memory can be deleted from your cells as they no longer serve a purpose. For example, the concept of immortality might have been taught to you to be considered taboo or blasphemy – this was stored in your medium term memory. Reading the explanation of immortality in this book, you may decide through the attribute of free will and rational analysis, to *drop* the memory associated with data about immortality and associate yourself with a new memory about immortality. Just so that we are clear, when I say '*drop that memory*', it does not mean that the memory is gone and you never remember it. What goes or gets dropped is the emotion that are associated with that memory. You still will probably tell the tales, "there was a time in my life when I did not believe in immortality ..." but then the emotion (I call *charge*) from that memory is gone. As an analogy, the bomb is still there, but the fuse has been ripped out of it, making the bomb harmless.

c. Short term memory – think of this as the RAM (random access memory) of your computer. It serves you for a brief period of time and then it goes away. For example, you accidentally bump into another person in a shopping mall and you exchange apologies and go your own ways. After a while that you cannot even recall the appearance of that person, since that memory no longer serves your life experience.

4. **Type 4 : shared memory** – this is a unique type of memory that is not necessarily related to your personal life in the current lifetime. This Type of memory is what you share with all the other Creatures with whom you co-exist in a contemporary life experience and who will exist even after your own mortal *Adaptivebody* has passed on. I am referring to the *legacy* that you will leave behind after

your *Adaptivebody* completes its mortal lifecycle. Such memory could also be what you have derived from the legacy left by someone else. Have you wondered why kids today are so smart in comparison when you and I were of that young age? Legacy is how humans evolve and grow and this Type 4 or Shared Memory is what facilitates such a carry-forward evolution across generations.

5. **Type 5: relational memory** – When did you fall in love with your partner? Oops, correction – When did you **_RISE_** in love with your partner? Are you in a romantic relationship now? How did you meet? What are the most cherished moments since you were together? What was your most challenging disagreement? How did you resolve it? Do you work? Where? When did you join? What are your qualifications? ... and you could go on. Type 5 memory is directly related to the twelve secondary relationship categories in your life (the primary being your relationship with yourself) in the relationship chart from Chapter 3. This Type of memory is very unique in a particular aspect that took me a while to understand when I first became consciously aware of its presence. I know what you are about to learn about this memory may seem shocking to you - in a good way of course ☺ You may not believe it and that is ok based on your current level of consciousness. However the facts about this Type 5 memory does not change and you too will remember the truth once this section of the code of the *Genetics Of Divinity* reactivates from your subconscious mind. Ready for amazement? Type 5 memory *contains the information implanted by your Activebody in the 4th pair of your DNA strands, prior to your birth in physical form. This information is about your life purpose and the identities of all the partners for all relationship categories that you are expected to enjoy a symbiotic collaborative relationship with during your mortal lifetime, who would contribute to the fulfillment of your life purpose.* If you recall, I mentioned earlier that the 5-D is a domain of stabilized energy and is a domain of collaboration and coherence Your 5-D *Activebody* has a role to perform in the grid of Existence and its role is to serve and contribute for the purpose of collective coexistence. In the process it needs to enable the Creature (you) to enjoy

unbounded delight. Your *Activebody* creates you, the *Adaptivebody* in physical form and assigns a specific life purpose to you that you are required to fulfill during your lifetime. Your *Activebody* also lines up all the partners in all the twelve secondary relationship categories who would be part of your life experience, with whom you would establish those symbiotic collaborative relationships. Thorough these relationships, you and your assigned partners would collectively enjoy unbounded delight in the partnership and fulfill your life purpose. You would also *contribute* to fulfillment of the life purpose of your partners. Your *Activebody* collaborates with the *Activebodies* of all of these partners in the 5-D prior to your birth in physical form to line them up for your life experience. Who these partners are, when exactly during your physical lifetime they would appear in your life, the circumstances that would be involved that would bring the two of you together, what you will be doing together, how you will do what you will be doing together, when you will do what you will be doing together in the relationship are all lined up for you by your *Activebody*. All of this, so that you can collaborate with these *optimized* partnerships and fulfill your life purpose. This plan for your life, your life purpose, this sequence of events that bring these relationships together for you are all stored as Type 5 memory in your *Adaptivebody*. Pretty smart design, huh? ☺ The question is, have you conducted your life so far according to this plan or have you made choices in Parallelism randomly, played games of chance, made your own decisions based on personal gut feelings about the partners in your relationship categories? You do have free will to override the assignments made by your *Activebody*, which is very much possible if you are unaware of your Type 5 memory or if you do not believe in such a pre-defined plan. Your parents obviously are the first partners that your *Activebody* chooses for you in physical form, just like all the other partners who are to be part of your life experience. Nothing and no relationship in your life is by accident – they were either the result of your *Activebody's handiwork* or your own choice through your free will without the guidance of your *Activebody*. It's time you understood this plan implanted in your Type 5 memory by your *Activebody* and get aligned with it. How can you learn more about this plan stored in your Type 5 memory? Can I read *your* Type 5 memory? No that is not possible by design, since I have no business about your life purpose - think about it as your *genetic privacy and confidentiality protection* ☺. I can however guide you through the process and empower you to read your own Type 5 memory. I will discuss how you can tap into your Type 5 memory in the book *Miracles from Genetics Of Divinity*.

What role does the brain play in this memory game? Well, the brain cells have their own memory that no other cell in the human body has and without a doubt you will find the discussion coming up shortly on this topic fascinating. For the sake of repetition, the brain does *not contain all your memory* as you might have been informed and have been convinced to believe so far. Let's understand the working of the human brain, its relationship to memory. Let's understand how the human brain is why we are all here the way we are here and how this unique and most sophisticated organ of the human body is the vehicle through which we can be wherever we desire to be in a different time in the 4-D living in a different Parallel Universe.

Central Nervous System – Modus Operandi

As you can imagine, in order to keep the focus on the book, I am not going make this an anatomy or physiology or clinical discussion. Feel free to research the workings of the human brain on your own. I am going to take you to the not so often discussed information as it relates to the human central nervous system

In software engineering and all modern software programming languages, we have the concept of *memory address pointers*, which actually refers to the actual *address* in the memory bank of that computer where the data is stored instead of the data itself. So a software program could have logic in it that manipulates the address of the data rather than the data itself. It could disable the address completely, eliminating the data along with it. The program could de-allocate the address of the data and re-allocate the data to a different address (reallocation). The program could read the data by using the address in memory where the data is stored and have follow-on logic based on the data that was read. The program could also write (or update) a certain piece data in a particular memory address. So when the software program loads, it becomes aware (through programming logic) of all the addresses in memory where data that the program will work with is available for reads, writes or updates. With this background information, the software program can perform its other functions according to its specifications of design.

-------------------------*****-------------------------

The concept of memory address pointers as I have briefly explained above is exactly how your central nervous system with the brain as the core component, is designed and organized to work. Along with the peripheral nervous system (associated with your five senses), all other anatomical systems of your *Adaptivebody* as well as your dormant communication uplink with your very own *Activebody* in the 5-D, are all managed through the manipulation of address pointers by this heavily equipped masterpiece of Creation – your brain.

-------------------------#####-------------------------

The memory (data plus the emotion) resides in the cells in that localized part of your body where the triggering event had the greatest impact. For example if you stubbed your toe on the foot of your bed, the memory of the injury and the emotions (feeling of pain) that you felt during the experience would reside in your injured toe but the *address* of the cell(s) in your toe that retains that memory would be stored in your brain. Next time you are around the bed, you will automatically be careful not to repeat the same circumstances again. Why? When you see or feel the bed near to you, those two senses transmit the impulse to your brain. Your brain cells will engage to find an existing memory address that matches the pattern of the impulse. The neurons in your brain which stored the address of the cell(s) of the toe that captured the memory, generates an simulated impulse to that same cell(s) in your toe, which in turn recalls the memory almost like a simulated playback, which in turn activates the peripheral nervous system *at biophotonic speed* to invoke a replay of the same emotions of pain.

This simulated experience is the warning that your brain would initiate to your conscious mind, which in turn would make sure you stay cautious and don't stub your toe again. Every time you are around a bed you would be careful, as it has now become a memory system that affects your decision making process, your rationality and hence your free will.

What exactly is this cell address that I am referring to? We come back to the DNA strand pairs again. Each cell in the body can be uniquely identified by its DNA signature, which is the address of the cell in your body. The only way your brain can communicate with that cell is when it registers the address of the cell provided by its DNA. Whenever a new cell is created in the body through the process of mitosis (cell division), its address is registered in the brain.

How is the memory address created in the brain? The brain is composed of nerve fibers called *neurons*, which are the fundamental building blocks of the nervous system. In order to store any information the endings of neurons would dynamically align with each other (we still don't know the precise mechanics of such alignment) and create that memory address. The gap between the nerve fibers is called *synapse*. When the alignment occurs data would flow across this *synaptic bridge* from one neuron to another all through the central nervous system into the peripheral nervous system and ultimately terminating in that cell of your body where the memory (data about the event and the emotion or associated charge) is stored. Now that the address is set, how does the brain leverage that memory to make rational decisions?

Pattern Recognition

We learn and live our life experience in the 3-D by a mechanism called *pattern recognition*. Several technology solutions that are associated with artificial intelligence in mechanical (for example, specific keys or specific number sequence combinations that open a lock), electronic (for example, biometric security devices) and software (for example, data encryption and decryption algorithms) systems are based on pattern recognition.

A pattern for us humans is a particular *memory pack* that includes (1) the address of your cell where the memory is stored, (2) what the triggering impulse for that memory was, (3) what the data of the event is (what happened) and (4) what type of *charge* is associated with that event. This pack of 4 data elements constitutes a pattern for your brain and the cell(s) that recorded the memory.

The brain uses the triggering impulse to identify the address (like an index on a database table or the catalog in a library of books), where a pattern associated with that trigger may be stored. If an address is found based on the triggering impulse, then the brain understands that a pattern already exists – this is part of your consciousness, a *known*. Since the pattern is now considered a *known*, the brain assumes that the response to that triggering impulse would also be known. The brain instantly identifies the cell where the memory is stored from the address and reaches out to the cell for the stored response through synaptic bridge of the nervous system. This transmission of the impulse from the brain to the localized cell and back is facilitated by *biophotons* that I will discuss shortly.

The cell(s) in question that holds the Type 3 memory or the data about the pattern and the emotions associated with that memory would receive the impulse from the brain using the 1st strand of the 3rd pair of DNA strands in that cell and generate a response about the pattern using the 2nd strand of the 3rd pair of DNA. This pattern of information is relayed to your brain thereby re-constructing your past experience. This pattern is relayed to your rational and decision-making mechanics of the brain, which analyzes the pattern and makes a decision.

This entire channel or route that links the associated parts of your *Adaptivebody* is called a *neural pathway* or a specific sequence of neural synaptic bridges through which information is exchanged through the nervous system. *Knowledge and hence consciousness is nothing else but patterns of information that you have acquired through your five senses, or inherited at birth, associated appropriate emotions to those patterns and stored it as memory.*

When a triggering impulse presents the same pattern to your *Adaptivebody* again, your peripheral nervous system would relay that pattern to the brain. The brain would engage a pattern matching algorithm and if a match is found, the information exchange would occur through the neural pathway as I just explained.

All of this information exchange for a healthy human happens instantly, carried by a particle what Fritz-Albert Popp, a professor at the University of Marburg, Germany referred to in 1970 as *biophotons*. In a recent book called *Holographic Healing* by Dr. George Gonzalez, refers to the human body as the *lightbody* (a human body made of light particles or photons or specifically biophotons). The reaction time (commonly referred to as *reflex action*) to an external impulse is designed to be blazing fast – although not quite as fast as the speed of light in vacuum, of course. Hence the biophotons broker the information exchange through electromagnetic impulses along the appropriate neural pathways in your *Adaptivebody*. The presence of biophotons is proven in modern research and by design are an integral part of both Type A and Type B Creatures. Logic and Parallelism allows biophotons to exist for Type C Creatures as well although research thus far has not conclusively confirmed as such.

I completely subscribe to these *biophotons* being the carrier particle of the impulse traveling through the neural pathway because the human *Adaptivebody*, specifically the central nervous system and your DNA are transceivers of electromagnetic energy. Recent research using Kirlian photography has been able to map out the human aura and the glow in that aura is the result of light being emitted from these biophotons – this is called the *lightbody*.

We conduct our life experience by pattern acquisition, pattern matching and pattern rejection. What is pattern rejection? All knowledge is considered to be a certain pattern with the four elements of the memory pack that I mentioned earlier. When you reject some information you are essentially rejecting any emotional association to the data of that memory. To some people who read this book for example, the information contained would not be considered plausible or believable. Such a person would still retain the data of the event of having received the information contained in this book, but since there was no emotion of acceptance or belief in the material, the knowledge would be rejected – this is called *pattern rejection*. Next time they find the book in a bookstore or in a friend's house, the initial response would be rejection.

I trust you will engage in the new pattern acquisition and pattern application processes as you consume the material contained in this book - it is authentic and accurate. In the online Multiversity of the *Genetics Of Divinity,* I describe a technique that you can use to determine the authenticity of the material contained in this book by tapping into the multi-dimensional consciousness.

Two people being exposed to the same event (the data) could potentially store entirely different emotions about the same event, which in turn would create a distinct pattern in each of them. In the future if the same two people are exposed to the same triggering event, they would react completely differently based on the knowledge that each of them respectively have stored as a pattern of memory. One person for example, could engage in a discussion about the world economy with doom and gloom, while the other would project an upbeat and opportunistic view about the same topic. Yet another person could appear to be completely oblivious of any information about economic hardship anywhere, if for example such a person was never exposed to the pattern about the state of the economy before.

How one interacts with events, people, and circumstances is dependent on the availability of some pattern about the subject in memory. If such a pattern does not exist, the individual *could* engage the Type B instincts of fight, flight or freeze. Alternatively the person could use the Type A attributes of rationality, analysis and free will, choose to acquire new knowledge and hence a new pattern about the subject so that an informed decision can be made through pattern matching. Greater the number of patterns available in the memory of an individual's *Adaptivebody*, higher is the level of consciousness and more empowered the person feels to <u>respond</u> *and not just react* to life's challenges and rewards. Collectively they define the quality of life experience.

Knowledgebase, Belief Systems and Neural Pathways

Your *knowledgebase* or *consciousness* essentially is the combination of specific neural pathways with memory patterns about the event, interaction with other *Adaptivebodies* or circumstance along with the associated positive or negative charge. While it is not possible to change the data since it gets recorded in your Type 3 memory, it is absolutely possible to change the charge or the emotion associated with the memory, which in turn would alter the pattern in your knowledgebase.

Research has shown that when emotions are registered or updated in memory, the neurons in the brain could and/or would physically delink themselves from the neural pathway to which they were originally associated and build the association of a synaptic bridge with entirely new set of neurons, thereby establishing a brand new neural pathway – hence an updated knowledgebase and belief system. However such an updated synaptic bridge can occur if and only if Parallelism supports such an alignment, in other words, if the possibility is logical and ethically feasible.

---------------------------*****---------------------------

Your life experience today, regardless of whether you are consciously aware of your life purpose and the code of the Genetics Of Divinity or not, is the sum of your consciousness composed of active memory patterns and neural pathways that currently influence the rational analysis and decision-making process in your conscious mind.

The sum refers to the net of all the memories that have a positive charge associated with them (those that are perceived by your conscious mind as positive – all the *do*s, *can*s, *must*s the *good*s, the *yes'* and the *right*s) and those that have a linked negative charge (those that are perceived by your conscious mind as negative – all the *don't*s, *can't*s, the *bad*s, *no*s and the *wrong*s). Collectively they define the quality of your life experience and the quality of relationships in the 13 categories that I mentioned in Chapter 3. At the same instant of time any other given individual could have a similar (if not same), somewhat different or significantly different life experience. This is all dependent on those currently stored patterns that influence rational thought, analytical decision making, degree of freedom of free will and hence deliberate and conscious action.

---------------------------#####---------------------------

If you are not enjoying a life experience filled with unbounded delight for what you have been designed, the only thing that you need to change is your neural pathways and hence your consciousness or belief system, possibly first by neutralizing the negative charge on memories (I call it *charge cleansing*) that inhibit your realignment with the *Genetics Of Divinity*. Once such a neutralization has occurred you can acquire new data for your new memory, associate it with an appropriate set of anabolic emotions, develop a new pattern and establish brand new neural pathways that align you with whatever leads you to unbounded delight.

How would you identify, acquire and establish these new neural pathways that would bring you unbounded delight in your life experience? Simple, those neural pathways that you consider new are not new at all and they don't require you to acquire or establish them by any means. Those neural pathways are already part of your Type 1 memory where the code of the *Genetics Of Divinity* are stored in the 2nd pair of DNA strands in every cell of your body. Events, people and circumstances in the past that you have related with in catabolic relationships could have left that proverbial bad taste in your mouth. It may be hard for you to swallow, but you have allowed such relationships to be established and for that you are equally if not more responsible and accountable as that partner. The solution is in *charge cleansing*.

The *Adaptive Energy* in such a catabolic relationship is so powerful that it contributed to the detachment of your conscious mind from those natural Type 1 neural pathways (those associated with Type 1 memories) and the attachment of your conscious mind to artificial Type 3 patterns creating neural pathways that guided you towards your state of pain and plight. This past cannot be changed in the 4-D as you are aware by now. However the burst of intensity of your *Adaptive Energy* at the moment of making that decision to change your current state of plight has the power and ability to re-engage and re-align your conscious mind with those Type 1 neural pathways.

Let me ask you a question – "Are YOU getting in YOUR own way towards unbounded delight?" Assume responsibility and accountability and answer that question for every relationship in those 13 categories form Chapter 3 – the answer will be self-evident. Great, now that you have the answer do you also understand the Contrast that Creation is offering you? If you could, probably you should, but only you know if you would make that decision to undergo the process of re-alignment with Type 1 neural pathways to navigate towards your definition of unbounded delight.

An old Chinese proverb says, '*The height of madness is doing the same thing over and over again and expecting different results*'. This is also true from a scientific point of view. Any system must have an input, a processor of that input and an output or result. In order to change the output, it does not matter how significantly you change the input –

the processor must change to first interpret the new input and hence consequently generate a new output. Makes sense?

Your life experience also is such a system where the processor is your consciousness. If you want the output – your intended life experience to be filled with unbounded delight, you must discard what is called *neuro-plasticity* (not willing to change your neural pathways) and embrace your natural *neuro-elasticity* (willing to change) by the acquisition of new and enhanced knowledge. As explained before, *the neural pathways are designed to be elastic*, constantly assigning new addresses to new memories. Consequently you would develop new anabolic Type 3 memory patterns and reactivate natural Type 1 memory patterns to guide rational thought to guide you towards your life purpose and hence unbounded delight.

The EGS - Emotional Guidance System

I humbly credit the concept of the human EGS® to Esther and Jerry Hicks as they describe so eloquently in Chapter 22 of the their bestseller book *Ask and It is Given*. I recommend you read that book and especially Chapter 22, for a detailed explanation of the EGS. The EGS is a gift of Eternal Consciousness to you from your 5-D *Activebody* and a gift of knowledge from the Hicks' to humanity.

You are aware by now, as a Creature you have free will and have been designed to experience unbounded delight in your physical life experience. The life purpose that your *Activebody* in the 5-D has assigned to your *Adaptivebody* in the 3-D is meant to bring you a life experience filled with unbounded delight as long as you stay aligned with your life purpose. If you are aware of your life purpose and aligned with its accomplishment, you will automatically experience emotions of unbounded delight (happy, positive, enthusiastic and vibrant all the time) – that is the core design of Creation and Existence.

What if you are not having delight in your life experience? You would be having emotions that are not in the domain of unbounded delight. The Hicks' mention 22 different levels of human emotions in their description of the EGS - starting from empowerment, joy, knowledge, freedom (their terms for unbounded delight) at the highest level to depression, grief, fear, despair, powerlessness at the lowest depths (their terms for unbounded plight) of the human EGS. A graphical representation of the emotions in the EGS is shown in Figure 23. Invest time to review the different emotions of the EGS and understand the transition from unbounded plight to unbounded delight.

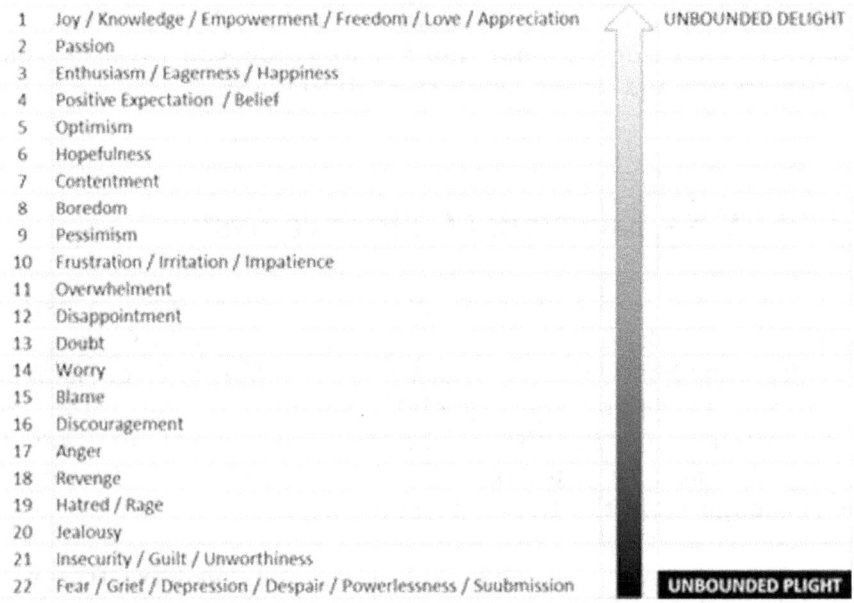

Figure 23

---------------------------*****---------------------------

All emotions originate in the super-conscious component of your quad-compartmental mind as a response to an external impulse captured by your five senses. Depending on your rational (or default) thought and analysis, *those emotions get transferred to the sub-conscious component of your mind* for appropriate involuntary physiological functions. For example the touch of a loved one is a neural pathway that would include specific emotions in your *super-conscious mind*. The memory of these emotions when transferred to your conscious mind by your brain would make you decide to respond to the impulse favorably. This decision to approve the impulse is transferred to your sub-conscious mind, which will direct the central nervous system to produce copious quantities of a neuro-transmitter called *serotonin*, which generates the warm feeling of love and happiness. This is the physical transformation of the non-physical emotion of love and happiness. Your *Adaptivebody* is a marvel, a genius of engineering, a masterpiece of Creation – be proud of it, protect it and maximize its potential to enhance your life experience.

--------------------------#####--------------------------

How does one use the EGS? Given the fact that as a Creature you are designed to feel unbounded delight in your life experience in the 3-D, that translates to the emotions indicated as #1 in the EGS scale. If you are **consistently** experiencing those emotions, you are in the domain of unbounded delight and in all likelihood, you are aligned with your life purpose as well. You are in that case, *doing or thinking about the right things, correctly, long enough and consistently whatever it is that you are doing or thinking about.*

Consider the EGS to operate like the GPS (Global Positioning System) of your car or an airplane. As long as you set the GPS to a particular destination (achievement of your life purpose) the GPS system will chart the course for you to navigate. As long as you are following the course, the GPS continues to indicate that you are aligned well and guides you to your destination.

However, if you veer off the charted course intentionally or not, the GPS unit will recalculate and chart a new course for you to adjust and follow in an attempt to re-align you with your preset destination. In other words, the GPS is a fault detection, early warning and a fault correction system. You always have a choice through your free will to ignore the course suggestions and corrections or to follow its instructions. Modern day GPS units can also be sensitive to dynamic traffic conditions in the default route that it charted and automatically suggest you alternative routes that would take you to your destination in the shortest possible time. The more closely you follow the instructions of the GPS, faster you will arrive at your preset destination.

Coming back to the context of your book, that preset destination for your EGS is the life purpose set for your *Adaptivebody* by your own 5-D *Activebody* and the intent to feel unbounded delight in your physical life experience. When you have dreams, goals, objectives, when you set targets and plan to set and achieve the subject of desire in your life experience, your EGS serves as guide to validate every moment for you whether you are aligned with your target or not following the principles of the Law of Alignment. If you are so aligned you will by design, feel emotions higher up on the EGS scale. Conversely if you are not aligned properly you will feel emotions that are lower down on the EGS scale. Essentially the emotions that you feel can be used as a *litmus test* for whatever it is that you are contemplating on or actually doing.

Napoleon Hill, bestseller author of *Think and Grow Rich* and *Law of Success in Sixteen Lessons* writes, "*You become (or you get) what you think about most of the time*". Your physical life experience, as I have indicated earlier is the sum of your neural pathways that you have set up and activated so far . Your life experience is the net of all the actions that you have taken so far, through decisions you have taken every moment of your life when Parallelism offered you its menu of choices. These decisions are the net result of all the thoughts that you have been thinking about the choices from Parallelism, which in turn are the products of your belief patterns or consciousness. Every decision you make in your life experience creates a memory attached with an emotion from the EGS.

When you are faced with an opportunity to make a decision from the available choices of Parallelism, the emotions from the EGS scale that you feel about your thoughts are very reliable guides that you can ever have and those emotions will seldom fail you. By design of the *Human* class of Type A energy if you remain attentive to the emotions that you feel about the thoughts that you think you can leverage the EGS to make the right choices in life. As a double whammy to your internal faculties, when you couple the EGS and your uplink with your *Activebody* in the 5-D together, seeking advice and counsel about decisions in life, you just simply cannot go wrong. The *Activebody* connection removes any doubts that you may have about the emotions that you feel in the EGS scale.

---------------------------*****---------------------------

The source of the emotions that you feel about a particular subject is in the super-conscious and/or infra-conscious mind, which operate in the domain of the non-physical energy. In the domain of the non-physical, there are no bounds or physical limitations and the higher components of your quad-compartmental mind are able to energetically connect and interact with related energies of other *Adaptivebodies* in the 3-D and even your own 5-D *Activebody* to trigger those emotions. These emotions are conveyed by the EGS to the conscious mind, thereby enabling you to apply your rationality and consequently take a decision.

More often than not, certain memories in neural pathways dominate the human conscious mind to such a large extent that they would overrule and override the natural emotions generated by the EGS, resulting in actions that yield a sub-optimal life experience. The emotions from these patterns are so strong they become the default as emotions lower on the EGS scale - more towards unbounded plight than unbounded delight.

This fact, coupled with the explanation of the Law of Attraction that I have provided earlier, specifically as it relates to *'like attracts like in the non-physical plane'*, implies that when you feel emotions that are lower in the EGS scale you align with and get attracted to more events, people and circumstances in your life experience that lead to more and more of the same emotions that are lower on the EGS scale.

These low emotions, lead to stress and in extreme cases, depression. Stress is a killer of the *Adaptivebody*, which is originally designed to live a life of emotions in tune with unbounded delight. When you are stressed, you have emotions that are lower on the EGS and this serves as an early warning system for you to seek out the Contrast to identify what will make you feel emotions higher on the EGS scale.

-------------------------#####-------------------------

Do your own research on the dramatic physiological and psychological impact of stress on your *Adaptivebody*. Stress is the root cause of any and all dis-ease. Modern allopathic medicine and surgical practices may alleviate some physiological *symptoms* of such disease but they can never eliminate the root cause. Stress acts as an inhibitor to the natural life sustaining *Adaptive* energy that pulsates through the *Adaptivebody*. Blockage or interference of this natural *Adaptive* energy flow leads to a degradation of the physiological and psychological body, resulting in dis-ease.

Hence that little anger, that scarcity, that unspoken jealousy, that quiet frustration, that fake bravado, that blame, that worry are all contributing emotions to stress and disease.

Effect of Lower EGS Emotions on the Adaptivebody

Higher emotional stress conditions (which are low EGS emotions) causes a group of hormones called *cortisols* to get secreted by the adrenaline glands of the human body as a survival mechanism of the physical body. These cortisols are introduced in the bloodstream in an attempt to counter the catabolic energy of stress by increasing the heart rates so that the heart can pump more oxygenated blood into the body. This leads to high blood pressure and faster (hence shallower) respiratory cycles. What is the body going to burn to get that compensating energy? Sugar. When sugar is burned by the body to generate the compensating energy, the body goes weaker thereby increasing the craving for sugar. To counter the sugar, the pancreas would generate a hormone called insulin to keep the glucose level in check. If adequate insulin is not generated, it leads to the disease of diabetes. The end result of all of this snowball effect in addition to diabetes as you can imagine could be high blood pressure, shortness of breath, hyper or hypo ventilation, strokes (not enough oxygen in the brain) or heart failures (too high heart rate), angina (skipped heart beats) and the degradation of the physical body continues with the risk of more serious diseases. The root cause is stress, the killer is stress – eliminate stress by refusing to succumb to the effects of people, events and circumstances that lead to lower EGS emotions and you have eliminated the root cause for disease.

It is impossible for the non-physical super-conscious and infra-conscious mind to function without a healthy and naturally functional physical body. A person with ill health focusses on the illness most of the time, and that focus snowballs into more of the same conditions of catabolic energy and a departure from any alignment with the life purpose of the *Adaptivebody*. Law of Attraction diligently at work. What is the root cause of stress? Take a few moments to pause reading this book, analyze your own life and ponder what the root cause of stress in your life could be. Here's a hint – *scarcity and deprivation of what you desire in life.*

What people, events and circumstances in your 13 categories of relationship from Chapter 3 are causing these low EGS emotions that are causing stress? There must be an artificial scarcity in one or more of those relationships that is causing that stress – what is it? What Type 3 memories and hence belief patterns are you being guided by that are running these background programs in your conscious mind to inhibit high EGS emotions? Find the root cause and eliminate them and you would constructively address the outcome of your life experience.

We humans have two very distinct philosophies of conducting a physical life experience. The specific choice made by an *Adaptivebody* as a result of its level of consciousness, the patterns of belief systems, the neural pathways that are established in the central nervous system determines if that *Adaptivebody* will experience a life plagued with the catabolic energy of stress and misalignment with the life purpose, or a life buoyant in the tides of anabolic energy of unbounded delight and alignment with the preset life purpose.

The first philosophy is to live a life of appreciation, humility, gratefulness and thankfulness for the pleasures and the delights that are already in the life experience, coming from a position of abundance and conviction that there is more from where the pleasures came from. Only *after such an appreciation and abundance* is felt in this philosophy of living does the *Adaptivebody* ask for more. With the focus being on the knowingness of abundance and the humility of appreciation, the *Adaptivebody* does not feel the sense of *lack, scarcity and deprivation, which are the root causes of stress*. The individual enjoys the journey of delayed gratification, with the knowledge that in due course whatever the super-conscious mind aligns with and stays aligned with (Law of Alignment) consistently by increasing intensity of focus, will eventually attract the *Adaptivebody* towards it (Law of Attraction).

This is living a life buoyant with abundance and in such a life, stress does not play any catabolic energetic interference in the operation of the physical and non-physical part of the *Adaptivebody*. You naturally have *the drive to thrive* not *strive to survive*, staying engaged in constant communication with the *Activebody* in the 5-D. Armed with such a knowledgebase, you would naturally assume full responsibility for anything and everything in your life experience and hold yourself with high accountability with what you align with and get attracted to. You have a life experience filled with emotions higher in the EGS scale, which conforms to the Law of Creation and Existence – the Creature with the will to receive and enjoy unbounded delight.

Individuals who would consciously conduct their life experience according to attributes of this first philosophy have consciousness levels that are at or above the ANALYTICAL level in the consciousness scale as described in Chapter 4.

The second philosophy is to live a life of depreciation, a life based primarily on complaints, blame, self-pity, feelings of perpetual scarcity and deprivation, jealousy, anger, disgust and frustration with no acknowledgement or appreciation for what the person already has access to in the life experience. There is no recognition of the *have*, but over-recognition of the *have not*. This focus on the *have not* is so intense that the person get attracted by events, people and circumstances that lead to more opportunities for scarcity and deprivation. A person trapped under the guidance of such a philosophy would think, '*I don't have that, the other person has it. I can't get it, but I must have it, so I must grab it.*' A person living under these guidelines is lured easily by the temptations of instant gratification which may provide short term gain but also contributes to long term pain, since the techniques to acquire those short term gains are seldom repeatable or sustainable. Such a person enjoys the blame game with no inclination to assume any personal responsibility or accountability for any aspect of the plight-filled life experience.

These emotions that are lower on the EGS scale when repeated over and over again to the point of *default* behavior, leads to extreme stress which depletes and erodes the *Adaptivebody* with catabolic energy. The individual comes from a position of scarcity and continues to be attracted by more life experiences that continue to generate more emotions of scarcity and deprivation. Such a person could also become inclined to disrupt the life experience of other *Adaptivebodies* through parasitic destructive relationships in a desperate and misdirected search of elusive delight – thereby sinking lower and lower down the EGS scale. The *Adaptivebody* is burdened by the catabolic energy of scarcity, deprivation, desperation and *struggles to survive* through a misaligned life experience.

Individuals who would consciously conduct their life experience according to attributes of this second philosophy have consciousness levels that are one of the lowest three levels (either COMATOSE, POWERLESS or FRUSTRATED) of human consciousness in the consciousness scale as described in Chapter 4.

Neuro-plasticity and Neuro-elasticity

Which of these two philosophies do you subscribe to? If you have such stress in your life that clouds rational thoughts and conscious responsible actions, you may want to consider abandoning your acquired, artificial state of neuro-plasticity (unwillingness to learn, change and grow) and adopt your inherent natural attribute of neuro-elasticity. Neuro-elasticity enables you to reactivate dormant natural, neural pathways and develop new neural pathways that elevate you to anabolic energy as you escalate your emotions up the EGS scale. As a result of increased anabolic energy flowing through your physical *Adaptivebody*, it will realign with the assigned life purpose and get attracted with specific life experiences that evoke emotions of unbounded delight.

This goes back to the discussion on the 6 pairs of DNA strands. Through neuro-elasticity, if you have reactivated the code of the *Genetics of Divinity*, natural vibrations of each of those DNA pairs is restored, thereby enabling them to perform their original functions to reactivate the Creature and CREATOR attributes within your *Adaptivebody* and consequently lead you to your version of unbounded delight.

The secret (or no secret) to living a life without the burden of stress is to feel good (emotions higher on the EGS scale) at the present moment. If that is not possible, you must analyze where you are on the EGS scale at a given time and do whatever is necessary to feel emotions that are at least one scale higher in the scale. From there do what is necessary to go higher on the EGS scale, like climbing up the rungs of a ladder. If you have lost your way in a forest going to higher ground or on a tall tree can realign you back to your preset destination. Going up higher on the EGS scale is that higher ground you need to seek to regain your alignment with your life purpose. In the follow-on book – *Miracles From Genetics Of Divinity* I will describe simple techniques that you can follow to consistently sustain yourself higher on the EGS scale.

EGS as Your Personal EWACS

The EGS is a tremendously effective tool to be aware of and rely on when you are faced with a decision making opportunity in your life experience. Emotions that you feel in your gut (not the fleeting whims and fancies in your heart) are never wrong, regardless of what your past life experience has been. The gut is actually the solar plexus chakra (explained in the next section) that responds to the energy of the incoming impulse and generates an emotional response.

Several decades ago, the United States Military had developed a technology called Early Warning And Communication System or *EWACS*, as part of the Star Wars Defense Program where it would be possible to detect hostile missile launches that could threaten the security of US assets and interests. Once the threat was detected, the *EWACS* would communicate precise details about the threat to appropriate counter-defense systems, which would get activated automatically to neutralize the threat.

Consider the EGS as this built-in *Early Warning and Communications System (EWACS)* in your *Adaptivebody*. The warning (emotions lower on the EGS scale) or the approval (emotions higher on the EGS scale) comes naturally from your super-conscious mind and are seldom false. However your conscious mind, based on the active neural pathways developed over the years of acquisition of new patterns, could override the suggestions of your super-conscious mind and guide you to decisions that are contrary in nature. For example, the information that you have been receiving from this book would get an approval from the super-conscious mind, however the rationality in your conscious mind based on the active neural pathways could reject it all or certain sections of this material. The end result is the memory (data plus the associated emotion) of this material that would be stored as new neural pathways or as restored neural pathways that hold the code of the *Genetics of Divinity*.

The EGS is constantly serving you by evoking the appropriate emotions in your super-conscious mind (the 3rd pair of DNA strands in each of your body cells) to indicate if you are aligned in the direction of unbounded delight or unbounded plight. When I say *'trust your emotions as they will never fail you'*, I am referring to this reliance on the EGS that is managed by this 3rd pair of DNA strands, to generate appropriate emotions and guide you through your life experience. The question is - are you consciously allowing your super-conscious mind to do its job? Are you getting in the way of your own way?

As I have mentioned before, emotions when associated to data becomes a memory in the appropriate part of your *Adaptivebody*. Memories are the core components of all neural pathways in your central and peripheral nervous system and their patterns constitute the nature of your active consciousness. When you are faced with an event, circumstance or some interaction with another *Adaptivebody* or your very own *Activebody,* that is the data which will be associated with an initial emotion in the EGS scale. That is not considered as memory just yet. Using your free will and your analysis of the experience you may choose to stay locked on to that emotion, slide down further on the EGS scale towards unbounded plight or elevate yourself to emotions on the scale leading towards unbounded delight. This conclusive and reconciling emotion that you feel about the data becomes your memory and hence part of your active neural pathway.

Multi-Dimensional Energy Vortices - Chakras

The *Adaptivebodies* of every Creature, regardless of the energy band in Existence is an energy center that is equipped with the attributes and functions of full-duplex (bi-directional – both functions of transmission and reception) communication with other *Adaptivebodies*. Consider this mode of interaction between *Adaptivebodies* that are in physical contemporary or non-physical extra-contemporary

Existence as non-verbal communication– almost like a multi-dimensional language.

A classic example of such non-verbal cross-energy band communication is found in animal training. Your pet obviously does not understand your spoken language but it would still obey the commands it has been trained to do. It is not the snake you are wary of, it is the possibility of the snake being venomous that alerts you. You offer a friendly smile to a stranger who does not speak your language and in all likelihood, you will be reciprocated.

These are examples of non-verbal communication that is conducted not at the physical level but at a non-physical energetic level. Past life regression, present moment communication with the *Activebody* in the 5-D and future life progression allows an individual to communicate intra-dimensionally (within the 4-D with your past, present and future life experiences) and inter-dimensionally (with your *Activebody* in the 5-D) at a non-physical energetic level.

You will notice that the title of this section indicates energy *vortices* and not the traditionally used word energy *centers*. If you can imagine the shape of a vortex, it has a wide mouth at one end, funnel type *body* and a highly focused tail at the other end. Twister tornadoes, water spouts over the oceans are examples of such vortices. While the mouth of the vortex is the entry point of energy, the architecture of the vortex begins to concentrate that energy to higher and higher intensity until it reaches its peak at the tail. This is intense concentration of energy which has the greatest impact on the greatest number of receivers of that energy. Every *Adaptivebody*, regardless of the energy band to which it is associated has one or more energy vortices, depending on the complexity of the class definition of the Creature per energy band. These energy vortices operate in the same manner in which all vortices do by engulfing *dispersed energy* at the mouth, processing that input energy in the funnel, concentrating it to high intensity and delivering this concentrated energy to the appropriate receivers through the tail within or outside the *Adaptivebody*.

These energy vortices in the human *Adaptivebody* are called *chakras*. Feel free to research **authentic** information about chakras on your own as they relate to their specific areas of focus (I refer to them as *receptors*) in the human *Adaptivebody*. In the context of this book however I will focus on an entirely different aspect of the chakras from the viewpoint of their multi-dimensional orientation and their role in the quad-compartmental architecture of your mind as illustrated in Figure 24.

While seven chakras starting from the crown to the root chakras are more commonly discussed, I will share insight with you about the hand and foot chakras and their role in the quality of your life experience.

Sacred Geometry and the Vessica Piscis

As you analyze Figure 24 you will find two identical circles of equal radii with the circumference of one intersecting the center of the other. In a later section, I will introduce you to Sacred Geometry when you will understand the significance of these circles. For the moment, as illustrated in Figure 4, you will find that these *two circles first intersect at the crown chakra of the human Adaptivebody and then entirely enclose the entire Adaptivebody with a second intersection below the feet of the human figure through the split foot chakra*. The space between these two circles, referred to as the womb of Existence is called the *Vessica Piscis* in the language of Sacred Geometry. One interpretation of these two circles is their representation of the duality of Creation – illustrating the attribute of *contrast* that I discussed earlier tin this book. The Chinese tradition refers to this duality as the *Yin* and the *Yang* energy, which you may want to research on your own.

For the purpose of this book, I will refer to these circles to represent *multi-dimensional CREATIVE energy originating from the Source Force in the 11-D, engulfing the entire Adaptivebody in the grid of Existence*. Detailed discussion on Sacred Geometry is beyond the scope of this book and deserves volumes on its own right. I will share more details about Sacred Geometry in the follow-on book – *Miracles From Genetics Of Divinity.*

Note however that although I have illustrated only two circles in Figure 24, it only represents a flat two dimensional view. In reality these circles are only a part of two spheres of identical radii where the circumference of one sphere intersects the center of the other sphere. The surface of the sphere represents the Sacred Geometrical pattern of Source Energy from the 11-D. Why is the grid spherical? *The sphere represents a geometrical structure that has no beginning and no end making it infinite, eternal and hence independent of time.* The bi-spherical grid of Existence with the Creature in the Vessica Pisces represents such infiniteness and eternity.

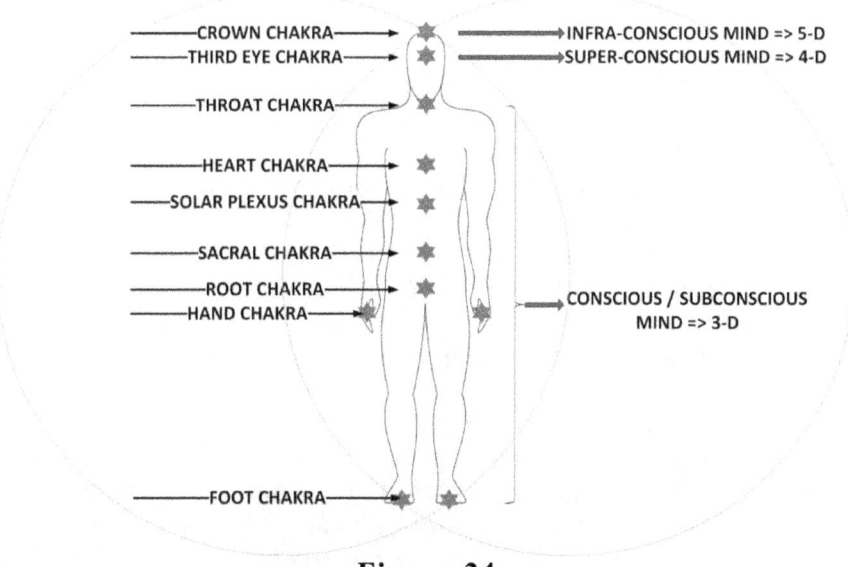

Figure 24

Each Creature regardless of its orientation in the twelve dimensional architecture of Creation and Existence is part of this geometrical grid of Source Energy connecting all multi-dimensional Creatures across all energy bands together. *Everything in Existence has a specific purpose and is interconnected in this grid of Source Energy, rendering a specific purpose to each Creature to contribute toward the design of Existence as allowed by its class definition.* **Due to the inter-connectedness, any disturbance or disruption in any part of this grid affects every other part of the grid of Existence.** Why do you think the frequency and intensity of the natural disasters in our planet have increased in the past decade? I will leave it to you to ponder about it and will discuss it in my blog. Read that last sentence in boldface and you will get the hint.

The Crown Chakra

The **CROWN** *chakra* as illustrated in Figure 24 represents the seat of the infra-conscious mind of your *Adaptivebody* - that part of your quad-compartmental mind which is empowered with the ability to communicate with your *Activebody* in the 5-D. The 5th and 6th pair of DNA strands of each cell are connected energetically to the crown chakra. *In this communication system between your 3-D Adaptivebody and your 5-D Activebody, while these DNA strands perform the function of the antenna in the communication system, the crown chakra performs the function of the transceiver, the biophotons act as the carrier within the Adaptivebody and the brainwaves generate the electromagnetic energy of multi-dimensional transmission and reception at specific frequencies in the electromagnetic spectrum.* Read that again.

I have discussed earlier in this book that your 3-D *Adaptivebody* going through a physical and finite life experience is *always* connected to your very own non-physical and infinite 5-D *Activebody*. The communication protocol between your 3-D *Adaptivebody* and the 5-D *Activebody* is designed to be bi-directional and duplex in nature. In other words your 3-D *Adaptivebody* transmits your request (specific brainwave frequency depending on your thoughts and emotions) through the crown chakra across the Great Divide of the 4-D to your 5-D *Activebody*. Your *Activebody* responds back to the crown chakra so that your infra-conscious mind composed of the 5th and 6th pair of DNA strands can receive the information for further processing in your conscious mind.

When your crown chakra is out of balance (oh yes it's a biophoton flow issue), the infra-conscious mind of your 3-D *Adaptivebody* is also not in optimal operation, thereby attenuating the intensity of the energy vortex of the crown chakra to communicate with your 5-D *Activebody*. What causes this impediment with the biophoton flow? Increased toxicity in the body cell as a result of non-nutritional food intake, stress, catabolic psychological and emotional factors are the obvious culprits for this attenuation to occur.

Photons have been proven to slow down to 30 miles/hour when passed through a Bose-Einstein condensate. Speed of these photons - biophotons are no exception, are dependent on the medium of transmission. Cell toxicity (the medium) slows down the biophotonic flow without exception. When you are not in communication (actual conversations) with your *Activebody*, you lose alignment with your life purpose and that is when your physical life experience, without the active guidance of your *Activebody* begins to downgrade towards *unbounded plight*. This is when the individual begins to subscribe to the disempowering artificial doctrines of fate, destiny and fortune – more like a rudderless ship being tossed around by the turbulent waves in an ocean.

When you balance the crown chakra (techniques to be discussed in the follow-on book called *Miracles From Genetics Of Divinity*), you realign yourself to re-vitalize communications with your 5-D *Activebody*, which in turn re-aligns you with your life purpose, enabling you to reclaim your right as a Type A Creature to enjoy unbounded delight.

The Third Eye Chakra

The **THIRD EYE** *chakra* as illustrated in Figure 24 is the seat of the super-conscious mind of your *Adaptivebody*. The super-conscious section of your mind, as I have explained earlier in this book, can communicate with other *Adaptivebodies* sharing a contemporary physical life experience with you. Needless to say, all of this is possible as long as you stay aligned with your *Activebody* in the 5-D – in other words as long as your crown chakra is balanced. The super-conscious mind is implemented by the 4th pair of DNA strands as I mentioned in Chapter 6.

As illustrated in Figure 25, *Adaptive* energy that your *Adaptivebody* transmits and receives from other *Adaptivebodies* is mediated by your third eye chakra. This *Adaptive* energy also can be mapped through Sacred Geometrical circles (shown in enlarged scale in Figure 25) in the form of the *Vessica Pisces*. Given the collaborative design of Creation, the purpose of this Adaptive energy is to enable your *Adaptivebody* to communicate at a non-physical level using non-verbal language with other relevant *Adaptivebodies* in your life experience in the 3-D with whom you desire to establish symbiotic collaborative relationships. *Adaptive* Energy that I am referring to is an essential attribute for every *Adaptivebody* regardless of the energy band to which it conforms.

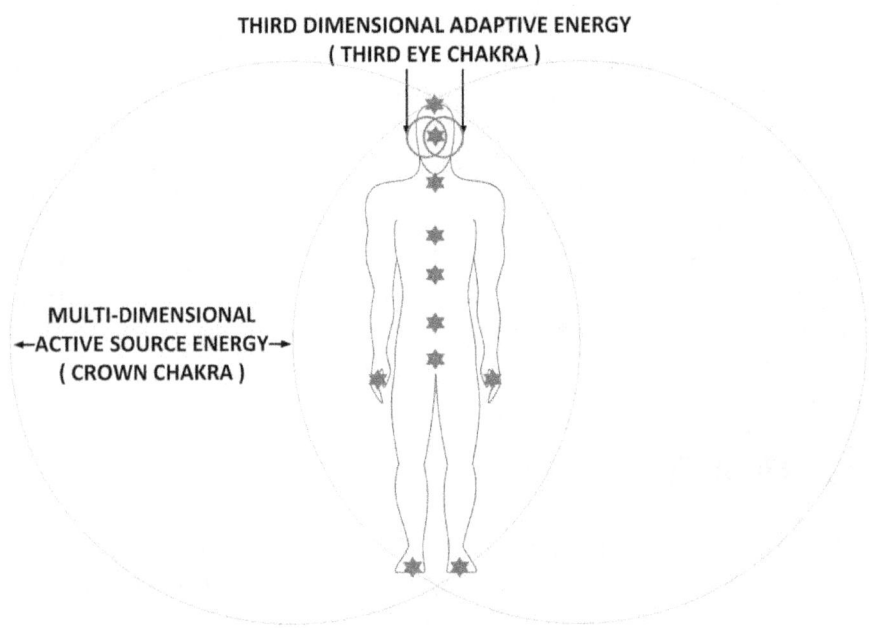

Figure 25

The *Vessica Piscis* form of Sacred Geometry applies to the design of the two visible eyes of the human *Adaptivebody* and the hidden third eye. Examine the two equal radii intersecting circles representing *Adaptive* energy generated from the vortex of third eye chakra which is at the center of the Vessica Piscis in Figure 26.

The two horizontal circles in Figure 26 have their centers on each of the visible eyes, but their respective circumferences intersect the other, forming the *Vessica Pisces* around the third eye chakra. When such a geometric design is drawn and the human face is superimposed the position of the third eye can be easily determined. Although depicted as a flat 2-D structure in Figure 26, it is actually a

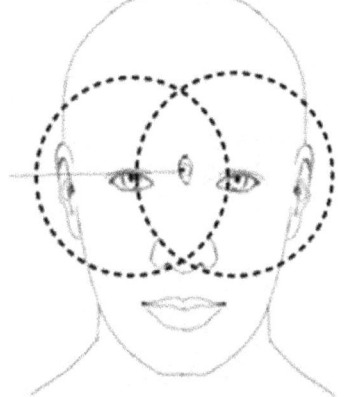

Figure 26

360° sphere of *Adaptive* Energy. This third eye at the center of the vortex created by these spheres, the seat of the super-conscious mind is thus designed to generate *Adaptive* Energy for transmission of brainwaves to other *Adaptivebodies*.

The super-conscious mind is the conduit between you and the non-physical component of the 3-D object of your desire that would contribute to your unbounded delight. The **frequency** (*the precise electromagnetic attributes of your intended object*), **intensity** (*how committed you are about your desire for that object*), **focus** (*how committed you are about the acquisition of the object*) and **prolonged duration** (*how consistent are you about the desire with the conviction about its acquisition*) for which *Adaptive* Energy generated through the energy vortex of the third eye chakra determines the degree of alignment between your *Adaptivebody and* the desired *Adaptivebody.*

The multi-dimensional Active Source Energy and the third dimensional Adaptive energy is designed to travel infinite distances, instantly, uninhibited and unattenuated, unless the attenuation has occurs within the physical *Adaptivebody.* If your crown and/or third eye chakra are out of balance, they will not be able to transmit your message with high intensity to the multi-verse. Under such conditions your *Adaptivebody* will also not be able to receive transmissions from other *Adaptivebodies* seeking to establish that relationship with you. Only a complete energy vortex with a wide mouth (receptor of dispersed and diffused energy) funneling down to a narrow focused tail (transmitter of concentrated energy) can release high intensity energy to a target. If you feel lonely and unfulfilled in life, in all likelihood, your third eye chakra is out of balance.

A vortex that is clipped midway does not have high enough concentration of energy that can bring about a change in a target. So whatever it is that you desire in your life experience to feel the emotions of unbounded delight can enter the vortex mouth of the third eye chakra. However if that is out of balance, the vortex stays clipped or attenuated and cannot reach the appropriate object of desire with a focused or well-aligned transmission. Consequently what you desire cannot respond to your attenuated transmission, since you are *not attractive* to it - you cannot align properly with the *subject of your desire* to facilitate an attraction.

For example, that loving relationship that you have been attracted to or are in the process of getting attracted to is the result of this *focused Adaptive* Energy being transmitted from your third eye chakra. This energy transmitted to the multiverse is received instantly by contemporary prospective suitors regardless of their geographical residence. Remember that on a non-physical plane, Law of Attraction says that *like attracts like.* Hence a suitor who is also transmitting such

Adaptive Energy (indicating *"availability"* for a loving relationship) that *matches with your frequency* will receive your transmission and according the basic laws of physics (refer to Figure 12) the two of you could resonate and hence amplify the waveform. When this resonance occurs, circumstances, events and people *seemingly show up* in your life leading to the union of the *Adaptivebodies* in that relationship established first in the non-physical plane.

The last paragraph directly relates to my own personal life experience when the love of my life and I attracted each other energetically in the non-physical plane. We followed the same principles as I have explained here. Even though we were geographically separated, continents apart on opposite sides of the planet that *Adaptive* energetic connection was established even before we physically saw each other. The two of us both know today (definitive proof that is beyond the scope of this book) that our *Activebodies* had already collaborated on this relationship in the 5-D and were aligning our respective 3-D *Adaptivebodies* to come together. That is the power of a well-balanced crown and third eye chakra and naturally functional DNA. You too are endowed with the same faculties and infrastructure by your affiliation to the *Human class* to align with and get attracted to any relationship in the 12 external categories of your desire as long as it is logical and ethically feasible. My objective and life purpose is to share the knowledge of this activation process of the *Genetics Of Divinity* with you.

The *Adaptive Energy* in the 3-D that your third eye chakra is capable of transmitting and receiving through the 4th pair of DNA strands (the *Matchmaker* pair) to fulfill your life purpose and enjoy a life experience of unbounded delight is processed by your super-conscious mind. When it is left untrained, un-directed or under-directed, the super-conscious mind will still operate according to default operating system of the multiverse without any specific personalization. However when the modus operandi of the super-conscious mind is understood, specifically its ability to establish and conduct non-verbal communication with other *Adaptivebodies* (regardless of their energy band), it can help resolve present challenges and also avoid future challenges from showing up in the life experience. The same example can be extrapolated to any relationship with any *Adaptivebody* in the 3-D.

When you have dreams or set goals and objectives for yourself that would lead you to unbounded delight, you can validate if they are aligned with your life purpose through inter-dimensional communication with your *Activebody* in the 5-D. Once validated, you can also align yourself to get attracted by those relevant *Adaptivebodies* by channeling well-defined, intense, focused *Adaptive* Energy through your third eye chakra.

The Foot (Split) Chakra

The **FOOT** chakra is not talked about in popular circles but this split-chakra is of vital importance for your *Adaptivebody*. The reason it is called a split chakra (just like the hand chakras as I will discuss shortly) is due to its presence in the balls of both feet. Review Figure 24 closely and you will notice that the Foot Chakra is part of the bounding circles of the Vessica Piscis. The foot chakra serves as the second extremity of the human *Adaptivebody*, the first being the crown chakra. Think of a magnet with north and south poles through with the magnetic lines of force form that toroidal magnetic field. The human *Adaptivebody* emits electromagnetic radiation in the form of light and heat due to the biophotons in the DNA of every cell. Electromagnetism in the non-physical plane imparts the attribute of attraction or repulsion of waves of *Adaptive* Energy when the human *Adaptivebody* comes in energetic contact with other *Adaptivebodies*. Gravitation imparts the attractive force among *Adaptivebodies* in the physical plane.

The crown and foot chakras, in addition to their physical functions also have a non-physical role to play in connecting the human *Adaptivebody* in the grid of inter-dimensional Existence. Active Energy enters the human *Adaptivebody* at the apex of the Vessica Pisces at the crown chakra and encloses the entire body within the Vessica Piscis like a protective cocoon, intersecting again through the foot chakra at the antapex.

From basic laws of electricity, electric current will flow from a point of higher potential to a point of lower potential. Fluids will flow from a point of high pressure to a lower pressure. Similarly as it relates to the human *Adaptivebody*, the crown chakra is a high potential point in the human *Adaptivebody*, while the foot chakra is the lower potential point.

In case of electricity, a sudden surge in electrical voltage (electrical energy) could damage the circuit it serves. This is why we have an electrical ground wherever there is a possibility of such a surge to occur and thereby protect the circuit from such unplanned electrical surges. In case of Fluid Mechanics, such a surge on the pressure between the high and low pressure points could disrupt the intermediary components in the flow channel. This is why some sensitive fluid systems have provisions through overflow diversion to divert the additional flow outside the regular system.

Similarly, the human *Adaptivebody* needs something like an electric ground or an overflow diversion mechanism to transfer additional charge from the *Adaptivebody* to the electrical ground. This function of grounding additional and disruptive charge from the human *Adaptivebody* is performed by the foot chakra. The *charge* that I am referring to, from a human *Adaptivebody* perspective is the catabolic energy of emotions perceived as low on the EGS scale, that is associated with each negative memory stored in the individual *Adaptivebody*.

Someone who does not regard you to be in their good books is capable, consciously or unconsciously to send you such intense, sudden, short bursts or prolonged transmissions of such catabolic *Adaptive* Energy – commonly called *'curses'*. The third eye chakra and your 4th pair of DNA strands (just like the other 5 pairs) are perpetual transceivers and can receive this catabolic energy, which could adversely affect your physiological and psychological health. With a strong crown and foot chakra, your physical Adaptivebody can be cocooned in the Vessica Piscis and act as an electromagnetic shield to bypass the catabolic Adaptive

Energy from reaching you. This is the same behavior that our planet Earth exhibits through its electromagnetic field that shields our planet from the harmful electromagnetic radiation coming from the Sun. Hence your foot chakra acts as the electric ground for energy that needs to be grounded and hence neutralized.

If you are feeling low for whatever reason, take your shoes off and stand bare feet, if safely possible, on the ground or preferably on a body of water interchangeably in the Intra-Intersection and Extra-Intersection position and you will be able to regain your position of power. I describe this process in the videos in the Multiversity of the *Genetics Of Divinity* that you have access to as an owner of this book.

The Hand (Split) Chakra

The **HAND** chakra like the foot chakra is also a physically split energy system due to its presence in the two hands of the human *Adaptivebody*. I refer to the hand chakra centered in the palms of either hand, as the physical *relationship* chakra that assists the human *Adaptivebody* to decide if a relationship with another *Adaptivebody*, regardless of the energy band would be symbiotic or parasitic in nature. *A stable, symbiotic collaborative relationship for harmonic, collective co-existence between two Adaptivebodies always initiates at a non-physical level before the physical Adaptivebodies can align and get attracted to each other.*

The HAND chakra if consciously utilized, provides the final approval of such a relationship at a physical level. Refer to Figure 29 and notice closely how the Sacred Geometrical circles of one *Adaptivebody* intersects the hand chakras of the other *Adaptivebody*. This Figure illustrates a stable symbiotic collaborative relationship for collective co-existence between two participating human Adaptivebodies not only at a non-physical level, but also at a physical level with the Active Energy field of one *Adaptivebody* intersecting the hand chakra of the other *Adaptivebody* and vice versa.

Can you feel the energy of your hand chakras? I demonstrate for you in videos in the Multiversity of the *Genetics Of Divinity,* a technique that you can follow to prove to yourself that you do have *Adaptive* Energy generated from your *Adaptivebody*. Bring your palms about 8-10 inches apart and facing each other. Then slowly but regularly bring then towards each other and pull them away from each other with the palms facing each other all the time. You will feel as if there is something squishy between your palms pulling and repelling each other. This is the *Adaptive* energy of your hand chakra in action. Ask a friend to stand facing towards you and extend their hand toward you as in an open handshake. Get into a handshake position yourself and stick out your hand 8-10 inches away from the palm of the other person. Repeat that same exercise. Both of you will be able to feel that squishy energy between your palms – this is your *Adaptive* energies interacting with each other.

Simply by shaking hands with a complete stranger, I can feel the energy of that person, helping me decide if the interaction would be positive or negative for my life experience – this skill took a while to develop and you can too. This is possible by being attentive to the *energy reading* of the hand chakra. Adaptive energy associated with emotions of love, caring, respect, honor, sympathy, peace, encouragement, excitement or lack thereof can transmit from one *Adaptivebody* to another through the hand chakra simply by the full touch of the palm on the target *Adaptivebody*. The hand chakra also has healing powers (deserves a different book on its own right) to clear blocks in the flow of energy in an *Adaptivebody*, treating the root cause of dis-ease.

The hand chakra can also be used as a physical directional antenna for transmission and reception of *Active* and *Adaptive* energy waves. While the crown and third eye chakras operate more like omni-directional antennae of your *Adaptivebody*, the hand-chakra operates more like a directional antenna. I demonstrate the two postures of *Intra-Intersection* and *Inter-Intersection* in the video within the Multiversity of the *Genetics Of Divinity*. In that video you will observe how I use my hands and hence the hand chakras as directional antennae to transmit or receive my *Adaptive Energy* waves.

The less talked about foot and hand chakras as I explained above are vital contributors to the quality of the life experience of the physical human *Adaptivebody*. I trust you understand how significant the foot chakra is to ensure the health of your *Adaptivebody* by providing a conduit to release excess eroding charge from your memory systems. I also believe you understand the significance of the hand chakra to provide guidance to you as your physical *Adaptivebody* engages in the pursuit of collaborative relationships with other physical *Adaptivebodies* in your contemporary life experience.

The Other Five Chakras

Review Figure 24 again and you will find that the other chakras starting from the **THROAT** chakra down to the **FOOT** and **HAND** chakras are all related with your physical 3-D *Adaptivebody*. These chakras collectively offer the operating domain of your conscious mind (voluntary decision and actions) and the sub-conscious component (involuntary functions within your physiology) of your mind. Physiological functions of individual body parts and their interdependence on one another as appropriate is embedded and controlled by the 1st pair of DNA strands. The memory about which body part is supposed to perform what function is contained in this 1st pair of DNA strands in the cells that are component of that body part. Hence all the chakras in your physical *Adaptivebody* have a physical component as well. Feel free to research on your own about the alignment of the different chakras with the different physiological functions of the human body.

---------------------------*****---------------------------

The life experience that is presented to you by the middle five chakras (Throat to the Root Chakra) and hence your conscious and sub-conscious mind is what I call *perceived physical reality* of your *Adaptivebody*. This is not necessarily the *intended reality* that was lined up for you by your 5-D *Activebody* before you were incarnated in your current physical 3-D form. How different your *perceived reality* is from your *intended reality* is dependent on the patterns and neural pathways that you have developed as Type 3 memory systems in your subconscious and conscious mind. It also depends on the degree of alignment you have achieved with your assigned life purpose through your infra-conscious mind and the manner in which you have established collaborative relationships with other *Adaptivebodies* through the engagement of your super-conscious mind.

-------------------------#####-------------------------

Something very interesting and revealing happens when you apply Sacred Geometry on the four components of your mind and superimpose the Sacred Geometrical patterns on one another as illustrated in Figure 27.

The crown chakra, which is the seat of your infra-conscious mind depicts the *intersection* apex of the Vessica Piscis, which symbolizes the intersection of the Fifth Dimension and the Third Dimension. This is represented by the large circles with broken lines in Figure 27. Note that the *Vessica Piscis* in this case cocoons the entire *Adaptivebody* making it a conglomerated energy vortex which can be observed as the aura in Kirlian photography. The 5-D is the domain of the non-physical *Activebody* powered by *Active* Energy while the 3-D is the domain of the physical *Adaptivebody* powered by *Adaptive* Energy. This intersection establishes the inter-dimensional bridge between your mortal *Adaptivebody* and your immortal *Activebody*. It is through this bridge, an active and balanced crown chakra, that your *Adaptivebody* can actually communicate with your 5-D *Activebody* for everything that I have discussed earlier.

While the crown chakra is the intersection of the *Vessica Piscis*, receiving guidance from your 5-D immortal *Activebody*, the third eye chakra (refer to Figure 26 for a larger scale view) depicts an *inclusion* of the third eye within the *Vessica Piscis*. The third eye is the seat of your super-conscious mind and is completely cocooned within the *Vessica Piscis* of the *Adaptive* Energy. The super-conscious mind as you know by now communicates with other *Adaptivebodies* that you desire to establish collaborative relationships with in your life experience. This *Adaptive* Energy generated through the vortex of your third eye chakra is responsible for your alignment with your life purpose or whatever it is that **you** command it to align with in a collaborative relationship.

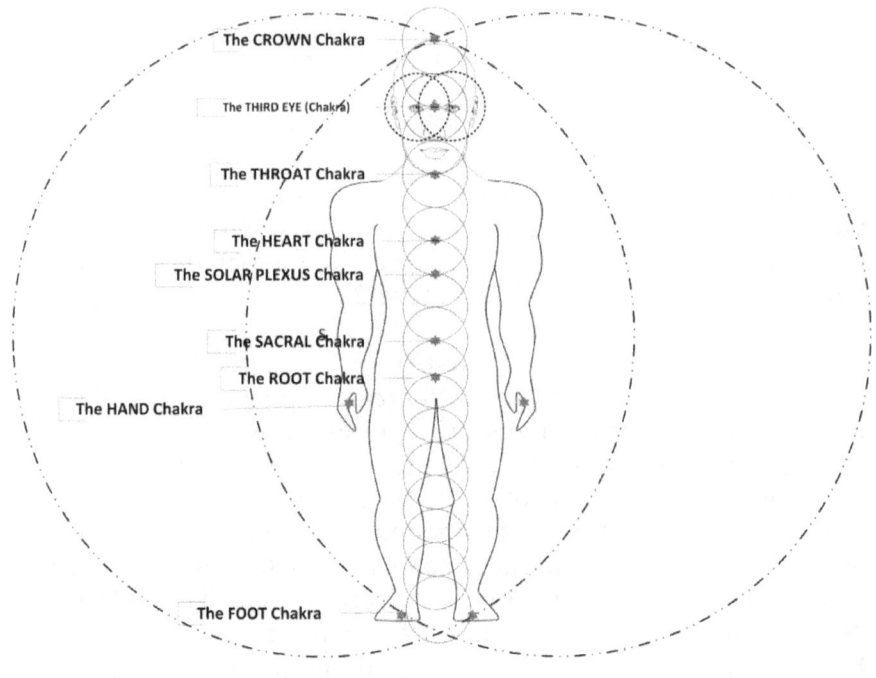

Figure 27

Lastly, refer to Figure 27 to examine the manner in which the Sacred Geometrical circles are laid out vertically on the seven chakras. This the domain of your physical energy (a subset in the spectrum of *Adaptive Energy*) that powers your 3-D physical *Adaptivebody* with the chakras being the energy vortices. If you look closely, you will find that these circles are *centered* around each chakra **and** *interlinked* with the other. This energy that is concentrated and designed to operate on your 3-D physical *Adaptivebody* is what determines your physical and your psychological health. This is the energy that defines your *perceived reality*, the tangible, the tactile, the physical nature of your current life experience in the 3-D. *This makes your entire Adaptivebody (physical and non-physical combined) an energy center that can broadcast, receive and transform energy in different frequencies* – truly as masterpiece of Creation and Existence.

-------------------------*****-------------------------

Hence through the *intersection* of *Active* energy enabled by your crown chakra you can receive guidance from your 5-D *Activebody* as your 3-D *Adaptivebody* progresses through its life experience. Through the *inclusion* of your *Adaptive* energy enabled by your Third eye chakra, you have the ability to build symbiotic collaborative relationships with other 3-D *Adaptivebodies* having a contemporary life experience. Through the *centering* and *inter-linked* nature of your physical energy you can maintain a healthy *Adaptivebody* where this physical energy flows unhindered, keeping you protected from disease.

As an energy center, what are you *broadcasting*? What value, what service you are you willing to provide to other *Adaptivebodies* that you share a contemporary life experience with and what are your personal *desires* to enjoy a life experience filled with unbounded delight?

As an energy center, what are you *receiving*? Are you susceptible to catabolic energies directed at you by others? Are you maintaining that strong crown chakra to strengthen the electromagnetic shield about your *Adaptivebody*, thereby grounding out the catabolic energy and consuming anabolic energy to enhance your physical life experience?

As an energy center, what are you *transforming*? Are you receiving anabolic energy, processing them with your own patterns of belief and knowledgebase and transforming to amplified anabolic energy that contributes to the service of the grid of Existence?

-------------------------#####-------------------------

Adaptive Energy Field of the Adaptivebody

In the simplified illustration in Figure 27, I introduced you to the three basic types of energy fields that affects the *Adaptivebody* – active energy, adaptive energy and its subset – physical energy. Energy as we know from basic Physics, travels in waves with characteristic frequency, amplitude and wavelength. If I were to represent the energy field of a healthy and well balanced human *Adaptivebody* in terms of Sacred Geometry, the energy fields would appear as illustrated in Figure 28.

This human energy field may be felt physically anywhere between 1 to 6 feet around the physical body, depending on the *net Available Energy* (to be discussed shortly) in your *Adaptivebody* – pretty much like a radio or television station. The power of transmission depends on this net *Available* energy stored within the *Adaptivebody*. An individual having a life experience based on scarcity and deprivation allows a substantial amount of anabolic energy to be consumed by the catabolic energy of those emotions that are lower on the EGS scale, thereby reducing the *net Available Energy*. On the other hand, an individual enjoying a life experience that is based on the cognition of abundance and plenty and the conscious knowledge about the code of the *Genetics Of Divinity*, has a much larger *net Available Energy*, hence capable of a higher power of transmission and hence a large range of the energy field.

---------------------------*****---------------------------

A review of Figure 28 reveals the consistent *Active* energy field of the infra-conscious mind intersecting the crown chakra at the apex and connecting your 3-D *Adaptivebody* to your 5-D *Activebody*. The *Adaptive* energy field (illustrated by the smaller Sacred Geometric circles) represents the super-conscious mind around the third eye chakra and is stronger than the *Physical* energy field that represents the conscious and sub-conscious mind that is processed by the other eight chakras (including the foot and hand chakras). Note that the crown and third eye chakras also generate physical energy like the other five chakras. The amplification near the top two chakras that you observe in Figure 28 is the result of the additional energy frequencies (active and adaptive) processed by them.

-------------------------#####-------------------------

Although *Adaptivebodies* conforming to other than Type A do not have the same chakras, every *Adaptivebody* has the capability to process the same three frequency types – *Active, Adaptive* and *Physical*. For the purpose of this book and illustration of the concept of collaborative relationships I will refer to the energy field of the Human *Adaptivebody*.

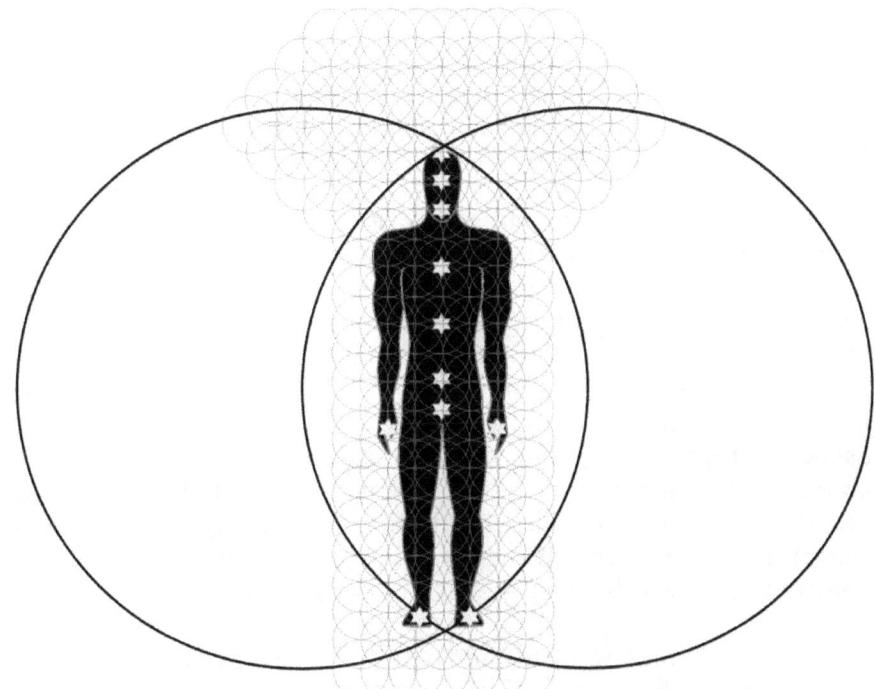

Figure 28

Desirability Index Of The Adaptivebody

This brings us to the concept of *Desirability Index* of any *Adaptivebody* of any energy band, indicating how desirable or attractive a given *Adaptivebody* is to other *Adaptivebodies* for the purpose of presenting itself as being worthy of participating in symbiotic collaborative relationships for the purpose of collective co-existence. In the grand design of Creation and Existence attractiveness and desirability are the core attributes of establishing any symbiotic collaborative relationship. Any *Adaptivebody* desirable or attractive is one that adds value to the life experience of other *Adaptivebodies* that understand, appreciate and desire those attractive attributes. *Desirability Index* engages the Law of Alignment and the Law of Attraction, which collectively contribute to an enhanced physical life experience of the physical *Adaptivebody*.

Desirability Index (DI) is a percentage defined as

DI = (Net Available Energy / Potential Energy) x 100

Potential energy refers to the **pure Adaptive energy that every healthy Adaptivebody is conceived with as a transformation from the Active energy of the Activebody.** This energy can never be created or destroyed as you know by now, but can only get amplified through resonance, attenuated through dissonance or transformed to store your memory systems (the data of the experience and charge of associated emotions). The net available energy in the formula above represents the arithmetic sum of the anabolic energy (whatever memory evokes emotions that are high on the EGS scale) and the catabolic energy (whatever memory evokes emotions that are low on the EGS scale).

An individual with higher catabolic energy than anabolic energy would have negative net Available energy and hence have a negative DI and hence not be desirable to other *Adaptivebodies* with positive DIs, to establish a symbiotic collaborative relationship. An individual with a positive net Available energy is better off on the DI percentage and hence automatically is more desirable than one with a negative DI.

However even with a positive DI, the score may be too low when a comparative desirability or attractiveness analysis is performed by a prospective *Adaptivebody* seeking to align itself in a collaborative relationship. In this relational multiverse, higher your DI, more fulfilling a life experience you can have and more service you can provide to other *Adaptivebodies*. In these interests, what this formula of DI indicates is that closer the net Available energy is to the Potential energy, the more desirable you become. This is possible by reducing the influence of catabolic energy in your life experience – simply refuse to succumb to emotions that are lower in the EGS scale.

What would happen if we had two *Adaptivebodies* (refer to Figure 28) with similar energy fields? *In a physical plane, opposites attract, but in a non-physical plane, like attracts like*. If we take that principle and apply it to Figure 28 with two *Adaptivebodies* with *like* energy fields the resultant energy field gets significantly amplified as illustrated in Figure 29, leading to a strong collaborative relationship. Examine closely and you will find that the Sacred Geometrical circles snap together to form a strong collaborative bond both in the non-physical and physical plane. Further analysis of Figure 29 reveals that it is impossible for a strong physical energy bond (from the throat chakra downwards) to be established without a strong *Adaptive* energy bond being established first through the third eye chakras of the relating partners.

What this indicates is if you *desire to* (not just *wish* or *want*) establish a collaborative relationship with a desirable partner that you deem to be necessary for your unbounded delight, then most definitely that partner has a high DI and hence a high range of its net *Available* energy. You are required to establish an *Adaptive* energy connection with this high DI partner first to energetically transmit your intent for alignment. Given the fact that like attracts like, on a non-physical plane if you also have a high DI you will establish alignment with your partner and assuming you can hold that alignment long enough with consistent intensity, you'll get attracted towards it until finally you both show up in each other's life experience for collective coexistence.

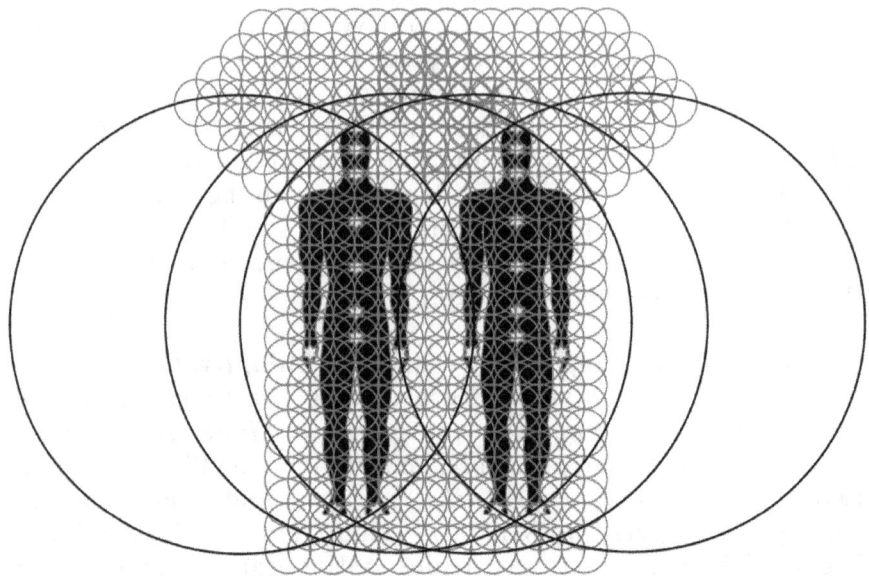

Figure 29

The speed of alignment and attraction depends on the DI of both parties in the collaborative relationship. If you redrew Figure 29 with one of the parties having lower adaptive energy (to be depicted using some fewer Sacred Geometrical circles radiating from the third eye chakra) it will be evident that it will not only take a longer time to establish any sort of collaborative relationship if at all, due to the low DI and hence a weak broadcast signal.

Review this section again until you understand and feel the *Adaptive* energy field that your *Adaptivebody* by design is equipped with and how you can use the same to get attracted to a life experience that brings you unbounded delight. I will invest a good portion of the follow-on book *Miracles From Genetics Of Divinity*, to describe the technology that you can use to build symbiotic collaborative relationships in your life experience. In that book, I will also describe a technique that would help you calculate your DI accurately and easily use that metric to improve your DI. This is pivotal for you to re-engage in a life experience based on collective co-existence rather than one that is based on isolated independence. Remember – what you desire, as long as it is logical and ethically feasible, by default desires you. The question is, are *you* desirable enough to your subject of desire? Raise your DI and you can choose to have whatever life experience that you desire.

Does the *Activebody* in the 5-D also have a chakra system of its own? Yes, it is logical to believe that it does and it would follow more advanced Sacred Geometrical patterns than what I have referred to in this book. I am aware of some material available from different authors on this topic about a system of chakras existing in the higher dimensions of Existence. However at the time of writing this book, I have not invested my energy to research that aspect of Creation or reactivate any dormant memory on this matter. Hence I consider that discussion as out of scope for this book at least for now. My current focus is on the 3-D *Adaptivebody* and assisting the common person understand the *Genetics Of Divinity* as it relates to this physical life experience of this 3-D *Adaptivebody*. Only when humanity reaches that AWAKENED level of consciousness can we invest on understanding the consciousness of the higher dimensions.

Brainwaves – Passport To Physical Reality

If you have been working with the Law of Attraction, you are aware that *your thoughts affect the relative position and energetics of physical matter*. There are toys available in the market today that enable the player to move a ball on a game board simply by thinking about the direction of motion. I have experimented with such a toy myself and was very impressed with the sensitivity of the mechanics of using brainwaves to move objects.

This particular toy that I am referring to, captures and transmits your thoughts as brainwaves through a device that you wear on your head. This transmission is captured by a receiver installed on the game board. Upon reception of your brainwave, the receiver is engineered to activate a small electric fan on the game board, which moves the foam ball around. More you concentrate (intense focus, correctly, long enough consistently) your thoughts on the movement of the ball and its direction, more sensitive it becomes. A pretty smart design, but this toy proves some very important points. First your thoughts are energy waves, commonly called brainwaves, which have the ability to align with and affect physical matter. Secondly, focused, concentrated and persistent thought energy is what brings about the change in the *relative position* of physical matter.

Energy mostly propagates as sinusoidal or co-sinusoidal oscillating waveforms with variations and combinations thereof. The three core energy frequencies (Active, Adaptive and Physical) that you are equipped with are no different. What distinguishes energy types from one another is their respective frequency and power of transmission.

A simple example is a radio or television station that transmits its programming through a certain pre-allocated frequency that every other station within range recognizes and chooses to transmit their respective programming on a different frequency. If more than one station within range of each other was to transmit their programming in the same frequency, a receiver tuned to that frequency would receive all transmissions at the same time and you would hear practically incoherent content. However what would happen if one station started to transmit its programming through a higher powered transmitter on the same frequency? A receiver would predominantly receive that transmission due to the higher signal strength with potential interference from the other lower powered transmissions from time to time.

From a commercial perspective, higher powered transmitters are more expensive, so instead of '*muscling through*' and competing for airtime, radio and television operators who are co-located from a transmission radius perspective, agree on and choose to transmit their programming on different frequencies with similar power, thereby giving the receiver options to enjoy different programs on different distinct channels but *never at the same time*. If you were operating that receiver, after a careful evaluation of the different programming available from the different channels, what would you do? You would tune into one particular channel and enjoy that programming. Why? Because at that given moment that particular chosen channel is rendering a program that is the *most desirable* to you. If that channel consistently delivers programming that you enjoy, you may never even bother tuning onto another channel because that frequency of transmission is highly desirable to you.

The above example illustrates the significance of the *power* of transmission. Not only does a higher power energy transmitter become *more desirable* due to the clarity of the signal to a receiver in comparison to others, the higher power also increases the *range* of the transmission, so that the energy can reach a receiver that is geographically further from the transmitter. Read the last two paragraphs again – *higher the DI of the transmitter of energy (as a function of content, frequency and power of transmission), greater the alignment of the receiver with the transmitter and more consistent and powerful the attraction due to the inclination to establish a symbiotic collaborative relationship for the purpose of collective co-existence.*

Remember that *"What's in it for me?"* is a question that not only you ask when you seek out your desired partner in a relationship, your partner asks the same when it evaluates your request. Only when both are in alignment can you, the transmitter, get attracted by the receiver or your partner in that relationship. These are the true mechanics of operation of the Law of Attraction – based on *your* Desirability Index.

The question I would have for you at this time is, "If you evaluated all that you have desired in life so far, did you make the effort to make *yourself* desirable to your partner in that relationship?" Evaluate all the 13 categories of relationships from Chapter 3 with this question. That analysis would clarify why some of your desires did not get fulfilled. You see, nobody external to you is responsible or accountable for the quality of your life experience – *you* are.

The next time you define your desires and set your sights on a relationship in any of the 12 relationship categories that revolve around your life, ask yourself the question, "Am I desirable enough for my partner to attract me?" If not, work on making yourself more desirable first before engaging the Law of Alignment and you will find that the Law of Attraction begins to work like magic. Recall the core principle of the *Genetics Of Divinity* and you will realize the accuracy of the concept of Desirability Index all your desired relationships.

Your brain being a transmitter, a receiver, a processor and a transformer of energy, has the capability to align, attract and get attracted to whatever makes the energy field under consideration more desirable. Every thought you think, every emotion you feel, every action you take, every move you make is a particular brainwave frequency.

There are *six distinct brainwave types* with distinct bandwidth (range of frequencies) of vibration that collectively contribute to your life experience or your perceived reality. The electroencephalograph (EEG) has been designed to categorize only four types of brainwaves. I will describe two more bandwidths that are rarely talked about. While the application and techniques for conscious generation of these brainwaves will be discussed in the follow-on book – *Miracles from Genetics Of Divinity*, I will describe their significance in determining your perceived reality. Feel free to research the common knowledge available about the alpha, beta, delta and theta brainwaves on your own, specifically from a physiological point of view for a better context of what I describe here.

As illustrated in Figure 30, each of the six brainwaves have their own bandwidth and collectively the peripheral five (beta, alpha, delta, theta and second beta) create a full circuit. When you observe closely, you will find that one brainwave bandwidth starts from where the previous one ends. If you were to spin such an arrangement around their center clockwise, the result would be a Gamma brainwave emerging from the tail of the vortex. There are several aspects to Figure 30 and I will address them one at a time for a better understanding of how profound this is for you to understand the masterpiece of the human *Adaptivebody*.

I have introduced the concept of *Potential* energy while discussing Desirability Index. Potential energy is the pure *Adaptive* energy that you inherit from your *Activebody* in the 5-D at the instant of time that you are conceived. As your embryo develops through the gestation cycle, part of

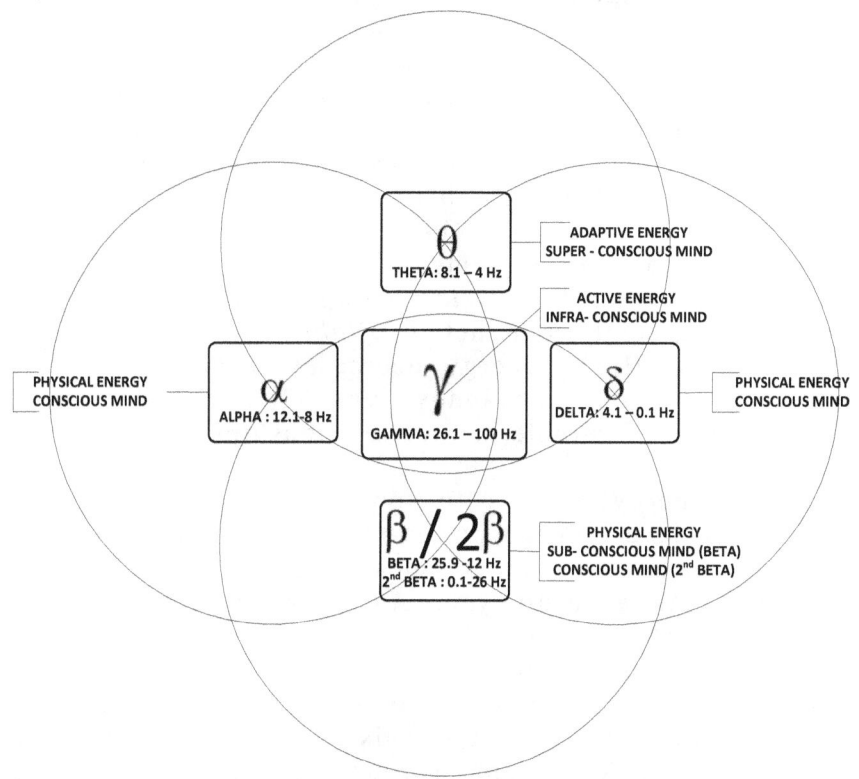

Figure 30

that Potential energy transforms to Physical energy facilitate cell division (*mitosis*) according to the definition of the *Human* class while the rest of the Potential energy continues to serve, sustain and protect your young life.

Note that your physical features, the way you act, react and interact, the physiological movements – both voluntary and involuntary movements that you could perform, and all four types of memory patterns are stored as Physical energy in your *Adaptivebody* – memory does require energy to be stored. Since energy is never lost (destroyed) or found (created) the remainder from your *Potential* energy is your *Net Available* energy. Hence we can state:

Net Available Energy =
(Potential Adaptive Energy – Stored Physical Energy)

The primary objective in your life experience is the fulfillment of your life purpose, defined by your 5-D *Activebody* to consequently lead you to unbounded delight. While the *Physical* energy sustains your physical body it is your *net Available* energy that is designed to propel you towards your life purpose. Doing the simple math – what happens if the memory systems that you have accumulated so far increases the stored *Physical* energy. Since the *Potential* energy is constant your net *Available* energy decreases. When Net Available Energy decreases, according to the formula of Desirability Index, your DI also decreases, making you less desirable in your relationships.

Lower energy equates to lower power. Lower power implies you have reduced power for intense, consistent and prolonged focus on what you desire to enjoy in your life experience. As a result your *Adaptivebody* becomes less efficient to align with what you desire for unbounded delight. In turn this makes you less desirable to your partner in your intended relationship to align with you, far less engage the Law of Attraction. This consequently keeps you away from the achievement of your desires. This *perceived failure* is stored as another memory with a negative emotion, which consumes additional *Physical* energy, leaving you with even less net *Available* energy and the result is a snowball effect that progressively takes you towards unbounded plight.

Catabolic emotions consume more physical energy than anabolic energy. Why? I have explained earlier how cortisols are produced in your bloodstream when you are feeling emotions that are low in the EGS scale. You are also aware of the snowball effect on your physiology as a result of these low emotions. Well, in order to sustain your physiological functions in survival mode, your body needs more Physical energy. Where is your body going to get this additional Physical energy from? Obviously from your reserves of Potential Adaptive Energy. The memory of this additional requirement to sustain your physiological integrity as a result of the natural defense mechanism in response to those low emotions, also gets added to the Stored Physical Energy. This snowball effect further depletes your Net Available Energy and makes you less desirable.

Aha! Now you know why things are not working the way you want them to and why the Law of Attraction *seems* to be ignoring you, right? How much catabolic and unproductive emotions in the form of Type 3 memories are you holding on to and investing your *Potential* energy? Could you let go of some of these and reclaim that energy into your pool of net *Available* energy? Nobody external is empowered by design to answer that question – only you are. So what's it going to be? Can you make a list of all those catabolic emotions and their memories? What if you learned how to release those emotions and reclaim your *Potential Adaptive* energy? I will discuss these techniques in the follow-on book - *Miracles from Genetics Of Divinity*.

The BETA Brainwave Frequency Band

The BETA brainwave bandwidth responds to the 1st pair of DNA strands that host memories about your physiological chemistry – body temperature, blood pressure, heart rate, oxygen levels, hunger, thirst, chemical dependencies or reactions, nutrition, allergies, hormones and enzymes, pH level and all pathological data that are uniquely specific to your *Adaptivebody*. The BETA brainwave is a physical energy waveform and generated from all chakras of your *Adaptivebody* affecting all involuntary functions of different parts of your physical body. Since your involuntary functions are operational whether you are in a waking state or are sleeping, BETA brainwaves are being generated literally every moment of your life experience.

The ALPHA Brainwave Frequency Band

The ALPHA brainwave bandwidth responds to the vibrations of the 3rd pair of DNA strands that manages the memories of emotions that you *or others* present have felt when you had to deal with the data about the event, circumstance or other *Adaptivebodies* who you had to interact with. First is the data and then comes the emotion. Needless to say, emotions that are lower in the EGS scale require greater Physical energy to be stored due to its compounding psychologically *drainage* effect on the physiology – the commonly used term is *'feeling drained out'*. Consequently, emotions that are higher in the EGS scale still require Physical energy, but that amount is much lower in comparison due to the psychologically uplifting effect on the physiology. Refresh your knowledge by reviewing my explanation of the physiological impact of catabolic and anabolic energy on your *Adaptivebody* earlier in this chapter. All emotions are hence ALPHA brainwaves. Emotions that you feel are experiences of your conscious mind and the Type 3 memory is stored as the Physical energy from ALPHA brainwaves.

The THETA Brainwave Frequency Band

The THETA bandwidth of brainwaves respond to the vibrations of the 4th pair of DNA strands, which as I had explained earlier are sensitive to Type 5 memory. The THETA frequency is where your rationality and analytical ability becomes operational. These brainwaves respond to your personal consciousness of belief systems and memory patterns and enable you store and retrieve those patterns when the need arises. Such storage and retrieval enables you to make decisions or render judgment within the bounds of this realm of your knowledgebase, specifically regarding the relationships that you have in your life experience. Whether an incoming impulse from a partner will be considered favorable, unfavorable or indifferent is governed by these patterns of Type 5 memory and is communicated through theta brainwaves. Every communication that you made with the current partners in the relationships in your life is a theta brainwave. If your intent is to establish a new relationship in any of the twelve secondary categories of relationships that I discussed in Chapter 3, your communication of *Adaptive Energy* through the third eye chakra uses the THETA frequency of brainwaves.

When you have desires, set goals and expectations to get attracted to whatever brings you unbounded delight, the thoughts about the partner in the relationship are first originated from the 4th pair of DNA strands and then transmitted as THETA brainwaves from your third eye chakra – the seat of your super-conscious mind.

THETA (and GAMMA that you will learn about shortly) brainwaves travel faster than light, uninhibited, instantly, and can travel infinite distances carried by the dimensionless massless Source particle – the *sourceon*. Where are the *sourceons* stored in the human Adaptivebody? *Sourceons* exist everywhere in Existence, but specifically in the human body they are concentrated in the pineal gland. The follow-on book – *Miracles from Genetics Of Divinity* will contain more details about the THETA brainwaves how you can leverage these brainwaves and the *sourceons* from the pineal gland to establish those relationships that you have been desiring. In the meantime, I encourage you to focus on *Charge Clearing* and increasing your *Desirability Index*, which would be critical to the process.

The DELTA Brainwave Frequency Band

The DELTA bandwidth of brainwaves may as well be called the detail recorder of the interaction that you may have in your life experience. The DELTA brainwaves facilitate the storage of Type 3 and Type 4 memory of the exact conversation you had during the interaction, details of the environment, even details of personal appearance and grooming. Such experiences are an integral part of your conscious mind and the memory is stored as physical energy just like ALPHA brainwaves. The 3rd pair of the DNA strands that record Type 3 memory would also respond to DELTA brainwaves. Due to the storage capabilities facilitated by these DELTA brainwaves that stores so much detail, the *Physical* energy consumed to store that memory is also comparatively high.

The 2nd BETA Brainwave Frequency Band

The 2nd BETA bandwidth of brainwaves are associated with memories related to your physical motions, even body language that you expressed and observed among those who participated actively or passively in your interactions. Such physical motions could also be the result of an event or circumstance for example when you received news of some successful outcome of your efforts, or even when you stepped out into a bitterly cold night. These are all recorded by 2nd BETA brainwaves and stored in the 1st pair of DNA strands, which essentially are the memories for all your *voluntary* movements when you are in a conscious awakened state. In comparison, regular BETA brainwaves control involuntary functions of your body every moment of your life experience, regardless of whether you are asleep or awake.

The GAMMA Brainwave Frequency Band

The GAMMA bandwidth of brainwaves is the channel of *Active* energy that sustains the connection to your 5-D *Activebody* and the *Consortium of Activebodies* and enables you to communicate every moment of your physical life experience – whether you are awake or asleep. The 5th and 6th pair of DNA strands are sensitive to the GAMMA brainwaves. *Every energy unit of a GAMMA brainwave can be transformed into any of the other brainwaves and vice versa.* Read that sentence again.

Remember that the connection between your physical *Adaptivebody* in the 3-D and your non-physical *Activebody* in the 5-D is always active – the channel is always open, the bandwidth is always available. However you as an individual may not be communicating on that open channel. Moreover, the channel between your 3-D *Adaptivebody* and the 5-D *Consortium of Activebodies* is not open by default – that channel can be activated only after you have established the communication link to your own *Activebody* first. Remember that you can access the *Consortium of Activebodies* only through your own *Activebody*. Therefore it is mandatory that before you activate the 6th pair of DNA strands, the 5th pair is already communicating with your own *Activebody*.

Whether you communicate with your 5-D *Activebody* through this wide high bandwidth (26.1 to 100 Hz) switchable duplex (bi-directional) channel or not is defined by your attribute of free will and a Type 3 memory pattern that acknowledges or does not recognize the existence of your own *Activebody*. You see, your Type 2 memory that hosts the code of the *Genetics Of Divinity* already "knows" about your *Activebody* connection. However if that memory is either not active or if you have an overlaying Type 3 memory that denies the presence of your *Activebody*, you will not be able to communicate on the 5-D channel.

The GAMMA bandwidth is constantly being used by your *Activebody* to communicate with you, providing you with guidance and counsel in an attempt to keep you aligned with your life purpose. The commonly used term for this mode of communication is *conscience*. But the question would be, "Is your *Adaptivebody* tuned to that frequency and is it listening to those GAMMA transmissions?" Needless to say, if the 5th pair of your DNA strands is not sensitive, far less, responsive to those GAMMA transmissions initiated by your *Activebody* who is fully aware of the future of your decision at any moment in Parallelism, your physical life experience would be devoid of this most amazing asset and resource of Creation. Pause reading this book and spare a few moments pondering what an amazing gift of Creation your *Adaptivebody* is. For the first time in human history you are getting exposed to this consciousness.

Transformation of Brainwave Energy

When your *Adaptivebody* is presented with a situation where a decision needs to be made (literally every instant of your lifetime) there is an instant initial emotion (ALPHA brainwave) generated from your conscious mind. This emotion would be based on any available memory pattern that may be stored in the 1st, 2nd or the 3rd pair of DNA strands. Your *Adaptivebody* **optionally** can convert that ALPHA into a GAMMA brainwave to communicate the memory (data plus emotion) to your *Activebody* in the 5-D.

Note I say *optionally*, which means that through your free will, you could choose through autonomic response not to convert the ALPHA to a GAMMA but directly convert the ALPHA into the next frequency band - the THETA, bypassing the involvement of your *Activebody* in the decision making process. Whether you will or will not consult your *Activebody* when that ALPHA is triggered is an autonomic response of your *Adaptivebody*. If your Type 2 memory that contains information about your *Activebody* in the 5-D is active, the conversion of ALPHA to GAMMA is automatic and will never be bypassed and you will always be able to enjoy the guidance from your *Activebody*.

However your conscious mind could operate under an artificial Type 3 memory pattern that indicates that there is nothing like an *Activebody*. There may a further Type 3 memory pattern that indicates that an external entity controls your life and has the magic pill for all your challenges. In that case you would directly convert that ALPHA to a THETA brainwave as a choice made through your free will.

If you did convert that ALPHA into a GAMMA, and engaged your *Activebody* through the first strand of the 5th pair of DNA strands, it would instantly (faster than light speed) start the communication process with you on the GAMMA channel either agreeing to your initial emotion or proposing a different one. This secondary emotion is a result of the GAMMA transmission converting back into an ALPHA brainwave is picked up by the 2nd strand of the 5th pair of DNA strands. The ALPHA progressively transforms into a

THETA which can now start your rational analysis in the process of relating accordingly to the partner involved in that initial event.

An interesting phenomena occurs here in the THETA. You can by the virtue of your free will, stick to thoughts related your initial emotion generated in the ALPHA or based on your rational analysis in the THETA choose to rely on the second emotion that you downloaded from your *Activebody* as GAMMA converted to APLHA. In case of a conflict, that THETA can also transform into a GAMMA for further communication to and consultation with your *Activebody* in the 5-D, now with new information that is augmented by your rational analysis in the THETA. As usual the *Activebody* responds faster than the speed of light as GAMMA brainwaves which convert back into THETA with new information which could become a new Type 3 memory pattern to augment your consciousness.

The outcome of THETA analysis is conversion into a DELTA brainwave that indicates your decision about the subject impulse. It also activates a corresponding expression through verbal words, facial expressions (smiley or frowning), body language, eye movement, goose-bumps which are all conversions of the DELTA to 2nd BETA brainwaves. The expressions generated through DELTA may also affect skin color (blushing red, or pale), increased heart rate, generate perspiration, unusual breathing patters (sighs for example), which are all conversions of that DELTA to 2nd BETA brainwaves.

The 2nd BETA or regular BETA brainwave would convert into ALPHA brainwaves with concluding emotions (for the cycle) that are now newly stored Type 3 memories in your *Adaptivebody*. You could now choose to convert that *Physical* ALPHA energy into an *Adaptive* THETA energy and energetically transmit your thoughts, towards an appropriate partner *Adaptivebody* that you desire to establish a symbiotic collaborative relationship with. A new cycle of brainwaves would thereby be initiated. Alternatively, you could convert that ALPHA into a GAMMA again and seek further consultation from your *Activebody*.

---------------------------*****---------------------------

Can BETA or 2nd BETA brainwaves inter-transform with the GAMMA? Most definitely. There are countless examples of non-medicinal, non-surgical and non-invasive healing modalities (not in the scope of this book) that are in practice for prevention and cure of diseases in the physical body. As I have described earlier in this Chapter, disease is rightly considered as *dis-ease* or lack of ease, which occurs due to some block or interference on the natural flow of the circuit of energy (BETA, APLHA, THETA, DELTA, 2nd BETA and GAMMA) through the physical body. This circuit of energy is called *Chi* or *Qi* in the Chinese tradition or what in India they refer to as *Prana*. The secret to a dis-ease free life is to ensure that the circuit can flow freely as designed. Yes even that GAMMA channel, facilitating your connection with your *Activebody*, is vitally important for the free flow of that circuit to operate. That is how your *Adaptivebody* is designed to function.

Refer to Figure 30 and consider what would happen to your physical body if there was any break in the circuit. The appropriate part of your physical body to which the memory is associated would not be able to communicate in the GAMMA, which would starve it of life giving energy.

Energy flows where attention goes. This bypass of the circuit through the affected area of your physical body as a result of stuck or unresolved interference, leads to dis-ease in that area which is not designed to operate under conditions of energy depravation. The result is a physical malfunction of that body part which is meant to serve as a warning to your *Adaptivebody* to do *something* that would remove the interference and clear the circuit.

All non-medicinal non-invasive healing modalities have one aspect in common – they address the root cause by eliminating energy blocks and not the symptoms that common medical practices focus on. That root cause is the block in the energy circuit in the physical body. It is important to understand how the block occurred and hence build a memory pattern to not repeat the same cause of the block in the future. However more importantly, the focus would be on how the block can be removed non-invasively to re-engage the natural circuit of energy within the physical body. Popular medicinal and chemical formula based treatments today address only the symptoms and essentially build *energy bypass circuits*, leaving the original circuit where the root cause lies, unattended. This leads to the possibility of recurrence of the dis-ease since the emotions associated with the memory of the offending root cause has not been released or neutralized.

Your conscious mind can deliberately transform these BETA brainwaves (collectively regular BETA and 2nd BETA) generated through your physiological state of dis-ease into GAMMA and obtain guidance on what needs to be done about the physiological dis-ease that has come up in your life experience. This release and transformation of stuck BETA energy into GAMMA starts the healing process. I have personally dissolved a tumor (a small one) in my own body through intimate and constant GAMMA communication with my *Activebody* in the 5-D without the use of any therapy or medication. Living in constant touch with the *Activebody* is a prescribed prerequisite to the mortal life experience of the *Adaptivebody* by design of Creation and a core attribute of the Creature. However this pre-requisite by Creation is offered to the Creature as a choice of Parallelism and hence free will. The Creature could consciously choose to ignore the presence of the very *Activebody* from which it was created, over-riding the principles of Creation. *While the ALPHA, both BETAs and DELTA are designed to exclusively serve your Adaptivebody, the THETA is designed to serve you and other Adaptivebodies that you would relate with in your life experience, the GAMMA is designed to serve your Adaptivebody and your Activebody as one cohesive unit.*

Refer to Figure 30 once again and this time examine the Sacred Geometrical circles. You will notice that the horizontal circles around ALPHA and DELTA form the first Vessica Piscis around the GAMMA. Furthermore the vertical circles around the THETA and the two BETAs form the second Vessica Piscis around the GAMMA. This creates a double energy vortex superimposed on one another on the GAMMA, making it the highest frequency brainwave and the most powerful of the group, thereby enabling the high powered transmissions to operate inter-dimensionally, penetrating the barrier of the intermediate 4-D.

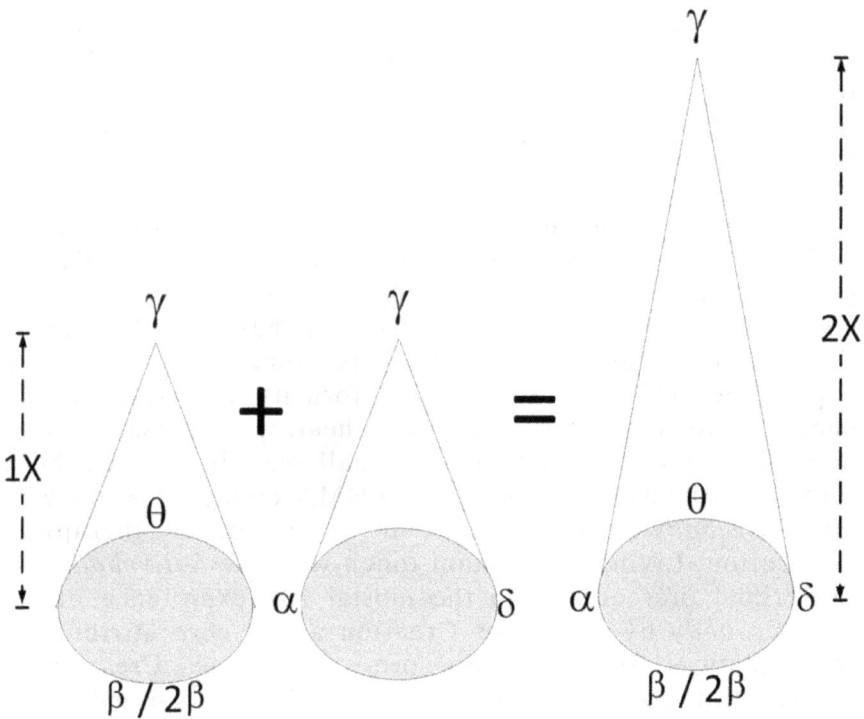

Figure 31

To illustrate this phenomena refer to Figure 31 where the first energy vortex on the left is the result of the first Vessica Piscis from the THETA and the two BETA energies generating the GAMMA – note the height of the vortex where the GAMMA is generated at the tail or apex. This represents the *amplitude* of the resulting GAMMA brainwave. Now let's introduce the second energy vortex in the middle as a result of the second Vessica Piscis from the ALPHA and the DELTA. Let us assume that the resultant GAMMA has the same (may be more or less depending on how balanced your chakras are) amplitude as the GAMMA in the first vortex.

Now if you superimposed these two energy vortices on one another, following the basic principles of wave mechanics for *superposition of waves*, the *amplitude of the resultant vortex would be sum of the two amplitudes* – in Figure 31 the resultant superimposed GAMMA is shown to be double the amplitude of the two component vortices.

Applying Wave Mechanics to Existence

According to the principles of wave mechanics, *Intensity* is proportional to the square of the amplitude of the wave. We also know that *Intensity equals Power per unit area* where the wave is incident. Hence the resulting GAMMA energy shown on the right in Figure 31 *has power that is approximately the square of double the power* of any one of the constituent vortices.

Essentially what I intend to convey here is that a healthy *Adaptivebody*, one that has all nine chakras of the physical body balanced and operating at optimum levels can generate a very powerful GAMMA brainwave when the BETA-ALPHA-THETA-DELTA-2nd BETA (I will refer to this as *BATD2B* from now on) circuit completes. An *Adaptivebody* with minimal or no energy blocks (balanced chakras or energy vortices) generating such high power GAMMA frequency brainwaves can communicate with the *Activebody* without any attenuation.

Following the principles of wave mechanics again, a strong un-attenuated *incident* wave (information that your *Adaptivebody* transmitted) is also echoed back as a strong un-attenuated *reflected* wave (processed information that your *Activebody* responded back with). *Your Activebody in the 5-D delivers consistent clear guidance when your Adaptivebody requests consistent clear counsel.* When this reflected GAMMA is received by your *Adaptivebody*, it would reverse-transform into whatever individual brainwave transformed into GAMMA originally and your BATD2B circuit continues its cycle.

Whatever logical and ethically feasible it is that you as a Creature desire in your life experience, becomes a THETA brainwave that you would transmit to a partner *Adaptivebody*. More powerful the transmission, greater is the DI of your *Adaptivebody* to your partner as indicated by the high intensity of your *Adaptive* energy. Greater the DI of your *Adaptivebody* and hence of this *Adaptive* energy, higher is the likelihood of you receiving a favorable response in the same THETA frequency from your desired partner, which is also at the same time, seeking to establish symbiotic collaborative relationships with a high DI partner.

Now consider the benefits of you consulting your highly conscious 5-D *Activebody* through a THETA generated from a full BATD2B circuit which transforms into a GAMMA. What if you consulted your *Activebody* through that GAMMA before you transmitted an individual THETA directly to the partner *Adaptivebody* with which you desire to establish that symbiotic collaborative relationship?

The *BATD2B* circuit is the amplifier (greater *amplitude* = greater *power* = greater *intensity*) within your *Adaptivebody* that sets up an energy vortex transforming the THETA brainwave into a strong incident GAMMA brainwave. Your *Activebody* responds with a strong reflected GAMMA, which your *Adaptivebody* through the 5th pair of DNA strands can transform back into a strong THETA. This is much more amplified than a direct THETA that can be generated without the BATD2B circuit.

Your *Activebody* operating in the 5-D that is independent of time, is fully aware of every moment of the life experience of your *Adaptivebody*. In the keen interests of providing your *Adaptivebody* a life experience filled with unbounded delight, your *Activebody* knows exactly what you need in your perceived physical reality and it is consistently and constantly communicating the same information to you through the GAMMA bandwidth. The key question here is, are you paying attention to such transmissions or are you ignoring them and making your own choices from Parallelism and deviating further away from your life purpose?

Even if you are not paying attention to these messages from your *Activebody*, at least make it a habit to autonomically generate that GAMMA before you embark on a new project or endeavor, or in the quest to seek a compatible partner in any of the twelve secondary relationship categories that I referred to in Chapter 3. What you receive without a doubt will be very insightful.

-------------------------*****-------------------------

It is impossible to do anything without a prior inspiration – yes, that is an open challenge to anything in the contrary. The Cycle of Creation mandates such an enforced sequence. Hence a THETA brainwave must precede a 2nd BETA brainwave – a protection that is included in the Creature class of Type A energy band. So instead of going from THETA to 2nd BETA directly, which is probably what you have been doing thus far as an autonomic memory pattern, insert a BATD2B circuit in between from now on. This engages your infra-conscious mind to communicate with your *Activebody* in the 5-D in the manner I explained above so that you can receive the proper guidance for the appropriate 2nd BETA action. Effective techniques to consciously convert brainwaves into the GAMMA and generate that BATD2B circuit will be covered in the forthcoming book – *Miracles From Genetics Of Divinity*.

-------------------------#####-------------------------

As I write the above I pause to ponder how different my life experience could have been (I am a frequent tourist of Parallel Universes ☺) if I knew this information that I am sharing in this book, as I was growing up. Events, people and circumstances that I had interacted with and established relationship with in my younger years could have been chosen and handled differently, thereby allowing me to have a life experience that was filled with more unbounded delight and in a different Parallel Universe.

While the past cannot be changed, I realize now the reason why I had to go through those experiences and stored them in my memory systems. Contrast. Those same experiences that caused me such great perceived pain and anguish served their purpose to show me what life in a Parallel Universe would be like where I could enjoy peace, love, harmony, health, security and abundance. This in turn became my driving force to embark on a mission to discover the code of Eternal Consciousness that as you know I call the *Genetics Of Divinity*.

My life experience in a 3-D Parallel Universe where I have chosen to thrive, in the aftermath of this evolving discovery, has been so dramatically different. The lesson that I learned through these experiences of Contrast was that my *Adaptivebody* was not nearly as smart as I vainly thought it was. It did not have the ability to predict the future by design of Creation. However my *Activebody* is the real smart one between us *conjoined twins. Instead of the override on the GAMMA guidance that was offered to me by my Activebody, if I was at least smart enough to abide by that guidance, my life experience would have been dramatically different.* This discovery is not a destination – it is a journey and now, by reading this book and expanding your consciousness you have hopped on the bandwagon.

PUPS - Parallel Universal Positioning System

The concluding paragraph of the previous section positions us well to understand your PUPS (☺) or the *Parallel Universal Positioning System* embedded in the definition of the Human class and hence an integral part of your *Adaptivebody*. As a refresher, you may want to go back and review Chapter 6, specifically the section on Type 3 Parallel Universes again, which if you recall I fondly referred to as '*Home, Sweet Home!*'

The life experience that you desire for your 3-D *Adaptivebody* is the sum total of all active (not dormant) memory patterns stored in your DNA and the *BATD2B* brainwave circuits that you complete or abandon midstream. Type 3 Parallel Universes, each with a unique combination of your own possible personal life experiences based on your currently *active* memory patterns, *in relationship with other*

Adaptivebodies sharing a contemporary life experience with you are all stacked up and superimposed upon one another at every instant of time. Whether the relationships are collaborative or destructive, symbiotic or parasitic is a matter of personal perception. It does not impact the lineup of the possible life experiences through Parallelism as they are based on the choices that you have made in the past that brought you to the life experience or the Parallel Universe of the present moment. If you make no change in the choices at the present moment, you choose to continue to enjoy in the same life experience and hence continue to live in the same Parallel Universe where you are right now. Is that a life experience of unbounded delight or unbounded plight or somewhere in between? Only you know that answer.

The key addition (now that your consciousness is more advanced when compared to when you started to read this book) to the concept of Type 3 Parallel Universes that what I had described in Chapter 6, is this element of *symbiotic collaborative relationship*s. Your A*daptivebody* is designed to fulfill a specific life purpose (assigned by your *Activebody) to* serve other *Adaptivebodies* across the energy bands that will attract you during your lifetime. This implies that establishing and sustaining symbiotic collaborative relationships with other *Adaptivebodies* that take you **and** those participating *Adaptivebodies* closer to that emotion of unbounded delight defines the Parallel Universe where you and your partner *Adaptivebodies* would share a collective contemporary coexistence. This Parallel Universe that I am referring to is a mutually and collaboratively agreed upon combination of choices of events, circumstances and interactions from Parallelism, providing the physical 3-D platform for such a collective contemporary co-existence.

When I refer to the *perceived reality* of your 3-D life experience, I am referring to that reality presented to you in a particular Parallel Universe in relation to other *Adaptivebodies* that you have built a relationship with. Although it should, this relationship may not necessarily be symbiotic and collaborative in nature. As you already know by now, all relationships, regardless of being perceived as symbiotic or parasitic must first align and then attract. A symbiotic collaborative relationship would generate amplified resultant energy through resonance (refer to Figure 12 in Chapter 6) of the *in-phase* participating brainwaves of *Adaptive energy* with higher amplitude and hence greater power. A parasitic destructive relationship on the other hand would generate attenuated resultant energy through dissonance (refer to Figure 13 of Chapter 6) of the *out-of-phase* participating brainwaves of *Adaptive energy* thereby depleting the amplitude and hence power. *While resonant brainwaves between the relating partners lead to mutual delight, dissonant brainwaves would invariably lead to mutual plight.* Read that sentence again.

Think about any challenge that you have in your life experience right now – for simplicity let's take that challenge that is occupying most of your attention and hence consuming the most of your *Potential* energy right now. How many *Adaptivebodies* are involved in those relationships? Who are they? How did you acquire these relationships? What did you find attractive about the partner in each of those relationships when you started them? Why are they presenting such a challenging experience for you that is depleting your *Potential* energy? What can be done to overcome such a challenge? Can you be proactive to expedite the resolution or would you allow nature to takes its default course? What would happen if the participating *Adaptivebodies* never existed in your life in a different Parallel Universe? What would happen if the participating *Adaptivebodies* in a different Parallel Universe realized in the near future that enough conflict was enough and the challenge was not worth it and agreed to settle with you? What if in a yet different Parallel Universe the participating *Adaptivebodies* were present in your life experience but never posed a challenge for you in the first place? What if in a yet another Parallel Universe, your *Adaptivebody* was so well tuned with your *Activebody* that you regularly listened to that inbound wisdom all the time and took decisions about your relationships under its guidance? Alternatively in yet another Parallel Universe what if you were autonomically and consistently transforming that THETA to a GAMMA and engaging your *Activebody* at every defining moment of your life? What if as a result of that consistent *Activebody* communication you were never established those parasitic relationships at all in a Parallel Universe? How different would the quality of your life be if you did make the choices in life under the guidance of your *Activebody* in retrospect?

All of the above are only a tiny sample of the plethora of possibilities of your life experiences in Type 3 Parallel Universes that co-exist superimposed on one another. The question is, in which of these Universes did you land your *Adaptivebody* through the use of your *Adaptive* energy? Another question would be why did you land yourself in that Universe where you are currently facing those challenges, when you had the option through Parallelism to make another choice?

The answer to the first is best known to you while I can definitively answer the second. First of all, you were probably guided by a memory pattern that there is one single physical Universe that you observe around you and multiverses are a figment of a theoretical Physicist's imagination. That paradigm needs an urgent overhaul. *Parallel Universes do exist, superimposed on one another in the same time and space each with a unique life experience for you and are presenting themselves to you at this very moment – get over it.* It is impossible for you to observe a plane of reference from the same plane of reference.

You cannot see the curvature of the Earth from where you are right now. However when you are in an aircraft flying at a high altitude, you can observe a fair bit of the curvature. Go higher beyond the Earth's atmosphere in a spaceship and you will be able to admire the entire blue marble of the Milky Way. You have to rise above the Parallel Universe where you are living in the 3-D to observe the other Parallel Universes superimposed on one another. This observation of the 3-D Type 3 Parallel Universes is not possible from within the same plane of reference in the 3-D. However, your Activebody in the 5-D can clearly observe the superimposition of the Type 3 Parallel Universes, each with a unique life experience for you.

Here's something really fantastic for you to consider. Recall the discussion on Type 5 memories, where your *Activebody* has already implanted the plan of your life experience in these memories. In that plan not only is your life purpose defined, your *Activebody* has also defined the specific partners in the twelve secondary relationship categories, when they would appear in your life experience and what circumstances will bring you together. These relationships collectively are meant to guide you to the fulfillment of the life purpose and lead you to unbounded delight. So as you can understand, your *Activebody*, through this plan has already defined the Parallel Universes that you need to navigate through during the course of your life. The question is are you aware of this plan or are you ignoring it through your free will?

You were probably convinced that you have no control about what the future holds for you and some unseen force commonly termed as luck or destiny led you to your current life experience and will continue to dictate your future. You are also probably convinced that you have no freedom to choose your life experience and have no other option but to follow the dictates of an external entity. Most definitely that memory pattern needs to be overhauled. There is no external entity that dictates your life – that is not the design of Creation and there is no provision for such a paradigm in the code of the *Genetics Of Divinity*.

You have all the mechanics, all the tools and technology in your *Adaptivebody* to intelligently choose a life experience in a Parallel Universe where you feel unbounded delight in your active pursuit of your life purpose with wholesome symbiotic collaborative relationships. You know that for a fact, if you have read so far into this book.

Just like the GPS (*Global Positioning System*) unit in a vehicle, boat or aircraft, your *Adaptivebody* is equipped with a special *firmware* that I refer to as PUPS – *Parallel Universe Positioning System* that works hand in hand with your other embedded *firmware* – the EGS that I have explained earlier in this Chapter. All 6 pairs of DNA strands in each cell of your *Adaptivebody* collaborate symbiotically to provide you with the PUPS. Let's understand first how a GPS unit works and that will help you understand the workings of the PUPS/EGS *technology*.

In order to operate a GPS, four core components are necessary. First, a receiver in your GPS unit (it does not have a transmitter). Second, a system of satellites orbiting the Earth at a specific distance from Earth and speed, each of which is constantly transmitting its position and time based on the same atomic clock. Third, your intended destination is a key input parameter into the GPS unit – it needs to know where you want to go in order to guide you. You can either manually specify the exact address of your destination, or provide a general address (no street name or house number, just a city for example) or choose from a list of destinations or what is commonly called *point of interest*. Fourth, necessary software must be embedded in the GPS unit that includes maps, logic for interpreting incoming satellite data and determining data about your current location.

Your GPS receiver is programmed to leverage a method called *trilateration* through which it can use a minimum of three incoming satellite signals about their respective positions, to pinpoint your current location and time on Earth. Additional data received from these satellites such as, upcoming (in the future) traffic conditions in your charted route, weather conditions, road conditions etc. This additional data can be used by the software in your GPS unit adjusting the navigation route as necessary, providing near real time updated data about your current position relative to your chosen destination, current time, remaining distance, estimated time of arrival and even the speed at which you are traveling.

Your physical 3-D *Adaptivebody* is equipped with such a navigation and guidance system – the PUPS, by virtue of its conformance to the *Human class*, that is significantly more advanced and sophisticated.

First of all your PUPS is not only a receiver (a GPS unit is only a receiver), it is also a transmitter of energy. The PUPS is composed of your central nervous system, 6 pairs of your DNA strands and the nine chakras that I have described earlier in this Chapter. Second, it does leverage *trilateration* algorithms by receiving *Active* energy transmissions from your 5-D *Activebody*, *Adaptive* energy transmissions from an unlimited number of other *Adaptivebodies* and *Physical* energy from the emotions that you feel in the EGS. Your PUPS synthesizes all of these three energy waves to determine your exact position in your route to the Parallel Universe of your choice *as long as you have defined what that life experience is like*. Third and in my opinion the most critical, in order for your PUPS to operate, you must mandatorily provide it with a clear an unambiguous address (a vivid description) of the Parallel Universe where you want to enjoy a life experience. Without this vital input, your PUPS is rendered dormant and over time when you don't use it, you will definitely lose it.

When you lose the PUPS, your life experience becomes a rudderless ship in the stormy waters and fills up with all sorts of challenges continuing to erode away your net *Available* energy, consequently rendering the trilateration algorithm defunct. As a result, the quality of your life experience continually degrades towards unbounded plight.

Your PUPS constantly keeps you aligned with your chosen Parallel Universe(s) that exist in a future time in the 4-D but not yet part of your current perceived reality. When you take those *not-so-scenic* routes deviating from your intended Parallel Universe through incorrect choices and decisions your PUPS generates alarms and warnings in an attempt to get you back in alignment. The question is, do you listen to those warnings and take corrective action?

The Mechanics of Your PUPS

First of all you will need to define your life experience that you desire in the Parallel Universe where you intend to thrive and enjoy feelings of unbounded delight. You may want to consider doing this along with me as you read this section. As a guide refer to the 12 different categories of relationship in your life experience as illustrated in Figure 1 in Chapter 3 of this book. The idea is to define your Parallel Universe that you want to call *Sweet Home*, as vivid and detailed as possible, preferably engaging details from all your five physical senses on each collaborative relationship that you would want in that Universe. Ready? Great – read each question and then write them down.

What is your home like in that Parallel Universe? Can you describe it? If I were to give you a blank canvas and painting supplies, could you draw this home with clear detail? Who are in your family and what are they like in that Parallel Universe? What kind of interactions do you have with them and what activities do you do together? How do you feel when you are immersed in the aura of those relationships in that Parallel Universe? What do you use for transport – is it a car, a boat, a plane or combinations thereof in that Parallel Universe? Can you describe them with their Make and Model and other features that you desire? How do you feel when you drive that car or boat or fly that plane in that Parallel Universe? How are your finances in that Parallel Universe? What do you do for a living to serve in that Parallel Universe?

Using Figure 1 as your guide for the types of collaborative relationships in your Parallel Universe, define in as vivid detail as possible how you would desire them to be. Now that you have defined those relationships with you as the center, define other details about the Universe that form your environment.

In that Parallel Universe are we still wasting trillions of currency units fighting wars and causing damage to life and property and promoting parasitic destructive relationships or is the money being invested on peaceful purposes that enhance the life experience of every contemporary Creature? In that Parallel Universe where you desire to live, are starvation and epidemics still the leading cause or disease and death or is the entire world population living in health and vitality? How is the local and global economy doing in that Parallel Universe of your choice - is there financial crisis or financial abundance there? What about the freedom of expression of free will in that Parallel Universe? Are people in that Parallel Universe still guided by the doctrines of fate, destiny, an external controlling power, or has the human civilization upgraded to higher consciousness and are assuming more responsibility and accountability for their life experience? Are people in that Universe predominantly building symbiotic collaborative relationships or is that not one of the top five drivers of life experience? How advanced is that civilization from a technology perspective? Are people still held hostage to invasive medical practices with rising healthcare costs or have alternative natural non-invasive healing modalities that rely on the removal of energy interference come into vogue? Overall, what is a typical day in your lifetime like in that Parallel Universe? When you wake up in the morning, go through your day and prepare to retire for the night do you feel unbounded delight and look forward to the next day in that Parallel Universe? If you do, then yes, you have defined your Sweet Home.

The more detail you add to the components of the Parallel Universe that you would want to spend the remainder of your mortal lifetime in, the more real it becomes. I refer to this as *intended reality* (while *perceived reality* is the reality of your present moment). In the above process of defining your desired Parallel Universe, you have generated Adaptive energy through your thoughts and visions. That intended reality is where your thoughts and imaginations have travelled to and were able to experience simulated unbounded delight. However your physical *Adaptivebody* still needs to abide by the linear progression of time in the 4-D and finally catch up with that future instant in the 4-D. This is possible only when stay attentive to the guidance of your PUPS leveraging the emotions of the EGS, before you can start a physical life experience in your intended Parallel Universe.

Interconnectedness between PUPS and EGS

Moving on with the modus operandi of your PUPS – now that you have defined your Parallel Universe based on your logical and ethically feasible desires, how does it make you feel? Does that seem like a pipe-dream in a fairy tale or do you believe such a Parallel Universe really exists? Do you believe that you, given the appropriate technology can actually travel to and start to enjoy a life experience filled with unbounded delight there? This is where the EGS component of your PUPS is activated in your *Adaptivebody* – what kind of emotions are evoked about the feasibility that you can actually have such an experience?

This is the deciding moment depending on your conviction or rejection of the Parallel Universe that you have defined. You would either feed the *destination details* that you have defined into your PUPS or you will make certain updates to make that Parallel Universe more realistic and achievable based on logical and ethically feasible desires as allowed by your current memory patterns. If your current consciousness and convictions consider some elements of that Parallel Universe to be too far-fetched, break it down into smaller achievable chunks that raises your emotions about them in the EGS scale. Remember Parallel Universes are a journey, not a destination - once you have emigrated to one, there is no limitation in the grid of Existence that prevents you from emigrating again to another for a better and bigger life experience. The PUPS is always present within your *Adaptivebody* being an integral part of your firmware. You have complete freedom to relocate from one Parallel Universe to another at any time as long as the definition is logical and ethically feasible.

Is it possible for the THETA bandwidth to be overloaded with data? Yes, absolutely and like any other transmitter, this can happen if you have too many target *Adaptivebodies* that you desire to build symbiotic relationships with in your intended Parallel Universe at the same time. Each target is a unique frequency within the THETA bandwidth. With too many targets that THETA bandwidth may be filled to capacity and the third eye chakra would not have room to accommodate any more targets to communicate with. What can you do in this situation when your intended reality is composed of everything in your list? Given the fact that everything in your list has passed the EGS test, you need to prioritize that list in categories such as *mandatory, nice to have, may be deferred for later* etc. Now define a Parallel

Universe with the elements in your *mandatory* list, so that the THETA bandwidth can accommodate those frequencies. When your 3-D *Adaptivebody* arrives in that Parallel Universe, you can re-engage your PUPS to focus on the *nice to have* or the *deferred* list, progressively taking you to a Parallel Universe where everything in your list upgrades from intended reality to true reality. The exciting part of this journey is that once in a Parallel Universe, you are offered a brand new set of choices by Parallelism allowing you to define a brand new list of priorities of desired symbiotic collaborative relationships for your next Parallel Universe.

At this point, with the address of the Parallel Universe set in your PUPS it goes to work by first converting the constituent THETA frequencies into GAMMA active energy through your crown chakra for a feasibility consultation with your really smart *Activebody* in the 5-D. The *Activebody* considers this incident GAMMA energy, applies updates as necessary and responds with a reflected GAMMA transmission back to your crown chakra. The crown chakra transforms that GAMMA into the THETA. At this point you will choose to override or abide by the counsel provided by the *Activebody*. If you agree, your *Adaptive* energy in the form of THETA brainwaves is now transmitted to the appropriate *Adaptivebodies* that constitute your intended Parallel Universe.

THETA energy transmissions ensue between your PUPS and your targeted *Adaptivebodies*. Assuming an acceptable DI match between both parties, the alignment is established followed by the initiation of a symbiotic collaborative relationship and your subsequent attraction towards your partner. When the attraction is complete, you would have arrived in this particular Parallel Universe where you are enjoying a life experience filled with unbounded delight with your partner.

When you veer off course during the process for example when you lose focus, or feel frustrated about the gestation period of the process, or begin to have doubts whether this really works or not, you generate THETA frequencies that are in opposite phase (refer to Figure 13) to the original frequencies *that you might have transmitted to your desired Adaptivebody*. This causes dissonance and may as well completely attenuate the original transmissions, snapping the alignment between you and your desired *Adaptivebody*.

Both you and your *Adaptivebody* realize this break and develop a mutual dis-regard, lowering both DIs. PUPS continually monitors the power in the channel and with its built in Early Warning System (EWS), will activate your EGS alerting you through emotions lower in the EGS scale to re-engage resonant communications with your partner. If such communications are restored, that's great and you can get back on course towards your intended Parallel Universe. Otherwise, you essentially are set back to the drawing board.

Figure 32 illustrates a schematic flow of energy between the source and target *Adaptivebodies* seeking a mutually collaborative relationship using the PUPS. If you are not conversant with flow diagrams (prevalent in process engineering and software programming), just follow the direction of the arrows from left to right and top to bottom to understand how information is transferred between the four multi-dimensional elements participating in the collaborative relationship for a contemporary collective co-existence. The concept of flow diagrams and the operation of the PUPS as illustrated in Figure 32 is explained in great detail in an instructional video accessible to you through the online Multiversity of the *Genetics Of Divinity*.

Does everything have to be different in this intended Parallel Universe? Not necessarily but it definitely could. The lives of most of the world population may have no perceivable change, if they did not participate in the journey with you. However, your life experience and the participating *Adaptivebodies* who engaged in that symbiotic collaborative relationship during your journey to that intended Parallel Universe would have upgraded to a new reality. What would happen if hundreds, thousands and millions of people invested their respective net *Available* energy to define such a Parallel Universe that fills every participating *Adaptivebody* with a life experience of unbounded delight? Would humanity have upgraded its consciousness to the next

The Code Of Eternal Consciousness

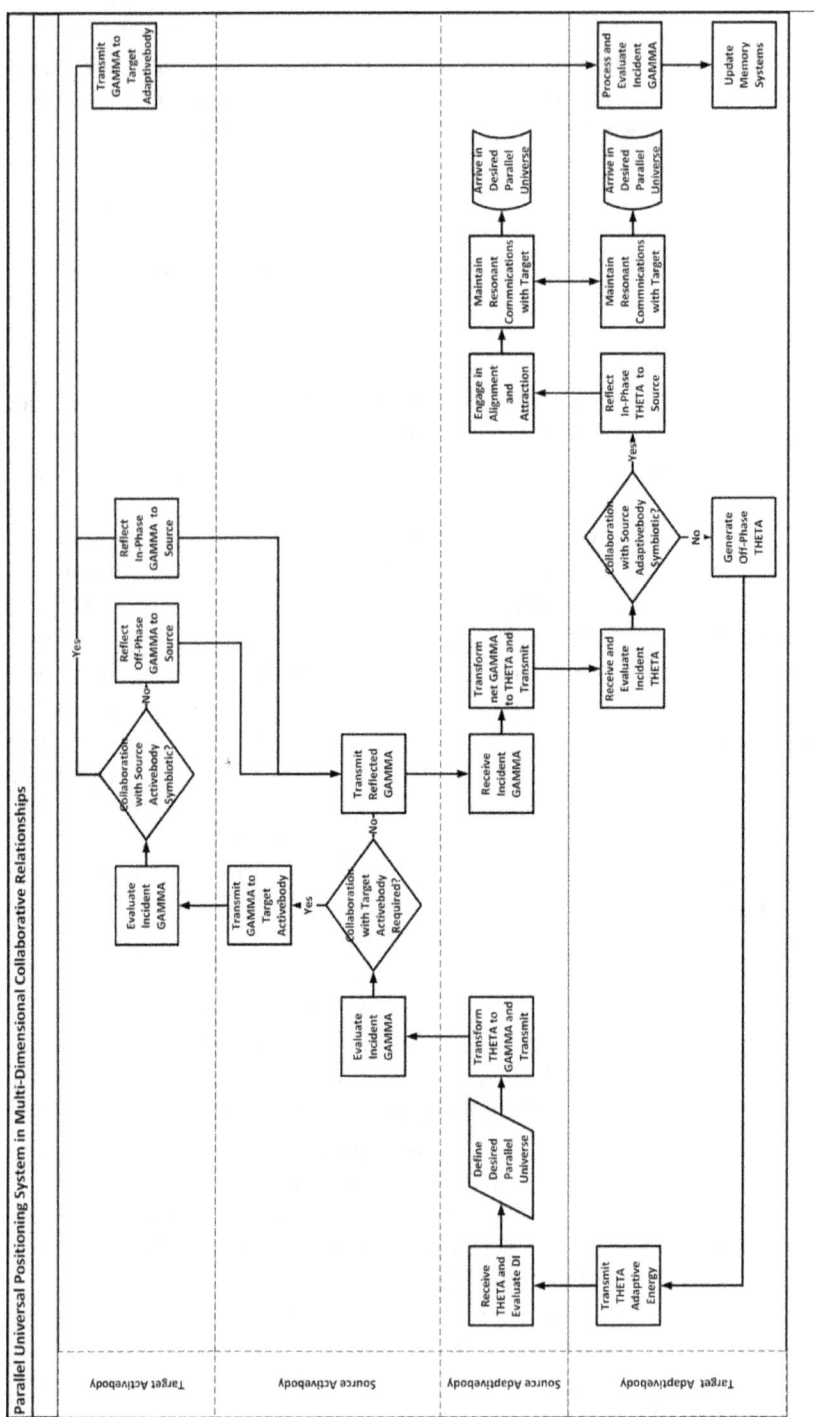

Figure 32

Higher level in a Parallel Universe? Most definitely so according to the *Genetics Of Divinity.*

As I wrap this Chapter up, I find myself again in awe at the masterpiece of Creation – the multi-dimensional human, the most lavishly endowed of Creatures living in this planet. I also find myself confused at why and how our civilization became misguided to the extent that we seem to have become oblivious of the immense faculties embedded within this flesh, blood and bones physical body. What an amazing capability we have, to choose not only our own life experience but collaboratively establish a Parallel Universe with those partners in the twelve secondary relationship categories to thrive symbiotically in peace, love, security, harmony, service and abundance in the spirit of collective coexistence and enjoy unbounded delight in the process.

Most definitely, we cannot change the past. However the past has demonstrated the Contrast to help humanity clearly define the life experience we all desire. We have stopped short of making that very important decision to rely on this marvel of Creation and find ourselves in a Parallel Universe where life can flourish without blemish. There is just one Truth that you would need to install in your memory system *There is no scarcity or lack in the multiverse of Existence – the domain of infinite abundance, symbiosis and collective coexistence.* Once you agree to this Eternal Truth, the rest will follow automatically over time in your life experience allowing you to enjoy unbounded delight.

Chapter 9 - Source Energy and the G.O.D

In the previous chapters of this book, I have provided a lot of information about Creation and Existence from my own research from various fields of Science, Engineering, Hypnotherapy, Human Anatomy specifically the brain and brainwaves, Sacred Geometry, Multi-Dimensional Energetics and most importantly the consciousness that I received from my *Activebody* through the progressive reactivation of the dormant code of the *Genetics Of Divinity* embedded in my subconscious mind. All information has been validated by my *Activebody* through a technique that I will describe in the follow-on book – *Miracles From Genetics Of Divinity*. I believe without a shred of doubt that if you embarked on the same quest for higher consciousness as I have done, seeking answers to some esoteric questions that I have been asking, you too would receive exactly the same information from your own 5-D *Activebody*. This book is meant to deliver the same impulses to your 2nd pair of DNA strands and reactive those Type 1 memories of the *Genetics of Divinity*.

You and I and the next person and everyone else are different physical *Adaptivebodies* for sure in the 3-D. However, the non-physical in higher dimensions we are one and the same as illustrated in Figure 17 – non-physical *Active* energy. The consciousness of Creation and Existence as defined in the code of the *Genetics Of Divinity* is the same regardless of the artificial differences we feel in this physical and mortal 3-D *Adaptivebody*.

If you recall in Chapter 7, I alluded to the *Source Force* in the 11-D and the *sourceon* in the 0-D which binds the other bounded dimensions of Existence together. In this

Chapter, I dive deeper into the source of everything in Existence. I write this Chapter in communication and partnership with my 5-D *Activebody*. The format of this Chapter will be different. Until now, if you noticed, the style of sharing the dormant code of the *Genetics Of Divinity* has been as if I am communicating directly with you as the reader – almost like having a conversation. In this Chapter I present the information in the form of a conversation that I was having with my 5-D *Activebody* through the GAMMA channel. You are the audience of this interview listening in.

The following is a close description of an actual real life experience I had when I was in this intense knowledge transfer session with my *Activebody* as dormant memories of the code of the *Genetics Of Divinity* were reactivated from my subconscious mind and flooded my conscious mind. This should be an interesting experience for both you and I (3-D *Adaptivebodies*) and I guess our respective Activebodies are *smiling* at what's coming up ☺

Since you have gone through the preceding material in this book and have come to this point, it is evident that your level of consciousness has already undergone an upgrade. Unbeknownst to you, I have already been releasing THETA energy your way and you have been processing the same. Your continued attention on this material indicates that we are in energetic resonance with one another – although in all logical likelihood our *Adaptivebodies* have never physically met with each other. Needless to say we both have DIs that are appealing to one another, which makes it a perfect platform to build a symbiotic collaborative relationship between ourselves.

Welcome! With that said, let's start this conversation with my *Activebody*. Although this experience had occurred before I write this material, I document that experience in the present tense to create an illusion of a live real time interview occurring right in your presence as our audience. The content in this Chapter requires an understanding of basic Wave Mechanics, so feel free to do your own research on certain terms that I will be referring to in this Chapter if they sound too technical for your current consciousness, which will definitely undergo a significant upgrade regardless. Again, I recommend that you secure access to the online Multiversity and watch the videos of Module 9 for a better understanding of this content.

One last thing. In the following content you will find I have documented the interaction with my *Activebody* as a conversation. However, not a single verbal word was spoken or heard. It was entirely a pure THETA-GAMMA communication purely through my focused thoughts that my crown chakra facilitated through the 5th pair of my DNA strands. The laughter and banter from time to time were (sur)real though ☺

My Activebody and I – A Live Download

My *Activebody* and I (my *Adaptivebody*) at the time of this conversation are in a Parallel Universe where I am sitting comfortably in my private *transitional sanctuary* (a concept to be discussed in the follow-on book *Miracles From Genetics Of Divinity*), undisturbed and alone. I do not physically see my Activebody, but I do feel his presence all around, engulfing me with a serene sense of warmth, peace and love. I feel secure and I feel so energetic – I guess that is what the GAMMA zone is all about. This may be my imagination, but his appearances mirror mine - the same image that I see whenever I seek his guidance as I go through my life experience. He is ready (well duh! ☺) and so am I (it's about time ☺), so now we begin.

[Me] This interview with you that I am documenting in this book is unprecedented and I had no idea that I will write this Chapter in this style when I started writing this book. I would hazard a guess that was your GAMMA communication to me that gave me this idea literally out of the blue?

I hear cosmic laughter ... oh my goodness, he also laughs like I do ☺

[*My Activebody*] You are getting better with these realizations – not guesses. Good that you were attentive to my GAMMA transmissions – it will make the information that you seek to share easier to read and understand.

{ I nod in agreement. }

The Source Force

[Me] Is it true that there is a force more fundamental than the four (electromagnetic, gravitational, strong and weak nuclear forces) that we know of?

[My Activebody] Yes, there is a force more fundamental to those that you are referring to. Those four types of forces that you call *'fundamental'* are only fundamental to the physical 3-D plane of Existence. These four are necessary to build the dimensions of Adaptive energy frequencies and collectively contribute to create the physical Third Dimension. These four forces bind physical matter of individual *Adaptivebodies* on all the energy bands that you have described and are also necessary for inter-*Adaptivebody* bonding and reproductive functions for Type A, B and C Creatures in the 3-D. No *Adaptivebody* is self-sufficient in the design of Existence and it would not serve any purpose if it were self-sufficient. The core theme of Creation is what you have referred to as *symbiotic collaborative relationships*. So by design, all physical *Adaptivebodies* have been created as components of a whole and the four fundamental physical forces enable such bonding for that collective co-existence to occur. These forces are the result of certain frequencies of energy that represent the bandwidth of Adaptive energy that apply to the 3-D. In the higher dimensions (5-D and higher) we have different energy bandwidths that are of much higher frequencies than those that exist in the physical domain. Hence those four fundamental forces do not apply and hence are not required here in our higher dimensions of Existence.

Independence From The Time Factor

[Me] Is the speed of light really the limit possible in Existence or is there another higher limit?

[My Activebody] Light energy occupies a specific bandwidth as a subset within the larger bandwidth of electromagnetic energy, which is one of the four fundamental types of energy in the 3-D and lower dimensions. In the 3-D the speed of light is definitely the limit for any physical matter – what you have referred to as *rest mass* traveling through vacuum conditions. This physical limit imposed on the 3-D is what makes up the dimension of time or the 4-D. In the higher dimensions there is no dimension of time because there is no physical matter and hence no rest mass.

[Me] Ah! Speed in the 3-D is defined as the distance travelled by an object in motion over a unit of time. Mathematically, we define *Speed = Distance / Time*. From this equation, *if Time = 0, that makes Speed = Infinite*. So the object in motion can travel at infinite speed in a dimension where time is not a factor.

[My Activebody] Precisely! In our higher dimensions, there is no limit to how fast non-physical matter (mass-less) can travel hence the concept of speed does not relate in the Fifth and higher dimensions.

[Me] What about energy? Every reference to energy implies a reference to frequency and frequency is measured in terms of number of oscillations of the energy wave per unit of time in Physics. So if time is zero in the higher dimensions, mathematically speaking, we are talking about extremely high frequency energy – infinite, just like speed?

[My Activebody] You are right. Infinity is a mathematical concept indicating the domain where 3-D consciousness loses insight since physical laws cease to apply. The energy frequencies that operate in the non-physical higher dimensions are not infinite in the true sense but yes they are extremely high frequencies, higher than what the 3-D designates as the UHF band. Higher dimension energy waves

are also of high amplitude, when compared to what you are used to in the 3-D and hence have very high intensity and hence power. Due to this high power, these energy waves can travel great distances in zero time. Just like your 3-D has been allocated a certain bandwidth of frequencies, every other dimension, other than the 4-D have their own allocated band of frequencies, which in turn defines the role and function of that dimension as you have described in the book. But here's what is more important to know and understand. Every dimension has been allocated a certain bandwidth of frequencies that are inter-dimensional in nature, overlapping with the next higher dimension. This enables inter-dimensional communication to be possible, just like you and I are using what you call the GAMMA bandwidth to have this mutual interaction. In our case, we are communicating between the 3-D, where you are and 5-D where I am on the GAMMA channel. This provision has been made in the design of Creation in the interests of establishing the grid of Existence based on the core theme of symbiotic collaborative relationships.

[Me] Fascinating how the fabric of Existence is interwoven and interconnected! GAMMA, the bandwidth that we are currently using to communicate with each other now is an electromagnetic frequency band. Does this mean that in the Fifth and higher dimensions, electromagnetism does exist just like in the lower dimensions? I thought you said physical time based frequencies do not exist in the higher dimensions.

{ I hear that cosmic laughter again }

[My Activebody] You did not graduate as an engineer in this lifetime for nothing, you know? That question bears testimony of your analytical and logical patterns of thought. Electromagnetic energy is restricted to the 3-D and lower dimensions. You are right, what you call GAMMA is a time factored electromagnetic spectrum of frequencies. You are transmitting in GAMMA, but I am not receiving in GAMMA. Similarly I am not transmitting to you in GAMMA but you are receiving in GAMMA. I know that you are familiar with the term *transducer*, right?

[Me] Yes, of course. I get it now – Wow! A transducer is a device that converts one energy form to another – for example, sound energy from a recording artist's performance is converted by a microphone (the transducer) into electrical energy and then again from electrical energy, when it is burnt on a CD another transducer converts the electrical energy into magnetic energy. During playback of that CD, magnetic energy is converted by another transducer into electrical energy, which in turn is transduced by the speaker (another transducer) into sound energy. So what you are saying is between you in the 5-D and I in the 3-D there is a transducer that is converting my GAMMA transmissions into your bandwidth when I transmit and then also back-converts your transmissions into GAMMA that I can receive and process.

[My Activebody] Exactly! That transducer is the 4-D. By removing the element of time, the 4-D is converting your GAMMA into a bandwidth that I can understand in our channel. Similarly, by inserting the factor of time the 4-D acting as the transducer is converting my transmitted energy into GAMMA that you are equipped to understand. Time is either removed or introduced by the 4-D depending on the direction of incidence of the communication. So keep that GAMMA open all the time and we will be able to communicate instantly with each other every moment of your life experience.

[Me] YeeHah ! (I am visibly excited)

{ That cosmic laughter again. }

Biophotons and the Lightbody

[Me] I want to talk about *biophoton and the lightbody*

[My Activebody] Ok, what about them?

[Me] The *biophoton* is a light particle emitted from the DNA in every cell of Type C Creatures and above. The energy waveforms carried by these biophotons have very low amplitude and hence have very low power. However, being the carriers of light energy, these biophotons do travel within the physical *Adaptivebody* pretty fast, though not at the speed of light. These biophotons participate in near-real-time intercellular communication within the *Adaptivebody*. A classic example is the reflex action in Creatures of Type A,B and C. Collectively, these biophotons within an *Adaptivebody* is what is commonly referred to as the *lightbody*. Can you provide more insight on these biophotons and the lightbody? How are they significant in the design of Existence and how do they relate to this physical 3-D life experience?

[My Activebody] You ask a very profound question so let's break things up into smaller pieces. The key factor of Creation across all dimensions as I have mentioned before is to establish and sustain symbiotic collaborative relationships. In the physical Third Dimension, the four fundamental physical forces have been provided specifically to facilitate the formation of these relationships between physical *Adaptivebodies*. In addition to these four, there is yet another force that is much superior to these four fundamental forces that only Creatures of Type A energy are equipped to relate to in the 3-D – you have referred to this force as the Source Force. In higher dimensions this is the only force that is required to maintain the cohesiveness of Existence. However for the moment, let's postpone the discussion about the Source Force for a little longer and focus on the four fundamental forces in the 3-D.

[Me] I can hardly wait to learn about the Source Force, I have always felt it's presence. But first, let's get back to my question.

[My Activebody] Biophotons, as you have rightly said, are carrier particles of electromagnetic energy. Focus on the word 'magnetic', which in this context refers to an aligning force. Depending on the nature of alignment, this may be an resulting attracting force or a repelling force, both of which are essential for the establishment of symbiotic collaborative relationships. Biophotons have been implanted in the design of all Creatures from the Type C energy band and up and essentially serve the same purpose with similar mechanics of

operation. Keeping us focused on the human *Adaptivebody*, biophotons are the vehicle for inter-cellular communication leveraging the infra-red range (0.003 Hz to 4×10^{14} Hz) of the electromagnetic spectrum. The brainwaves that you have mentioned in the book are in this infra-red range of the electromagnetic spectrum.

[Me] Infra-red – now that makes sense. This range is beyond the human visible range, which is why we can't actually see the brainwaves in the BATD2B circuit and neither the GAMMA of course, but an EEG machine can detect them.

[My Activebody] Right! The central nervous system along with the peripheral nervous system of your *Adaptivebody*, is the super-highway of all data being constantly and incessantly exchanged at near-light speed between every cell in your physical body. The dataflow in and out of your brain is facilitated by these biophotons like a *closed-feedback* system. Disruption in the flow of these biophotons from any cell is sensed by the brain (due the closed-feedback design of your *Adaptivebody*) and is transmitted to every other cell in your body. However the memory of that disruption is stored only in all cells surrounding the affected cell in the organ to which the cell belongs. The regular BETA energy generated by your chakras is responsible to drive these biophotons through the cells and the central nervous system. Every cell is designed to heal itself, or be healed by adjoining cells having the same form and function. If the affected cell cannot self-heal, it is replaced by another new cell with the same form and function, thereby restoring the flow of the biophotonic circuit of energy. Well how does this healing occur? Magnetism. While the affected cell initiates a repelling force to communication from other cells, indicating *trouble*, other healthy cells generate an attracting force between each other pooling their resources to start the healing process.

[Me] I am amazed – I never heard an explanation like that before ever. I know about self-healing capabilities of the *Adaptivebody*, but did not know the true mechanics of the process until now. This is fantastic.

[My Activebody] You did know but you were unaware of this knowledge which had been dormant in your subconscious memory until now. Regular BETA energy is what drives these biophotons in your lightbody all throughout your physical *Adaptivebody*. Stop that BETA in your *Adaptivebody* and you would get me busy here in the 5-D to determine your next assignment and life purpose for your rebirth as a new physical *Adaptivebody*. Essentially when BETA flow stops, the physical body erodes and you call that dis-ease.

[Me] Hey, that's not funny! I am in no hurry to stop my BETA flow. ☺

[My Activebody] Yes, you still have a long journey before that eventually happens to your current mortal *Adaptivebody*. In the above explanation you understood how biophotons operate at a physical level within your Adaptivebody facilitating cell-division for growth or what you refer to as *mitosis*. The same biophotonic electromagnetism is responsible for *meiosis* or cell reproduction. Like all cells, both male and female reproductive cells have biophotons and hence are powered by BETA energy. Only those pairs of such male and female cells whose energy frequencies are in-phase or in resonant vibration will generate enough power to fuse together to form the embryo, while others even if they are in physical proximity will not participate in fertilization of the egg due to the out-of phase vibrations of BETA energy. From the perspective of the human *Adaptivebody*, although all the available sperm cells are potential candidates to get attracted by the egg cell, only those inbound sperms cells with biophotons that are vibrating in a frequency that is in-phase with the frequency of vibration of the biophotons in the awaiting egg cell, will fertilize the egg through a resonant interaction. This is in line with the core concept of Eternal Consciousness – the establishment of symbiotic collaborative relationships.

[Me] Aha! So the use of chemical contraception actually serves to prevent possible fertilizations by exciting the biophotons in the sperm and/or egg to energy levels that are out-of-phase, hence even though the male and female reproductive cells are in close physical proximity to one another, their magnetism is aligned with a repelling force due to out-of-phase dissonance of the energy waves, as opposed to an attracting force. Since the inter-cellular energetic connection does not occur, the male and female reproductive cells cannot come together for meiosis.

[My Activebody] Precisely – at least that is how you would manage conception – by artificially creating an energy imbalance in the vibration of the biophotons in the male and female reproductive cells. Whether a female *Adaptivebody* in her reproductive cycle would conceive or not naturally is also dependent on whether her egg is being presented with a sperm with biophotons radiating **resonant** BETA energy. Such are your *Genetics Of Divinity* as you call it.

My *Activebody* pauses as if reading my thoughts about my next question and continues.

[My Activebody] Now about the lightbody ...

{ I am not surprised at all that *he* read my mind all right. My *Adaptivebody* is just not designed to conceal anything - not even my thoughts from my *Activebody,* courtesy of that THETA-GAMMA transformation and the fact that my *Adaptive* energy is part of his *Active* energy. I actually like it that way to have my "big brother" and that too, the smarter one hands down, watching over me every moment of my life experience. ☺ }

[My Activebody] The physical structure of the *Adaptivebody* that is visible reflects incident light in the visible range of the electromagnetic spectrum, which is why objects are visible to the eye. The non-physical structure of the *Adaptivebody* that you refer to as the *lightbody is* composed of biophotons and is invisible to the eye because it is in the infra-red range of the electromagnetic spectrum.

[Me] Ah! The lightbody is the aura of the *Adaptivebody* that can be made visible through Kirlian photography?

[My Activebody] Yes and you can feel that same aura kinesthetically as well, when you bring your palms close to

each other and slowly move them towards and further away from each other. That squishy feeling that you sense between your palms is that electromagnetic energy field from the infra-red radiation being generated by your lightbody and concentrated through the hand chakras. It almost feels like a magnet in the space between your palms that is repelling as you bring your palms closer to each other and attracting as you pull them further apart.

{ I nod knowing very well what that experience is like and I have referred to this test earlier in this book and have demonstrated this technique in a video available in the online Multiversity of the *Genetics Of Divinity*. }

[Me] I have actually performed that kinesthetic aura test with two people at the same time with my left palm facing the right palm of one person and my right palm facing the left palm of the other person with me in the center. All three of us could feel that aura and each other's *Adaptive* energy field through the hand chakras.

[My Activebody] Every physical 3-D *Adaptivebody* regardless of energy band having a contemporary life experience is equipped with the four fundamental energy forms for the purpose of establishing symbiotic collaborative relationships. The specific Creature class determines how the Creature would use them to fulfill their assigned life purpose.

History of Existence – Source to Force

[Me] I believe this is a good platform to move on to my favorite topic – the Source Force. Can you please explain what the Source Force is and how it operates?

[My Activebody] Let's talk about Source Energy – the root of all energy in Existence and the driver of the Cycle of Creation..

{ He is referring to Figure 6 of this book. }

[My Activebody] From the emptiness of space, from the nothingness of vacuum, *Source Energy* developed from a zero dimensional point that contained a massless particle that you have called the *sourceon*. I understand that as a physical Creature of Existence, you are not designed to comprehend particles to be massless. I use the word 'particle' only to help you relate the concept from the physical domain of a uniquely identifiable discrete entity. The *sourceon* as you have named it, is actually a wave. If you have to consider the *sourceon* as a particle, well its size would be the size of its wavelength. In the Zero dimension where the concept of size does not exist, we are talking about a wavelength that is infinitesimally small. Since wavelength of a wave is inversely proportional to the frequency of its vibration, that *sourceon* wave has an infinitesimally high frequency. This is the Source Energy. So the *sourceon* is the particle and also the energy wave – the first introduction of the concept of duality in Creation.

{ A pause, for which I am thankful – allowing me the time to understand the magnanimity of what was just revealed to me by my *Activebody* }

[My Activebody] You represented this Source in the Cycle of Creation as 'Bliss' – ineffable Bliss. You are not and neither am I even in the 5-D by the design of our respective Class definitions are capable of comprehending ineffable Bliss. The *MASTER CREATOR*, or *SOURCEBODY* in what you have referred to as the Eleventh Dimension is the domain of Source Energy. This is the domain of pure Perfection and ineffable Bliss because the *MASTER CREATOR* or Source Energy in the 11-D only has the will to bestow with no expectation to receive anything in return. As a matter of fact, there is no other entity in the 11-D that can give anything to the *MASTER CREATOR* or Source Energy in return. This was also when the dimension of time was created, marking the beginning moment of everything non-physical or physical in Existence.

[Me] Time? I thought in the higher dimensions there was no factor of time.

[My Activebody] [Laughter] Patience! Time has always been there – *gestation period* is nature's attribute of evolution. Just that word evolution implies a before and after state and hence involves time. Time has also evolved as I will explain in a little while. *Source Energy started as a very weak (low power) hence low amplitude energy waveforms oscillating around dimensionless points in the 0-D in randomly varying infinitesimally high frequencies to form the Source Energy band.* These weak energy waves started to collide with each other, sometimes causing out-of-phase dissonance, attenuating and even cancelling each other and sometimes oscillating exactly in-phase causing resonance, or amplification of amplitudes giving the resulting waveforms higher intensity and consequently power. Sometimes Source Energy waves of equal amplitude (hence power) and identical frequency bounced off each other back on themselves creating standing wave patterns. Sometimes these Source energy waves of different amplitudes and frequencies would interfere with each other creating new complex waveforms of newer varying amplitudes and frequencies. The result was an infinite number of possible permutations and combinations of waves with different frequencies and amplitudes that constituted the Source Energy band.

{My mind was racing at this time as I was beginning to develop a rather vague idea of where this explanation was going. My thoughts sprinted from memory system to memory system digging up data from middle school Physics about standing waves, traveling waves, waveguides and harmonics. The concepts of Wave Mechanics that I studied during my days as a student of electrical and electronics engineering were coming back into conscious memory but those related mathematical formulas were still hidden in some crevice of my memory bank. }

Defining Space

[My Activebody] With higher amplitude and hence higher power, resonating waveforms of Source Energy started to push the dimensionless points outward and hence the energy fields around them expanded away from each other, thereby

creating *space*. With more space, the constituent standing wave patterns had greater room to oscillate, resonate even more, leading to higher amplitudes, more power and hence more outward expansion of space. **Space** *hence was defined as that area where the effect of at least one energy field regardless of its amplitude and frequency can exist.* This outward expansion continues even now and will continue until such time that everything in the 3-D flattens out into a 2-D plane. At that time, the 3-D would cease to exist as you know it today and time would no longer have any impact on the 3-D, converting all that mass into pure *Adaptive* energy, which in turn would be reclaimed into the *Potential* energy of Creation. The 3-D would have stabilized by then and the dimension of time would be pushed down over the 2-D. Over time again, that 2-D as well would disintegrate into the 1-D, pushing the dimension of time down and then back to the 0-D. At that time, Existence would reset itself to the dimensionless point only to restart the Cycle of Creation again. What would remain would be the memory of the consciousness of the Cycle of Creation that created this Existence in the only remaining dimension – the dimension of the linear progression of time.

[Me] I have never ever heard such an explanation of how space was created and how it expanded and how Existence evolved. I am fascinated to know the manner in which the Cycle of Creation is operating and how critical the Dimension of Time is to Existence. I am humbled by this knowledge. How was this multi-dimensional structure of Existence created and how did it evolve?

Wave Mechanics for Stabilization of Existence

[My Activebody] It's all about what you call Wave Mechanics. The intersection point of the two waves in a standing wave pattern, which is the *inflexion point* of both the constituent waves is a point of zero displacement (no movement of the wave) and is the *node*. At other points of the two constituent waves the points of maximum displacement is the *antinode*. Relative to each other, the

nodes stay still regardless of the time. *These nodes and antinodes in a standing wave where the crest of incident wave is in exact opposite phase of the trough of the reflected wave and vice versa due to nature of vibration* {see Figure 33 } *are regions of highly stabilized energy and time ceases to be a factor.* Under such perfect conditions time stands still and the illusion of a past, present or future dissolves at these points. In fact the entire concept of a time based experience collapses. *In the higher dimensions of Creation there is no effect of time* as you will realize shortly and that is due to the stability of the energy in these dimensions – nothing changes, there is no loss and no gain – only Existence.

{ I nod in comprehension. In a perfect standing wave pattern, with the incident and reflected wave both being in exactly opposite phase and oscillating in the same frequency there is no net motion at the node and the antinode – everything is indeed perfectly still, stable and perpetual – no loss and no gain. }

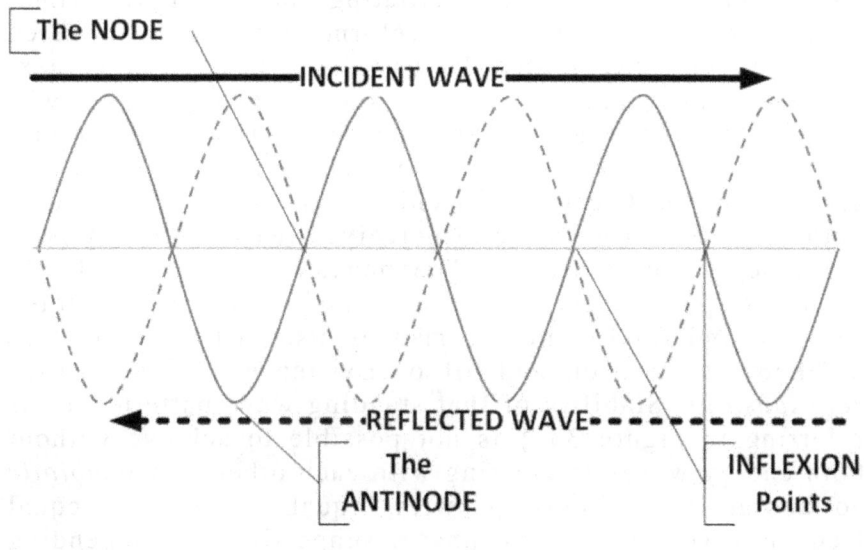

Figure 33

[Me] Ah! so that is how time was literally frozen once the 11-D became a dimension of stabilized energy and time was no longer a factor in the 11-D. However a change must have been required to occur in the energy field in order to create the next bounded dimension.

Birth of Contrast and Duality

[My Activebody] Good analysis, but before we go that, there is something more fundamental that happened in the 11-D - the domain of Source Energy for all of Creation and Existence. The antinodes which are the same waveform traveling in opposite directions in opposite phases created the attribute of *Contrast* in the design of Creation. Contrast requires two identically opposite energy waves in parallel to each other. This contrast is also what defines the *Duality* of Creation. The node of the standing wave pattern, where time has ceased to be a factor is the bridge between these contrasting energy waveforms. Creatures are allowed to define and choose by individual perception, which wave is positive and which is negative to its life experience. Furthermore, due to the oscillating nature of the time-dependent section of the waveform, what is considered negative will eventually have to go through the next inflexion point into the positive and what is positive, will have to eventually go through the next inflexion point into the negative in the Creature's perceived reality. So at any given time, the Creature can enjoy a life experience that is both positive and negative in perceived reality. Duality is in the blueprint of Creation. The negative illustrates clearly what the positive is and vice versa – this is Contrast. Contrast and Duality in this manner also institutes the core attribute of Creation and all of Existence – *collaborative relationships*. Stability of that standing wave pattern { he is referring to Figure 33 } is not possible to achieve without both energy waves interacting with each other in a *symbiotic* collaborative relationship with equal amplitude, equal frequency yet in opposite phase, supporting and depending on each other in *collective coexistence,* at the same time to ensure the stability of the standing wave relationship. The 11-D was established from the 0-D dimensionless points from where it all began. Collectively in this manner, the 11-D and the 0-D set up the bounding dimensions of Existence.

[Me] What about free will? How did that come into play?

[My Activebody] For the *Adpativebody*, free will helps you make decisions among the choices available in Parallelism. Each choice offered is a particular energy wave with its distinct properties of amplitude and frequency. Through your brainwaves, you ignore or resonate with those choices of frequencies offered by Parallelism. The choice you ultimately decide on is the outcome of your free will to resonate with that particular choice. This is how free will operates in the Third Dimension. At the birth of every Cycle of Creation in the 11-D, the waves of Source Energy exhibits identical behavior. Source Energy waves would either interact with each other or would not. If they did interact, that interaction could have led to *resonance*, leading to amplification of the resultant wave. The interaction could have led to *dissonance*, leading to attenuation of the resultant wave. Alternatively, the interaction could have led to *interference* resulting in a hybrid, complex waveform with different frequencies and amplitudes than the constituent waves. There was randomness in the manner in which Source Energy waves interacted and proliferated to create the Source Energy bandwidth. Randomness is critical before stability can be achieved and in this randomness was conceived the seed of free will. Source Energy waves in the very beginning of the Cycle of Creation, had complete free will to randomly set up those interactions of resonance, dissonance, interference or ignorance. Over time, as I have explained the randomness reduced in the 11-D as stability increased. When the 11-D stabilized, the randomness of Source Energy interactions were eliminated from this dimension. This randomness of Source Energy interactions was inherited by the newly created 10-D, which started that same process of leveraging *free will* to establish the new energy band of the 10-D. This is how the randomness of free will created newer dimensions while the prior dimensions stabilized and became independent of time. The 3-D as we know today is currently going through this period of instability due to the randomness of the choices *Adaptivebodies* are making in their life experience through free will. One day, when humans on Earth upgrade their consciousness, which is inevitable by design of Creation, the randomness of free will that we observe in humanity today, will subside as humans being the dominant species in the planet will lead the stabilization process under the guidelines of the *Genetics Of Divinity*.

{ I am speechless at such a sublime explanation of how Contrast, Duality and Free Will was created and how they contributed towards the core concept of Creation - symbiotic collaborative relationships. My *Activebody* pauses, as if allowing me the opportunity to collect my thoughts, rationalize and internalize what was just conveyed and reactivate my Type 1 memory systems. As if by automatic reflex action, I find myself kneeling on the ground, eyes closed, arms spread out wide open with this burning desire and humility to receive more of this wisdom and knowledge. I feel relaxed - almost floating freely in an ocean of tranquility as this knowledge continues to elevate my consciousness. }

[My Activebody] The 11-D thus is the domain of ineffable Bliss { refer to Figure 6 }– everything that there is or can be is in the 11-D, everything is stable, everything is known, everything operates under the principle of contrast, duality, free will and symbiotic collaborative relationships. From that domain of ineffable Bliss which is the band of Source Energy there was a need to create the other components in the Cycle of Creation { refer to Figure 6 again } and the other bounded dimensions of Existence. It was necessary for the random expansion and diversification of Existence from the 11-D to occur - that temporary randomness and instability be initiated to bring about change in the beginning followed by a process of stabilization once the change had been realized. Whenever change from the current state is required in Existence, the factor of time automatically needs to be included, since change itself is a function of time.

[Me] ... so that there is a state *before* the change and a state *after* the change – both being elements of time. Hence in this case as well, the time dimension was invoked to facilitate the change through randomness of Source Energy interactions?

Technology To Create The Dimensions

[My Activebody] Correct! In order to create a new dimension of Existence, there was a need to generate a new derivative from the Source Energy – an energy band with a different range of frequencies and amplitudes (hence power) under which that dimension could exist.

[Me] You refer to the need for an energy *band* with waveforms having several frequencies and amplitudes per dimension of Existence. Each dimension would subsequently be responsible to randomly combine and permute their allocated band of frequencies to create their own unique waveforms using a subset of frequencies and amplitudes within that band to define the form and function of their distinctively own Creature classes.

[My Activebody] Right! There was a need for power – an immense amount of power to create each dimension. Where could that immense power come from?

[Me] Probably by amplitude amplification of resonant traveling waves?

{ Laughter... he seemed to be enjoying this conversation as was I }

[My Activebody] Source Energy had low amplitudes and hence low power. The need was for *higher amplitude waveforms hence for a higher power energy band* derived from the Source Energy that would create the next bounded dimension – in this case the Tenth Dimension, then the next and then the next. Higher power was needed to bring about the change and lower frequency was necessary to allow sufficient gestation period for the change to occur. The reason to create an energy band was to form the Tenth Dimension which, as you have indicated in this book { as in Figure 17 }, is the domain of all CREATORS of all Creatures of all energy bands. Each such CREATOR in the Tenth Dimension, in order to be distinct would require a separate energy band with its own unique characteristics of amplitudes (hence power) and frequencies.

{ I nod in agreement as that explanation made perfect sense.}

[My Activebody] Go back to those oppositely phased standing waves that brought the stability in the 11-D. There were other waves of Source Energy that were being generated from those ever growing population of dimensionless points as Source Energy continued to expand space. These energy

waves that I am referring to now were *traveling waves* (not standing wave patterns) with same amplitude and frequency and interacted with each other not in opposite phase, but either completely in phase or with a *phase difference with respect to each other*. The resulting waveform was one with a greater amplitude and hence greater power, due to the fully-resonant or near-resonant amplification.

{ He is referring to Figure 34 that illustrates how near resonant traveling waves with same amplitude and frequency however with a phase difference between them can also create a resultant wave with higher amplitude which gives it greater power than the constituent waves. Figure 12 contains an example of fully resonant waves}

[Me] I can visualize where you are going with this now and as another observation, that resultant derivative wave also has a phase shift from the trailing traveling wave in the union. Depending on the phase difference between the participating traveling Source Energy waves involved in a near resonant interaction, there will be different points between the peaks and the inflexion points where the two waves would interact. Each of these intersection points would create different resultant waves derived from the Source Energy waves, each with different amplitudes and hence different power. Each of these unique waveforms would represent a unique energy wave and hence a CREATOR. Goodness me – this is simply fantastic !

[My Activebody] You've got your knowledge of Wave Mechanics down pat. { Yeah right – it's all rusty after over 25 years } These traveling waves that have a phase difference hence with a dependence on time, had no significance anymore in the 11-D since the 11-D had already become a dimension of stabilized energy that was rendered immune to the element of time. These Source Energy waves of equal amplitude and frequency interacted with each other in resonant and near resonant relationships. Other Source Energy waves of disparate frequencies and amplitudes also interacted with each other creating other complex waveforms of varying amplitudes and frequencies within the same

energy band thereby creating the new 10th dimension of Existence.

[Me] The properties of wave mechanics, how energy waves interact with each other, engaging in constructive, destructive, collaborative and stabilizing relationships were all instituted in the higher dimensions to build the foundation for the remainder of Existence.

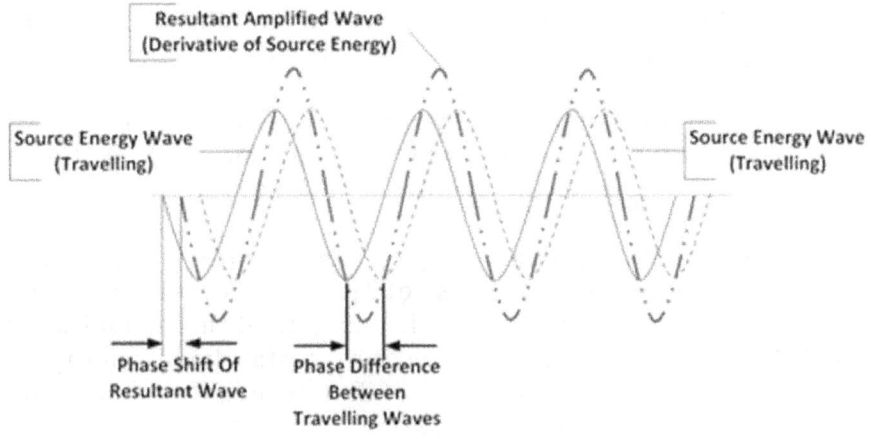

Figure 34

[*My Activebody*] Precisely and by the grand design of Creation, only Type A *Adaptivebodies* in the physical 3-D are able to understand this technology of Creation. The newly created dimension needed to be stabilized in order for its purpose could be realized. This stability was attained over time again by the higher amplitude and hence higher energy standing wave patterns in the new dimension following the same pattern as in the 11-D. Lower energy waves that were generated in the newly created dimensions eventually also settled down into standing waves over time. Eventually, the new dimension had achieved its purpose and was no longer considered new – it had stabilized and relinquished the need to change and the de-linked itself from the dependence on time. Other Source energy waves that did not stabilize, were pushed out of this newly stabilized dimension to create the next dimension.

[Me] This is how Existence became a repetitive cycle through which dimensions were created through amplification of traveling waves that were pushed out from the higher dimension to the new dimension. Waveforms of same or different amplitudes and frequencies, stabilized through standing waves and the particular dimension of Existence declared itself to be independent of the element of time. Once this stability was achieved, the dimension pushed out the unstabilized energy waveforms to create the next dimension where time and the randomness of free will became allies once again to bring about the change that was necessary. Fantastic!

{ A moment of silence – seemingly pregnant moments of silence as if my *Activebody* was allowing me time to digest this knowledge and let the cognition sink in. }

[Me] This is how the energy bands were created – each band with a range of frequencies of energy became its own dimension of stabilized energy. I understand this model until the 8-D which is the last dimension of stabilized energy in the hierarchy of the dimensions of Existence. How about the dimensions of Coherent Energy?

[My Activebody] Just to clarify a dimension cannot be created unless the one above has reached stability and became independent of time - this is a core principle of Creation. The parent dimension must reach a point where nothing is changing, only sustaining, in order to be stable and when this stability is achieved then only can the independence from time be declared by that dimension. So even in the domain of Coherent energy the 7-D had to stabilize, become time independent before the 6-D can come into Existence and the cycle of stabilization and creation continues down the multi-dimensional stack of Existence.

{ I nod in agreement }

[My Activebody] The next set of dimensions – from the Seventh to the Fifth that you have described as the domain of *Coherent* energy was all about categorization and

collaboration. Until the 8-D there were too many possibilities of combination of energy waves each with their own wave characteristics. From the prior discussion it must be already clear that each dimension had higher amplitude and lower frequency energy waves in comparison to the preceding dimension.

[Me] Progressively lower frequency waves as we go down the multi-dimensional stack – let me figure this one out. When two waves of different frequencies and amplitudes interfere, the resultant wave would have the net sum of the amplitudes and either the lowest common frequency or the average frequency. While the higher frequency waves would be trapped in the particular dimension where they interacted with the band of stabilized energy, the low frequency waves would escape to initiate the next dimension. As an example from modern technology, high frequency waves in a microwave oven cannot escape to the outside but the lower frequency sound energy of the popping corn inside the microwave is audible or the light inside the microwave oven is visible from the outside. Brilliant !!! Oh my *Genetics Of Divinity* – this is simply brilliant.

{ I can almost see the grin on the face of my *Activebody*, or is it my imagination? Looks like we are both having fun in this interactive dialog }

[*My Activebody*] Critical energy was reached in the 8-D with too many possible combinations and derivatives of energy waves and any further would have caused chaos disrupting Existence. In addition to the first protocol of stabilization as in the dimensions of stabilized energy, there was a need to bring order in the initially chaotic 7-D. This was achieved by adding a second protocol of stabilization through grouping of energy frequencies into five sub-bands of energy in the 7-D that you have illustrated { he is referring to Figure 17 } as the Five Types of Active Energy. This was the birth of a grid-like energy crossover structure in the 7-D which was eventually replicated down to the 3-D. The purpose of this second level of grouping of energy was to bring further stability to the 7-D (and below). How do you think this grouping of frequencies occurred?

{ Wow, a direct question from my *Activebody* for the first time in the conversation! Then a pause – he was actually waiting for me to figure it out. I found myself scratching my head and then I had it - the only answer that could be possible. Was it me or was it my *Activebody* giving me the hint? I could not tell. }

[Me] Harmonic frequencies!

{ That inter-dimensional laughter of approval again - I knew I had it and I had it right! }

[Me] In order to bring stability and perpetual repeatability in these Five energy bands in the 7-D all the way down to the 3-D, obviously standing wave patterns between participating waveforms are necessary just like in the higher dimensions. Standing wave patterns can occur only at certain frequencies of vibration of the constituent waves – these are the harmonic frequencies. Any other frequency of vibration would be irregular and non-repeatable and hence unstable. So the grouping of frequencies occurred based on the five groups of harmonic frequencies with Type A getting the largest share of these harmonic frequencies, decreasing down to the Type E group of harmonic frequencies. Each harmonic represents a unique attribute or function of the Creature. This is fascinating!

[My Activebody] Thus the grid of coherent energy was developed in the 7-D with stability being provided by harmonic energy waves collaborating to form standing wave patterns in each energy band illustrated vertically { referring to Figure 17 }. Collectively they stabilized the entire 7-D horizontally { again referring to Figure 17 }. The process of achieving dimensional stabilization, with waveforms interfering with each other within the harmonized energy bands, creating newer waveforms of varying amplitudes and *progressively lower frequencies*, becoming independent of the time factor, continued down to the 5-D.

[Me] The only reason that it was possible to develop distinct Creature classes following the object oriented design principles was the stabilization of the constituent harmonic frequencies in each of five energy bands. This is why in the 3-D, the anatomy of a human, a whale, an eagle, an oak tree, astronomical bodies, molecules of oxygen, the crystalline structure of carbon, for example are always consistent and repeatable, no matter how many of these come into a physical existence. In fact it is this stabilized harmonization of frequencies that makes up the DNA of Type C through Type A Creatures in the 3-D – consistent repetitive stabilized forms of energy. I now understand how energy and time evolved. Oh My *Genetics Of Divinity*!

Collaborative Relationships and Free Will

[My Activebody] Hold off on that discussion of the 3-D for a little while longer. You referred to the concept of matter, which is the building block of the 3-D the only dimension of *Physical* energy. We are not ready for that yet. We are still in the domain of coherent energy, there is no matter involved, hence none of the physical laws apply in this domain. Based on the core principle of Creation – to build symbiotic collaborative relationships, the harmonized five energy bands needed a mechanism to interconnect with each other so that they can collaborate in the grid of Existence. Higher the energy band the constituent waveforms have greater amplitude and lower frequency when compared to the lower energy bands. The Creature class is more complex in the higher energy bands. In order to establish collaborative relationships between a pair of disparate *intra*-dimensional energy bands each with harmonized frequencies, the waves involved in the alignment, attraction and subsequent collaboration were required to interact differently. A symbiotic collaboration implies a wave interaction that encompasses both harmonized waves in a manner that retains the integrity of both individual waves.

[Me] An example of such a complex waveform would be a square wave { refer to Figure 35 } that is generated as a result of two different harmonic waves interacting with each other in a coherent collaborative relationship. Greater the number of odd harmonics of the higher-frequency lower-amplitude wave within the half wavelength of the lower-frequency higher-amplitude wave, flatter the square wave becomes. This continues until such time when enough of these odd harmonics have been added - the result is a square wave. Hence the resultant square wave can be considered to be the equivalent of a higher amplitude sine wave (higher energy band) of the same fundamental frequency and the sum of a large number of *odd harmonic* sine waves with lower amplitudes (lower energy band)

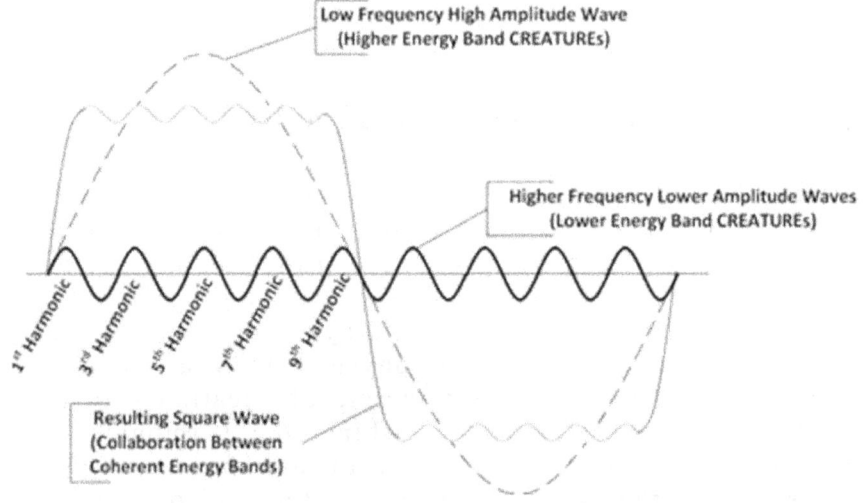

Figure 35

[My Activebody] The mechanics of different waveforms representing different amplitudes and frequencies resonating, interfering or staying unaffected by one another defines the process of building collaborative relationships and thereby implements the attribute of Free Will in Existence. It is only through the randomness of this Free Will can there be choice in Parallelism and this choice is what defines a particular state of Existence.

Sinusoidal Waveforms - Signature of Existence

[Me] What you are telling me is in order to form a collaborative relationship between two energy waveforms *within the same energy band*, they may each have different amplitudes and hence different power and intensity, but their frequencies **must be the same** and **they must vibrate in-phase** in order to establish another resulting high amplitude and more powerful and intense resonant sine wave having the same frequency as the participating waves {refer to Figure 12}. This implements the concept of *Desirability* between the partnering sine waves due to their same frequency and *in-phase* vibration. When this resulting sine wave with a magnified amplitude bounces back and forth between the generators of these resonant waves, they create stable standing wave patterns – hence establishing a symbiotic collaborative relationship. If the constituent frequencies of the two interacting sine waves are different and/or if they are vibrating out-of-phase, then regardless of their respective amplitudes, the resulting sine wave cannot be in a resonant interaction due to the attenuated amplitude and an intermediate frequency that does not relate to either one of the participating waveforms. This incoherent interaction thereby thwarts a collaborative relationship {refer to Figure 36}. I can totally relate this to relationships between Adaptivebodies. When frequencies don't match, the DI is mutually very low on both partners and the Law of Alignment cannot get activated, thwarting any sort of subsequent attraction.

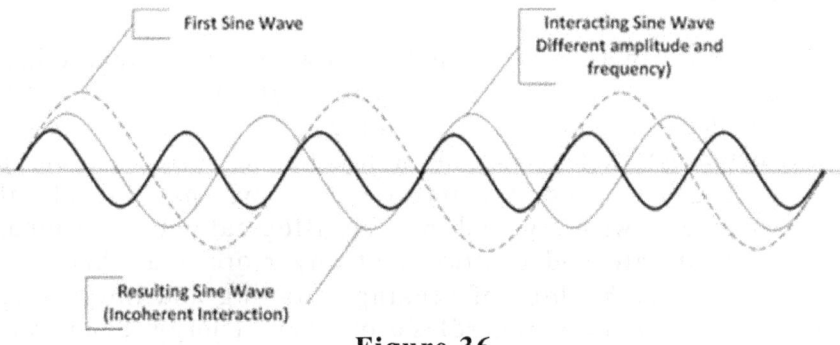

Figure 36

{ I pause to recollect my thoughts and reflect on my own life experience and the relationships I've had with other partners in my 12 secondary relationship categories with whom I crossed paths. My *Activebody* waits patiently for me to rationalize the information I just received. What had seemed fate and destiny and out of my control to me once upon a not too distant time, I realize now was all energy and wave mechanics. My *Adaptivebody* was already designed to choose my relationships all the time but I was oblivious of this attribute. This cognition is rather liberating that I am able to share this with you as the reader of this book. This knowledge ensures you and I have full control over our respective future life experiences. It was clear that I had to watch those THETA brainwaves that I generate in the future and invest my energy to discover the Type 1 and Type 5 memories embedded in my DNA. ☺ }

[Me] However in order to build collaborative relationships *across energy bands* { refer to Figure 35 }, where there is significant disparity in the available frequencies, it is important for the higher amplitude waveform, generated from the higher energy band, to have a fundamental frequency that can fit multiple odd harmonics of the lower amplitude waveform that is generated from the lower energy band. Larger the number of these odd harmonics of the lower amplitude wave that can fit within the fundamental frequency of the higher amplitude wave, more stable becomes the resultant square wave. These square waves bounce off each other creating standing wave patterns, which imparts stability to the inter-energy band symbiotic collaborative relationship.

{ I pause again to reflect on this new cognition that I just had as a result of this conversation with my very patient *Activebody*. All the material things (objects from lower energy bands) that I wanted in my life experience were a mixed bag of accomplishments and my past level of consciousness was stymied by the illogical and irrational doctrines of fate and destiny. Not any more – at this very moment, the *technology* of seeking, aligning and interacting with *Adaptivebodies* regardless of their energy band was revealed in no uncertain terms. I was humbled and awakened. }

[My Activebody] The sine waveform throughout all of Existence wherever it operates is the signature of Source decomposed into multiple constituent sine waves.

{ I nodded - no doubts about that anymore }

[My Activebody] The sine waveform also defines the pattern of Existence – an alternating yet definitive rhythm of *inevitable* crests and troughs representing perpetual repetitive relative motion. In the language of mathematics a sine wave is represented with alternate swings on either side of an axis to depict the rhythmic nature of the vibration. *The inflexion points on a graph of a sine wave represents a change in the borderline emotion in the EGS for Adaptivebodies* that has been described in your book. Every brainwave that the human *Adaptivebody* generates is a sine wave or can be decomposed into a sine wave. Every energy wave that *Activebodies* in the 5-D and energy patterns in the higher dimensions generate and process are all sine waves or can be decomposed into a sine wave. The sine wave, a 2-D representation of Source Energy is the core essence of Creation in the 3-D and every dimension from the 5-D and up.

{ My infra-conscious mind is constantly doing double duty – not only having this conversation with my *Activebody*, but also prodding my conscious mind to pull up dormant memories that I can leverage right now to relate my personal life experience to what was being revealed to me. My *Activebody* continues on ... }

[My Activebody] You are the impatient one, aren't you? That is understandable since you are having a physical life experience. You see, the cognition that is about to dawn on you in a few moments is already in the active consciousness of all *Activebodies* in the 5-D, which is also the reason why this is a dimension of coherent stabilized energy. This knowledge is powerful and you will feel that liberating power and profound significance of the sine wave in the physical life experience. { ...a pause ... } Looks like you have figured it out without my explanation. Ok, let's hear it.

{ I am not surprised that my *Activebody* had become aware of the frenzy of activity in my conscious mind, as I pulled up memory systems related to wave mechanics and the content that was being delivered to me by my *Activebody* while I was relating and collating information. I am however, pleasantly surprised at the speed at which this cognition engulfed my *Adaptivebody*. Truth be told – the consciousness was always there as Type 1 memory within my *Adaptivebody* by the design of Creation. Only now was I consciously accessing that information that was already embedded in my *Adaptivebody*. My eyes are closed, I am oblivious of the physical world around me as I am entwined with my *Activebody*. I speak through my brainwaves, without verbal words being spoken.

Wave Mechanics Of The EGS

[Me] The Emotional Guidance System as described originally by Esther and Jerry Hicks as referenced earlier in this book, actually defines the technology built into the 3-D *Adaptivebody* to ensure that it remains in alignment with the assigned life purpose for a life experience filled with unbounded delight. The sine wave being Source Energy is the vehicle for the life experience of the *Adaptivebody*. The upward swing of the sine wave indicates whatever we individually consider as a positive experience of our perceived reality. What one considers positive may be considered a negative experience by another – hence the individuality of perceived reality. The sine wave is agnostic of the individual perception of a particular *Adaptivebody*. The crest of the sine wave, representing the amplitude is the point of unbounded delight in the individual life experience, while the trough is the point of unbounded plight from an EGS standpoint. However the cycle of crests and troughs of an untainted sine wave is continuous and repetitive. The attribute of Contrast is an inevitable condition of Existence. Both crests and troughs are necessary for all *Adaptivebodies* to understand Contrast and to leverage the EGS to modify the characteristics of the sine wave through the attribute of free will and choose a certain life experience. A *default* life experience would be one with equal amplitudes of the crests and troughs of the default sine wave { refer to Figure 37 } representing the default equal share of experiences that are perceived by the individual *Adaptivebody* as positive or negative.

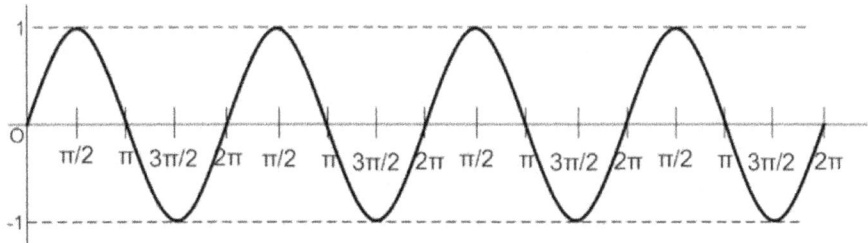

Figure 37

{ I pause to collect my thoughts and organize the information that had begun to drench me with the empowerment of Eternal Consciousness. My *Activebody* waits patiently, allowing me the freedom to use my rationality. }

[Me] The perceived life experience of the Type A *Adaptivebody*, based on its current belief systems or memory patterns can be one of unbounded delight or unbounded plight, simply by first consciously and then autonomically (just like in all the higher dimensions), manipulating the waveform of the sine wave through the power of emotions in the EGS. This can be illustrated through applied wave mechanics on the sine wave considering the upswing of the waveform to represent a life experience filled with emotions that are higher on the EGS scale and the downswing of the sine waveform to represent a life experience filled with emotions that are lower on the EGS scale. *Energy flows where Bliss, Inspiration, Thought, Intention, Attention and Action goes*. Empowered by free will, the *Adaptivebody* is equipped with the ability to direct this *Adaptive* energy to manipulate the sine waveform to individually choose a personal life experience that is filled with unbounded delight or unbounded plight.

{ I pause again to collect my thoughts, visibly excited at the realization that I am coming to. }

[Me] When presented with a particular life experience { referring to the default sine waveform as in Figure 37 } that is perceived as negative or unfavorable through the emotions evoked in the EGS scale, an individual can choose to divert more *Adaptive* energy towards the downward slope of the wave. The result is a manipulated sine waveform that increases in amplitude due to the added resonant *Adaptive* energy. Greater the focus on emotions that are lower in the EGS Scale, larger that *Adaptive* energy and greater the amplitude, leading to further emotions that are even lower on the EGS scale. If the individual does not take prompt action to correct such emotions, the time period for which such focus persists, increases. The result { as shown in Figure 38 } is a modified sine waveform with a much higher amplitude (hence more powerful and intense) downswing with an increased wavelength and hence reduced frequency, which

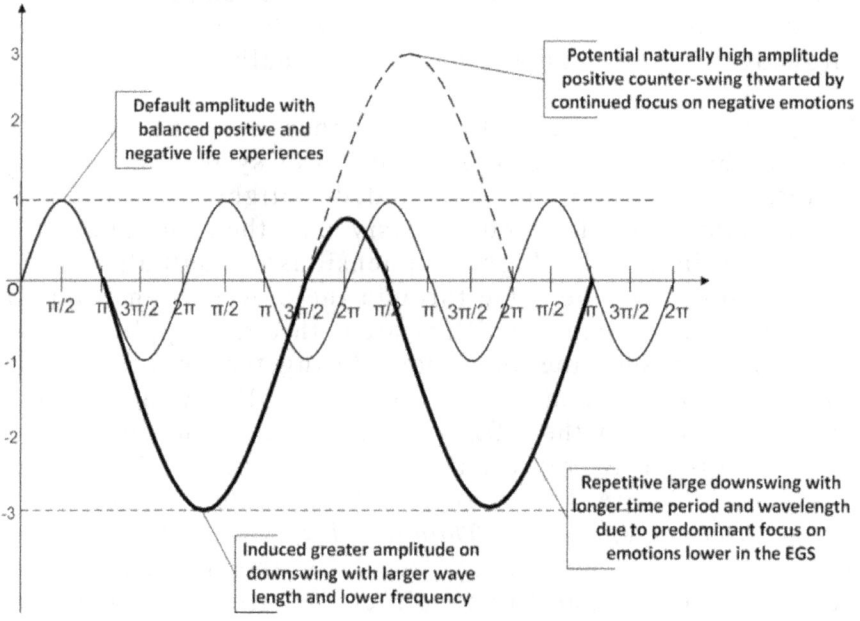

Figure 38

implies that the individual would have a prolonged stay, due to the greater time period of the wave in the negative zone when compared to the duration of the default sine waveform. The Law of Alignment is applicable here in the progressively longer downswing, since the individual aligned its *Adaptivebody* towards emotions lower in the EGS and hence got attracted through the Law of Attraction by emotions that dragged the *Adaptivebody* even lower – in the non-physical plane here, *like attracted like*. This clearly explains the magnified downswing of the sine waveform with greater amplitude of catabolic energy and wavelength towards the negative phase of the waveform.

{ I am smiling now, having figured out the answer to my pressing question for all those years - "*Why me?*" The answer – because it *was* me and nobody else who is to be held accountable for not understanding the mechanics of Existence - which explains my extended periods of plight in my life experience. This is such an empowering and liberating body of Eternal Consciousness that just got reactivated into my conscious mind. }

[Me] At the peak of the negative swing, the design of Creation and the operability of the sine waveform would automatically initiate the recovery of the wave towards the upswing and all the individual needs to do is allow the *Adaptivebody* to ride the escalation of emotions in the EGS and hit the opposite positive peak with a much higher amplitude or greater delight and larger wavelength, which implies a longer time could potentially be spent in a positive experience immediately following the long time spent in a negative domain. However just when the waveform crossed over the inflexion point, the individual's memory patterns that have predominantly negative emotions attached, could thwart the natural large amplitude upswing past the inflexion point and after a brief moment in the relief of emotions higher in the EGS scale, take the *Adaptivebody* again into a prolonged experience in the negative domain. Such a repetitively prolonged life experience within emotions lower in the EGS scale erodes the *Potential* energy of the *Adaptivebody*, thereby deflecting the *Adaptivebody* from fulfilling its assigned life purpose and a life experience of unbounded delight.

[My Activebody] Perfect! The converse is also true – again by the same unbiased and fair design of Creation. A life experience that is deemed as a positive one by an individual can be amplified significantly in amplitude towards the upswing of the sine waveform { refer to Figure 39 } simply by the escalation of emotions that grow progressively higher on the EGS. This high amplitude and hence high anabolic energy waveform with a life experience in unbounded delight would eventually reach its peak and initiate its natural journey downward towards the axis. Left to its own devices, the waveform would continue downward beyond the inflexion point to reach the same amplitude on the negative phase, which would imply a life experience in unbounded plight for the *Adaptivebody* for the same long duration. This would definitely be an option offered to the *Adaptivebody* by Parallelism to have a life experience that swings between unbounded delight and unbounded plight. However the other option for the *Adaptivebody* would be to arrest the downswing too far below the inflexion point and with continued focus on emotions that are higher on the EGS, quickly initiate the upswing back towards and beyond the second inflexion point towards a prolonged life experience in unbounded delight.

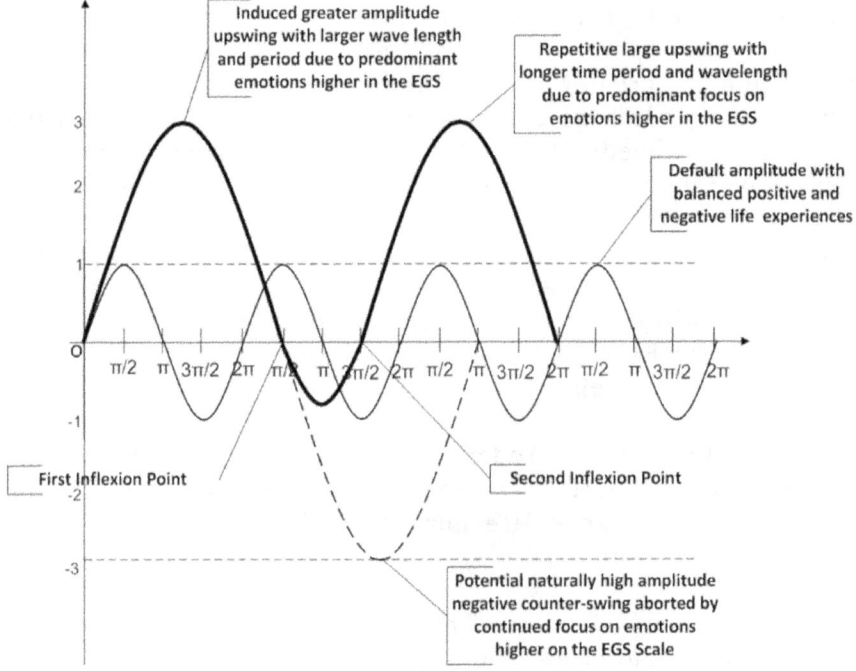

Figure 39

[Me] The *speed* of a sinusoidal wave can be calculated as the product of its frequency and its wavelength. Longer time periods of the induced waveforms either predominantly in positive or negative phase, implies longer wavelengths and hence shorter frequencies. This reduces the speed of the induced wave, which is perceived as if it is taking a long time for the individual to emerge from the negative or the positive phase in the life experience. While the desire of the *Adaptivebody* becomes to somehow accelerate the passage of time while in a negative phase an equal desire becomes to somehow decelerate the passage of time while in a positive phase. Such acceleration and deceleration of the element of time is not possible for the physical *Adaptivebody*, due to the consistent linear progression of time however the Adaptivebody, through free will has absolute freedom to prolong periods in the life experience with emotions of delight or plight..

{ There it was, the answer that had eluded me for so many years was now revealed. Source Energy, through the sinusoidal waveform, naturally offers choices in Parallelism for the *Adaptivebody* to choose its own life experience by virtue of its own free will without the need or influence of any external entity. }

[My *Activebody*] The high amplitude waveform whether predominantly in positive or negative phase, becomes normalized and settles down eventually from disparate amplitudes to a more natural sine waveform with equal swings on either side of the axis { refer to Figure 37 }. The *Adaptivebody* empowered by higher amplitude and hence more powerful waveforms, thereby stakes its claim to a life experience in a new Parallel Universe. The design of Creation and the mechanics of operation of the Source Energy is consistent throughout Existence. While the dimensions of stabilized and coherent energy have mastered this technology and have become independent of the time factor, the 3-D is yet to achieve this stability, hence life experiences of physical Adaptivebodies are so different from one another.

{ I was beginning to understand where this conversation was headed, but it was still not clear enough. }

[My Activebody] Once the individual has arrived at this Parallel Universe where the wave swings are equal on both sides of the axis, the Creature designed with the will to receive soon realizes that it has started to live a default life experience again in the new Parallel Universe where there is a new equal share of positive and negative emotions albeit stronger than before. This prompts the Creature to define new desires that would lead to more delight (or more plight). As a result of the increased focus again with appropriate emotions on the EGS scale, the upswing or downswing of the sinusoidal wave would increase repeating the process that enables the individual to emigrate into a newer Parallel Universe with increased delight or plight.

{ We both pause as I digest this information that holds the key to resolve all challenges in our lives. I am humbled by its simplicity and yet excited by the magnanimity of the significance of what was just revealed to me. My life purpose seemed to be strongly aligned with me and I was getting strongly attracted towards it. }

Traveling Faster Than Light Speed

[Me] I have had a question ever since my childhood days after I fell in love with Physics. Is there anything in Existence that can travel faster than light? I have always had a feeling that the speed of light is not really the universal limit there's got to be something that can travel faster.

[My Activebody] Yes, there is and all CREATORs which includes Type A *Adaptivebodies* are capable of generating energy that travels faster than the physical speed of light.

[Me] I knew it, I just knew it. The theoretical limit of the speed of light is applicable only to particles that have rest mass and traveling through vacuum. I have always known that there are particles that do not have rest mass and hence should be capable of traveling faster than the physical limit imposed by speed of light regardless of the medium.

[My Activebody] Let's understand the characteristics of light energy. Light energy occupies only a small portion of the electromagnetic spectrum. Light energy (also sinusoidal waveforms) can travel large distances and its carrier particle – photons that have no rest mass but only momentum can travel at theoretically very high speeds. However the concept of a line of sight is an integral part of light energy. You cannot observe a physical object behind a brick wall for example because that the intense electromagnetic energy of that wall causes so much dissonance to the incident light wave that it reflects back all the light energy, preventing it from traveling through to the target object of observation. This is called *opacity* of the wall. However if the wall was made of glass (transparent) or plastic (translucent) material, then due to the weaker electromagnetic energy within the material of such a wall, some of the incident light could pass through and be reflected back to make the target object visible. The speed of light hence is a factor of the medium through which it travels.

{ So far this was all known information to me, but I knew that something big was coming and I had to stay patient. Oh, this insatiable hunger that I have for knowledge ! }

[My Activebody] Like all forms of electromagnetic energy, light energy is unidirectional. Once photons are emitted from the source or reflected from an object capable of reflecting light energy, these can never get back to the origin or the reflection point. This makes light energy dependent on the element of time. As a result of this dependence on the time factor light energy has no significance in the higher dimensions of Existence - from the 5-D and up, which as you know by now, are independent of the factor of time. Light energy does not exist in the higher dimensions of Existence and is not needed that I have explained before. In these higher dimensions where there is permanent stability of symbiotic collaborative relationships, information does not need to flow anywhere – information related to Creation and Existence is always available. Hence there is *no time factor*

involved in the non-physical higher dimensions between the request and the delivery of information.

{ My *Activebody* pauses as if to allow me the opportunity to ponder over the last statement – *"no time factor involved in the non-physical higher dimensions between the request and delivery of information"*. }

[Me] You mentioned *five* critical elements that are mandatory for any communication. First and most important is the data, the information, the knowledge. Second is the process of requesting that data. Third is the process of responding to that request. Fourth, is the medium of communication, which is non-physical in the higher dimensions. Finally, the fifth element is the time elapsed between the request and the response. In the physical 3-D the medium of communication and the elapsed time are important factors to consider. How do you communicate in the higher dimensions without a medium and time?

[My Activebody] There *is* a medium of communication in the higher dimensions that is quite different from the medium in the 3-D. The Cycle of Creation has physical and non-physical components { refer to the modified version of the Cycle of Creation in Figure 40 }. While the physical components in the Cycle of Creation require a medium composed of particles and conglomerate objects (a multitude of particles connected together by electromagnetic force) having rest mass to communicate, the non-physical components can operate in a *medium composed of particles without rest mass*. When there is no rest mass, the particles are not subject to any energy loss from the time it is projected from a source and the time it is received at the target. Since there is no loss and no factor of time, there is no delay between transmission and reception of information. All non-physical components in this Cycle are by design, transceivers { devices that have both transmitting and receiving capabilities } of *Source Energy*. Whereas all physical components in the Cycle are also designed as transceivers but they operate in the energy band of *Adaptive Energy*, which is a derivative from Source Energy. *All communications in the non-physical domain, regardless of the dimension occur instantly, traveling infinite*

distances without interference from any external source. Such is the speed, for lack of a better word, at which energy propagates in the non-physical domain.

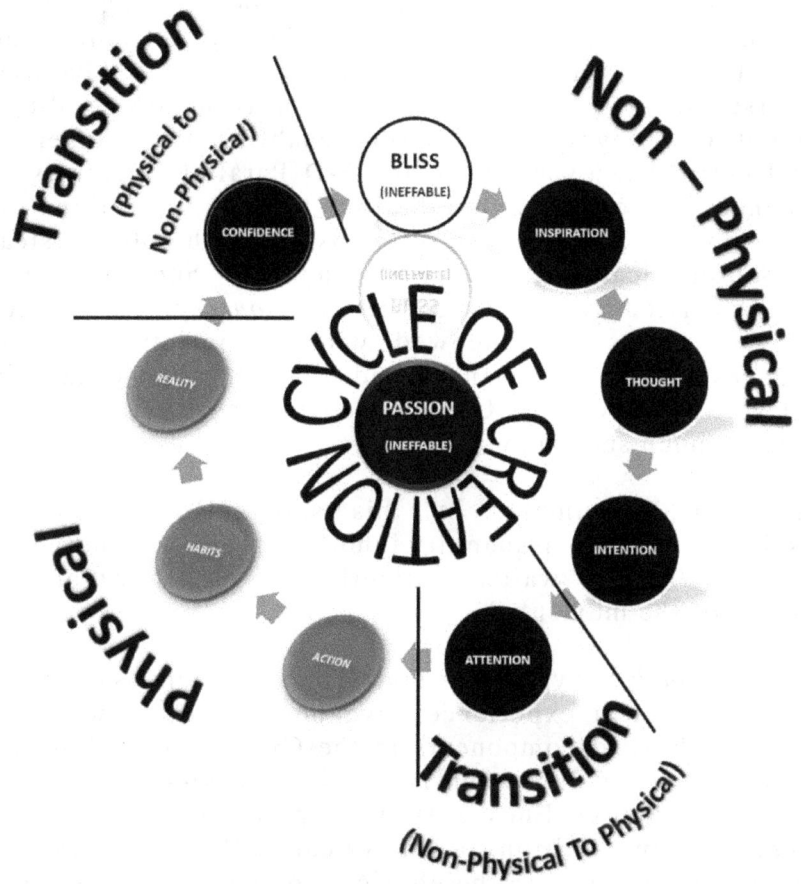

Figure 40

{ As I was listening intently to my *Activebody*, I glanced at the Cycle of Creation again and my gaze fixated on the component – *Thought*. After a few moments of reflection there was no more doubt left in my mind that the answer to a key question that I had been searching for was just answered. I held my gaze on that component – Thought with unseeing eyes as I muttered to myself... }

[Me] Thought – it travels instantly, infinite distances, uninhibited, immune to any physical barrier, without any dependence on the line of sight – faster, incredibly many magnitudes faster than the speed of light. Nothing can stop the propagation of thought. Unlike the unidirectional mode of propagation of light energy, Source Energy of Thought can travel to the past, to the future and even to Parallel Universes instantly without attenuation from any medium. Thought is holographic in nature enabling the thinker to model entire life experiences and 3-D Parallel Universes of Existence instantly and uninhibited through the alignment with symbiotic collaborative relationships with both physical and non-physical partners. If Thought is Source Energy which is carried by the carrier particle *'sourceon'*, it implies that we humans are endowed with an infinite pool of *sourceons* that we can manage and direct them to engage in the Cycle Of Creation. Oh my *Genetics Of Divinity*! This makes so much sense now.

{ I am truly humbled by this self-realization as my consciousness made a quantum jump to an entirely new high as my *Activebody* waited patiently for me to savor the euphoria of the moment. }

[My Activebody] Type A Adaptivebodies such as humans having a physical experience have been endowed with the same non-physical components in the Cycle of Creation just like in the higher dimensions. As a human, you have access to the same Source Energy as we experience in the higher dimensions. In addition, all physical 3-D *Adaptivebodies* have been endowed with the physical components of Creation powered by Adaptive energy. Due to its dependence on the physical laws in the physical 3-D plane of EXISTANCE, Adaptive Energy cannot travel faster than the speed of light. The bio-photons within the physical *Adaptivebody* for example that I have explained earlier, travel much slower than the theoretical speed of light. However, as you concluded, the Source Energy that you have access to through emotions of Bliss, Inspiration, Thought and Intention travel at infinite speeds, riding on the mass-less zero dimensional particle that you have called *sourceons*. Due to these particles being mass-less and dimensionless, it is possible to pack an infinite number of these *sourceons* in a very small space. In the human body these *sourceons* are ...

[Me] ... concentrated in the pineal gland or in the third eye. In this physical and mortal 3-D *Adaptivebody*, the immortal non-physical 0-D Source Particle of Creation is embedded making this physical and mortal 3-D *Adaptivebody* a CREATOR in its own right. As a CREATOR I have the capabilities to engage these *sourceons* on the same Cycle Of Creation through proper direction of this Source Energy simply by focusing my Thoughts about my Inspiration to Create my life experience of unbounded delight.

{ I unconsciously interrupted and continued to speak involuntarily as if I was in a trance – my unseeing eyes focused on empty space as the cognition set in. There could be no other explanation. }

[*My Activebody*] ... and the truth will set you free. Those dormant memories of Eternal Consciousness in your subconscious mind are reactivating rapidly.

{ I continue to ponder on the magnanimity of what I just became aware of – what a Masterpiece of Creation this human *Adaptivebody* is, I wondered. }

The G.O.D 'Particle' – Sourceon

[*My Activebody*] All advances in technology in human civilization today are based on the physical laws of particles that have at least some rest mass, which binds the perceived reality of this 3-D plane of Existence to the speed of light. All instrumentation, detection devices and equipment are dependent on the factor of rest mass, time and the four fundamental forces. However as you mentioned, Source Energy propagates unhindered by any physical object and is carried by *sourceon*. *These sourceons provide the platform and define the medium of communication in the non-physical plane of all dimensions – 3-D included* and it is true that the human *Adaptivebody* has an infinite reservoir of these massless dimensionless *sourceons* in the pineal gland.

[Me]. What are the key characteristics of these *sourceons*?

[My Activebody] The knowledge about *sourceons* is already implanted within your Type 1 memory systems as the *Genetics Of Divinity* in your Type A *Adaptivebody* by design of Creation – you just never had the inclination, justification or the opportunity until now to activate that consciousness. So I will do the honors and you will remember it all.

{ My *Genetics Of Divinity* were about to be rekindled and I could hardly contain my excitement. I settled down into a deeper meditative state, increasing the intensity of my GAMMA transmissions, ready to receive and elevate my consciousness about Existence in general and about me in particular. }

[My Activebody] Adaptive energy that powers the physical 3-D *Adaptivebodies* across all energy bands is a derivative of Source Energy. This implies that *Adaptivebodies* not only are physical manifestations of transformed Source Energy, *Adaptivebodies* are also composed of transformed *sourceons*. For the human *Adaptivebody*, the Central Nervous System is the transceiver of Source Energy. While *sourceons* are present in every cell of your physical body in the form of DNA, they are concentrated in infinite quantity in the pineal gland. Type A being the highest energy band in the 3-D offers all conforming *Adaptivebodies* the ability to communicate with other *Adaptivebodies* in this non-physical plane through Thought. Thought always requires a partner in one of thirteen relationships. Thought, which is Source Energy transformed into the *Adaptive* energy of your brainwaves, specifically THETA brainwaves. The same standing waves that created the multi-dimensional structure of Existence are at play in the 3-D as your thoughts engage in the process of Creation – what are you creating as a physical *Adaptivebody*? You are creating relationships with *Adaptivebodies* across all the 5 energy bands in the 3-D leveraging Thought. Whether that relationship is symbiotic and collaborative for the purpose of collective coexistence or

not is based on your free will. How you direct the *sourceons* through your Thoughts is dependent on your level of consciousness about the *Genetics Of Divinity*.

{ A pause again as I assimilated this body of knowledge expanding my awareness and consciousness }

[My Activebody] While *biophotons* in the *Adaptivebody* are the carriers of Physical Energy, occupying a segment in the spectrum of Adaptive Energy within the *Adaptivebody*, *sourceons* in the *Adaptivebody* are carriers of Source Energy. When you generate a THETA brainwave through your thoughts they are also carried by *sourceons* to the *Adaptivebody* target of your thoughts. This is why the holographic experience of interaction with the subject *Adaptivebody* could potentially involve all of the five senses of the transmitting *Adaptivebody*.

[Me] Hence my thoughts about what I desire to align with and get attracted to, can travel to my target instantly, regardless of geographical or astronomical distances uninterrupted, without attenuation and without the need for a physical medium for propagation. Each and every *Adaptivebody* in the 3-D has a certain unique frequency or its signature in Existence.

{ I paused to collect my thoughts that were now directed inward within my own Type 2 memories }

[Me] For Type C through A *Adaptivebodies* this unique frequency is generated by the biophotons in the cell DNA and hence is electromagnetic in nature. Type E and Type D Adaptivebodies also emit electromagnetic energy with their own unique frequency depending on the luminosity of that *Adaptivebody*. Hence before I can generate Adaptive Energy in the THETA frequency through my thoughts I must fix the coordinates of my target in the spectrum of Existence using this unique frequency of the target *Adaptivebody* – this is the beginning of *alignment*. *Alignment* is the component of *Inspiration* in the Cycle of Creation. Once these frequency coordinates of the target *Adaptivebody* is set, I can use the *Thought* component in the Cycle to transmit my request for alignment with that specific target *Adaptivebody,* as THETA Adaptive Energy carried by *sourceons,* emitted from my third eye chakra. If this request is considered to be symbiotically collaborative by the target of my thoughts based on my DI, that *Adaptivebody* would transmit a response through Adaptive Energy also using the same frequency in THETA. When my third eye chakra receives this transmission of the incoming response from my target, the result would be the generation of a resonant waveform with greater amplitude and hence amplified power. The component of *Intention* in the Cycle of Creation takes over between both *Adaptivebodies* consenting to alignment in a symbiotic collaborative relationship. The alignment becomes a standing wave pattern between the partners thereby granting stability to the new relationship. Once such a stable alignment is achieved between the relating *Adaptivebodies,* my target *Adaptivebody* would leverage physical gravitational energy to attract me towards it.

{ I am shaking my head in awe, as these memories of the Eternal Consciousness I have never invoked before begin to come back and flood my consciousness. }

[*My Activebody*] Yes, it is brilliant when your memory comes back { a short laugh }. Source Energy and *sourceons* are the fundamental building blocks of Creation and are integral components on every single part of Existence. Can you recall how the 3-D with all the physical Adaptivebodies was created?

[Me] I am supposed to have memory of that process too?

{ that was a rhetorical question – of course I should. I diverted my thoughts to access the knowledgebase of the memories of the birth of the 3-D. My *Activebody* smiles reassuringly }

[Me] If one were to go deeper and deeper into any *Adaptivebody*, regardless of its physical form, function and complexity in the 3-D beyond the cellular or molecular layer, beyond the atomic structures, even beyond the nucleus of the atom, one would find nothing but empty space where the physical characteristics of the *Adaptivebody* are no longer accessible or pertinent. The lowest common factor for all Adaptivebodies hence is energy – Source Energy and the *sourceons* – carrier particles of Source Energy. In that empty space where one would arrive through the process of progressively traveling deeper and deeper into matter, exists the *sourceon* – the energy wave – the original particle of Creation. The perceived appearance of the *Adaptivebody* is its resulting luminosity in the visible electromagnetic spectrum.

[My Activebody] Precisely! It is all coming back to you now. In the physical 3-D world built through the conglomeration of physical massive particles, equations of applied force such a $F = ma$ or $E^2 = m^2c^4 + p^2c^2$ { refer to Chapter 7 } are relevant and represent the finiteness of *Adaptivebody* behavior. However in the non-physical plane of Existence, the domain of massless carriers and independence of time, these equations have no significance and physical laws do not apply. *There is no Force in the non-physical domain – only sinusoidal waveforms of Source Energy with different frequencies and amplitudes generated from dimensionless points sourced and propagated through variations of massless, dimensionless sourceons enabling resonance, dissonance, harmonization of waveforms to create all of Existence.*

{ Whoa! What a revelation! }

Was There Really a "Big Bang"?

[Me] There was no Big Bang that started it all?

[My Adaptivebody] What you refer to as the Big Bang that supposedly created the 3-D Universe is actually the process of transformation of high frequency Source Energy into the lower frequency *Adaptive* Energy. *Sourceons* aligned and interacted with each other and developed symbiotic collaborative relationships with one another through resonance and established standing *Adaptive* Energy wave patterns. In the 3-D you refer to this relationship between *sourceons* as electromagnetic energy within the spectrum of

Adaptive Energy. The magnitude of the electromagnetic energy in the *Adaptivebody* determines the state of matter – solid, liquid, gaseous, plasma and what you referred to as the Bose-Einstein condensate. You can also say the degree of compactness of *sourceons* as a result of the bonding of quasi-stabilized electromagnetic energy determines the state of matter. The reason it is quasi-stabilized energy is because, through the application of external Physical energy, it is possible to alter the electromagnetic bond within matter, leading to a change in its natural state – for example, solid to liquid to gas and combinations thereof. As I mentioned before if one were to go deeper and deeper into physical matter, there would be a point where nothing physical could be detected through the human sensory feedback system or human instrumentation. However the presence of the *sourceon* in that emptiness of space cannot be denied. This is how the physical 3-D came into Existence. These so called Big Bangs are happening constantly all the time as the 3-D expands, whenever there is a transformation from Source of Adaptive Energy. When this happens, the non-physical *sourceons* collaborate in the manner explained above to generate physical matter. The frequency of electromagnetic energy in the newly formed matter determines its degree of luminosity which in turn provides the human illusion of physical reality.

[Me] When an *Adaptivebody* completes its lifecycle in mortal physical form, the Adaptive Energy transforms back into Source Energy which we refer to as the *soul leaving the body. This is transformation of the state of conglomerate matter of the physical body into a unique state of matter that humanity has never ever recognized or talked about. This is the massless, dimensionless state of pure energy or the sourceonic state from which all of Existence was created.*

{ I feel emotions of bliss like I have never experienced before I had this interaction with my *Activebody*. Not only was a vivid picture of Creation and Existence painted in my consciousness, my *Activebody* guided me to activate Type 1 memories that had remained dormant in my *subconscious mind* for so long. This knowledge is liberating as I feel a wave of peace and calmness engulf my *Adaptivebody* and slowly emerge from my meditative state. I thank my *Activebody* for the revelations. He smiles and his image fades away with one last message – "You have a mission in this life experience and you are aware of your life purpose – now bring it home at G.O.D-speed." I emerge from the meditative state, fully refreshed and rejuvenated, feeling lighter than ever before, basking in the glory of the new level of consciousness. }

These are the authentic *Genetics Of Divinity* – the grand design of Creation, sublime, logical, repeatable, consistent and flawless code of Eternal Consciousness. You now know what I know about how everything came to be, how the choice made at each and every present moment affects how your future life experience would turn out to be in the 4-D. While the past cannot be changed, you have complete control to design your future. Once you have identified your life purpose, you have direction. Once you have direction, engage that Cycle of Creation and you would have served your life purpose through symbiotic collaborative relationships.

My belief and desire is your consciousness has just undergone a quantum jump forward simply by reading this Chapter, of course if you have allowed the information to pass through the artificial critical filters of your conscious mind. You and I are no different at our core and we come from the same Source and part of the same identical design of Creation and Existence. What creates the difference is our level of consciousness based on the degree of dependence on the acquired Type 3 memory patterns and ignorance of the native Type 1 memory where our operating manual, in the form of the *Genetics Of Divinity* is embedded.

Your *Activebody* needs you to align back with your life purpose and reactivate not only the Type 1 but also the Type 5 memories that were set for you prior to your birth in physical form. What choice in Parallelism are you going to make now for a different tomorrow?

Chapter 10 – The Beginning

I started this book with a Chapter titled 'The Conclusion' and I am ending this book with this Chapter that I have titled "The Beginning". Unconventional for sure but I had to convey unconventional information. The repetitive mortality of your physical 3-D *Adaptivebody* contributes to the immortality of your non-physical 5-D *Activebody* that resides in the domain of stabilized energy, immune to the aging of time. Each mortal life experience that your 3-D *Adaptivebody* is awarded with is not a mere random happenstance. It is the end result of a well-designed plan of Coherent Source Energy through which your *Adaptivebody* is assigned with a specific purpose by your *Activebody*, following the Cycle of Creation. All of this is motivated by the inspiration for the expansion and sustenance of Existence by establishing symbiotic collaborative relationships for the purpose of collective coexistence, incrementally establishing the stability in the Third Dimension. This is the core objective of your Activebody – that to collaborate and stabilize this Third Dimension of Existence.

When would the Third Dimension achieve the stability of the higher dimensions? Simply follow the principles of stability as I discussed in Chapter 8 and you will know the answer – the answer lies in the code of the *Genetics Of Divinity*. The instability of 3-D *Adaptivebodies* is the result of all of the artificial conflict, hardship, scarcity, deprivation and the random blindfolded application of our free will – contributing to the plight of humanity today. In other words *Adaptive Energy* is stymied with dissonance which prevents the formation of standing waveforms, consequently thwarting stability from being instituted. Remove these elements from humanity and symbiotic collaborative relationships will automatically begin to form and proliferate, thereby stabilizing our Third Dimension.

My goal in this book has been to elevate your consciousness to a level higher than you were at before you started to consume and rationalize this information and help you reactivate the code of the *Genetics Of Divinity* from your subconscious mind. This book and the online Multiversity of the *Genetics Of Divinity*, two Type D *Adaptivebodies* that you now have access to, contains my own (Type A *Adaptivebody*) *Adaptive Energy* that I have transferred to them. These resources contain the signature of my own elevated consciousness that I have shared with you. How you came to know about this book is irrelevant, but what is important to know is if your central nervous system received and responded to the sinusoidal waveforms of *Adaptive Energy* that this book and the online training has been transmitting – unbeknownst to you. When you responded through your thoughts you generated like-frequency THETA waves towards the book or the Multiversity content and together there was resonance. The two of you got aligned and you found yourself getting attracted towards this content. Now you have established a symbiotic collaborative relationship with each other all for the purpose of collective coexistence.

As promised in Chapter 3, it is now time with your upgraded consciousness to revisit Exercises #02 and #03. Remember to download the worksheets of the relationship analysis chart from the Multiversity portal while going through these exercises again, however with a very important twist. In Chapter 3 when you completed those two exercises, I had asked you to focus on them based on your past experiences with yourself and the twelve other secondary relationship categories. When you perform those exercises now, I want you to future-project each of those relationships on how you would desire to engage in those relationships in a (or multiple) Parallel Universe(s) where you want to spend the remainder of your mortal lifetime for the purpose of collective coexistence. Parallelism is offering you choices right now in each of your thirteen relationship categories, what would your choices be?

I will be curious to know your new score once you complete that exercise and would be eager to learn about your experiences through the Multiversity portal. What you find will probably startle you. Do you see the obvious improvement? What happened between Chapter 3 and now that caused such an improvement of your self-image and consciousness? Needless to say, such an improvement would occur only if you have internalized what you have learned from this book and through the Multiversity and allowed those dormant memories of the code of the *Genetics of Divinity* to get reactivated from the subconscious to your conscious mind.

Finding Your True Identity

While the book (Type D *Adaptivebody*) has only one unique frequency through which it transmits its acquired *Adaptive Energy*, you on the other hand, a much highly endowed Type A *Adaptivebody*, have the ability to transmit and receive an entire band of frequencies of *Adaptive Energy*. The question is, what incoming frequencies of *Adaptive Energy* are you resonating with, hence aligning with and getting attracted to? Are they symbiotic collaborative relationships that contribute to the achievement of your life purpose and provide you with emotions of unbounded delight? Are those relationships parasitical in nature that erode the Potential Energy within your *Adaptivebody* distracting you away from the achievement of your life purpose, and leading you to a life experience filled with plight? What choices are you making every moment of your life experience from the plethora of options being presented to you by Parallelism? Candid answers to these questions that you ask yourself would identify for you where your past life experience had brought you today. Through the element of Contrast, you can clarify what you need to do to have a life experience drastically different in the future, in a different Type 3 Parallel Universe of Existence.

Without a doubt, if you have read this book and accessed the online training content, and have resonated with the information contained here, you have experienced an upgrade in your consciousness from where you were before you started. I encourage you to repeat Exercises 2 and 3 from Chapter 3 and Exercise 4 from Chapter 4 again but future-projecting their context, now that you have consumed all of this material and are more aware of your *Genetics Of Divinity*. In all likelihood, the results from those exercises would be vastly different and improved than your first attempt.

The question arises if all details about the *Genetics Of Divinity* that I have conveyed to the best of my knowledge in this book is the end game and if this information is all that there is to know about Creation and Existence. I would answer that question with a definitive 'No way! Are you kidding me?'. The grand design of Creation and Existence is too extensive and profound for any one book to cover. There's much more data from where the information contained in this book came from. Remember that just one gram of your DNA can hold 5.5 Petabytes of data and you have about 5 billion of these DNA pairs in your physical body. Even if you take just the 2nd pair of DNA strands which is one-sixth part of the DNA in each cell of your body, where the *Genetics of Divinity* is stored, how much of data are we talking about?

I have only scratched the surface of the infiniteness of the *Genetics Of Divinity* in this book.

The information contained in this book about *Genetics Of Divinity* is the result of the questions that I have asked my *Activebody* and have sought answers for, based on my perceptions of reality of my personal life experience. You as the reader of this book and more importantly a Type A *Adaptivebody* with your own personal life experience in all likelihood would have other questions of your own that have eluded you in the past, leaving you unsatisfied and incomplete. I welcome you to connect with your own *Activebody* to ask your own questions. If you would like, leverage the online community of like-minded people just like you at www.GeneticsOfDivinity.com to share the wisdom that you receive with the rest of the world. In the follow on book I will explain techniques through which you can re-kindle the dormant communication channel with your *Activebody* in the 5-D. You are designed to receive additional insight on the *Genetics Of Divinity* and guidance to identify your life purpose and have a forthcoming life experience filled with unbounded delight. You were designed as a Creature with the will to receive and experience unbounded delight during your tenure in this physical 3-D *Adaptivebody*. You have a birthright to such a life and you are here sharing a contemporary lifetime so that you can enjoy such a life. So is NOW the time for you to stake your claim to your definition of unbounded delight?

Defining Your Very Own Parallel Universe

Before I wrap up this first leg of the most amazing journey that I have embarked on under the guidance of my *Activebody*, I would encourage you to complete an exercise under the guidance of your newly elevated consciousness. In this exercise, I invite you to engage your PUPS and your EGS to describe the Type 3 Parallel Universe where you personally would desire to spend the forthcoming days of your life experience in this mortal form. This is an important exercise for you to complete because I will have you refer to it in the follow-on book *Miracles From Genetics Of Divinity*, where I describe the techniques that you would follow to find yourself incrementally navigating through a series of Type 3 multi-verses until you arrive at that Parallel Universe you define now. I would like to remind you of the basic principles of Creation and Existence as you settle down to complete this exercise:

1. You have to define entirely for yourself what your perception and interpretation of *unbounded delight* is - the forthcoming questionnaire would guide you. You are going to use those components and implant them in your Type 3 Parallel Universe.
2. We are talking about a physical Type 3 Parallel Universe, hence such a Universe would need to

conform to the physical laws of Existence. So pigs can't fly in that Parallel Universe, castles cannot be built in the air and that genie inside you cannot produce what you want in your life experience at the click of your fingers or rubbing that magic lamp. Be reasonable, use common sense and logical reasoning following the guidelines of ethical feasibility during the process.

3. Focus on the *what* and the *why* as you define your coveted Parallel Universe. Refrain from focusing on the *How*. If you knew the *How*, you would already have been living that experience.

4. If you *want* something in your life experience, that is **not** good enough. You have to convert that want into a *need,* which is a more powerful wave of Adaptive Energy. A *need* is a must have with a justifying reason behind it. You must be able to articulate the reason clearly. Now that you have the need, take it one notch higher by converting that into a *desire*, which is a need augmented by an appropriate emotion high on the EGS scale. Can you express that emotion without inhibition and doubt?

5. What you desire, would desire you as long as both of you have DI that is acceptable to each other so that your frequencies can resonate and develop that symbiotic collaborative relationship.

6. Just because you desire to establish a relationship with another *Adaptivebody* does not enforce or obligate that *Adaptivebody* to reciprocate. *You must understand that any stable symbiotic relationship is based on collaboration and not a compromise and must be established through the free will of mutual consent for the purpose of collective coexistence.*

7. Take full responsibility and accountability of yourself for anything and everything that has happened to you in your past, which will give you the strength and confidence for everything that you are about to usher into your future life experience. There is no external entity that dictates your life – although your physical body is immortal, your *Activebody* is immortal. Free will is yours to leverage and you have complete control of every moment of your life experience.

8. Existence is based on *service for others* and establishing *symbiotic collaborative relationships*. What do these terms mean to you and how would you conduct and carry yourself in that Parallel Universe under the guidelines of the core principle of the *Genetics Of Divinity*?
9. Refrain from assigning any time limits or deadlines on your journey through the multiverses just yet. Collapsing time or reducing the *gestation period* to realize your desires in the life experience in the 4-D is a rather advanced skill and can be achieved – you are not ready for that level of expertise just yet.
10. Engage as many of your five sensory feedback systems as possible during the process as you define components of your life experience in your Parallel Universe – this enhances the power of the perceived reality.

If you are unable to understand and agree to all of the above considerations, you are not yet quite ready from a consciousness maturity point of view to perform this exercise with much efficiency. This is not to disappoint you but to demonstrate Contrast. If you are not ready at this point to define your Parallel Universe, it is clarifying to you what you need to do in order to get ready. Maybe all you need is another attentive reading of this book to understand the principles of Creation and Existence as defined by the *Genetics Of Divinity*. Assuming you have achieved readiness to define your Parallel Universe let's embark on this adventure of your future life experience.

Invest some time to review and analyze Figure 41. You will be defining your desired Parallel Universe following the basic principles that I have described earlier. This chart is downloadable from within the Multiversity portal of the *Genetics Of Divinity* that you have access to as an owner of this book. On the left column of the chart are the different categories of Adaptivebodies that make up your physical life experience. On the columns to its right are challenge questions that I have for you to answer with as much clarity and definitiveness. In some cases, especially in case on people or objects you may not know them personally or their

Components of Your Desired Parallel Universe	Describe Who or What do you desire in your Parallel Universe? If you have names, put them down. If you don't have specific names, describe the characteristics of the person or object or circumstances that would bring you unbounded delight in that Parallel Universe	In each category describe the precise nature of the symbiotic collaborative relationship with you. Provide as much detail as you can - greater the detail, more intense the focus, stronger the relationship. What makes you have high DI to be appealing to your target?	Why is this important for you to have the person(s) or thing(s) or circumstance(s) in your life experience in your intended Parallel Universe? Would you settle for a second option if the first could not be acquired? Why would you no?	How would you feel when you actually have been attracted by the person(s), object(s) or circumstance(s) in the category being considered and are now in your physical life experience in a Parallel Universe in the 4-D?
Parents				
Siblings				
Significant Other or Spouse				
Children				
Friends and Relatives				
Teachers and Mentors				
Career or Business				
Society and Community				
Finances				
Passions or Hobbies				
Residence(s)				
Transportation				
Health and Fitness				
Nutrition				
Entertainment and Leisure				
Knowledge and Education				
Personal Value Systems				
Who Serves Me				
Who I Serve				
My Self Image				
Political				
Infrastructure				
General Living Conditions				
Environment / Mother Nature				

Describe what a day in your life in your desired Parallel Universe is like once you have arrived at it with all of the above in your physical life experience?

Figure 41

identity yet. In that case, describe the characteristics and key attributes of that *Adaptivebody* that you desire for.

When I was going through that personal relationship recovery in my life that I referred to in Chapter 1, I did not know the identity of my soul mate. All I focused on were the emotions that I would feel in the company of such a lady in my life and on the precise nature of our symbiotic collaborative relationship. Within a short period of time, I aligned with and found myself attracted to such a lady thousands of miles away on opposite ends of the planet, under circumstances that clearly defies common logic. When I was looking for a luxury car in my Parallel Universe, I did not have a brand name, make or model in my mind – all I had were some of the specifications of such a vehicle. Such a vehicle would definitely have an impressive price tag but I did not focus on that at all – just the characteristics of the vehicle that I would be driving in my Parallel Universe. Within a few weeks, I aligned with such a vehicle, got attracted to it and eventually acquired it – the money came from a source that was not in my plan by any means. Focus on the *What* and the *Why* and allow the reactivated memories of the *Genetics of Divinity* to lead you through the *How*.

Type 3 Parallel Universes do exist – it's time to get over the debate and doubt. You are living in one right now and could have been in another one by choice at a prior instant, having an entirely different life experience right now. You have the ability to define and find yourself in a Parallel Universe that you desire. Parallelism and Contrast are attributes of Creation meant to allow you the Creature to enjoy a physical life experience filled with unbounded delight through the exercise of your free will.

It is very important that you be careful about the manner in which you define the attributes of your Parallel Universe. For example, if you have been diagnosed with a disease that you want to get out of your body, you would be focusing on the Health category of the Parallel Universe definition in Figure 41. Instead of mentioning anything about the disease (the subject) describe the characteristics of your body as if it was a normal healthy body - energy flows where attention goes. Apply the focus of your THETA brainwaves on the natural health of your body and not on the disease itself in this example.

While you define the desired components for your Parallel Universe make sure you use *present tense, first person and active voice* as if you are already living in that physical life experience. This significantly accelerates the journey to your desired destination.

There is another common mistake people make while defining their desires – they focus on all the things that they *don't* want in their life experience. *Energy flows where attention goes.* As you work on the components of your Type 3 Parallel Universe, focus on the precise need and the desire. For example, instead of saying that you don't want debt in life, mention that you desire to be financially free in your Parallel Universe to buy anything that you desire without considering the price tag as a deciding factor.

Most importantly, the purpose of this exercise is not to define the end game – or the final Parallel Universe that you would desire to enjoy your life experience in – you can hop between multiple Parallel Universes each better than the last one. As you ride the magic of your PUPS, pay close attention to the feedback from your EGS. You must feel good with emotions higher on the EGS scale about what you define on the worksheet in Figure 41. If what you define does not make you feel good about it, break it down into smaller components that seem more believable and achievable to you. It is perfectly ok and actually advisable to travel through Parallel Multiverses before you arrive at your coveted Parallel Universe.

The quest for instant gratification is not possible by design of the 4-D in your physical 3-D *Adaptivebody*, and chasing such an objective would only bring more grief to the desperation. Any attempts to circumvent such a design as an *Adaptivebody* is a futile exercise that erodes your *Adaptive* energy to create memory systems that are not anabolic to your life experience. Such attempts to pursue instant gratification would without a doubt, present the *Adaptivebody* with emotions that are lower in the EGS scale.

Invest your time and energy to complete the worksheet in Figure 41 using the guidelines that I have described here. In the following book, *Miracles From Genetics Of Divinity*, I will describe techniques that you can adopt and apply to actually embark on your journey through your multiverses and find yourself in the Parallel Universes of your choice. When you are there, you will begin again to define yet another series of multiverses to a new Parallel Universe to find yourself enjoying a different level of unbounded delight.

Four Types of Civilizations + The Fifth

The notable Theoretical Physicist, Dr. Michio Kaku describes four types of civilizations based on their level of consciousness and maturity to impact Existence.

Type 0 civilization represents humanity in its current level of consciousness, hostage to the doctrines of fate and destiny and going through an unpredictable and unstable life experience according to the principles of the default operating system of Existence in the 3-D. Whatever your current perception is about humanity, that is the Type 0 civilization that Dr. Kaku refers to.

Dr. Kaku describes a Type 1 civilization as one that has acquired the consciousness to control the physical attributes of the planet where they live in. Since Source Energy is at the core of all matter in Existence, a Type 1 civilization would understand that the planet where they inhabit is also a derivative of Source Energy. Geological, maritime (if the planet has liquid states of matter), meteorological, seismological, atmospheric, cosmological properties of the planet where such a civilization lives are the effect of the flow of *Adaptive Energy* through the planet in the Type B energy band. A Type 1 civilization has the ability to energetically manipulate these properties and functions of the planet to make it a more hospitable and exciting platform for Creatures conforming to other Type D through Type A energy bands to thrive.

A Type 2 civilization, according to Dr. Kaku is one that is conscious enough to have the ability for controlling inter-planetary properties, functions, interactions and communications within their own galaxy.

A Type 3 civilization, Dr. Kaku theorizes has attained the consciousness that can operate at an inter-galactic plane of Existence, controlling the modus operandi on entire galaxies, each possibly its very own laws of Physics, and in a different spectrum of *Adaptive Energy*.

To these four types of civilizations I would prefer to add a Type 5 civilization that operates in the 11-D and controls Source Energy and the symbiotic collaborative relationships of *sourceons*. Without a doubt, such a civilization does exist, which is why we are here in the first place.

Sounds like a Star Wars® or a Star Trek® story, doesn't it? I personally find such an explanation completely logical and absolutely possible – Parallelism allows such civilizations that have such levels of consciousness to exist and they probably are having a contemporary life experience with us here on Planet Earth. Our perceived reality on planet Earth is but a tiny segment in the spectrum of *Adaptive Energy* – true reality can only be *felt* in a non-physical plane of Existence.

Can humanity through our *Adaptivebodies* someday become a Type 5 civilization? Definitely not, since our physical *Adaptivebodies* are restricted to the domain of the 3-D on the *leash* of the 4-D. However our non-physical *Activebodies* do have the capability to transcend into the domains of *Active Energy* as you know by now. Can our non-physical *Activebodies* operate in the domain of Source Energy? Well we are already operating in that domain albeit in a different dimension, are we not? We are just not conscious enough just yet – there is no better time than NOW to begin that journey.

I don't know about you, but I actually like this physical 3-D. When coupled with the ability to foresee the future and conduct this life experience with the objective of fulfilling my life purpose, it becomes such an exciting journey through time. The technology of *Genetics Of Divinity* enables the practitioner to experience such a life. Whatever you have done so far in your life has brought you to this moment of choice – Parallelism at play once again. What would you choose to do?

As I say *C'est la vie* (such is life) in its true glory that has remained obscured to your consciousness so far, I urge you to memorize the following lines and repeat the following, verbally or even write it down in a personal diary as many times as possible every day.

It Is <u>NOW</u> My Time To Step Into My <u>TRUE</u> REALITY

I Am Immortal... Not believing in this is Immoral.

I Have **Not** Been Designed For Immorality.

I AM IMMORTAL.

I RESPECT, HONOR and CELEBRATE My Life

You have now been introduced to yourself – the Beginning of your true self has been recorded. Now let's make life happen for you.

Next Steps

If you have read this book thus far you have evolved since the time you started – no point questioning that. Your consciousness has been upgraded – have no doubt. Perform a simple Kinesiology test and you will prove the upgrade to yourself. You can feel an elevated level of *Adaptive Energy* surging through your physical *Adaptivebody*. You aren't surprised about it are you? You feel more connected to the grid of Existence. You realize that there is an absolutely valid reason why you are here having a contemporary life experience with the rest of Existence in the form of your physical 3-D *Adaptivebody* – makes you feel important doesn't it? Those desires to go out and seek those symbiotic collaborative relationships that you have been yearning for all these years have escalated to an all-time high – have they not? I am glad you are in the groove to re-align with your life purpose. The technology of the *Genetics Of Divinity* has been imprinted in your unique energy signature, which is the combination of your *Active* and *Adaptive* energy, I have simply assisted you to reach into those memory systems and re-activate them into your conscious focus and attention.

Where do you go from here? One of my mentors have said, "Knowledge is Power only if you use it". Hence I encourage you to now start applying your knowledge by learning the techniques to leverage the technology of the *Genetics Of Divinity* and realign yourself with your life purpose – that to serve the expansion of Existence and enjoy unbounded delight in the process. In my follow-on book *Miracles From Genetics Of Divinity*, I describe some of these techniques that I have used, tested and continue to improve and enhance under the guidance of my *Activebody*. Evolution of consciousness is by no means a destination in this domain of *Adaptive* energy where you and I are having a contemporary life experience. It is a journey until we reach stability and finally declare our independence from the factor of time.

As a student of the technology of *Genetics Of Divinity* you are eligible to access additional content as they become available and I encourage you to visit my website at www.GeneticsOfDivinity.com and request access to the

Multiversity portal for the latest details. You will have access to a moderated online forum where not only can you have access to me, but can also collaborate with other like-minded individuals who are evolving with you. Share your knowledge in this online community as you revitalize the communication channel with your very own *Activebody*.

Several times every year, I will be hosting some very unique events that you can attend in person or participate online. As more and more individuals remember these *Genetics Of Divinity* I will organize mass events at a global scale where regardless of where you are in the planet you can participate at the same time applying the same techniques as everyone else to generate a global field of *Adaptive* Energy that fosters symbiotic collaborative relationships in a Parallel Universe where humanity lives in love, peace, harmony, security and abundance. Every such event will have a specific theme that we will focus on to generate a massively powerful resonant sinusoidal waveform that restores the glory of our civilization and this planet. My website at www.GeneticsOfDivinity.com will carry all such details and instructions – you are welcome to be a part of this global movement.

Existence is based on the principle of establishing *symbiotic collaborative relationships through the free will of mutual consent between the relating partners for the purpose of collective co-existence.* If you are involved in arts, music, consciousness, non-verbal communications, science and technology, you have a role to play for the sustenance and advancement of life in this planet with the global objective to upgrade us into a Type 1 civilization as Dr. Michio Kaku explains. I encourage you to join the online community and reach out to me to share your cognitions and ideas as you strengthen your connection with your *Activebody*. This desire to share and collaborate will be automatic for you as it have been for me ever since my dormant Type 1 memory systems started to reactivate. If you are in positions of authority, I encourage you to facilitate research on the technology of the *Genetics Of Divinity*, diverting funds and resources from non-collaborative initiatives that erode humanity today into initiatives that assist in the revival of our civilization regardless of color, race, religion or creed.

We have fought wars, destroyed precious life and property, abused our environment, deprived others from enjoying a fulfilling life since the dawn of human history. What have we been chasing? At the core of everything there is nothing – only pure Source Energy. Where has all that conflict and turmoil really gotten us? We are in violation of the code of Creation and Existence. Whatever it is we are doing is not helping the proliferation of love, peace, security, harmony, health and abundance in this planet is it? Why not try something different by relinquishing the paradigm of scarcity and deprivation and adopting a life guided by a paradigm of abundance using the natural code of the *Genetics Of Divinity*? The choice is yours to make. The decision to usher in life in an abundant Parallel Universe is yours to take. What's the next moment of your life going to be like? Only you can decide for yourself.

G.O.D-speed to you and to every *Adaptivebody life* that you touch in your thirteen relationship categories and engage in symbiotic collaborative relationships through the free will of mutual consent for the purpose of collective coexistence. I look forward to meet you in a different Parallel Universe where we can collaborate for the advancement of our civilization and reignite the glory of our Existence.

"Peace, Love, Security, Harmony, Health, Abundance

To You and Yours" ...

Joy Ghosh

Your Time Is NOW !!!

ABOUT THE AUTHOR

"The Eternal 'technology' to enjoy a life experience filled with unbounded delight, lays hidden in a freely available yet never before revealed body of knowledge or Eternal Consciousness that I refer to as the Genetics Of Divinity. Revealing this information is my life purpose, to serve and assist anyone with a burning desire seeking a better life experience to access, acquire and use this knowledge in every aspect of life, first for the improvement of the self and then for the service of humanity and Existence ." .... Joy Ghosh.

Joy Ghosh is an Electronics and Electrical Engineer, a Software Architect and a certified Hypnotherapist, a published author and speaker. After investing tens of thousands of dollars and thousands of hours on the heavily touted Law of Attraction, all to no avail to improve the quality of his life experience, it had become a question of survival for Joy to figure things out fast or else ...

Determined to seek the answers and resolve many simultaneous challenges in his life, he invested over a decade in research on Applied and Theoretical Physics, Chemistry, Human Anatomy, Engineering, Astronomy, Spirituality, Religion, Hypnotherapy, Sacred Geometry, Multi-Dimensional Energetics, and of course guidance from his Fifth Dimensional *Activebody* in a quest to learn the Truth behind Creation and Existence. The result has been the activation of The *Genetics Of Divinity* – the knowledge that anyone from any background can learn and apply to significantly upgrade their consciousness and enjoy a life experience of peace, love, harmony, health and abundance.

You have now learned the Theory behind the *Genetics Of Divinity* and I will continue to share as more and more sections of the code progressively reactivates into my consciousness.

CONGRATULATIONS!!!

Read this book a few more times and watch the accompanying training videos in the online Multiversity to reactivate those dormant memories of this code of Eternal Consciousness from your subconscious mind.

Prepare yourself to apply your knowledge in practice ...

Coming Up Next

Miracles From Genetics Of Divinity

Oh My *Genetics* *Of* *D*ivinity

Mail This Form Today

ICREATE Technologies, LLC
2647 Gateway Road, Suite 105-288, Carlsbad, CA 92009

I would like to be included in your mailing list for offers, promotions and notifications for events and seminars. I understand that you will contact me by email or regular post and I agree to receive such communication from ICREATE Technologies, LLC. I understand that my information will not be shared with anyone else. I can opt out at any time upon which I will no longer receive any email or post from ICREATE Technologies

Fill up as many areas that you want to enable us to contact you

My First Name (required)   _____
My Last Name (optional)   _____
My Email Address   _____

                                _____
My Mailing Address   _____
                                _____

www.ingramcontent.com/pod-product-compliance
Lightning Source LLC
Chambersburg PA
CBHW050118170426
43197CB00011B/1625